Costume and Identity
in Highland Ecuador

previous page: Warp-resist patterned poncho, probably from Magdalena or Rumipamba, eastern Imbabura province. Wool warp-faced plain weave. 1.52 x 1.42 meters (60 x 56 inches). The Textile Museum 1984.46.1, Latin American Research Fund.

this page: Belt woven by José Miguel Limaico, Ovalos (Natabuela), Imbabura province. Cotton plain weave with both supplementary-warp and supplementary-weft patterning in acrylic. 3.015 x .045 meters (9 feet 10¾ x 1¾ inches). The Textile Museum 1989.22.13, Latin American Research Fund.

facing page: Salasaca belt, Tungurahua province. Cotton plain weave with acrylic supplementary-warp patterning. 2.58 x .06 meters (8 feet 5½ x 2⅜ inches), excluding ties. The Textile Museum 1986.19.33, Latin American Research Fund.

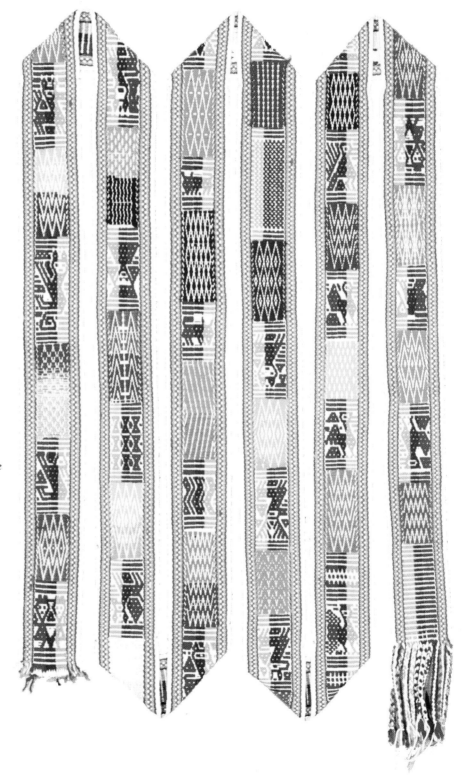

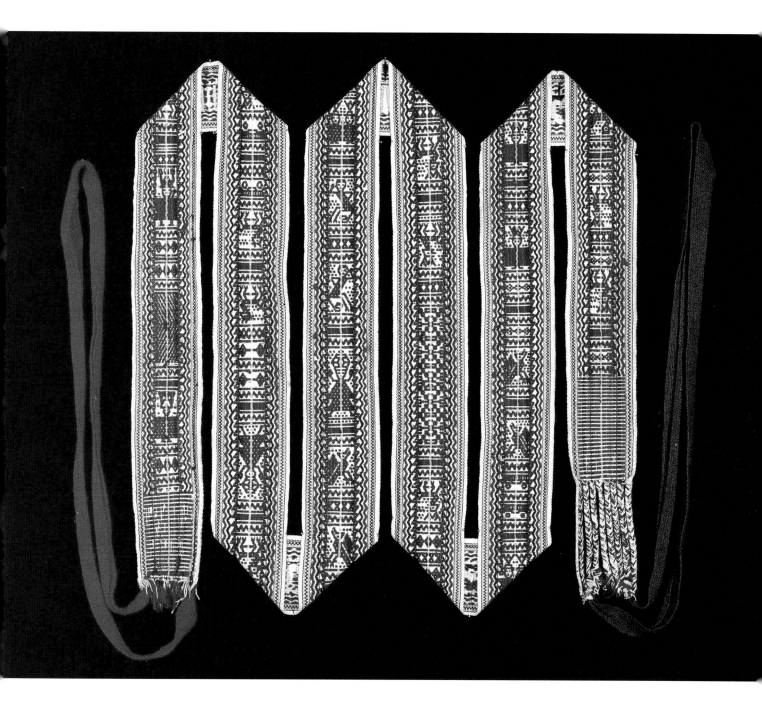

Costume and Identity

A Samuel and
Althea Stroum Book

in Highland Ecuador

Edited by **Ann Pollard Rowe**

Text by *Lynn A. Meisch,*
Laura M. Miller,
Ann P. Rowe,
and others

The Textile Museum
Washington, D.C.

University of Washington Press
Seattle and London

title page: Paño cachemira (cholo woman's shawl), made in the Bulcay-Gualaceo area, Azuay province. Warp-faced plain weave, warp-resist dyed, with knotted fringe, wool. Slightly more than half of the total 2.63 meters (8 feet 7½ inches) length is shown. Width: 79.5 centimeters (31 inches). The Textile Museum 1986.19.56, Latin American Research Fund.

This book is published with the assistance of a grant from the Stroum Book Fund, established through the generosity of Samuel and Althea Stroum.

Copyright 1998 by The Textile Museum
Printed in Hong Kong
Designed by Veronica Seyd

Library of Congress Cataloging in Publication Data

Costume and identity in highland Ecuador / edited by Ann Pollard Rowe;
    text by Lynn A. Meisch . . . [et al.].
       p. cm.
    "A Samuel and Althea Stroum book."
    Includes bibliographical references and index.
    ISBN 0-295-97742-6 (alk. paper)
    1. Costume—Ecuador. 2. Ethnicity—Ecuador. 3. Ecuador—Social life and customs.
I. Rowe, Ann P. II. Meisch, Lynn, 1945– .
    GT693.C67 1998
    391—dc21
                                   98-24521
                                   CIP

Contents

Preface *ix*

Acknowledgments *xiii*

Maps, *following page xvi*

1. The Land and the People *3*

2. Ecuadorian Textile Technology *16*

3. Indigenous Ecuadorian Costume *39*

4. Otavalo, Imbabura Province *50*

5. Northeastern Pichincha and Eastern Imbabura Province *84*

6. Cotopaxi Province *110*

7. Tungurahua Province *126*

8. Bolivar Province *162*

9. Central Chimborazo Province *167*

10. Eastern Chimborazo Province *207*

11. Southern Chimborazo Province *222*

12. Cañar Province *230*

13. Azuay Province *254*

14. Loja Province *263*

Conclusions *280*

Glossary *282*

References Cited *287*

Index *300*

Contributors *306*

Shigra from the area west of Salcedo, Cotopaxi province, purchased in the Otavalo market. Simple looping with agave fiber yarns. Height: 26.5 centimeters (10½ inches). The Textile Museum 1988.19.95, Latin American Research Fund.

Preface

This book describes the contemporary daily and fiesta or ceremonial costumes of the indigenous peoples of highland Ecuador, as they relate to ethnic identity. We use the term *costume* to include not only clothing but also jewelry, hairstyles, and other bodily adornments. By fiesta or ceremonial costumes, we mean those that indigenous people consider their finest traditional dress, which they wear for such special occasions as weddings, baptisms, market days, and church services.

We have not attempted to cover the subject of masquerade, that is, festival costumes worn to disguise or change identity, called *disfraz* in Ecuador. Such costumes are a rich tradition in highland Ecuador, but require a different kind of background research and would require an entirely separate book to do them justice. The clothing and weaving traditions of the indigenous peoples of lowland Ecuador are omitted as well, not because they are not interesting or relevant to our subject, but simply because the authors have not done field work in these areas. Fortunately, there is some information on these areas already in print, which we refer to here.

Highland Ecuador is in any case a coherent cultural unit from a number of perspectives. It is divided from highland Peru not only politically but also geographically and by loom style. The loom style changes again in Carchi province adjacent to the northern border. Some nearly identical costume elements can be found in more than one area, reflecting common historical processes. The modern push for land reform and recent indigenous political activism generally are necessarily taking place within the modern national boundaries. This activism, in which indigenous people are seeking recognition of the value of their traditions, is directly relevant to the question of indigenous identity and its expression in costume.

The concept and content of the book are based primarily on the field work of Lynn Meisch and Laura Miller. In order to provide further information on areas where Meisch and Miller spent less time, some contributions from others who have done anthropological field work in highland Ecuador were solicited. These sections—on Mariano Acosta by Marilee Schmit Nason, Zumbagua by Mary J.

Weismantel, Pulucate by Rebecca Tolen, and eastern Cañar by Lynn Hirschkind—in addition to accompanying costume descriptions, provide background on indigenous life that helps explain the continuing use of distinctive costume and illuminates the context of costume change. As a group, these sections reveal the kinds of regional variations that are found in other aspects of the culture that condition or reflect those found in the costumes.

Initially, we planned to produce a single book on indigenous costume and weaving of highland Ecuador. However, the full text proved to be too lengthy to be published in this form. Therefore, we have divided the material into three volumes, to be published separately. The present book focuses on the regional variations in the costumes and on issues of indigenous identity; a second volume will present evidence for the historical development of the costumes; and a third will describe the textile technology. Our information on the costumes of Carchi and southern Pichincha provinces has been reserved for the historical volume, since a distinctive indigenous costume is no longer in general use in these areas.

The introductory text in chapter 2 on fibers, spinning, and weaving is designed to be understandable to those who have no background in these matters. It is intended to explain these subjects sufficiently so that the later references will be clear. It also highlights those technical features that are particular to Ecuador.

It should be kept in mind that most of the field data reported here were gathered during the 1980s. The precise dates of the field work are given in the text or notes to each section. Change has been occurring very rapidly. As recently as the 1960s, most indigenous clothing was still handwoven, but by the time of our field work that was no longer the case. We did, however, have the opportunity to record a number of traditions that were on the point of disappearing. We hope that we have succeeded in drawing the broad outlines for each of the highland areas where an indigenous textile tradition existed at the time of our work. In cases where we have only partial information, we include it anyway, both so that it will be available to others and to highlight the need for further work. Of course, additional changes have taken place during the 1990s, and some of the traditions described are already becoming a thing of the past.

Although there is no single self-referential term used uniformly by all of Ecuador's indigenous groups, *indígena* (Spanish for *indigenous person*) is currently the most common and accepted designation. It is employed by the national indigenous federation CONAIE (Confederación de Nacionalidades Indígenas del Ecuador), so we will follow their lead. Since our text is in English, however, we usually translate the term as *indigenous person*. Although the term *Indian* is often used in North America, it has acquired insulting connotations in South America. As it is in any case a misnomer, we prefer to avoid it.

Orthography

Most, but not all, highland indigenous people speak Quichua, as the Inca language is now known in Ecuador. Sometimes indigenous people also call it *runa shimi*, the people's language, or *Inka shimi*. The question of what orthography to use in transcribing local terms is a thorny one, since the language was not written until after the Spanish conquest, and even then, extensive texts have been uncommon until recently.

The language has also differentiated into a number of dialects, so that, for example, the pronunciation in Ecuador has softened from what one hears in the Cuzco region, as often happens when a language spreads to a new area. The sound pronounced "s" in Cuzco has become "sh" in northern Ecuador (e.g., *simi* [language] versus *shimi*) and "j" in southern Ecuador, "p" has become "b" (so *chumbi* [belt] instead of *chumpi*), and the sounds made in the back of the throat that are also difficult for English- or Spanish- speaking people to pronounce are absent in Ecuador. Moreover, in Ecuador alone there are three different Quichua dialects, with varying pronunciation and vocabulary. There is further no agreement among indigenous groups in Ecuador about what orthographic system should be used. In this book, we have used different systems depending on the context of the word.

In order that they should look as familiar as possible to residents and travelers in Ecuador, most place names have been spelled the way they appear on the maps of the Instituto Geográfico Militar. These maps do not use a consistent system, but the majority of the spellings are with Spanish orthography. For example, the sound that would be pronounced "w" in English is written "hu" or "gu" in Spanish, since the Spanish alphabet does not include the letter "w" (for example, Huairapungo, Zumbagua). Likewise, words familiar in the English and Spanish literature on South America (such as *Inca*) are spelled in the traditional way.

Modern terms have been spelled according to a phonetic alphabet devised by linguist Lawrence Carpenter (1982), which does include letters such as "w" and "k" that do not occur in Spanish. A sound often written as "o" in Spanish is usually pronounced closer to "u" in Quichua. Thus, the word for the Inca-style pin is written *tupu* instead of *topo*, and the word for the woman's wrapped dress or skirt is written *anaku* instead of *anaco*. The spellings generally reflect local pronunciation in Ecuadorian dialects.

We have not used the Quichua plural suffix (*-kuna* or *-guna*); terms (italicized) are given only in the singular, even if the sentence introducing them uses an English or Spanish plural. When the term is not being defined but used as an unitalicized noun in the sentence, plurals are added in the English (and Spanish) manner by adding "s" to these words. However, we often use a translation of a term unless an English word would be unnecessarily ambiguous. When a Quichua or Spanish term is given in the text, it means that the use of this term was specifically recorded in the place being described. Commonly used terms are also defined in a glossary at the back of the book.

In giving the derivations of words, we use the abbreviations *Q.* for Quichua and *S.* for Spanish. In a few cases the origin of a local term could not be determined.

Spanish words that have been incorporated into Quichua are generally given in both their Spanish spelling and Quichua pronunciation so that their derivation from Spanish is clear. It should be noted that the Spanish language sound that is written "ll," which is pronounced like the "y" in "yes" in southern Ecuador and in many Spanish-speaking countries, is pronounced "zh" (French "j") in northern highland Ecuador by Spanish-speaking as well as by Quichua and bilingual residents. We write it as "ll" so that the Spanish words will not look unfamiliar to readers literate in that language.

If our informants are literate, we have spelled their names the way they do, if we know. It should also be noted that indigenous women do not take their husband's name when they marry, though all children receive their father's family name.

Maps and Photographs

We have attempted to include on the maps as many as possible of the places mentioned in the text. However, some communities could not be located on any of the maps currently available to us, and in most cases we have omitted them rather than insert them in only an approximate location. We have tried to provide a general description of the location of such places in the text. In other cases, neighboring communities would not all fit on the scale of the maps used. Again, the approximate location is indicated in the text.

When the photograph credit reads, "Photo by . . . ," the photograph was generally produced from a black-and-white negative. When it reads, "Slide by . . . ," the photograph was produced by converting a color slide to black and white.

Acknowledgments

In any project of this kind, we researchers are wholly dependent on the hospitality of the people whose lifeways we want to record. In this regard, we wish to express our great appreciation to all those who explained their costume and dyeing, spinning, and weaving traditions to us, shared meals, and otherwise made us welcome. Those who provided data presented in this book are mentioned by name in the appropriate places, but here we would like to say thank you to everyone involved in this monumental project.

Lynn Meisch's initial work in southern Ecuador in 1977–79 was funded by Fulbright-Hays, with a grant toward film expenses from the Institute for Intercultural Studies. She also worked under the United States Agency for International Development (USAID) as a textile consultant in Otavalo from September 1985 to July 1986 in a project requested by local weavers. From October 1992 through January 1995, she conducted dissertation field work in Ecuador on transnational contacts and indigenous ethnic identity, some of which overlapped with work on this book. Her dissertation research funds were provided by Stanford University's Institute for International Studies, the Wenner-Gren Foundation for Anthropological Research (Predoctoral Grant No. 5483), and the National Science Foundation (Doctoral Dissertation Grant No. NSF DBS-9216489).

Laura Miller's initial work in Ecuador in 1984–86 was also supported by a Fulbright Fellowship. Meisch and Miller also received assistance in the summer of 1988 from the Bead Society of Los Angeles. Ann Rowe's first visit to Ecuador in 1986 was supported by a grant from the Organization of American States.

When this book and the accompanying exhibition were in the planning stages, Dr. Margaret McLean, then Director of the Center for Field Research (the field research arm of Earthwatch), suggested to Meisch and Miller that the project was suitable for Earthwatch funding. We thank her for her suggestion and support, which resulted in our fielding a total of six Earthwatch teams in Ecuador during the summers of 1988 and 1989.

The money used in Earthwatch projects comes from volunteers who also provide their labor to assist in the work. Volunteers who recorded data that appears in this book are credited in the notes and photograph captions, but this list acknowledges the financial support of all team members.

The volunteers in team 1 in 1988, based in Latacunga, Cotopaxi province, were Stephanie M. Burns, George W. Crockett, Patricia Grooms, Ellen R. Hanley, Carol J. and William H. Holmes, Constance Kenney, Marjorie Klockars, Sara Laas, Pamela Y. Lipscomb, Bonnie O'Connor, and Darby C. Raiser.

Volunteers in team 2, based in Ambato, Tungurahua province, were Helen Daly, Betty L. Davenport, C J and Edna A. Elfont and their daughter Dayna M. Elfont, Helen and Leonard Evelev, Marjorie Hirschkind, Carol Mitz, Sheila F. Morris, Maritza Mosquera, Norma Jean Nelson, Adelle M.P. Pollock, and Roberta Siegel.

Volunteers in team 3, based in Riobamba, Chimborazo province, were Dianne B. Barske, Barbara U. Buech, Jean V. Fuley, Jean L. Hayden, Edward and Helen Healy, Judith A. Kelly, Renate Kempf, Kathleen A. Jahnke, Emily M. Marsland, Ellen T. McQueary, Lorraine S. O'Neal, Robyn J. Potter, and Louise Taylor.

Volunteers in team 1 in 1989, which worked mainly in the eastern Imbabura area, consisted of Monique Andre, Gayle Bauer, Barbara Johnson Borders, Bettye Dennison, Elizabeth S. Drey, Nancy A. Fleming, Iris Garrelfs, Leslie Grace, Eileen Hallman, Patricia (Patt) C. Hill, Jennifer Lantz, Joy Mullett, and Linda L. Ruby. Leslie Grace had visited Lynn Meisch in Ecuador in 1978, and first suggested to Lynn the idea of studying and collecting complete costume.

Volunteers for team 2, which was based in Riobamba, were Jean Dayton, Jack M. DeLong, Mary Ewing, C. Robert and Celia S. Foss, Bee and Ken Henisey, Sandra Lewis, Kevin G. O'Brien, Suzanne Powell, Naeda B. Robinson, Carol Siegel, and AlJean D. Thompson.

Volunteers for team 3, which again was based in Riobamba, were Sandra Baker, M. Catherine (Kate) Beamer, Lari Drendell, Jacquelyn Engle, Cynthia M. Ferguson, Louise Hainline, Kirby T. Hall, Margaret E. Jacobs, William I. Mead, Patricia L. Meloy, Mary C. Shook, and Nancy C. Tucker.

Earthwatch also provided funds to cover the expenses and honoraria for local assistants. Our assistant for teams 1 and 2 for both summers was Breenan Conterón, an Otavalo woman from Ilumán, who made a particularly significant contribution to our work. Chuck Kleymeyer of the Inter-American Foundation in Arlington, Virginia, put us in touch with Carlos Moreno of COMUNIDEC in Quito. Carlos's background as an adult literacy instructor in Chimborazo province opened innumerable doors for us. In addition, his sons became valuable research assistants to our Earthwatch teams: Fernando Moreno Arteaga for team 3 in 1988 and Carlos Moreno Arteaga for teams 2 and 3 in 1989. Julio Chérrez S. also provided assistance to team 3 in 1989.

Several other people also participated in the Earthwatch research. Mrill Ingram, then of the Earthwatch staff, joined team 1 in 1988 to cover the project for the Earthwatch magazine but she also participated in our research. Her airfare was donated by Ecuatoriana airlines. Maria Aguí, a filmmaker, joined team 2 in 1988.

Dr. Lawrence K. Carpenter, a linguist at the University of North Florida in Jacksonville, was a visiting scientist for teams 2 and 3 in 1988 and team 2 in 1989. Although he contributed to the team research reports in 1988, his untimely death in 1990 prevented our obtaining a contribution from him for this book. Ann Rowe participated in team 2 and part of team 3 in 1988, as well as team 1 in 1989.

Other people in Ecuador were very helpful during the Earthwatch research. We are particularly grateful to Gail Felzein, a Peace Corps volunteer based in Ambato, who in 1988 introduced us to invaluable contacts throughout the province. Among these, Gonzalo Hallo, adult literacy instructor with the Dirección Provincial de Educación, helped us with introductions to the Chibuleo community. Sylvia Forman, an anthropologist with the University of Massachusetts at Amherst, helped us by giving us the names of her friends in Majipamba and by her enthusiasm for the project. Our hope that she might also write something for this book was unfortunately not realized before she died in 1992. However, she generously bequeathed her textiles to The Textile Museum, where they have been available to contribute to the project. In Chimborazo, Sra. Marta Borja of the Hacienda Gustús Grande was also helpful.

People in Quito who provided particularly valuable assistance were Costanza Di Capua, Ernesto and Myriam Salazar, and Jill and John Ortman of La Bodega Artesanías and Centro Artesanal. We would also like to thank past and current staff of the Fulbright Commission, especially the director, Gonzalo Cartagenova, and Helena Saona, Jenny de Castillo, Maria Mogollón, and Maria Eugenia Freile, as well as the late Presley Norton of the Programa para Antropología en el Ecuador.

Since 1977, many current and former staff members of CIDAP (Centro Interamericano de Artesanías y Artes Populares) in Cuenca have gone out of their way to help our research, including the director, Claudio Malo González, and librarian, Betti Sojos, as well as Diana Sojos de Peña, Ana Francisca Ugalde, René Cardoso, and Blanca Inguiñez.

In Otavalo, Margaret (Peg) Goodhart and Frank Kiefer, former restaurant owners and now proprietors of the Hotel Ali Shungu, and Guillermo Cobos and Lia Gallegos of the Residencial El Rocio, fed our Earthwatch teams and were helpful in innumerable ways. The staff of the Instituto Otavaleño de Antropología went out of their way to be helpful to us, especially Edwin Narváez Rivadeneira, the general director, and Hernán Jaramillo Cisneros, investigator and director of the journal *Sarance*. We would also like to thank Mariana and Matt Long and Shannon Waits-Escobar, who hand-carried film and manuscript chapters between Ecuador and the United States.

At The Textile Museum, the support of the Latin American Research Fund, a generous gift of Marion Stirling Pugh and the late Major General John Ramsey Pugh, was critical. The fund supported the acquisition of the Museum's collection of Ecuadorian textiles, some of which is illustrated here, paid Ann Rowe's travel expenses in 1988 and 1989, and made possible several aspects of the preparation of this book. The Textile Museum is also grateful for financial assistance from Don and Inge Cadle, Florence and Roger Stone, Hope Patterson, Nancy Wilson, and Hector and Erica Prud'homme.

Photography of The Textile Museum's Ecuadorian collection was funded by a grant from the National Endowment for the Arts. This work was ably coordinated by Christine Norling of The Textile Museum staff, and the excellent photographs were taken by Franko Khoury. Additional photographic sessions and processing were coordinated by Christine's expert successor, Amy Ward. The maps were drawn on computer by Laurie McCarriar, based on pencil sketches by Ann Rowe.

I am also grateful for the support of Ursula E. McCracken, Director of The Textile Museum, for the project, even when it took far longer than planned. I would like to extend my thanks to the Board of Trustees and staff of The Textile Museum for their encouragement throughout. Their support was practical as well as verbal, since many staff members took on extra projects, particularly exhibitions, in order to free my time for writing and editing.

Considerable editing of many of the sections in this book proved necessary in order to create a coherent volume. I am grateful to the authors for their willingness to adapt to this situation. In addition, I appreciate very much the efforts of the anonymous readers for the University of Washington Press and the helpful support of its staff, including Michael Duckworth, Marilyn Trueblood, and Veronica Seyd. I also owe an uncountable debt to John H. Rowe, who not only read the entire costume text, but also provided much advice and constant moral support throughout the gestation of this oversized project.

Ann P. Rowe
Washington, D.C.
March 1998

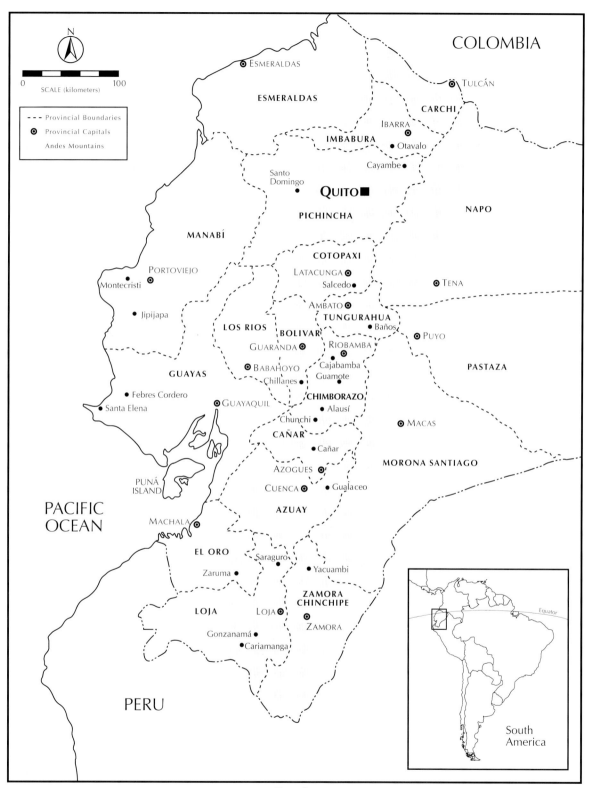

COLOMBIA

⊙ ESMERALDAS

⊙ TULCÁN

ESMERALDAS

CARCHI

IBARRA ⊙

IMBABURA

● Otavalo

● Cayambe

Santo
Domingo ●

QUITO ■

PICHINCHA

NAPO

MANABÍ

COTOPAXI

LATACUNGA ⊙

⊙ TENA

PORTOVIEJO ⊙

Salcedo ●

● Montecristi

AMBATO ⊙

● Jipijapa

TUNGURAHUA

LOS RIOS

BOLIVAR

● Baños

⊙ PUYO

GUARANDA ⊙

RIOBAMBA ⊙

PASTAZA

● BABAHOYO

Cajabamba ●

● Chillanes

Guamote ●

GUAYAS

CHIMBORAZO

● Febres Cordero

● Alausí

⊙ MACAS

● Santa Elena

⊙ GUAYAQUIL

Chunchi ●

CAÑAR

● Cañar

MORONA SANTIAGO

PUNÁ
ISLAND

AZOGUES ⊙

PACIFIC
OCEAN

CUENCA ⊙

● Gualaceo

MACHALA ⊙

AZUAY

EL ORO

Saraguro ●

● Yacuambi

Zaruma ●

ZAMORA
CHINCHIPE

LOJA

LOJA ⊙

● ZAMORA

Gonzanamá ●

● Cariamanga

PERU

Equator

South
America

Ecuador

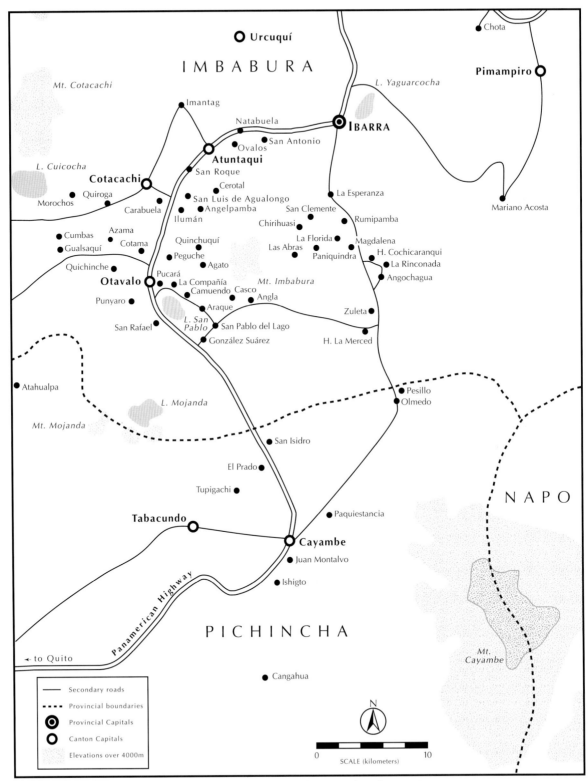

Southeast Imbabura and Northeast Pichincha Provinces

xviii

PICHINCHA

to Quito

Mt. Iliniza

Mt. Cotopaxi

COTOPAXI

NAPO

SCALE (kilometers)
0   10

— Secondary roads
- - - Provincial boundaries
◉ Provincial Capitals
○ Canton Capitals
 Elevations over 4000m

• Cuicuno

• Mulaló

Saquisilí

Salamala   • Macas

Poaló •

Panamerican Highway

• La Calera

Zumbagua

Latacunga

Pujilí

Salache •

• Rumipamba

Collana •

Salcedo

• Papaurcu

Cusubamba •

○ **Píllaro**

Chachilbana •

Quizapincha •

Ambato

Pasa •

San Alfonso

Pilahuín •

Santa Rosa

Palogsha •

• Nitón

Simiátug •

Salasaca

○ **Patate**

San Luis •

• Milquilli

Pomatúg

Cevallos

San Vicente •

Río Blanco •

Angaguana

Pelileo

Teligote •

TUNGURAHUA

Mt. Carihuairazo

Mocha

Quero

to Guaranda

Baños

Mt. Tungurahua

BOLIVAR

Mt. Chimborazo

Cotopaxi and Tungurahua Provinces

Secondary roads
Provincial boundaries
Provincial Capitals
Canton Capitals
Elevations over 4000m

N

0   10
SCALE (kilometers)

TUNGURAHUA

BOLIVAR

Simiátug

to Ambato

Mt. Chimborazo

Cuatro
Esquinas

Guanujo

GUARANDA

Santa Fé

Magdalena

San Lorenzo

San José de Chimbo

Santiago

San Miguel

Chillanes

Pallatanga

San Vicente
Nitiluisa

San Juan

Chanchahuán

Cajabamba

Majipamba

L. Colta

Santiago
de Quito

San Bernardo

Llinllin

Columbe

Tiocajas

Panamerican Highway

Guamote

Tuntatacto

Guanando

Penipe

Guano

Los Elenes

Cubijíes

RIOBAMBA

Yaruquíes

Cacha

San Luis

Punín

Troje

Pulucate

Cebadas

Chismote

Chambo

Molobóg

Licto

Pungalá

Flores

Alao

Mt. Altar

Mt. Sangay

CHIMBORAZO

Palmira Dávalos

Palmira

Cochapamba

Sanganao

Tixán

Alausí

Nizag

Pumallacta

Sevilla

Achupallas

Letrapungu

Osogochi

Chunchi

MORONA
SANTIAGO

Chimborazo and Bolívar Provinces

xx

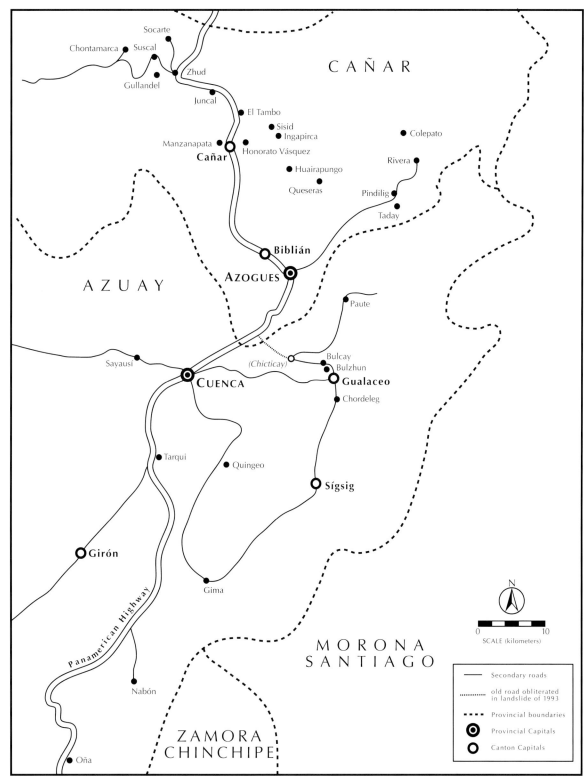

Socarte

Chontamarca   Suscal

Zhud

Gullandel

Juncal

El Tambo

Sisid

Ingapirca

CAÑAR

Colepato

Manzanapata   Cañar

Honorato Vásquez

Rivera

Huairapungo

Queseras

Pindilig

Taday

AZUAY

Biblián

AZOGUES

Paute

Bulcay

(Chicticay)   Bulzhun

Sayausí   CUENCA   Gualaceo

Chordeleg

Tarqui   Quingeo

Sígsig

Girón

Panamerican Highway

Gima

MORONA
SANTIAGO

N

0   10
SCALE (kilometers)

Nabón

——————   Secondary roads

················   old road obliterated
                 in landslide of 1993

– – – –   Provincial boundaries

◉   Provincial Capitals

○   Canton Capitals

ZAMORA
CHINCHIPE

Oña

Cañar and Azuay Provinces

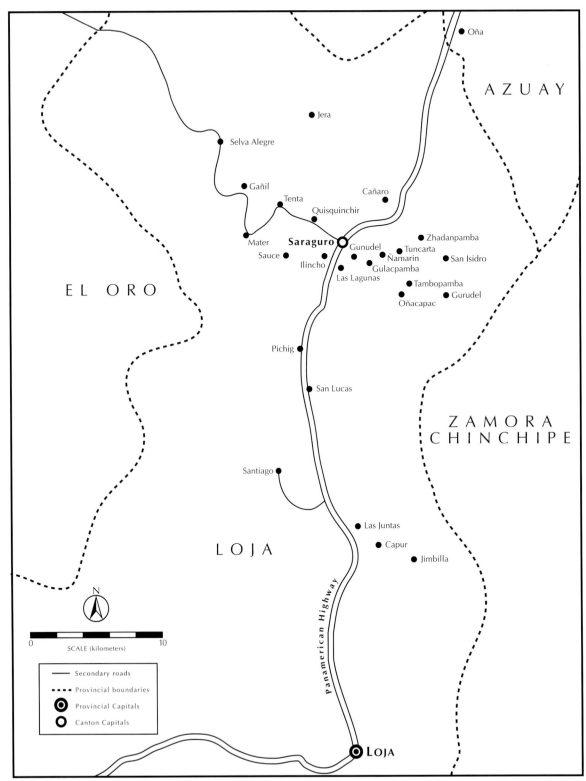

AZUAY

Oña

Jera

Selva Alegre

Gañil

Cañaro

Tenta

Quisquinchir

Zhadanpamba

Mater

Saraguro

Gunudel

Tuncarta

Sauce

Ñamarin

San Isidro

Ilincho

Gulacpamba

Las Lagunas

EL ORO

Tambopamba

Gurudel

Oñacapac

Pichig

San Lucas

ZAMORA
CHINCHIPE

Santiago

Las Juntas

Capur

LOJA

Jimbilla

N

0   SCALE (kilometers)   10

—— Secondary roads
- - - Provincial boundaries
◉ Provincial Capitals
○ Canton Capitals

Panamerican Highway

LOJA

Northern Loja Province.

Costume and Identity
in Highland Ecuador

Chapter 1

The Land and the People

The Geographic Setting

Ann P. Rowe

Imagine a country the size of Oregon that has extremely wide variation in ecological zones, from mangrove swamps and dense tropical rain forests to temperate valleys and snow-capped mountains with permanent glaciers. Such a country exists in Ecuador, which is situated directly on the equator and where altitude equals latitude, so that gaining or losing elevation is equivalent to moving north or south away from the equator.

The country has three main geographic zones: the Pacific coastal lowlands, which are hot and wet; the Andes, which are the second highest mountain range in the world, forming a north-south spine through the country; and the lowland Amazon basin rain forests to the east, usually referred to in Ecuador as the Oriente. The coastal lowlands are broader and the Andean highlands narrower than in Peru, Ecuador's southern neighbor.

The coast

The coastal zone of Ecuador also forms a marked ecological contrast with that of Peru. The Peruvian coast is one of the driest deserts in the world, which is the chief factor in the preservation of so many archaeological textiles in that area. Off the coast of Ecuador, however, the cold Humboldt current that flows northward along the Peruvian coast turns out to sea, and warm waters flow southward from Central America, causing a wetter climate. There is a rainy season from mid-December to mid-May, though with regional variations.

Formerly, the peninsula between Guayaquil and Manta was forested, but in this century the forests have been almost entirely cut down. Rainfall is unreliable, and people in this area subsist on fishing and raising cattle. To the north and east it is much wetter, supporting tropical forest vegetation, and tropical crops such as cotton, papaya, pineapples, and now sugar cane, coffee, bananas, and bamboo. The most heavily populated region is the Guayas basin, lying inland from the dryer coastal area. The western slopes of the Andes rise precipitously, covered with tropical vegetation.

Some 49 percent of the population lives in the coastal area and is a mixture of indigenous, Spanish, and African peoples. The indigenous population is for the most part not readily distinguishable as such. Nevertheless, remnants of indigenous weaving and metalworking traditions have recently been documented in some fishing villages on the coast (Klumpp 1983; Hagino and Stothert 1984; Alvarez 1987), and there are two small indigenous groups living in the northern tropical forested areas near the western slopes of the Andes who have maintained a significant amount of their traditional culture into the twentieth century.

The Chachis (called Cayapa in the earlier literature), now numbering some five thousand people, live mainly along the Cayapa River in the northern province of Esmeraldas. Their weaving was recorded by Samuel Barrett (1925), although now the native costume is worn only by old women and for fiestas (Einzmann 1985). The Tsachila (called Colorado in the earlier literature, because of their extensive use of red body paint) number only about one thousand, and live in the vicinity of Santo Domingo in Pichincha province. They wove until recently, but now wear clothing woven for them by Otavalos.[1] Although their weaving technology has not been documented in detail, it was apparently similar to that of the Chachis. These two groups speak Barbacoan languages (related to Paez and Guambian in Colombia), and both have an oral tradition of having migrated from the highlands in the province of Imbabura, probably as an escape from either the Inca or the Spanish conquest.

The highlands

The Andes mountains form two parallel chains with a fertile valley between them where most people live and which in Ecuador ranges in elevation from 2,200 to 2,800 meters (6,750 to 9,000 feet). The mountain chains include a series of spectacular snow-covered active volcanoes, and the area is also prone to earthquakes. The central valley is further divided like a ladder by other mountainous or desert areas into smaller basins, which also tend to coincide with indigenous ethnic divisions. The exact number of these basins varies slightly depending on who is counting them, but there are ten of sufficient importance to be represented in this book.[2] Rain is frequent in this area, too, ranging between one and two meters (39–79 inches), though it is dryer between June and October. Annual average temperatures range from 12 to 18 degrees Celsius (54–66 degrees Fahrenheit) on the valley floor. The different basins vary among themselves in fertility and amount of rainfall and temperatures, but in general the climate is pleasant.

Originally, the lower elevations of the central valley were forested, up to an elevation between 3,000 and 3,500 meters (9,840–11,480 feet). The forests are now gone, the land instead used for either agriculture or grazing animals. Above this altitude there is an area of colder grasslands, called the *páramo*, which is frequently overcast and rainy (Fig. 1). Some 48 percent of Ecuador's population lives in the highland valleys and most of these are indigenous descendants of the prehispanic

1. Ramón Aguavil Calazacón, personal communication 1993, conveyed to me by Robert L. Mix.

2. A convenient English summary of the various Spanish language sources on Andean geography is provided by Salomon 1986, chap. 1.

1 *Llangahua boys on the páramo near Mount Chimborazo, Río Blanco, Tungurahua province. Their ponchos are, left to right, red, two dark red, and blue (see chapter 7). Photo by Lynn A. Meisch, 1988.*

peoples of the area. Their lifeways include a broad and varied mixture of pre-Inca, Inca, Spanish, and modern elements. Traditionally, they are rural agriculturalists and/or artisans, but an increasing number are living in towns and cities, working as wage laborers or selling goods.

In the central valley, maize is the most important indigenous crop at lower elevations, often intercropped with beans, lupine (*tawri* Q.), or quinoa (Fig. 2). At higher elevations, crops include barley and fava (broad) beans, introduced by the Spanish, as well as a variety of indigenous tubers, including potatoes, ocas, mashua, and ullucos (or mellocos). Sometimes the lower elevations of the páramo may also be cultivated, while the higher elevations are used mainly for grazing animals. In prehispanic times, the domesticated Andean camelids, namely llamas and possibly alpacas, would have been kept. Now there are mostly sheep and cattle, though a few llamas can still be seen in the central provinces. Regardless of elevation, many indigenous households raise guinea pigs (*cuy* Q.), an Andean domesticate, for fiesta feasts, and some also raise chickens or rabbits.

The Ecuadorian high valley has a milder climate than that of Peru and Bolivia both because of its proximity to the equator, which is not far north of Quito, and because the altitudes are lower. The puna grasslands of Peru and Bolivia range between 3,900 and 5,000 meters (12,800–16,400 feet). They end at about the latitude of Trujillo, and in turn the northern páramo narrows sharply north of the Cajamarca basin, at the latitude of Huancabamba, forming a natural geographic break. Harry Franck, who walked the length of the Andes north to south in the early twentieth century, describes the border terrain thus, "another of those sudden changes of climate left the dripping forested mountains behind me, and underfoot was a desert-dry world" (1917:214). There is also a dramatic change in the species of wildlife present, with as many as 80 percent different (Miller and Gill 1990:51, citing Wing 1973:3).

The extent of the cultural distinctions is unclear archaeologically, but today the type of loom used changes at about the same latitude. Other features, such as spinning methods, continue across the border and trading has certainly occurred.

The border with modern Colombia has a less pronounced geographic break, and differentiation has depended primarily on politics. The border area was culturally unified in the pre-Inca and Spanish colonial periods, but the northern border of the Inca empire was in the same place as that between the modern republics. The loom style changes again in the northernmost province of Ecuador (not at the border), although certain other cultural features continue into the

2 Agricultural fields of indigenous farmers, on the hillsides near Pilahuín, Tungurahua province. Slide by Ann P. Rowe, 1988.

southern part of Colombia. For example, animal fibers are found in southern Colombia, though further north, only cotton is used. While this feature appears to predate the Inca conquest, it is likely that some elements of costume and belt-weaving techniques spread northward during the colonial period (Cardale Schrimpff 1977:46).

The Oriente

The Oriente includes the eastern slopes of the Andes, and gradually flattens out to the east. It has very heavy rainfall, with tropical rainforest vegetation. Climatically and culturally it is similar to the eastern tropical areas of Peru and Colombia. It is much more sparsely inhabited than either the highlands or the coast, and the various indigenous peoples have preserved many of their prehispanic cultural features. Most of these peoples, although they make such items as baskets and hammocks, do not do much weaving and their culture does not relate to the highland traditions that are the chief subject of this volume.

The Shuar and Achuar (called Jivaro in earlier literature), living in the southern part of this area, while of predominantly tropical forest culture, do have a weaving tradition that seems to bear some relationship to adjacent highland areas (Bianchi 1982). Another group, the rainforest Quichua (called Canelos Quichua in earlier literature), has been heavily influenced by highland traditions, including language and costume.

Ecuador's claim to Amazonian territory was reduced by half as a result of an invasion by Peru in 1941 and a settlement in Río de Janeiro in which Peru was supported by the United States (see Whitten with Fine 1981, note 4, for references). This event remains a very sore point in Ecuador, and most maps printed in Ecuador show the country with a boundary drawn according to the pre-1941 claim, with a dotted line marking the protocol of Río de Janeiro. Maps printed elsewhere, on the other hand, show the disputed territory as belonging to Peru, which today actually administers the area.

Historical Perspective

Ann P. Rowe

At the time of the Inca conquest, the territory that is now Ecuador was divided into many small and often antagonistic political units, which were smaller than the known linguistic units. At least six different languages were spoken in the highlands. From north to south, these languages were Pasto (in what is now Carchi province), Cayambi (Imbabura and northern Pichincha), Panzaleo or Lata (southern Pichincha, Cotopaxi, and Tungurahua), Puruhuay or Puruhá (Chimborazo and Bolivar), Cañar (Cañar and Azuay), and Palta (Loja).[3]

Records from early in the period of Spanish occupation indicate that people living in the highlands commonly traded with people living on the outer slopes of the Andes for products that could not be grown in the high valley, such as cotton and chili peppers (see, e.g., Salomon 1986). The passes to the western slopes are

3. This list is based on information from John H. Rowe.

3 Ingapirca, Cañar province. This site, which has the most impressive prehispanic ruins in highland Ecuador, was an important local center, with an overlay of fine Inca style stonework. Photo by Lynn A. Meisch, 1978.

more numerous than those to the east, so the majority of the trade networks were in this direction. This trade appears to date well into the prehispanic past and cotton was in fact an important component of the highland textile tradition until comparatively recently (see, e.g., Doyon-Bernard 1994). Coca, another tropical product, was cultivated in prehispanic times, but at some point early in the colonial period it ceased to be either grown or used in Ecuador.

The Inca empire

The Inca empire originated in Cuzco in what is now the southern highlands of Peru. It began its expansionist policies under Pachacuti Inca Yupanqui, who reigned between about 1438 and 1471. The highlands of what is now Ecuador to as far north as Quito were conquered toward the end of Pachacuti's reign by an army under the command of Pachacuti's son and successor Tupa Inca (Fig. 3).[4] Although Tupa Inca also campaigned in Guayas and Manabí on the coast, and established some sort of foothold, it does not appear that this area was as thoroughly incorporated into the empire as were the highlands.

Tupa Inca, who reigned from around 1471 to 1493, was succeeded by his son Huayna Capac (died 1528), who had been born in Tumi Pampa (modern Cuenca) during the campaign. It was Huayna Capac who conquered the northern highlands of Ecuador. The Inca army marched as far north as the valley of Atres in what

4. This account of the Incas in Ecuador is based on information from John H. Rowe.

is now southern Colombia, but the territory actually incorporated into the empire ended at the current border between Ecuador and Colombia. Huayna Capac also went to the coast, but was interrupted by news of an epidemic of a European disease that killed his designated successor and many other important people, and to which he also shortly succumbed.

The Incas divided the territory of highland Ecuador into two provinces, one governed from Quito and the other from Tumi Pampa. The border between them was around Mocha in what is now southern Tungurahua province. The Incas introduced their language and ordered their subjects to learn it, and this process was well under way by the time the Spanish arrived. The Spanish found it convenient to continue this policy, with the result that the indigenous highland Ecuadorian languages all died out in the colonial period.

The Incas also had a regular policy of moving people from previously conquered areas to newly conquered ones, often on a large scale, as part of the pacification process. Many people were moved from one part of Ecuador to another as well as from Peru and even Bolivia into Ecuador. These resettled people were called *mitma* or *mitmaq* in the Inca language; the Spanish wrote this word as *mitima*.

Following Huayna Capac's death, there was a civil war between two of his sons: Huascar, who was Huayna Capac's next choice in Cuzco, and Atau Huallpa (Atahualpa), who was the governor of Quito. The key event in terms of Ecuador was a battle at Ambato in 1531 in which Atau Huallpa defeated Huascar and subsequently massacred large numbers of Cañar men and boys for having fought on Huascar's side. Subsequently Atau Huallpa succeeded in having Huascar and his family captured and killed. This civil war greatly facilitated the Spanish conquest.

The Spanish empire

The Spanish under Francisco Pizarro arrived on the Ecuadorian coast in 1531, but first proceeded to Peru where they captured Atau Huallpa in 1532 and put him to death the following year. A Spanish force under Sebastián de Benalcázar conquered Ecuador in 1534, with assistance from the Cañares, who were happy to fight against the supporters of Atau Huallpa.

The Spanish naturally introduced numerous aspects of their own culture into Ecuador, including their language, the Roman Catholic religion, food crops such as barley, fava beans, citrus fruits, etc., animals such as sheep, cattle, pigs, and chickens, and technology such as the treadle loom and ironworking.

The Spanish administration was very oppressive for Ecuador's indigenous population. Populations declined dramatically through the introduction of European diseases. Spanish officials took much of the best land for themselves, relocating indigenous communities. Large tribute quotas were demanded in both labor and goods, including textiles. The Spanish forced some indigenous people to move long distances to provide labor for their mines or armies. Other people left their ancestral homes hoping to avoid the tribute and labor demands. Indeed, over half of the indigenous population was living elsewhere than their original lands by the end of the seventeenth century (Alchon 1991:82–85).

Because Ecuador lacked any appreciable mineral wealth, the economy was centered on agriculture and on textile production in factories (*obrajes* S.) using Spanish equipment (see, e.g., Cushner 1982). The fabrics produced were plain-weave and twill-weave yardage of cotton and wool in various grades. They were mostly exported to other parts of the Spanish empire. Working conditions in these factories were notoriously bad, and the pay amounted to little or nothing. By the eighteenth century, the Ecuadorian obrajes were suffering competition from fabrics made in Peru and in Europe, and the economy stagnated (Tyrer 1976). Lowered income from obrajes caused the Spanish to raise tribute levels, sparking numerous localized armed rebellions (Moreno Yánez 1985).

The Republic of Ecuador

Spanish policies to raise money in their South American lands also alienated the local elites of Spanish descent, who responded by initiating an independence movement, which succeeded in 1822. The modern state of Ecuador was founded in 1830. Nevertheless, the new republic continued to treat its indigenous population in the same way as had the Spanish crown. Legislation that might seem to offer prospects for reform often had little real effect. For example, tribute was abolished in 1857, but income from exports of cocoa and Panama hats had by this time effectively supplanted it (Mörner 1985).

The predominant (though not exclusive) pattern was that much of the agricultural land was owned by a small number of whites, who ruthlessly exploited indigenous labor to operate these estates (called *haciendas* S.). A common form of exploitation was debt peonage (*concertaje* S.). An indigenous family received wages insufficient to cover necessary expenses, as well as the use of a plot of land (*huasipungo* Q.) within the estate. A new constitution in 1906 officially separated church and state, which simply meant that former church haciendas were rented to private individuals by the state and management was as oppressive as before (Muratorio 1981:510; Weismantel 1988:65). It is only since the 1964 Law of Agrarian Reform that this pattern has begun to break.

The modern political geography of Ecuador divides the country into twenty provinces, of which ten include the highland areas. These in turn are subdivided into cantons, which are subdivided into parishes. Although originally ecclesiastical, the parishes now have a secular organization. They are composed of individual communities and hamlets.

Indigenous Identity in Ecuador

Lynn A. Meisch

There is no census count of the indigenous highland population, but out of a total population of 10,990,900 for the country in 1993 (*El Comercio*, August 29, 1993), it is estimated that some 40 percent is indigenous (Corkill and Cubit 1988; CONAIE 1989), the vast majority of whom live in the highlands. There is enormous diversity among and within the different groups. As CONAIE (Confederación de Nacionalidades Indígenas del Ecuador), the national indigenous organization, puts it, "We indígenas are immersed in the structure of Ecuadorian society and for that reason we are campesinos, workers, business people, artisans, etc.; some of us work in the country, others in the city, some of us receive salaries, others do not" (1989:261). In the sierra alone, indigenous people range from illiterate, Quichua monolingual, Roman Catholic families farming small holdings on the páramos of Cotopaxi province, who have never been farther than Latacunga, to wealthy Otavalo Evangelical Christian (or Mormon or Catholic) weaving and merchant families, whose bilingual and trilingual offspring have degrees from universities in Latin America, Europe, or the United States, and who have traveled widely internationally to sell textiles and perform music.

Ethnicity in Ecuador is complex and subtle. In the country as a whole there are differences between how people identify themselves and how they are identified by others, having more to do with social class than with physical characteristics (phenotype). In addition, there are differences in the ethnic categories used by people living in the sierra and by those on the coast. Because this volume features indigenous highland costume, we are mainly concerned with indigenous ethnic identity in the highlands.

From an indigenous perspective, the fundamental distinction in highland Ecuador is between *blancos* (whites) and *indígenas* (or *runa,* the Quichua word for a person or human, used by indigenous people to refer to themselves).

The term *mestizo* (meaning mixed European and indigenous ancestry) is sometimes used by people to identify themselves or others and is sometimes hyphenated with the term *white,* as in *blancos-mestizos,* to indicate the nonindigenous population. There are many Ecuadorians of mixed descent, some of whom consider themselves white, others of whom consider themselves indigenous. These distinctions are not racial but social. Many people who call themselves *blancos* or *mestizos* have darker hair, skin, and eyes than do people who call themselves *indígenas.*

Today, there are four main visible or public determinants of indigenous versus white identity in highland Ecuador: language, residence, income, and dress. Of these, dress is the most important. Indigenous people can speak Spanish rather than Quichua, live in Quito or other large cities or even abroad rather than in their natal communities, and have incomes that far surpass their neighbors who are considered white, as is the case for many Otavalos, but as long as they wear traditional costume they are considered indigenous, both in their own eyes and in the eyes of other Ecuadorians. The situation is different in Ecuador's Amazon basin, where language and territory, rather than costume, are the main markers of indigenous ethnic identity (Hendricks 1991:61; Whitten 1976:2, 213).

Ecuadorian society has been highly stratified, with indigenous people considered to be at the lowest social level. The details of such stratification and the interactions of people from different levels vary from one area to another. White social stratification and attitudes do not concern us here, however, except as they impinge on indigenous self-perception.

Ecuadorian indigenous people are currently claiming and sometimes receiving rights that place them on parity with whites, while insisting on the importance, value, and preservation of their cultural traditions, including the use of a distinct dress. This book coincides with a general resurgence of indigenous identity, pride, and political activisim in Ecuador. Antonio Males, a historian and an Otavalo, sums up the situation:

> In order for an Indian (*indio*) in this country to be considered a citizen, he must transform himself into a white (*mishu*), dress like one, behave like one, and think like one, which is to say, turn against his own brothers and sisters; and of course, an Indian cannot be an intellectual and remain an Indian. But we are demonstrating that Indians can be citizens, that we can be intellectuals while considering ourselves Indians, with our own language, culture and history (1993:162, Meisch translation from Spanish).

1964 and Beyond

Lynn A. Meisch

Ecuador underwent a major agrarian reform in 1964 that over the long run profoundly changed indigenous–mestizo-white relations. The impetus for the 1964 Law of Agrarian Reform was pressure from the Alliance for Progress of the Organization of American States and the fear of a Cuban style Communist revolution in Ecuador. The law ended serfdom (huasipungo) on the haciendas, giving former huasipungeros title to their plots, with a minimum of five hectares (12 ½ acres) of productive land per family. The law was circumvented in some instances and implemented in others only through armed confrontations (indigenous people fighting with machetes, hoes, sticks, and rocks), particularly in Cañar and Chimborazo. Still, many families received land, and the law encouraged some hacienda owners to sell parcels rather than get entangled in violent struggles or interminable court disputes. State (formerly church) haciendas were abolished, as for example in Zumbagua (see Weismantel 1988).

In some communities, indigenous people have formed cooperatives, which usually involves a number of families pooling their money to buy a large tract of land that is used for communal farming or grazing. This does not mean that the families give up their individual parcels. In fact, land tenure is astonishingly complex because the indigenous custom is to divide land and property equally among all children. This means that parcels get smaller with each generation and that both men and women bring to their marriage land and property, which they hold in their own name unless they acquire additional property jointly. Families often end up owning parcels of land all over the area, often at different elevations, making it possible to grow a variety of crops. The disadvantage is that frequently there are great distances between fields or they are located far away from the family's home.

Significant population growth has meant that many people inherit too little land to live on, so they must leave the community and make a living elsewhere.

Despite the reform, many large estates remain in the best valley bottom lands. A German friend once commented that Ecuador was the only place he had ever been where the cows grazed in the valleys and the crops were planted on the mountainsides. A trip through Ecuador's Valley of the Volcanoes offers stunning panoramas of enormous, green landholdings on the valley floor, some stretching as far as the eye can see, occupied by a herd of dairy cattle or a prize bull. The mountainsides of the eastern and western cordilleras that flank the valley are a patchwork of tiny, steep, cultivated plots whose indigenous owners look down daily on the white-owned estates below. Some of the valley haciendas are legitimate farms, although they could easily be reduced by three-fourths and still be viable, with the fields redistributed to landless farming families. Other estates, 28 percent of them according to CONAIE, run a few head of cattle to prove that the land is not *tierra baldía* (abandoned or unused), thereby exempting it from land reform (Macas 1991:10).

The CONAIE leadership is not happy with the 1964 agrarian reform, considering it a tactic to "help suppress the forms of agricultural production that were an obstacle to development; likewise a measure that contributed to calming the indigenous insurrection" (ibid.:8). Even if the land reform was imperfect, however, the law gave people freedom. Abolishing huasipungo meant that people could choose to farm their own land, or sell it or rent it out and try life in the city; freedom to go to school, to open a small shop in front of the house, to become an artisan, to get an education, to travel. Not everyone wants to stay down on the farm.

The government apparatus established to handle agrarian reform is called Instituto Ecuatoriano de Reforma Agraria y Colonización (IERAC). The colonization part is significant. The government encouraged colonization of the Oriente as a safety valve for unrealized aspirations in the sierra. The official position was that this territory was unoccupied, which must have come as a shock to such groups as the Shuar, Achuar, rainforest Quichua, Siona, Secoya, Huaorani, and Cofán, who had lived there for centuries, if not millennia. Colonization pitted indigenous people against one another in a contest for rainforest land, which is unsuited to intensive agriculture and cattle ranching and which does not have a large population carrying capacity. It is no great surprise that one of the first well-organized, successful indigenous federations was the Shuar Federation in the southern Oriente, established with the help of the Silesian mission in 1964 (see Salazar 1981).

Social reform continued piecemeal. In 1970, six years after the abolition of huasipungo, *precarismos* (S., sharecropping) was also outlawed and in 1973 rent in the form of labor. In 1972, to push for completion of land reform, indigenous people from six highland provinces founded ECUARUNARI (Ecuador Runacunapac Riccharimui: Q., Ecuador Indígenas Awaken). ECUARUNARI limited its membership to indigenous people, stated its nonviolent intentions, and identified with the Roman Catholic Church, which, influenced by liberation theology, had supported land reform and other social justice programs in Ecuador. The 1960s and 1970s also saw increasingly successful Evangelical Protestant missionizing, particularly in Chimborazo and Tungurahua provinces, and these indigenous people formed their own organizations (Muratorio 1981; Stoll 1990, chap. 9). Throughout the decade, ECUARUNARI organized and grew, establishing contact with other Ecuadorian indigenous and workers groups and with indigenous federations in Colombia, Peru, and Bolivia.

The increased migration of colonists from the sierra to the rainforest in the sixties and seventies coincided with Ecuador's oil boom, which put additional pressure on groups in the central (Whitten 1985) and northern Oriente, where large oil reserves were found. Such groups as the Cofán and the Huaorani are engaged in a continuing battle to prevent oil drilling in their reserves. Various Oriente indigenous groups formed federations to block colonization and oil exploration, culminating in the establishment of a regional organization, Confederación de Nacionalidades Indígenas de la Amazonia Ecuatoriana (CONFENAIE) in 1980.

The same year, ECUARUNARI and CONFENAIE held a congress and established a national executive council (CONACNIE) to coordinate plans among indigenous organizations, contacting or helping organize fledgling federations on the coast. In 1986, CONACNIE became CONAIE. CONAIE has emerged on the national scene as the largest, best organized, and most powerful federation of indigenous peoples. In keeping with the diversity of the groups of which it is composed, there is no rigidly enforced CONAIE party line. It is impressive that CONAIE has welded these disparate ethnic groups into a national organization and come up with some agreement on an overall agenda.

At the top of the list of CONAIE demands is land: land titles for indigenous communities and the settlement of major territorial disputes throughout the country in a timely manner without prohibitive legal fees. According to CONAIE, 50 percent of the holdings smaller than five hectares (12.5 acres) account for 4 percent of the land surface and support 3 million inhabitants, while holdings greater than 100 hectares (250 acres) account for 50 percent of the land and are populated by 200,000 persons (Macas 1991:8). The demand for genuine land reform, however the details are worked out, is the glue that binds the indigenous movement.

Another item on CONAIE's agenda is education. The generation born after the abolition of huasipungo in 1964 has had more opportunity for education and is therefore more literate than their parents and grandparents. In 1988, under pressure from CONAIE, the Ecuadorian government established a department for intercultural and bilingual (indigenous language and Spanish) education, DINEIB, which functions in fifteen provinces with 3,600 teachers and 80,000 indigenous students (Paz y Miño 1994), although it is hampered by a lack of funds and shortages of bilingual teachers. In the highlands, this program means instruction in Quichua, with the purpose of ultimately completing schooling in Spanish. The bilingual program has resulted in a number of publications in indigenous languages that are far more culturally sensitive than what has been propagated in the regular textbooks (see Stutzman 1981). The 1980s also saw the rise of an ambitious publishing program of books, not only about indigenous affairs but by indigenous people, many of which are cited in this work. An adult literacy program was functioning in 1988–89 when we were doing research for this volume, and many of the people involved in this campaign were helpful to us.

In order to call attention to the need for land reform and for the immediate settlement of a number of pressing land disputes, CONAIE called a coordinated, nationwide strike in May of 1990. The insurrection succeeded in bringing the country to a halt for a week and served notice that indigenous people were serious and that they could effectively paralyze the country. Likewise, Monday, October 12, 1992, the 500th anniversary of Columbus's arrival in the Americas, was observed by indigenous people in Ecuador as "500 years of indigenous resistance and survival," in opposition to the Ecuadorian and Spanish governments' celebration of an "encounter of two worlds." The week leading up to the twelfth saw large indigenous and campesino strikes and demonstrations in cities and towns throughout the country, and thousands of people participated in marches, including an enormous march from Riobamba that was halted at the entrance to Quito by the army.

CONAIE's effectiveness was again demonstrated by the amendment in July of 1994 of another agrarian reform law that it felt favored the large landowners. Thirty years after the 1964 agrarian reform, the issue is again on the table, only this time indigenous people and campesinos are active participants in the events that affect their lives, and they are a force that cannot be ignored.

Chapter 2

Ecuadorian Textile Technology

Fibers

Ann P. Rowe and

Lynn A. Meisch

The leaf fibers

There are two important leaf fibers used in Ecuador today, both of the family Agaveaceae, but belonging to two distinct genera, *Furcraea* and *Agave*. The flowers of *Furcraea* species are pendulous rather than erect as in *Agave* species. Plants of both genera have long fleshy leaves, usually with spiny edges, which emerge from a base low on the ground (Fig. 4). The fibers lie lengthwise in the leaves.

The species of furcraea and agave common in the Ecuadorian Andes are found between 700 and 3,000 meters (2,300–9,840 feet) in elevation, but grow best somewhere around 1,700 meters (5,575 feet). They grow wild in many areas, but are also often cultivated into lines around crop fields. Extracting the fiber from the pulp in the leaves is a laborious process involving shredding, soaking, beating, and washing, and then further hand separation. The leaves may also be crushed to form a soapy lather for washing hair and clothing, and the end spines can be used as needles.

Although similar in appearance, in the techniques used for processing them, and

4 At left is an agave plant, with wide curving leaves; to the right, a furcraea plant, with straighter, narrower leaves. Peguche, Imbabura province. Photo by Lynn A. Meisch, 1985.

often indiscriminately called by the same names, furcraea and agave in fact differ in some respects and may be used for different purposes. In this text we will refer to the plants as furcraea and agave, for the sake of clarity.

Furcraea andina is the species of furcraea found in Ecuador and, as its name suggests, is native to the Andean area (Towle 1961:32–33). Its leaves are a brighter green and are stiffer and narrower than those of the agaves commonly found in Ecuador (Fig. 4, right). The fibers are used to make rope and sandal soles, as well as coarse woven sacks, and in some areas are also used to make looped bags (*shigras*). Looping is a technique of prehispanic origin in Ecuador, in which a needle is used to draw the end of the yarn through previous work at the edge of a fabric (Fig. 5). New fibers are twisted onto the end of the yarn when it grows short.

Agave on the other hand is native to Mexico, where many species, useful for varying purposes, were and are still cultivated (Gentry 1982). One of these species, generally identified as *Agave americana*, seems to have been introduced into South America sometime in the later colonial period (Yacovleff and Herrera 1934:268). It has fleshy bluish-green leaves that are wider than those of furcraea and curve slightly (Fig. 4, left).

Currently, agave is the preferred fiber for making shigras in Cotopaxi province. The plant is more frequently used as a boundary marker than is furcraea. If the bud of the stem is cut out, a sweet sap (*chawarmishki* Q.) collects in the resulting hole and is used as a sweetener and as a drink for medicinal purposes. The leaves are also fed to animals.

Today there is a profusion of local names for these plants in Ecuador. Both are called *chawar* or *tsawar* in Quichua and *penco* in Spanish (pronounced "pinku" by many Quichua speakers). A related Spanish word, *penca*, refers to a fleshy leaf of such a plant. Furcraea is called *yuraj chawar* or *tsawar* (Q.) or *penco blanco* (S.), *yuraj* and *blanco* both meaning "white," while agave is called *yana chawar* or *tsawar* (Q.) or *penco negro* (S.), *yana* and *negro* both meaning "black." The tall stem that grows when the plant is mature may be called *palo* (S.), *ojo* (S. for "eye"), or *maguey grande*, which is the Mexican term. The fiber from both plants is called *cabuya*, or sometimes *pita*, throughout Ecuador. To add to the confusion, sometimes the plants themselves are called *cabuya*. *Cabuya* is a Taino word introduced into Ecuador from the Caribbean by the Spanish.

Both agave and furcraea are grown, processed, and fabricated into goods throughout the Ecuadorian sierra. However, the most important centers for furcraea growing and processing are in Imbabura and Chimborazo provinces, while Cotopaxi and Tungurahua grow more agave.

Cotton

The species of cotton native to South America, *Gossypium barbadense,* is found in the northern and central Andes in those zones low and warm enough to support it. It occurs sporadically on the Pacific coast, in some subtropical inter-Andean val-

5   *Diagrammatic construction of simple looping, the structure used for Ecuadorian shigras. From Emery 1980, fig. 9.*

leys, on the western and eastern slopes of the Andes, and in the Amazon rainforest. Indigenous cotton, called *algodón criollo* in Spanish and *utcu* or *chillu* in Quichua, is generally cultivated as a large-sized perennial garden crop, mixed in with other plants, rather than as a distinct field crop. It is often described as bush or tree cotton and can grow as tall as 4.5 meters (15 feet). It grows in marginal soil and requires little maintenance. It can be harvested continuously for up to six years, starting 8–10 months after planting (Vreeland 1978, 1986).

Cotton fiber occurs as the seed hair of the plant. When living it is tubular, but after it is picked, the shaft collapses and twists, giving it a dull, fuzzy appearance. The length of the fibers in American cottons is greater than that of Asian cottons, and modern hybrids are all derived chiefly from these American species. Cotton is difficult to dye with natural dyes, and of those known, indigo is the only one currently used in highland Ecuador.

Camelid hair

The fiber-producing animals native to the Andean area are related to the camels of the old world, both belonging to the family Camelidae. There are four Andean camelids: the wild guanaco and vicuña, and the domesticated llama and alpaca, all closely related. The hair of all these animals was used for textile products

6 Ecuadorian llamas, Zumbagua, Cotopaxi province. Slide by Mary J. Weismantel, 1984.

in prehispanic times, but that of the alpaca and vicuña is the finest.

Although there is historical evidence for the presence of guanacos and vicuñas as well as llamas in Ecuador in prehispanic times, only the llama survived the early colonial period to the present day. They are currently found in small numbers in the central provinces of Cotopaxi (Fig. 6; see also chapter 6), Tungurahua, and Chimborazo. Several modern attempts have been made to introduce additional llamas, as well as alpacas and vicuñas.

The llama (*Lama glama*) stands about 5 feet (1.5 meters) tall. Male llamas were and are used as pack animals, for loads up to about 75 pounds (34 kilograms). The meat is also eaten. In Ecuador today, the only place we found in which the hair was said to be spun and woven is the Llangahua area in Tungurahua province on the páramo below Mount Chimborazo (see the section "Other Indigenous Peoples," chapter 7).

Sheep's wool

Sheep, including Merinos, a Spanish breed with particularly fine wool, were introduced almost immediately after the Spanish conquest. (See the section "Eastern Cañar," chapter 12, for information on the modern indigenous use of sheep.)

Sheep's wool differs from other animal hairs in being covered with tiny scales, and it is this property which defines it as "wool." Thus, the term wool properly applies only to the fiber of sheep, and not to camelid fiber, which has very few scales, and those faint. The scales make sheep's wool feel much rougher than camelid hair.

They also cause the fibers to mat together if they are rubbed against each other in the presence of moisture. The fibers can be made to adhere solely by this means, a technique called felting, used for example in making the European style hats still worn in many parts of Ecuador. This characteristic is also exploited in European fabric production, by weaving wool fabric rather loosely, and then applying hot water and friction to shrink it and cause the surface fibers to felt, a process called fulling. Fulling mills were established in Ecuador in the colonial period, and the hand process is still occasionally used, for example to finish Salasaca ponchos.

Synthetic fibers

Synthetic fibers are polymers (long chains of small molecules) synthesized from petroleum or coal tar derivatives and extruded as continuous filaments. Polyesters were invented in 1941 and include such brand names as Dacron, Fortrel, and Trevira. Acrylics were first commercially manufactured in 1950 and include such brand names as Orlon, Acrilan, and Dralon. They are dyed and usually also spun into yarn in the factory. However, since factory-made yarn often has a slack twist, Andean spinners may re-spin it to add more twist or twist two strands together in order to make it more suitable for handweaving.

The acrylics (usually referred to as *orlón* in Ecuador, after the DuPont trade name) mimic the appearance of wool, but do not have scales and are therefore smoother and softer. They are usually cheaper than wool and require less processing, and therefore beginning in the 1970s have been increasingly used in Ecuador, especially areas such as Otavalo where there is a wool shortage. There are factories for acrylic yarn in Quito and Cuenca, and some acrylic is also imported. Polyester yarn is seldom used in handweaving, but clothing made from machine-made polyester fabric is readily available.

Dyes

Ann P. Rowe

Dyes were among the principal products of the Spanish American colonies, and although these products are no longer commercially significant, some natural dyeing does persist in Ecuador today. Cochineal (*Dactylopius* spp., called *cochinilla* or *grana*, both S.) is an insect that is parasitic on the prickly pear cactus and produces beautiful red and purple colors. It is native to the Americas and is still cultivated and used to dye wool by the Salasaca in Tungurahua province. Indigo (called *añil* S.), of which there is an indigenous American species (*Indigofera suffruticosa*), produces many shades of blue. It is a tropical plant, but can be processed into cakes that are easily transported. Natural indigo produced in El Salvador was available in highland Ecuador up until the late 1970s and was used for dyeing both cotton and wool in several areas. Now, however, only the more expensive synthetic indigo from Germany is available. Another natural dye still in common use is the bark of walnut trees (*Juglans neotropica*, called *nogal* in Spanish and *tukti* in Quichua), which produces various shades of brown. (See Jaramillo 1988a for more on these and other natural dyes.)

Most dyeing done today in Ecuador, however, is done with synthetic dyes, which are much easier to use than natural dyes. For example, they require no preparation and much less firewood. Synthetic dyes are locally referred to as *anilina* (S.), or "aniline," after the first synthetic dyes that were developed in the 1850s and 1860s. Since then, however, many other types of synthetic dyes have become available, and it is doubtful that those currently in use are "aniline" in the strict sense of the term. The powders are sold from tins, with the seller frequently combining powders from different tins to create the desired color. We have not made a special study in order to analyze the contents of these tins, and will therefore simply refer to them generically as synthetic.

Either the raw fiber, or the yarns, or the finished woven cloth can be dyed. All these techniques are practiced in Ecuador. Cloth dyeing is common in Tungurahua, Chimborazo, and Cañar provinces, as well as in Saraguro.

Spinning

Lynn A. Meisch

People have been spinning in Ecuador for millennia, twisting fibers into yarn for weaving, thread for sewing, and cordage for netted bags, fishing lines, sandal soles, and other uses (Figs. 7–8). Although the leaf fibers can be made into thread merely by rolling them between the hands or along the leg, this technique will not work with such short fibers as cotton, camelid hair, or sheep's wool. For these fibers, a spindle must be used, and a spindle can also be used for agave and furcraea. This technique of yarn making, of drawing out and twisting fibers together using a spindle, is called spinning in English. To spin is *hilar* in Spanish, *puchkay* in Quichua.

The prehispanic technique of spinning with a hand spindle persists in nearly every area of highland Ecuador today, despite the Spanish introduction of simple spinning wheel technology, which dramatically increases the speed at which spinning can be done. The main exception is Otavalo, where spinning wheels are used to assist in commercial textile production. This conservatism is probably due to the fact that spinning wheels are relatively bulky, and not as easily obtainable or adaptable to the contexts in which Ecuadorian spinning often takes place. For example, spinning wheels are not as portable as a hand spindle, and you cannot spin with one when traveling.

The hand spindles used in Ecuador today are between 30 and 60 centimeters (12 and 24 inches) long, with roughly the same diameter at their thickest part as a pencil, and are most often made from pampas grass stems, locally called *sigsig* (Q., *Cortaderia rudinscula*). This practice is so usual that the most common term for spindle in highland Ecuador is *sigsig*. In some areas, chontadura palm, eucalyptus, or other wood is used instead. Basically, any straight slender stick will do. The spindles are often carved to a tapering point at both ends; pampas grass tapers naturally.

Whorls (*tortero* S., *piruru* Q.) are usually added to serve as a flywheel and to help the spindle rotate. Today in Ecuador, whorls vary widely and include perforated potsherds, pieces of wood, cardboard, or cane, small potatoes or chili peppers, ceramic electrical insulators, and finely carved stone whorls (the latter in Saraguro, Loja province).

The spindle is generally manipulated with the right hand, and the unspun fiber with the left. While the right hand causes the spindle to rotate, the left hand pulls the right amount of fiber from the bundle, a process called drafting. As the thread forms, the arms are spread farther and farther apart. When they attain their maximum reach, the spinner ceases drafting and winds the yarn onto the spindle. The process then begins again.

In the Andean area, indigenous spinning methods can be divided into two categories, those in which the spindle is released, often dropped so that it is suspended by the thread that is being created (usually called drop spinning), and those in which the spindle is always held in the hand (hand-supported spinning). In drop spinning, both hands are available to draft the fiber; in hand-supported spinning, one-handed drafting is usual.

The long hair of camelids or sheep's wool can easily be spun with the drop-spinning method, and this technique is typical of Bolivia and southern Peru (see, e.g., Franquemont 1986a:315–16; Meisch 1986). In these areas, when the spindle becomes heavy or when extremely fine yarn is being spun, the tip of the spindle is sometimes rested on a plate, gourd, or piece of crockery on the ground so that the yarn does not break. The vertical position of the spindle, the finger motion used to set the spindle spinning, and the release of the spindle with two-handed drafting is the same in either case.

Cotton has a shorter staple than camelid hair and a smoother surface than wool, making it more difficult to spin because the fibers tend to slip past each other rather than grip before they are twisted together. Although drop spinning of cotton is practiced in some parts of the world—for example, Indonesia—in South America the spindle is always supported when the fibers are twisted. Cotton spinners I visited in Icla, in the department of Chuquisaca, Bolivia, held the spindle vertically, as in drop spinning, but they always supported the spindle in their laps or on the ground.

In northern Peru and Ecuador, however, the spindle is always held in the hand (see also Meisch 1980b, 1982; Vreeland 1986). If the spinner is seated, the tip may rest on the ground, but the spindle is never released. It is likely that this technology is based on the use of cotton, which has been the predominant fiber used in this area since well before the Spanish conquest.

There are two possible directions in which the yarn can be twisted, resulting in the orientation of the fibers in the yarn corresponding to the slant of the body of the letters S or Z. In Ecuadorian hand-supported spinning, there are two basic styles, one yielding S- and the other Z-twist. If the spindle is held more or less horizontally and rotated in the usual, most natural manner with the same thumb, index, and middle finger motions made when snapping one's fingers, the result is an S-twist (Fig. 7). If the spindle is held vertically and rotated with the same snapping motion (the thumb moving up and away from the body, the fingers moving toward the palm), the result is a yarn with a Z-twist (Fig. 8). Since a vertical spindle and the same finger motion is used in south Andean drop-spindle spinning, the resulting twist in this technique is also Z.

Sometimes, yarn is used immediately after its initial spinning. At other times, in order to make a stronger and more even yarn, two or more spun threads are twisted together, a process called plying. To ply is commonly called *torcer* (twist) in Spanish, though the more accurate *retorcer* is also used; the Quichua terms vary. In plying, the yarn is generally twisted in the opposite direction from that in which it was spun. S-spun yarn must be Z-plied and vice versa. In Ecuador, this is usually accomplished by holding the spindle in the opposite manner from spinning. For example, Cañari yarn is Z-spun with the spindle held vertically, so it is S-plied with the spindle held horizontally.

In Bolivia and southern Peru, yarn spun the reverse of normal has magical associations. Because in the southern Andes the spindle is held vertically and

7 *Rosario Sisapaca demonstrating hand-supported spinning with a horizontal spindle, yielding S-twist, Nitiluisa (San Juan area), central Chimborazo province. Photo by Lynn A. Meisch, 1989.*

8 *Rosario Sisapaca demonstrating hand-supported spinning with a vertical spindle, yielding Z-twist, Nitiluisa (San Juan area), central Chimborazo province. Photo by Lynn A. Meisch, 1989.*

dropped, normal yarn is Z-spun (S-plied) and left spun yarn (*llu'qi* Q.) is S-spun (Z-plied). This is not true in Ecuador, where what is "normal" (S- or Z-spun) depends on the community. For example, in Saraguro, S-spun yarn is considered normal or right spun and Z-spun yarn is considered the reverse, left spun. In Ecuador, when the spindle is held horizontally it is called *echado* (reclining) in Spanish and when it is held vertically it is called *parado* (standing up). No matter how the spindle is held, when it is rotating well it is said to be *bailando* (S., dancing).

The spindle is anthropomorphized in highland Quichua riddles. For example, "What is it? Just one leg with a hundred intestines," with the answer, "The spindle with wool yarn" (Kleymeyer 1990:78). Kleymeyer collected a number of riddles along this line, and I have heard the whorl called the spindle's pollera skirt, which twirls when a woman dances.

The kind of fiber, choice of spindle and whorl, the placement of the whorl on the spindle, the use of S- or Z-twist, the diameter of the yarn, its degree of twist, whether yarn is used as a single strand, doubled but not plied, or plied, and the gender of the spinner and plier vary among Ecuador's ethnic groups as well as within groups.

Context of spinning

It is important to remember that yarn is always spun for a particular purpose, with a particular textile in mind, and this affects the thickness of the yarn, the degree of twist, and whether or not it is plied.

Although spinning appears easy and effortless, especially when the spinner is also hiking up a mountain trail with a load of firewood, it takes considerable skill. Children learn at a young age, between four and six, sometimes with toy spindles and distaffs. They practice until they are competent, which is seldom later than age eight or nine, and often earlier.

In most of highland Ecuador the ability to spin well is still considered an essential feminine skill. "Now you are a woman; you can spin. Now you can get married," the Saragureños told me when I mastered their spinning techniques. Laura Miller received similar accolades in Salasaca when she learned to spin. Although spinning with the hand spindle is generally considered a female activity, most men and boys in spinning households can spin or are familiar with the process. Many males will spin at home, but will not do so in public, and were as helpful to me as females when I was learning. Spinning in colonial obrajes was done by males on European spinning wheels, so the use of the walking wheel is not as gendered as the use of the hand spindle.

It must be emphasized, however, that ideology (spinning as feminine) and practice frequently diverge. If there is a job to be done, gender often becomes secondary and males and females pitch in. Both sexes take pride in their spinning and plying because high-quality yarn is essential for high-quality textiles.

Because teasing, carding, and joining rolags are simple, repetitive tasks and can be done sitting down, these jobs are often assigned to old people or those with disabilities, who can thus be useful and contribute to the maintenance of the household. This also applies to spinning (depending on the abilities of the spinner) and plying. In one household we visited in Tungurahua province, a young man with a mental disability living with his elderly parents helped them by plying yarn, which they wove into warp-resist dyed blankets. His plying method was unusual because he did not wind the plied yarn onto his spindle but let it accumulate at his feet in a big kinky pile which his mother later made into skeins using a wooden frame niddy noddy. He just sat there and happily plied away.

How long does it take to spin the wool for a poncho, shawl, or blanket? The problem with doing time studies of spinning is that it is an intermittent activity, worked in around the day's more pressing activities: child care and cooking, work in the fields, feeding the animals, gathering firewood, trips to the market, and laundry, which are done by either or both genders, depending on local custom, although women predominate as cooks and baby watchers. Spinners often haul their work along with them, accounting for the cliché of the industrious Andean woman spinning as she walks along the road or herds her sheep. But like all clichés, it has its origin in truth, and I have invoked it myself. Healthy males and females rarely sit idle and will pick up their spinning and plying between other chores or even while doing other chores, as long as their hands are free.

In addition, there are many variables to consider. If fine yarn rather than coarse, thick yarn is used in a garment there are more threads per inch and it takes longer to spin the necessary amount. That is, the same amount of fleece might go into a garment with fine yarn as with thick yarn, but the spinner will need to produce many more yards of fine yarn. It can also take longer to spin two yards of fine yarn than two yards of coarse yarn because the wool has to be extremely clean, which means more careful teasing; there are more lumps for the drafting fingers to smooth out, which slows down the process; and the yarn is more likely to break. Spinning fine yarn therefore represents an enormous investment of time and labor and it is rather amazing that so many Andean spinners still do it. But spinning is a highly valued skill in traditional Andean societies where people still make their own clothing, blankets, and sacks.

Although I did not do extensive time studies, Edward and Christine Franquemont carried out a systematic study of textile production, including drop-spindle wool yarn spinning rates, in Chinchero, Peru (Franquemont 1986a). For the plain-weave poncho and sacks (*costales*) that are the most comparable to large, plain-weave Ecuadorian textiles, spinning, skeining, and plying took 70 to 75 percent of the total time (90 hours each for the sacks, 288 hours for the poncho) spent making these items. No wonder people are spinning all the time.

Loom Technology

Ann P. Rowe

The majority of the textiles presented in this volume are woven on a loom and the type of loom used naturally conditions the characteristics of the cloth woven and of the clothing made from it. Moreover, the indigenous looms differ dramatically from those introduced by the Spanish, and an understanding of the differences serves to clarify which elements of costume are indigenous and which are of Spanish origin. In addition, the form of the loom is one of the defining characteristics of the culture area under discussion, since indigenous Ecuadorian looms differ in key respects from those of Peru and Colombia (Meisch ms.). Since many of the local terms for the loom parts vary regionally, they will not be given here.

A woven cloth consists of two sets of elements arranged perpendicular to each other, the *warp* being the longitudinal set and the *weft* being the transverse set. Functionally, the warp is that set of yarns initially put on the loom before the actual weaving process can begin, while the weft is the set inserted over and under the warp yarns during the weaving process. The complete process consists first of winding the warp (called warping), second of attaching the loom parts or putting the warp on the loom, third of inserting the weft (weaving), and fourth of removing the loom parts or taking the cloth off the loom.

9 *Balanced plain weave.*
From Emery 1980, fig. 85.

In order to weave plain weave, in which each weft yarn interlaces over-one and under-one warp yarn (Fig. 9), the weaver needs to be able to separate the even and odd numbered warp yarns, first raising the evens above the odds, and then the odds above the evens. The weft is inserted in the space (called a shed) between them. The basic interchange of the two groups of warp yarns is called the warp cross. This cross is most clearly visible in a side view of the weaving (Figs. 10–13).

In indigenous Andean weaving technology, the warp is made the exact size wanted for the finished piece, and the size of the various loom parts more or less conforms to the size of the warp. Thus, a weaver will have different loom sticks for a belt than for a poncho. This technology contrasts with the European tradition of weaving a very long warp that is then cut up into smaller pieces for actual use. Usually, on a European-style treadle loom, one must cut the warp yarns in order to put them on the loom in the first place, since each one is individually drawn through the loom mechanism.

In most Andean weaving, on the other hand, the warp yarns are turned at each end of the fabric without being cut and several ways have been devised for attaching the various parts of the loom to the warp without the need to cut the warp yarns. Thus, each fabric will have not only the two finished side edges (selvedges) found on European style yardage, but it will have finished end selvedges as well. Therefore, traditional Andean costumes are made of square and rectangular fabrics that are completely uncut. Sometimes the edges of the rectangles may be decorated in some way, and two smaller rectangles may be sewn together to make a larger one, but there is no cutting and tailoring such as one finds in the European tradition.

Indigenous Andean looms

In Peruvian looms, the warp is stretched out flat, with the warp loops at each end bound to a loom bar (Fig. 10). In Ecuadorian looms, on the other hand, the warp is doubled back on itself, so that the length of the loom setup is only half the length of the actual warp (Fig. 11). The warp is not tied to the loom bars at all, but instead the end warp loops pass around a single stick, alternately from one direction and from the other, which is here referred to as the dovetail stick or cord (Fig. 11E). A stick is used in winding the warp, but usually a cord is substituted before the weaving actually begins.

Since the warp is not securely fixed to the loom bars in the Ecuadorian setup, extra devices are generally used. For example, many belt looms have a back loom bar that is slightly curved, which helps prevent the warp from slipping from one end of the loom bar to the other (Fig. 12). At the front of the loom, next to the weaver, a separate stick, called a roller bar, usually the same size and shape as the front loom bar, is placed on top of the warp next to the front loom bar, and the loops of the backstrap are secured to one bar while passing under the other (Fig. 13 shows one possible configuration). For belts, the warp is usually wound several

10   Profile diagrams of the Peruvian style backstrap loom, with the warp in a single plane bound to the loom bars on both ends. Shown with the sword holding the shed open, ready to insert the weft. A: shed rod shed open. B: heddle rod lifted. Drawings by Laurie McCarriar based on sketches by Ann P. Rowe.

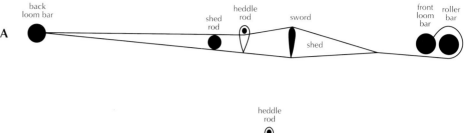

11   Profile diagrams of the Ecuadorian style backstrap loom, with the warp passing around both loom bars and the ends dovetailed around a cord. Shown with the sword holding the shed open, ready to insert the weft. A: belt loom with the cruzera shed open. B: belt loom with the heddle rod lifted; C: poncho loom with the shed rod shed open. D: poncho loom with the heddle rod lifted. E: detail of dovetailed join. Drawings by Laurie McCarriar based on sketches by Ann P. Rowe.

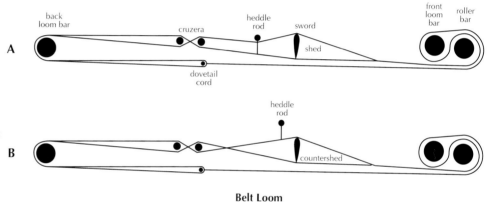

Belt Loom

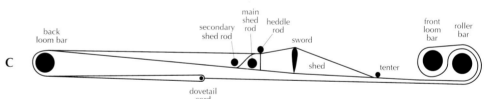

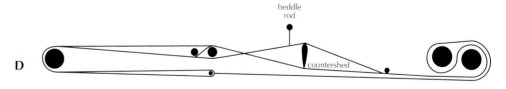

Poncho Loom

turns around both sticks to secure it; for wider fabrics the extra turns are optional. To adjust the position of the working area of the warp once some of the cloth has been woven, the weaver unwinds the warp from the roller bar and front loom bar, slips the entire warp around the loom bars toward him, and rerolls the warp around the two bars.

Each of the two sheds for plain weave is opened in a different way. A stick called the shed rod has alternate warp yarns above it and the others below it. When this stick is moved forward, the warp yarns above it are lifted (Fig. 11c). On wide looms it is usually of a fairly large diameter, to make the shed easy to open, but is light in weight since it is resting on top of half of the warp yarns. In many Ecuadorian wide looms, especially for wool ponchos, the regular shed rod is supplemented by a secondary shed rod, which passes under alternate warp yarns that are over the main shed rod (Figs. 11c and D, 13). Moving these two shed rods past each other helps open the shed.

In Ecuadorian belt looms, often the stick that functions as a shed rod is tied at both ends to a second stick behind it which marks the opposite shed, so that the cross appears between them (Figs. 11A and B, 12). Therefore it is usually called *cruzera* in Ecuador from the Spanish word for cross, *cruz*. The English term would be cross sticks, although this term does not usually refer to something that also functions as a shed rod. Sometimes one of the cruzera sticks is grooved. Three-stick cruzeras are found in looms with some mechanism for warp patterning. Of course, the grooves and the ties on the cruzera also help secure the warp yarns in the loom.

In order to lift the warp yarns passing underneath the shed rod, a stick called the heddle rod is used (Figs. 11B and D, 12–13). It is placed in front of the shed rod, and is usually thinner, resting on top of the warp. It has thread loops which pass between the warp yarns that are above the shed rod and encircle the warp yarns that are below it. Each of these thread loops is called a heddle. In South American looms, the heddles are usually made of a single continuous thread. There is a considerable variety of possible methods of forming the heddles and binding them to the heddle rod. In Ecuadorian belt looms, the heddle cord is looped in half hitches around the heddle rod, firmly securing the loops. In wider looms, the heddle cord winds around a heavy cord, which is in turn tied to the heddle rod. In order to open the shed controlled by the heddles (often called the countershed), the heddle rod is lifted with the left hand, and usually the shed rod is pressed down at the same time with the right.

To make sure the shed is clear and to bring the cross closely and evenly against the woven edge of the fabric, another stick, usually of a hard wood, called a sword, is used. It has a profile like an airplane wing with one sharp and one rounded edge. It is inserted into the shed, and its sharp edge is pressed down against the woven edge. Often the pointed end of the sword or of another stick made solely for this purpose, called a pick, may be first scraped over the upper surface of the warp in order to make sure all the warp yarns that must drop below the weft are in fact down. After the sword is inserted and pressed against the woven edge, it is turned on edge in the warp to hold the shed open for the weft to be inserted (Figs. 11–13). The weft, which has usually been wound on a narrow stick called a shuttle, is then inserted, and the weaver turns the sword flat again to beat the weft into place. For wide looms, the sword is pointed on both ends, but for belt looms in Ecuador, it usually has a handle on one end so that it is shaped like a knife (Fig. 12).

A device for maintaining the warp tension is essential to the effective separation of the warp yarns in forming sheds and for beating in the weft. In most of highland Ecuador, body tension is used. That is, the end of the loom nearest the weaver is affixed by ropes to a strong, broad strap that passes around the weaver's hips. The weaver leans back to increase tension on the warp—for example, when beating in the weft—and forward to decrease the tension—for example, to make it easier to lift the heddle rod. Usually the weaver also braces his feet against something, in order to achieve maximum tension with minimum back strain.

The variability in tension makes the warp yarns tend to draw together, so that most fabrics woven this way are either warp-predominant in count or warp-faced, meaning that the warp yarns are closer together than the weft yarns. On wide looms, sometimes a stick pointed at both ends or with metal nails or hooks at each end, called a tenter, is placed across the warp near the edge of the weaving, to help maintain an even width (Fig. 13).

For belt looms, the back loom bar is tied by a rope to a vertical support, usually a house post. For wider looms, the support for the back loom bar usually consists of two stout posts driven into the ground, usually permanently, or actually built into the house in a convenient place, sometimes inside, sometimes on a porch. The

12   Woman weaving a plain-weave band on the backstrap loom, Cacha, central Chimborazo province. The heddle rod shed is open. The dovetail cord is visible near the back loom bar. Photo © CJ Elfont/Light Isolates Photography, 1988.

13 *Rafael de la Torre weaving a poncho half on the backstrap loom, San Luis de Agualongo (Otavalo area), Imbabura province. His legs are braced against the square beam underneath the loom, although covered with a blanket for warmth. He is opening the heddle rod shed. Photo by Lynn A. Meisch, 1985.*

Opposite:

14 *Detail of a cotton double bag (alforja) from Cariamanga, Loja province, in warp-faced plain weave in alternate colors of warp. The Textile Museum 1989.22.3, Latin American Research Fund. See Fig. 262 for a full view.*

15 *Detail of a cotton warp-resist patterned shawl from Rumipamba, near Salcedo, Cotopaxi province. The Textile Museum 1988.19.15, Latin American Research Fund. See Fig. 111 for a full view.*

loom parts for wider looms are often very heavy; the sword alone may weigh two to three kilograms (5 or 6 pounds), so it requires considerable strength to operate the loom.

To summarize, the complete weaving sequence for plain weave on a backstrap loom is as follows.

1. To open the heddle rod shed, release tension on the warp by leaning forward slightly, take the sword with the right hand and place it on top of the shed rod, pressing the shed rod down and back, simultaneously lifting the heddle rod with the left hand.

2. Still holding the heddle rod, insert the sword into the shed formed.

3. Release the heddle rod, and bring the sword forward against the woven edge of the fabric, first gently, then sharply, simultaneously leaning back to increase the warp tension.

4. Release the tension slightly, turn the sword on edge to hold the shed open, and pass the shuttle through the shed.

5. Increase tension, turn the sword flat again and beat it again against the woven edge.

6. To open the shed rod shed on a wide loom, move the shed rod forward against the heddle loops and strum with the sword or pick both above and below it,

holding the warp tension firm. If a secondary shed rod is present, the two rods are also exchanged several times. In a belt loom usually the sword is inserted into the shed just below the cruzera and it is brought forward against the heddles and then removed.

7. Insert the sword into the shed in front of the heddle rod and beat against the woven edge.

8. Release tension slightly, turn the sword on edge and pass the shuttle through the open shed.

9. Increase the warp tension, turn the sword flat, and beat sharply again against the woven edge, afterwards removing it from the shed. Begin again at step 1.

The Quichua word for "slow" is the same as that for "good," *ali* in Otavalo (Meisch 1987:128), *aillilla* in Saraguro, a combination of meanings that is particularly appropriate for weaving on the backstrap loom.

Decorative techniques

Comparatively few decorative techniques are used in Ecuadorian weaving. The most common is the simple device of making warp stripes. The colors are arranged during the warping process, and the weaver weaves the cloth in plain weave. If two colors of warp are alternated one by one, one color will be lifted by the heddle rod, and the other color will be lifted by the shed rod. If the fabric is warp-faced, as is usually the case, this trick results in narrow horizontal bars of color (Fig. 14).

Another method of patterning a plain weave fabric used in Ecuador is to tie dye the warp yarns before the fabric is woven (Fig. 15). The yarns to be dyed are warped, and then usually grouped so that each different design need only be tied once. Then the groups of warp yarns are tightly wrapped with agave or furcraea fiber, or strips of plastic, in those places where the dye is not wanted. The yarns are then immersed in the dye pot, after which the wrappings are removed, and the yarns dried and then set up on the loom and woven. Because the yarns easily slip slightly out of position on the loom, the weaver may periodically try to readjust them. Nevertheless, the outlines of the designs are usually slightly blurred because of such slippage. Because the pattern is made by applying a "resist," something that will resist the dye, to the warp yarns, this technique is called warp-resist dyeing. Since this technique has been carried to fantastic heights in Indonesia, the Indonesian term *ikat* is often used instead, but we prefer the more descriptive terminology.

Three different structures or techniques besides warp-faced plain weave are found in Ecuadorian belts. The simplest to explain involves the use of supplementary-warp yarns (Fig. 16). That is, the belt has a ground of warp-faced plain weave, usually in white cotton, but after every second ground warp yarn a colored supplementary-warp yarn is added during the warping process. During weaving, these supplementary-warp yarns are manipulated by means of an additional heddle rod

16 *Detail of a belt in white cotton plain weave with blue acrylic supplementary-warp patterning. Left, the front; right, the back. Otavalo area, Imbabura province. The Textile Museum 1986.19.24, Latin American Research Fund. See Fig. 37 for a full view.*

or shed rod, and caused to float either above or below the ground weave. That is, they float on the front of the fabric to form the pattern, and on the back between pattern areas. The weaver may create a variety of designs by selecting which of the supplementary-warp yarns are lifted for each weft passage (called pick-up). Or for simple repeating designs, he or she may use additional heddle rods that control the supplementary-warp yarns needed for each part of the pattern.

The other belt structures are not based on plain weave, and may be best understood by referring to the diagrams. The first of these structures (Figs. 17–18) unfortunately has no generally accepted shorthand name and will be referred to here as a twill-derived weave (cf. Emery 1980:120–21). It is a simple weave, woven warp-faced, and in Ecuador is usually woven in three colors, one of which is white, warped in equal proportions, one white followed by one of each of the other two colors. The white yarns are all controlled by the same heddle rod, which is lifted for alternate shots of weft, thus interlacing over-one, under-one, forming narrow

17

19

18

20

17 Float weave based on 2/1 twill. The opposite face is structurally identical except that the warp-float areas are in reversed positions. From Emery 1980, fig. 214.

18 Diagrammatic construction of the weave shown in Fig. 17. Here the 2/1 interlacing order of the weft is apparent. From Emery 1980, fig. 215.

19 A complementary-warp weave with both faces formed by three-span warp floats in alternate alignment. The warp yarns are compacted sufficiently to nearly hide those that form the opposite face, which are normally a different color. From Emery 1980, fig. 244.

20 Diagrammatic construction of the weave in Fig. 19. From Emery 1980, fig. 245.

horizontal white bars. The other two warp colors alternately interlace 1/1 opposite to the white or float, usually over or under either three or five weft passages, one on the front and the other on the back. The colored floats line up horizontally, making wider horizontal bars (see also Fig. 51, center). In some belts, for example in Otavalo and Saraguro, one of the colors is always on one face of the fabric, and the other color is always on the opposite face. In other belts, for example in central Chimborazo, the two colors may periodically exchange faces (Fig. 105).

The third belt structure involves the use of complementary sets of warp (Figs. 19–20). That is, there are two sets of warp, each of a different color, that are co-equal in the fabric (Emery 1980:150; A. Rowe 1977, chap. 10). In any given area, one color is floating on the front of the fabric, while the second color is floating on the back. In an unusual poncho fabric woven in the Otavalo area, the warp floats span two weft yarns, but in belts they usually span three weft yarns. The underlying principle in each case is the same, however. In the belts, the three-span floats are in alternating alignment, that is, aligned in offset rows like brickwork, and the two colors exchange faces periodically to form designs. In Ecuador, there are several different techniques of weaving belts with this basic structure, but here we refer to it simply as a complementary-warp weave.

The European treadle loom

As noted above, the European treadle loom introduced by the Spanish operates under principles quite different from those of the indigenous Andean looms (Figs. 21–22). The concept of using foot treadles to operate the shed-changing mechanism probably originated in China and spread first to the Middle East and from there to Europe during the Middle Ages, around the eleventh or twelfth centuries (Hoffman 1979). As introduced into Europe, it was a method of production weaving on a commercial basis in which the weaving was done by professional male weavers. It first supplemented and then replaced the household weaving of textiles by women. In the Americas, it was also introduced as a commercial venture and the work was done by men, whether or not weaving was traditionally done by men in the area. Thus, the weaving in the infamous Spanish obrajes was done by men on treadle looms.

The reason why the treadle loom is associated with professional production weaving is simply that it is much faster to weave on this type of loom than on a simple heddle rod and shed rod style of loom. The treadles are connected with cords to a series of rectangular frames, called shafts ("harnesses" in North American handweaving terminology), containing the heddles (Figs. 21–22). Each heddle is separately made, often of string, and has an eye in the middle through which a warp yarn passes. For plain weave, a minimum of two shafts is required, one controlling the odd warp yarns, and one the evens (Fig. 21). Thus, in order to open the shed it is necessary only to press one or more treadles. There is no need to scrape the warp, insert the sword, and move it down toward the woven area.

Beating is done using a framework with closely spaced slats in it through which the warp yarns pass, located in front of the heddles. This framework, called a reed, is usually connected to the loom framework by means of a bar on each side that operates on pivots. Thus to beat the weft in, a single jerk with the reed against the cloth is all that is needed.

The weft is wound on a pin (called a bobbin), which is set in a smooth, hollow, wooden framework (called a boat shuttle since it is usually pointed on both ends) in such a way that the bobbin can turn within the framework, releasing the weft as it moves along the warp. The weaver thus can send the shuttle through the shed with a quick flick of the wrist, catching it on the other side with the other hand.

The weaving motion thus consists of (1) depressing the treadle(s), (2) throwing the shuttle and adjusting the weft position, and (3) pulling once on the reed. Each of these actions can take less than a second.

Further time savings are gained by the practice of putting a very long warp on the loom, enough for multiple garments. In some European looms, to accommodate the long warp, the bars on which the warp length and the finished cloth are wound may be set below and inside the plane of the cloth where the weaving is actually occurring. Each of these bars, called the warp beam and the cloth beam, respectively, is set up so that they can be rotated and secured in position. The

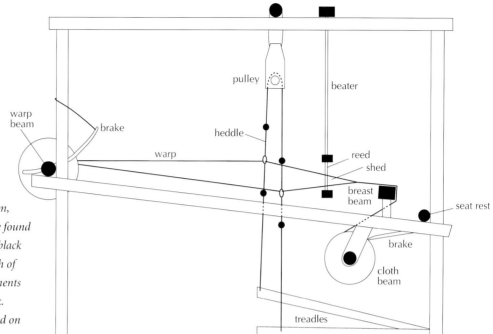

pulley

beater

warp
beam

brake

heddle

warp

reed

shed

breast
beam

seat rest

brake

cloth
beam

treadles

21 *Profile diagram of a treadle loom, based on the most conservative type found in Ecuador. Elements shaded solid black are bars that go across the full width of the loom. Dotted lines indicate elements passing behind the loom framework. Drawing by Laurie McCarriar based on a sketch by Ann P. Rowe.*

22 *Treadle loom in Cuicuno, Cotopaxi province. A swift, a rotating device for winding from a skein of yarn, has been propped over the upper left corner of the loom. Photo by Laura M. Miller, 1988.*

section of the warp that is the working plane of the cloth is supported by the breast beam and back beam. Figures 21 and 22 show looms with a breast beam but no back beam, which is a common configuration in Ecuador, but looms with back beams also occur.

European treadle looms have each of these parts built into a single framework that may even include the bench on which the weaver sits or against which he rests, thus becoming a substantial piece of furniture. In Ecuador, a variety of types of treadle looms are found, including some that may be similar to Spanish looms of the colonial period (Figs. 21–22) and others that include modern refinements.

Although plain weave is commonly woven on treadle looms, for which two shafts are sufficient, many treadle looms include four shafts, which make it easy to weave twill (Fig. 23). In twill weaves, the weft yarn, instead of interlacing over-one, under-one, interlaces over or under more than one warp yarn at regular intervals and these longer skips, called floats, are diagonally aligned from one shot of weft to the next. For instance, the weft might interlace over-two, under-two (the most common in Ecuadorian weaving), or over-two, under-one, or over-three, under-one.

23 *Diagrammatic construction of 2/2 twill weave. From Emery 1980, fig. 116.*

It is possible to produce twill weaves on the native Andean styles of looms, using additional or modified heddle rods, but in practice it is rarely done, and most contemporary twill fabrics are produced on treadle looms. An interesting exception is the poncho from Cacha in Figure 24, which was woven in imitation of a treadle-loom woven fabric (Fig. 25). Its warp loop ends and warp-faced structure betray its backstrap loom manufacture. We were unfortunately unable to record such a loom, but were told that multiple heddle rods were used to form the twill. In contrast, the poncho in Figure 25, which was woven on a treadle loom, has a balanced structure and cut warp ends.

Several Spanish fabric names, introduced in the colonial period, are still used in Ecuador to refer to different types of treadle-loom woven fabrics. *Lienzo* is a plain-weave cotton fabric, while *liencillo* is similar but more finely woven. *Bayeta* (related to the English baize, a thick "flannel" fabric) is a coarse wool fabric, while *paño* is a more finely woven wool cloth. *Jerga* is a coarse wool twill-weave cloth. However, the precise connotations of these terms can vary in different parts of Spanish America.

The Spanish style, handmade tailored garments, such as blouses, shirts, pants, and skirts, are made mostly of rectangles, cut with minimal waste of fabric. They are sewn with flat fell seams so that no raw edges of fabric are exposed on the inside of the garment. Closures consist of ties or buttons.

Context of weaving

While spinning is a quintessential woman's task in Ecuador, weaving is predominantly men's work in the highlands, although women are weavers on the coast and also in Carchi province in the north. In the highlands, some women do weave belts

24 *Detail of a poncho in 2/2 twill weave wool, woven on the backstrap loom. The weaving is nearly warp-faced and the warp ends are looped. Cacha, central Chimborazo province. The Textile Museum 1988.19.153, Latin American Research Fund.*

25 *Detail of a poncho in 2/2 twill weave wool, woven on the treadle loom. The weaving is balanced and the warp ends are cut. Central Chimborazo province. The Textile Museum 1989.22.47, Latin American Research Fund.*

in many areas and it is not considered odd, but very few weave the wider textiles on either the native backstrap loom or on the European treadle loom. An exception was the area around Chicticay in Azuay province where it was usual for women to weave even large fabrics on the backstrap loom. In other areas, for example in Bulcay, in Azuay province, or in Salasaca, a woman who weaves is considered strange, although a few do it anyway.

Many of the weavers we recorded, both backstrap-loom and treadle-loom weavers, make ponchos or blankets on commission, referred to as *pedido* (S., request) or *obra* (S., work). In these cases the customer, generally another indigenous person, supplies the yarn to be used and consequently specifies the colors of the cloth to be woven. The weaver may or may not also do plying or dyeing for the customer. This is a common type of arrangement for weaving in the whole Andean area. A more Europeanized system, where weaving is done on speculation for sale to unknown customers in the market, is also occasionally found, but more often for belts or treadle-loom woven fabrics than for larger backstrap-loom woven items. Of course, people also weave garments for family members. And these arrangements are often combined in one household, for example, weaving for the family and weaving on commission, or weaving on commission and weaving on speculation.

Although some people weave full time, especially in the Otavalo area, many people make textiles in the interstices of the agricultural calendar or whenever nothing more pressing is going on. In these cases, weaving is a supplement to the household economy, not the sole means of support. This system lends itself well to weaving for domestic use, since one can spend as much time as one likes, with a correspondingly beautiful result, on a textile for someone who is loved. It can also work adequately with barter within a society where values are shared. However, it is open to exploitation in a situation in which a small cash income is a supplement to subsistence living, so that the cash remuneration is often not proportional to the amount of time that the work actually takes.

Spinning and weaving are inherently slow processes, especially using indigenous methods, a fact that may be difficult for those of us removed from these processes to appreciate. But it is no accident that the industrial revolution in Europe began with spinning. Once cash income becomes the predominant goal, the amount of time spent on the process becomes critical, and technical and artistic compromises naturally follow. Although there are exceptions, the belts of Cañar and Salasaca, which are made mostly for domestic use, are generally finer than the belts in Otavalo and Chimborazo that are made for sale.

Another level of compromise is involved when the textile is made for sale to someone outside the community, who usually has different tastes and needs, as well as being unaccustomed to paying for the amount of time it takes to weave a textile by hand. In Ecuador, the textiles woven for whites, local or tourist, are often totally distinct, in technique, in design, and in function, from those woven for local use (as, for example, in Otavalo). This process is entirely logical. Indeed, the Otavalos understand it better than most development workers.

I have used the term "compromise" from the perspective that a textile woven by the slowest method for traditional use is often the most beautiful (*ali, aillilla*), and it is these textiles that primarily concern us here. But there is a wide range of quality in most types of textiles, and certainly commercial weaving has been extensively practiced for centuries in Ecuador.

Chapter 3

Indigenous Ecuadorian Costume

Lynn A. Meisch and Ann P. Rowe

How boring life would be if we wore clothing only to keep warm or preserve our modesty. Imagine a world inhabited by people wearing plain white or black robes, with identical hairstyles for males and females—no decorations, no colors, no jewelry, no differences, no fashion statements. Throughout the world, however, costume invariably expresses a wide variety of cultural values in a uniquely visible and portable way. Costume is more widely practiced and more readily visible in more contexts than any other form of human expression (see Wobst 1977).

For those familiar with the meanings of clothing in a given culture, it is often possible to determine the gender, age, marital status, degree of wealth, social rank, religion, and occupation, as well as the geographic or cultural affiliation of a person, by observing their clothes. Special clothing may also be worn for specific types of events such as weddings or other celebrations or rituals, or for mourning. In addition, clothing may convey general information about trading contacts or historical events, such as a military conquest. Costume also expresses such abstract cultural values as pride or submission, conformity with or rejection of the dominant social order, and the relative status of men and women in the society.

The messages conveyed by clothing can be interpreted in order to predict the behavior of a person and condition the behavior of the observer accordingly. Anthropologically speaking, therefore, understanding the messages that clothing presents can provide significant insights into the cultures studied.

Because costume is thus sometimes considered a code to be deciphered, it has become fashionable in recent years to use the metaphor of costume as a "language" that can be "read" (Barthes 1977, 1983; Bogatyrev 1971; Turner 1980). Such semiotic theories derive from Saussure's work in structural linguistics (1960), which holds that language is paramount and which compares all signs to words or texts, sometimes literally, sometimes metaphorically. Written texts are so important in our own society that it seems natural to make this comparison. Clothing does not have a grammar and syntax, however, nor can it be decoded in a one-to-one correspondence like a true code (McCracken 1987:117). Clothing is effective in communicating multiple messages precisely because it does so visually, in a way that language does not.

The analogy of all signs to language is particularly inappropriate for traditionally nonliterate cultures, including Andean societies, which had no writing before the arrival of the Spanish. Rather than being a representation of language and hence a poor cousin of writing, ancient Andean textile art was instead a primary medium itself (Franquemont 1986b:86).

It has also been noted that "many clothing messages are more like music: they are expressive in an indirect and allusive way. There is rarely a single meaning attached to each article of clothing. Instead, its meanings depend on the context— Who wears it? When? Along with what other clothes? What was the history of the garment?" (Steele 1989:6). In other words, costume is a visual medium that communicates in a manner distinct from language, carries a heavy symbolic weight, and has many levels of meaning that are culturally dependent and must be learned.

In this volume, we treat costume as a symbolic system conveying multiple messages, including cultural, political, and economic information that is situationally dependent. For example, within a community, subtle details of an indigenous person's costume can identify him or her as wealthy and of high status locally, while the identical dress on the national level marks the person as a member of a perceived low-status, stigmatized group (*indio*, an insult). In the United States, Canada, and Europe, where Indians are frequently exoticized and romanticized, an indigenous person wearing this same costume may receive preferential treatment.

Many of the cultural values apparent in indigenous Ecuadorian costumes are pan-Andean. For example, the fact that the indigenous cultures are relatively egalitarian (among themselves) is reflected in minimal differences between the clothing of wealthier and poorer people or between community leaders and more peripheral members.

Although women's costume is significantly more conservative than men's (a feature with multiple causes), it is not greatly different from men's in terms of its practicality or amount of decoration. This reflects the relative equality of men's and women's status and work, even though the particular roles are different and are also reflected in the basic forms.

Older children are often dressed exactly like adults, reflecting their status as miniature adults. As soon as they are old enough they are given household chores within their capabilities. Acculturative pressures such as school attendance may alter this situation, but in some parts of Ecuador (unlike some other Andean countries) children are permitted to wear ethnic costume to school.

Costume and
Ethnic Identity

26 *Breenan Conterón of Ilumán, Imbabura province, wearing Otavalo costume, with Earthwatch volunteer Suzanne Powell in the Hotel Whymper, Riobamba. Photo by Lynn A. Meisch, 1989.*

---

1. Casagrande (1974) notes that people from Otavalo, Saraguro, and Salasaca would typically put on their best indigenous clothes for a photograph, while people from Pichincha and Chimborazo would put on western-style clothes if they had them (see also Whitten 1981:275, note 1). Casagrande concludes from his own observations and from interviews that the main source of these attitudes was whether people were able to live relatively independently or were subject to the hacienda system.

As we have seen, costume is a major visible or public determinant of indigenous identity in highland Ecuador. In view of the fact that indigenous people, at least until relatively recently, have been assigned to the lowest social level and are immediately judged as such by their dress, it might seem remarkable that so many do wear a distinctive costume. Moreover, commercial clothing is usually cheaper than traditional dress.

In fact, attitudes toward indigenous dress vary considerably from one area to another, and in some areas distinctive costume has indeed been disappearing. In other areas, such as Zumbagua, where people have less cash income than in areas like Otavalo, there is less pride in being indigenous, and people may feel ashamed to wear their distinctive costume in public although they feel comfortable in it at home.[1]

For some people traditional dress seems to be taken for granted, and they are not especially self-conscious or analytical about it. Other indigenous people have a strong positive sense of their identity, which they are interested in maintaining, and wear a distinctive costume as a matter of choice. Thus, wearing the appropriate costume often reflects self-determination, not to mention pride, in an indigenous ethnic identity. Movimiento Indígena de Chimborazo (MICH), one of the indigenous federations in Chimborazo province, included a statement on dress in the history of their organization: "In each community we utilize different dress and this differentiates us from one another, but in no way does this signify social inequality or that we are not one people; rather it permits us to reaffirm our condition as indigenous people" (MICH 1989:174–75, Meisch translation).

For example, Breenan Conterón, our Otavalo research assistant in 1988 and 1989 (Fig. 26), wrote about her costume in our Earthwatch team notebook:

"I am an Otavaleña indígena who lives in Ilumán. My dress consists of a headcloth (*fachalina de cabeza*), which in Quichua is called a *sucu* (light) *fachalina* or *huma huatarina* (head wrap). I also wear an embroidered blouse, then a white anaco and then a black anaco. In order to hold up these two anacos I wear two belts, the mother belt (*mama chumbi*) and baby belt (*huahua chumbi*). On my feet I wear sandals (*alpargates*), on my arms I wear bracelets (*manillas*) and at my neck a bead necklace (*gualcas*). I wear this dress every day and when I leave my town for other cities in my country, Ecuador, I always wear this dress because in this way I value and respect my ancestors, who fought to maintain their culture, tradition and customs. I have great pride that through my inheritance and in my blood I carry this culture." (Meisch translation from Spanish and Quichua).

Costume is also the most important way in which indigenous people identify themselves as members of a particular ethnic group, subgroup, or community. The most distinctive and internally uniform costumes are generally found among groups whose sense of ethnic solidarity is strongest, such as the Otavalos, Salasacas, Cañaris, and Saraguros. In other areas, such as Pichincha, Cotopaxi, and Chimborazo, where the hacienda system was particularly pervasive and oppressive, people identify with their community rather than with an ethnic group, and the costumes tend to be more acculturated as well as more diverse.

The Ecuadorian government's policy of *mestizaje*, the assimilation of the indigenous population (Stutzman 1981), demands that indigenous people abandon a custom (distinctive dress) that most consider essential to their selfhood and culture. The contemporary use of traditional dress by indigenous people is partly an assertion of ancient autochthonous values, and partly a strategy of resistance to discrimination, depending on the situation and the meanings that individuals ascribe to their dress. For the demonstrations and protests associated with the 1992 Columbus Quincentennial in Ecuador, indigenous people throughout the country wore their finest traditional dress as a political statement.

Dress is so important that two of twenty-one points in a bilingual Quichua-Spanish CONAIE publication on human rights and indigenous people relate directly to costume. Point number five reads, "We have the right to create our own textile industry in order to dress ourselves with our own clothes (*churana* Q.; *vestidos* S.), and not to be forced to wear foreign clothes that carry the destruction of our culture" (1988:6, Meisch translation from Spanish). The two pictures accompanying the text show a woman spinning yarn on the walking wheel and a man weaving on the backstrap loom. Point number nine reads, "Our children have the right to have their dress (*churana* Q.; *vestimientas* S.) respected in centers of education. We cannot permit the imposition of uniforms that are foreign to our reality and identity. This imposition brings the loss of our cultural values and is the imposition of the dominant society." (ibid.:8, Meisch translation from Spanish).

Fiesta and Ceremonial Costume

In Ecuador, as in most places, people wear the richest costumes for fiesta and ceremonial occasions, either masquerade (more often men than women) or traditional dress. In some cases, fiesta clothing is similar to everyday clothing, but new clothing is worn for the first time for a fiesta. It is common to wear newer clothing for occasions such as church services and market days, and older clothing for everyday.

In some instances, a reversal of this practice occurs: a style that formerly was worn on a daily basis but which is obsolete will still be worn on ceremonial occasions. Sometimes old clothes are saved for this purpose, and sometimes replicas of the older styles are made. This practice is common among indigenous communities worldwide. The Otavalo wedding costume is a good example from Ecuador. In areas of Ecuador where rapid costume change is occurring, fiestas are now the only occasions on which traditional, non-Euro-American clothing is worn by some segments of the indigenous population.

Fiestas and rites of passage differ markedly among the different ethnic groups of Ecuador, both in terms of which ones are observed and in the manner in which they are celebrated. Christmas (*Navidad* S.), for example, is one of the major fiestas in Saraguro, whereas in much of the highlands it passes almost unnoticed. Corpus

Christi (a movable feast usually falling around mid-June) is much more significant in Tungurahua and Cotopaxi provinces than it is elsewhere (Fig. 120). The feast day of the Virgin of Carmen on July 16 is celebrated in parts of Chimborazo (Figs. 201–203), whereas in Pichincha and Imbabura the feast days of Saint John the Baptist (San Juan Bautista) on June 24 and Saints Peter and Paul (San Pedro y San Pablo) on June 29 are the most important fiestas of the year (Figs. 71, 95).

The Catholic Church, unable to eradicate the prehispanic system of fiestas based on the agricultural and astronomical cycles, co-opted them. For example, the late June fiestas fall around the time of the winter solstice (June 21), which was celebrated by the Incas as *Inti Raymi* (Festival of the Sun). There is nothing Christian whatsoever in the masquerade-costumed circle dancing and music that most Otavalo men and boys old enough to walk participate in during the week of San Juan.

The Spanish practice of *compadrazgo*, a system of ritual kinship or co-parenthood, has been incorporated into Andean social observances. It is ubiquitous among both indigenous people and white/mestizo Ecuadorians of all Christian religions, including Mormons and some Evangelicals. A family asks an adult couple (preferably) or a person of either gender to be the godparents or godparent of their child for baptism, first communion, confirmation, or marriage. In Saraguro, and perhaps elsewhere, godparents are also chosen for a first haircutting ceremony (*rutucha* Q.), a ritual with Inca origins (J. H. Rowe 1946:282). Through these ceremonies, a couple becomes co-parents, *comadre* or *compadre* (S.), to the child's parents and *madrina* or *padrino* (S.) to the child.

Compadrazgo in Latin America has taken on a significance far beyond the Christian one of serving as a spiritual sponsor of a child. The custom has equally important social functions and serves to extend the social network of the family. Through the huasipungo era, families often asked the owner (*patrón*) or the foreman (*mayordomo*) of the hacienda to be compadres because these people had influence and power. It is still customary for people to try to arrange compadrazgo relationships that are beneficial to them and their children. It is acceptable to refuse a compadrazgo request and people do, often because of the expenses involved.

Compadrazgo embodies a fundamental Andean value, reciprocity. Compadres can turn to one another for loans of money, help at fiestas, etc. Children bring their godparents gifts of food, and the godparents give gifts in return, which vary depending on the wealth of the godparents and their closeness to their compadres and godchildren. The godparents may also hire a godchild over another person or help their compadres in other ways. For a researcher, having compadres and godchildren greatly increases our pestering quotient. For example, when Ann asked for photographs of the different ways the headcloth is worn in Otavalo, Lynn asked her goddaughter in Ilumán to demonstrate the styles.

Among the gifts the godparents give their godchildren are clothes, including clothes to wear during the ritual event: baptismal outfit and (in Otavalo) traditional costume, first communion or confirmation suit or dress, and for the wedding, for example, a veil and blouse for the bride and a shirt for the groom. Weddings are undoubtedly the most expensive event for the godparents (*padrinos de la boda*, godparents of the wedding), because it is also customary for them to give the bride and groom household items and to pay for the band; total expenses can run to U.S. $300. The padrinos de la boda are often dressed as richly as the wedding couple (Figs. 57, 125), while the parents wear something closer to ordinary fiesta dress. Baptism, first communion, and confirmation involve initial expenses of U.S. $25 to $50.

History of Indigenous Costume in Ecuador

The costume tradition of Ecuador before the Inca conquest seems to have differed significantly from that of Peru, although it must be considered that evidence is much more abundant from the coast (mostly in the form of figurines) than from the highlands (Bruhns ms). Nudity seems to have been common, with such body decoration as painting, jewelry, and headdresses. Alternatively, men wore a loin-cloth while women wore a wrapped skirt, generally without a belt (Figs. 27–28). These garments were probably supplemented with some sort of cloak or mantle in cold weather or at night. Another coastal male garment apparently of ritual function is a kind of tabard, with the sides open and usually made of some stiff material. The available evidence for northern highland costume suggests it was similar to that of the coast. Almost no evidence exists for the southern highlands, but men may have worn tunics.

Inca dress was influential in highland Ecuador, since if the Incas did not consider newly conquered peoples sufficiently clothed, as apparently was the case in the northern highlands of Ecuador, they ordered people to wear something similar to Inca dress (A. Rowe ms). Inca female dress (Fig. 29) consisted of a large square fabric (called 'aqsu or 'anaku, Classic Inca orthography) that was wrapped around the body and secured with straight pins (*tupu*) at the shoulders and with a belt (*chumpi*) at the waist (see A. Rowe 1997). They also wore a shawl (*lliklla*) over their shoulders that was secured on the chest with a pin similar to those used for the dress, and a headband (*wincha*). Male dress consisted of a knee-length tunic (called 'unku or *kusma*), a small breechcloth, and a large rectangular cloak. Both sexes wore leather sandals ('usut'a).

Inca style costume seems to have been considered sufficiently modest by the Spanish, who probably therefore reinforced Inca policy in the matter, so that ordinary people continued to wear Inca styles throughout the colonial period. However, the indigenous nobility soon adopted the use of European fabrics for some garments and male nobles started to wear hats and pants and sometimes European style capes (see, e.g., Caillavet 1982). By the eighteenth century (Fig. 30), ordinary indigenous men in Quito were wearing hats and loose calf-length pants, and the poncho was beginning to be worn (Juan and Ulloa 1748, vol. 1, lib. 5, cap. 5, ¶653, p. 367).

Indigenous pre-Inca, Inca, Spanish colonial, and modern elements all occur in

27 *Capulí figurine showing a woman wearing a long wrapped skirt with geometric patterns. Private collection, Cali. Photo by Karen O. Bruhns.*

present-day costumes. The broad outlines of the history of the region can thus be read in each costume.

Women's costume

Some elements of the contemporary women's costume are of obvious Inca origin. In Imbabura, southern Pichincha, and central Chimborazo provinces, a dress worn exactly like the Inca woman's dress and called by its Inca name, *anaku*, and fastened with tupus was in use until recently. In Chimborazo this garment (still in fact worn by a few old women) was woven on the backstrap loom, although elsewhere treadle-loom woven cloth was evidently used instead. In these areas, a half-length wrapped and belted skirt is now worn. The derivation of shorter, pleated, wrapped skirts, also called *anaku* and worn belted, is less clear, but the term and the use of rectangular fabrics is indigenous. The fullness may be the result of Spanish influence.

In southern Ecuador, from southern Chimborazo south, instead of the wrapped skirt described above, a gathered skirt of Spanish origin is worn, usually called a *pollera*. The fabric is sewn to a waistband in unpressed pleats, and the ends of the waistband are extended to form ties that are used to secure the garment. The skirt fabric may be cut with the warp either horizontal or vertical. The lower edge of the pollera may be embroidered, usually by machine. The pollera can be traced as far back as the eighteenth century in the Spanish American colonies, when it was an upper class garment (e.g., Juan and Ulloa 1748, vol. 1, lib. 3, cap. 3, ¶271, p. 163; lib. 4, cap. 5, ¶407, p. 228; lib. 5, cap. 5, ¶658, p. 369).

A related style of gathered skirt has a series of horizontal tucks near the lower edge. In the Cuenca area, this latter style is referred to as a *bolsicón*. By the 1740s, women in Mexico were wearing a long (ankle-length) version of this skirt (Carrillo y Gariel 1959). A skirt with this name was also worn in nineteenth-century Quito by mestizo servant women (e.g., Hallo 1981:105). Nineteenth-century illustrations of skirts with horizontal tucks are readily found, in the peasant costume of Europe as well as in other parts of Latin America, but the exact origin and distribution of this style of skirt has never been fully investigated.

Women's shawls in a square or rectangular style without fringe are derived from prehispanic precedents. They are sometimes called by the Inca term *lliglla*, most notably in Saraguro and the indigenous parts of Azuay, sometimes by other Quichua words describing its function (*fachallina, tupullina, washajatana, wallkarina*) and sometimes by Spanish terms either for a similar garment (*chalina, rebozo*) or derived from the types of Spanish cloth that were commonly used for the

28 *Capulí figurine showing a man wearing a patterned loincloth and a cloth draped over one shoulder, probably a folded rectangular cloak. He has a coca quid in one cheek. Private collection, Cali. Photo by Karen O. Bruhns.*

29 *Inca costume, as worn by the emperor, his wife, and a female attendant, drawn by Felipe Guaman Poma de Ayala, ca. 1615.*

Carlos d'Borgas del.t   Casanova fcp.t

purpose (*bayeta, bayetilla*). In many cases, these shawls are worn in the manner of Inca shawls, with the ends brought together and pinned on the chest with a tupu. If the corners of the shawl are tied or the shawl is draped under one arm, as is common in Imbabura, the Inca antecedent is less certain.

Relatively few modern shawls are actually made of backstrap-loom woven cloth, however. Examples made of treadle-loom woven cloth are hemmed on the ends so that they resemble the backstrap-loom woven precedent. Solid dark colors are usual. A style of shawl or carrying cloth of white cotton with narrow, colored wool weft stripes at intervals is found in several areas, including Salasaca, Chibuleo, and Chimborazo, and probably derives from treadle-loom woven yardage from the colonial obrajes.

Harder to answer is the question of the origin of the fringed shawls made in Azuay and Cotopaxi, frequently patterned with warp-resist dyeing. Such shawls are worn either instead of the prehispanic-style shawls, or as carrying cloths supplementary to prehispanic-style shawls. There is no known prehispanic precedent for the elaborate knotting of warp fringes found in these shawls, though the principle is a common European technique of finishing the cut ends of treadle-loom woven fabrics.

30 *Engraving published by Jorge Juan and Antonio de Ulloa in 1748 showing costumes worn in the Quito area at the time of their voyage in 1730. At left is the* Española Quiteña, *a Spanish woman, wearing a pollera and a shawl with both ends draped over one shoulder. To her right is the* India Palla, *an indigenous noblewoman, wearing a costume very similar to that of Inca women. The next figure is the* Indio Barbero, *or indigenous barber, a man of some status, who wears a lace trimmed shirt and pants with his tunic. Next is the* Mestiza Quiteña, *who wears a costume similar to the Spanish woman but less elaborate. At right are the* Indio Rustico *and* India Ordinaria, *an ordinary indigenous man and woman.*

This finishing technique is also found on Chinese square silk shawls that were imported to the Americas from the Far East, via the Manila galleon trade. These shawls, the so-called *mantones de Manila,* were embroidered with floral patterns and had 45-to-60-centimeter (18-to-24-inch) long knotted fringe on all edges. They became fashionable in Spain and her colonies in the late eighteenth and early nineteenth century (Robinson 1987:68–69). An example worn by a middle-class woman in Quito in the 1850s was depicted by the Ecuadorian painter Juan Agustín Guerrero (Hallo 1981:104).

In addition, the similarity of the Ecuadorian warp-resist dyed shawls to others found in Mexico (*rebozo*), Guatemala (*perraje*), and the north highlands of Peru around Cajamarca (*pañón*), tends to suggest a Spanish colonial period origin. In Mexico, the form can be traced as far back as the eighteenth century (see Castelló Yturbide and Martinez del Río de Redo 1971). In Ecuador we have no concrete evidence for it before the early twentieth century, although the manner in which it is often worn, with both ends tossed over one shoulder, can be traced back to the eighteenth century (Fig. 30).

The warp-resist dyeing technique is, in fact, known in prehispanic textiles from the Guayas basin (Gardner 1979, 1982, 1985), and the shawls are woven on the indigenous backstrap loom. Perhaps the style was created during the colonial period from an amalgam of influences.

Backstrap-loom woven belts are also called by their Inca name, *chumbi*. It is interesting that a distinction between a *mama chumbi* (mother belt) and a *wawa chumbi* (baby belt) exists in Otavalo, central Chimborazo, and formerly also in southern Pichincha, and the belts themselves are very similar among these areas. This distinction does not appear to be Cuzco Inca, but could be provincial Inca in origin. It is nevertheless probably not coincidental that these areas are the same ones where a full-length Inca style anaku persisted up until this century.

A type of belt with colored wool or acrylic supplementary-warp patterning on a white cotton ground is woven throughout the length of Ecuador except in Cañar and Azuay. Even the designs are similar among the different areas. There is nothing Inca about these belts, so a pre-Inca origin is possible, although concrete evidence is lacking. Perhaps the similarities in design are due in part to migrations and influences during the colonial period.

Women's blouses seem to be a relatively recent introduction, and in many cases do not even appear to date as far back as the colonial period. In central Chimborazo and in Otavalo, where the full-length Inca wrapped dress was also worn until living memory, blouses were not adopted until the half-length anaku became popular. In Saraguro, also, the blouse is known to be a twentieth-century introduction. The tailoring of the blouses is Spanish in inspiration, however. The blouses are often embroidered, sometimes by hand or sometimes now by machine.

The predominant way of dressing the hair, wrapping it with a narrow woven band, may well be pre-Inca, since it is neither Inca nor Spanish. The long, beaded earrings worn until recently in Otavalo and Central Chimborazo, and still worn by the Chibuleo and Pilahuín in Tungurahua province, may be indigenous, but the silver filigree earrings sometimes worn in east Imbabura and in southern Ecuador are Spanish (Anderson 1951).

The hats are certainly Spanish. The felting method with which they are made is a European technique based on the properties of sheep's wool; it was introduced early in the colonial period. While some indigenous men began wearing hats before the end of the sixteenth century, there is no evidence that women wore them before the nineteenth century. Although recent hat styles vary from one area to another so as to help serve as a means of identification, the style in any one area appears to have been changeable over time.

Most ordinary indigenous women probably went barefoot until relatively recently. Now, however, sandals or machine-made shoes are increasingly worn.

Men's costume

Inca influence is now much less apparent in men's dress. Although the man's tunic is scarcely seen in Ecuador any more, a simple version (often called *kushma*) actually was worn until recently in parts of Imbabura and Pichincha, as well as Salasaca, and it still is worn in Saraguro, woven on the backstrap loom. A related garment, also called *kushma* but without side seams, worn until recently in central Chimborazo and still worn in Cañar, may be a local pre-Inca version of this garment. Most recent Ecuadorian kushmas, whether sewn up the sides or not, are woven of a single loom panel.

Most Otavalo, Cañari, and Saraguro men wear their hair long and pulled back in a braid. Long hair is so important to the men of these ethnic groups that young indigenous men who serve in the Ecuadorian army are allowed to keep their braid. On rare occasions, men cut their hair, sometimes as a requirement for obtaining work on sugar plantations on the coast, but most re-grow their braid when they return home. The Incas did not try to influence the way people wore their hair, and Inca men wore their hair very short, so this style is probably Ecuadorian.

The rest of the men's costume, when it is not of modern manufactured clothing, is of Spanish colonial origin. Handmade pants are now seldom seen, but were worn until recently in many areas, and we were able to collect information on them. Most commonly these pants were of simple cut, made of undyed cotton yardage in northern Ecuador (through most of Chimborazo province) and of wool in southern Ecuador.

Since the tunic was worn by many indigenous men until relatively recently, the Spanish style shirt has less of a history than pants. Homemade shirts were, however, worn in a number of areas recently enough that we were able to record them, though now they are seldom seen. Machine-made shirts are now nearly universal.

Today, the pre-eminent indigenous item in the man's wardrobe is the poncho, or *ruana* (S.), as it is often called in the Ecuadorian and Colombian Andes. In function, it takes the place of the man's mantle, not of the tunic. It clearly derives from native technologies, being usually woven on the backstrap loom and made of two uncut panels sewn together. Its development into its current form, however, and its widespread use have their origin in the colonial period.

The earliest evidence for it is among Chile's Mapuche (called Araucanians in earlier literature) in the early seventeenth century (Montell 1929:239). The Mapuche are an indigenous group that resisted conquest by the Spanish for 350 years. They began fighting on horseback at about the same time as the early poncho evidence. It has been suggested that the poncho might have been invented for use on horseback (Montell 1929:240–41, citing Gómez de Vidaurre, written 1789), which is plausible given its practicality for this purpose, as well as its subsequent pattern of use.

Use of the poncho gradually spread northwards from Chile during the 1700s. The poncho had reached northern Ecuador by the 1730s, where it was worn by ordinary indigenous men (Juan and Ulloa 1748). By the early nineteenth century, it was worn by men of all classes for travel on horseback (Stevenson 1825 [2]:76), and mid-nineteenth-century watercolors reveal that it was even worn by upper-class women riders (Hallo 1981:70, 72). Among indigenous people, it is a male garment.

Many Ecuadorian ponchos are solid color or have warp stripes, but in several areas a style with warp-resist dyed stripes is or was until recently sometimes made. The association of this technique with poncho weaving may also be of Mapuche origin, since it occurs on Mapuche ponchos as well as on some Bolivian, Peruvian, and Ecuadorian ponchos with remarkably similar designs (A. Rowe 1977:19–22).

Some Ecuadorian ponchos are woven on treadle looms. One style, in a twill weave, white with narrow black stripes, sometimes cloth dyed red or purple, is now seen primarily in Chimborazo, but formerly was also used in Pichincha, Cotopaxi, and Tungurahua provinces. It was probably derived from obraje production.

In the Otavalo area, men wear sandals made of furcraea fiber (or rubber) soles and cloth uppers (*alpargatas* S). This type of footwear, as the name suggests, is probably of Spanish origin (Vicens et al. 1968, fig. 29, shows alpargatas of hemp from Ibiza, Spain). Sandals with leather or motor-vehicle-tire soles and straps are more apt to be called by the Inca term *ushuta*. In many areas, however, men go barefoot or wear factory-made shoes.

It is striking that in Ecuador there is less of a correlation between indigenous types of garments and indigenous weaving processes than one finds in southern Peru and Bolivia. It appears that local importance of the obrajes in the colonial period in Ecuador may have dictated the use of obraje fabrics for indigenous styles of clothing. Another factor may be that in the southern Andes the women did most of the weaving while men were the primary weavers in Ecuador. If indigenous men were forced to spend all their time doing other kinds of work, including weaving in the obrajes, they would have little time to weave at home. Still, it is noteworthy that the fabric was so often used for indigenous and not for Spanish garment styles. Thanks to this custom, it is a small step to using machine-made cloth for indigenous garments, as is done in Imbabura and Chimborazo today.

Chapter **4**

Otavalo, Imbabura Province

Introduction

Lynn A. Meisch

The green, fertile Otavalo valley nestles in the Andes at 3,000 meters (9,200 feet) above sea level, 105 kilometers (65 miles) north of Quito.[1] The town of Otavalo (population approximately 24,000) is the market and commercial center for some seventy-five small surrounding communities that are inhabited by indigenous people of the Otavalo ethnic group and by a small number of mestizos-whites. Ibarra, a half-hour drive north of Otavalo, is the provincial capital and is also home to a number of Otavalo indigenous people. Two volcanoes, Taita (Q., Father) Imbabura in the eastern cordillera of the Andes (Fig. 31) and Mama (Q., Mother) Cotacachi in the west, loom over the valley and figure prominently in local folklore. The volcanoes are considered a married couple, whose offspring is Urcu (Q., mountain) Mojanda, a smaller mountain that seals off the valley in the south. (See map, page xviii.)

A rough estimate of the Otavalo indigenous population in 1995 is about 60,000 people, including those who live outside the valley (perhaps 10,000). Many Otavalos are now bilingual in Quichua and Spanish as a result of increased school attendance, some are monolingual Spanish speakers, while some also speak English, French, German, Italian, or Portuguese in addition to Spanish (and often Quichua).

Beyond a doubt, they are the most prosperous and best-known indigenous people in Ecuador and perhaps in all of Latin America because of their virtual monopoly of the cottage industry textile trade and associated tourism in Imbabura province. There are now at least 130 to 140 indigenous-owned and -operated stores in Otavalo, not to mention the thousands of indigenous people who have stands at the Saturday market. There are also indigenous-owned restaurants, hotels, a tourist agency, and other businesses in town.

Evidence is available to suggest that Otavalos have been weavers and merchants for centuries (e.g. Salomon 1986:202). These occupations provided them with an effective strategy for coping with centuries of colonial oppression, both in terms of a livelihood and a sense of self. The products woven and sold varied according to market conditions. For example, beginning around 1917, Otavalos began weaving imitations of Scottish tweeds for men's suits, which they could market for less than

1. Field work in Otavalo was done over twenty-two years between 1973 and 1995, including short visits in 1973 and 1974, eight and one-half months in 1978–79, one month in 1981 and 1984, ten months during 1985–86, several weeks in 1987, parts of the summers of 1988 and 1989, the entire summer of 1990, several weeks in February 1991 and in the summer of 1992, throughout most of the interval from October 1992 through January 1995, and the summer of 1995. See also Meisch 1987 and 1991. I would like to thank Margaret Goodhart and Frank Kiefer for their useful comments on this chapter.

31 Village of Agato with Taita Imbabura in the background, Imbabura province. Slide by Ann P. Rowe, 1986.

the price of the imported cloth. By the 1940s, some indigenous people had sufficient income from textile sales to enable them to buy land and were visibly more prosperous than other indigenous people in Ecuador (Salomon 1973).

After World War II, tweeds became less profitable, and the Otavalos instead began producing other kinds of textiles to sell to the many tourists who come to their famous Saturday market. Jan Schreuder, a Dutch designer and painter, directed a weaving project at the Casa de la Cultura Ecuatoriana in Quito beginning in 1954 under the auspices of the United Nations' International Labor Organization and other agencies (*Handweaver and Craftsman* 1959). The project taught tapestry weaving (with double interlocked joins) to some forty indigenous people from both Otavalo and Salasaca.[2] Tapestry weaving took firm root in both areas. Subsequently, Peace Corps volunteers have helped to enrich the local design repertoire, for example, introducing M. C. Escher motifs in 1974. Wall hangings, purses, day packs, duffel bags, and pillow covers are still produced in the Otavalo area (Fig. 32).

The 1964 Law of Agrarian Reform released many Otavalos from serfdom. Although the Agrarian Reform law has proven to be an imperfect vehicle for land redistribution, with many large estates still existing in the region, the abolition of huasipungo freed many Otavalos to work for themselves, unleashing an impressive burst of entrepreneurial energy. Instead of weaving for the hacienda owner in return for the right to farm a plot of land, families were free to weave and to market their textiles for themselves or to hire themselves out to other indigenous people or whites. Some former huasipungeros are now among the more prosperous contemporary weaving and merchant families in the valley. The shortage of farm land, in spite of agrarian reform, has caused an increasing number of families to turn to full-time weaving or merchandising.

2. The *Handweaver and Craftsman* article corrects the idea I previously held that the Otavalos had copied the tapestry technique from the Salasacas (Meisch 1987:157).

32 *Tourist tapestries for sale in the Otavalo market, Imbabura province. Design sources include local people and costume, M. C. Escher, and prehispanic Peruvian and/or Ecuadorian motifs. The panels on the far right are imported from Peru. Photo by Lynn A. Meisch, 1992.*

The past fifty years have also seen increasing differences in wealth among indigenous families. At one end of the scale are families, usually the poorest, who are entirely farmers. Other families are primarily farmers, but may weave a poncho or a few scarves or belts each month on the backstrap loom to bring in extra cash. In the middle are families who both farm and produce textiles ranging from acrylic shawls to tapestries on treadle or electric looms, and who usually sell in the Otavalo market or to other Otavalo textile vendors. At the other end of the scale are families who are full-time merchants and who export quantities of sweaters or ponchos or tapestries all over the world. Many of these merchant families have their own stores in Otavalo or Quito and also sell in the market. These indigenous people are wealthy by any standard, paying $28,000 cash for a new Chevy Trooper, building apartment complexes, restaurants, and shops in Otavalo, and sending their children to the universities in Quito or abroad.

Otavalo weavers and merchants live in every city and major town in Ecuador where they sell textiles in Otavalo-owned shops and in local markets. There are permanent Otavalo expatriate communities in Popayán, Bogotá, and Cartagena, Colombia; Caracas, Venezuela; New York City, USA; and Barcelona, Spain. Some merchants sell their textiles in one locale in Ecuador or abroad and then bring back textiles and crafts from that region to sell in Otavalo. Others make special trips to Peru and Bolivia to import traditional textiles, musical instruments, alpaca-fur rugs, cotton and alpaca sweaters, and wool or alpaca pictorial panels (the latter from San Pedro de Cajas and Lima, Peru), which are sold in shops in Otavalo or in the market.

Textile merchants and traditional music groups travel throughout the world selling textiles, playing music and selling tape casettes and compact disks to finance their travels. In the summers of the early 1990s hundreds of young men and a few young women traveled to the United States and Europe to play music on the street. When I first began to do research in Otavalo in 1978 I knew one indigenous man who had been abroad on a trip to Peru with a Peace Corps volunteer. Fifteen years later I know hundreds of indigenous people who have traveled abroad, especially to the United States, Canada, Europe, and Central and South America.

Thousands of Europeans, North Americans, Colombians, and Ecuadorians attend the Saturday market in Otavalo, and exporters from these countries and Japan visit Otavalo throughout the year to buy crafts and to place orders. The textile industry has expanded beyond Otavalo and the surrounding indigenous communities to include the mestizo-white sweater knitters in Ibarra and Mira, the makers of high fashion clothing in Fuente la Salud near Otavalo and in Ibarra, seamstresses, stocking makers, the owners of artesanías (crafts) stores in Otavalo, hat makers in Ilumán, and leather workers in Cotacachi. The boom includes mestizo-white antiquities sellers, palm leaf (Panama) hat vendors, hippie jewelry makers, and vendors from other South American countries, basket, warp-resist dyed textile, and shigra vendors from the central sierra, and indigenous people from Salasaca (Tungurahua province), Cacha (central Chimborazo province), Tigua and Quilotoa (Cotopaxi province), Cañar, and the eastern Imbabura communities, all of whom sell in the Otavalo market. Some mestizo-white merchants visit Otavalo to sell artesanías to Otavalos who sell them in turn in their shops or in the market. They include the merchants who bring warp-resist patterned shawls from the Cuenca region.

The Otavalo crafts market in the Plaza Centenario (known popularly as the

Plaza de Ponchos, or Poncho Plaza in English), which was formerly held on Saturdays and Wednesdays, the traditional major and minor market days, had gradually become a daily market by 1992. Tour buses from Colombia and Quito now disgorge eager buyers at the edge of the Poncho Plaza during the middle of the week.

Costume

Lynn A. Meisch

As Ecuador and the Otavalo valley modernize with a vengeance, especially in terms of technology and transnational contacts (including access to Euro-American popular culture), indigenous people in the valley have chosen those aspects of modernity, particularly technology, that they deem useful while retaining a unique costume and many other customs that are distinctly Otavalo. As Salomon has pointed out, "Otavalo contradicts the steamroller image of modernization, the assumption that traditional societies are critically vulnerable to the slightest touch of outside influence and wholly passive under its impact" (1973:464). Increased prosperity among the Otavalos through the production and marketing of textiles has strengthened rather than weakened ethnic identity and pride in traditional dress.

The survivals in Otavalo male and female costume suggest that there is not an inevitable progression leading to the loss of traditional dress. Instead there has

33 *Elements of Otavalo women's costume for sale in the Otavalo market, Imbabura province. The women are wearing their headcloths in the uma watana style. Photo by Lynn A. Meisch, 1984.*

been gradual change with the new eventually becoming the traditional and, in some instances, the traditional becoming archaic and then disappearing. But something new always becomes defined as *churajuna* (literally, "clothing"), the Quichua term for traditional dress, so that there is still a distinct costume that identifies the group as an ethnic entity.

Every single item of men's and women's costume can be bought in the Otavalo market (Fig. 33). Frequently a family or a community will specialize in a particular item: headwraps in the barrio of San Juan, women's belts in La Calera and La Compañía, alpargatas in La Calera, backstrap-loom woven ponchos in Carabuela, and so on (Meisch 1980c:25). Some families make some of their clothes and buy the rest, but I know of no one in the Otavalo region who makes everything. Those families who specialize in making a particular item are not producing just for their own use, but in quantity for sale.

Women's costume

Women's dress in Otavalo is conservative (Pl. I). The blouse-and-slip combination, probably introduced sometime in the nineteenth century, is the main modern component.[3] Females, from babies six months old to elders, wear the same basic costume, with the babies and girls dressed like miniature versions of the adults.

The blouse (*warmi camisa* Q., woman and S., blouse) is basically made from squares and rectangles, which are gathered or pleated into a tailored shape (Fig. 34). The main piece (bodice) of the blouse is pleated at the shoulder and neckline and sewn to a narrow band at the neck. The sleeves, which have a diamond-shaped underarm gusset, are gathered where they join the shoulder and also gathered into a narrow band that encircles the upper arm. In the 1940s, the blouse was made of cotton fabric, frequently commercial muslin, but today is usually made of synthetic fabric (*tela caucho* S., rubber cloth). The upper blouse portion is usually of a different, finer fabric than the lower part, called *tela bajera* (lower cloth) in Spanish or *ura chaki* (to the feet) in Quichua.

White lace (*encaje* S.), which is usually purchased separately in the Otavalo market, is attached to the blouse in ruffles at the neck and sleeves. Sometimes the ruffles are machine embroidered to match the embroidery on the blouse. Some women and girls crochet an edging on the lace that is decorative and also protects the edge of the lace. For a while in the late 1970s lace imported from Spain enjoyed a vogue.

There is a band of embroidery across the front of the bodice and around the sleeves at the shoulders. The narrow bands at the neck and upper arm are also embroidered, usually in a simple scallop, zigzag, or chevron stitch. Some blouses are embroidered at home by women for their own use, others by indigenous or mestizo-white women who embroider blouses as a business. The latter are now mostly machine embroidered.

34 Otavalo style blouse, purchased in the Otavalo market and sewn together by Lucita Fichamba of Peguche, Imbabura province. Synthetic fabric, machine embroidered in blue rayon thread with white cotton thread on the back. Length: 1.34 meters (53 inches). The Textile Museum 1986.19.26, Latin American Research Fund.

3. Considerable information is available about Otavalo costume earlier in this century. The main sources on the 1940s, from which information cited hereafter is taken, are Parsons 1945 and Collier and Buitrón 1949.

35 *Detail of the blouse in Fig 34. This embroidered design has been in use for several decades.*

The type of leafy vine design seen in Figure 35, worked predominantly in a single color, is a common traditional design, but now is less often seen. Many of the machine-embroidered blouses now available in the Otavalo market have elaborate naturalistic floral designs. Embroidery thread ranges from cotton to acrylic to rayon, which is shiny and which women call *seda* (S., silk). In the 1990s some blouses had sequins or fake pearls added to the embroidery.

Women wear two waist-to-ankle wrapped skirts (*anaku*) over their blouse, navy blue or black over white. The ends of the navy blue one meet on one side, revealing the white one underneath (Fig. 33). The white (*yurak* Q.) anaku, is called *ukunchina* (Q., underskirt). It is wrapped with one big pleat that is folded back to front at the side, with the opening on the opposite side. The dark blue or black (*yana* Q.) anaku is wrapped over the white one with the single pleat and opening on the opposite side from the first anaku.

My indigenous comadres and goddaughters showed me various tricks for making and holding the pleats while two belts are wrapped over the anakus to hold them up. First, the white anaku is wrapped around the lower body with the two ends meeting on either the right or left side (let us say left for purposes of illustration). The left hand holds the selvedges together while the right hand pulls the fabric away from the waist on the right. This extra fabric is folded into a pleat with the opening toward the front of the body. The pleat actually starts in the small of the back in order to finish at the side. Young girls just learning to wrap their anakus can tie the baby belt temporarily around the white anaku or back up against the wall to hold the anaku up. Older women use their elbows to hold the white anaku at their waist; women and girls also help one another.

Next, the dark anaku is wrapped over the white one. One side selvedge is tucked into the opening of the pleat of the white anaku, the dark anaku is passed around the body with its other side selvedge covering the white pleat. The extra fabric of the dark anaku is folded into a pleat on the left side, with the opening towards the front of the body. In other words, the dark anaku is not just wrapped over the white anaku, but has one edge tucked inside the pleat of the white anaku. If the baby belt has been used to hold up the white anaku, it is loosened and removed, and the mama belt is wrapped tightly over both anakus, followed by the baby belt. Another trick is to tuck the top edges of the anakus under on the sides, then fold the end of the dark anaku inside the white one as the belt is put on.

In the 1940s, anakus were made either of local treadle-loom woven wool fabric or of finer imported material. Today most anakus are made from factory-made wool (*paño*) or acrylic cloth woven in Quito. The factory-made wool anakus are wrapped so that the side selvedge is vertical, with white lettering visible where the anaku opens on the side. This lettering on the side selvedge says, "Flanel [sic] For Export" or "Indulana," which is the name of the factory in Quito. Some dark anakus are made from velvet (*terciopelo* S.) and this is considered luxurious and elegant, as are anakus made from heavily felted wool cloth (*piel de foca* S., seal skin) imported from the United States. The size of The Textile Museum dark anaku (1986.19.3) is .95 by 1.55 meters (37 by 61 inches). The light anaku (1986.19.4) is .93 by 1.52 meters (36½ by 60 inches). A few women wear green anakus; this style has appeared since 1985 and seems to be a matter of personal preference.

Many Otavalo white and dark anakus have simple machine embroidery at the hem. Common anaku border designs include flowers (*sisa* Q.), zigzags (*kingu* Q.), and butterflies (*chabul* Q.), with small corn stalks enclosed in an oval at the corners above the border design. The embroidery is usually done in such bright colors as red, blue, yellow, green, and lavender. The floral and butterfly motifs usually involve embroidery thread of several different colors, while simple zigzag patterns are frequently done in just one color. Sometimes this single color is a shaded thread, that is, an embroidery thread that varies from light to dark. Anakus are sold with the embroidery already done and thus do not indicate village residence.

Women wear two belts. Underneath is the wide *mama chumbi* (mother belt), red with green edges and a cabuya weft to make the belt stiff and woven on the backstrap loom with four selvedges (Fig. 36). Over the mama chumbi is a long narrow belt, the *wawa chumbi* (baby belt) or *chumbi*, usually of white cotton with colored wool supplementary-warp patterning, also backstrap-loom woven (Figs. 37–39).

36 *Otavalo style mama chumbi, purchased in the Otavalo market, Imbabura province. Warp-faced plain weave with acrylic warp, furcraea weft. 1.30 x .10 meters (51 x 4 inches). The Textile Museum 1986.19.6, Latin American Research Fund.*

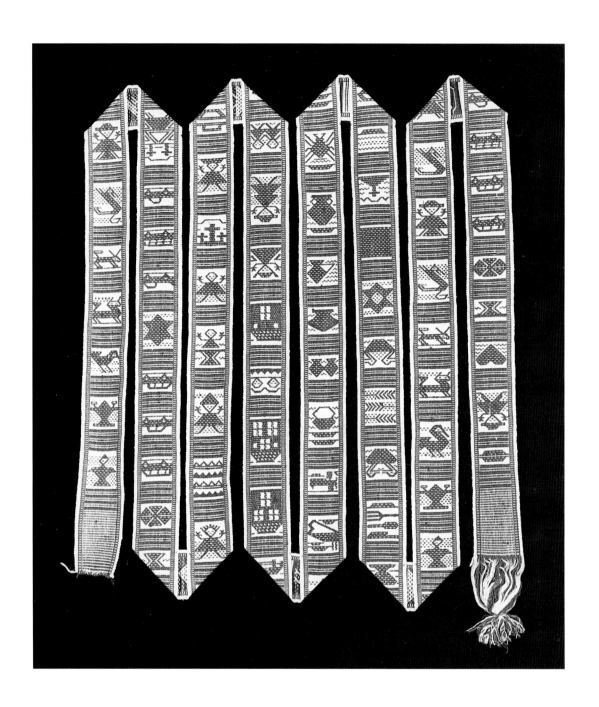

37 *Otavalo style wawa chumbi, purchased
in the Otavalo market, Imbabura province.
White cotton plain weave with blue acrylic
supplementary-warp pickup designs. 4.695 x
.05 meters (15 feet 5 inches x 2 inches). The
Textile Museum 1986.19.24, Latin American
Research Fund.*

58 Otavalo, Imbabura Province

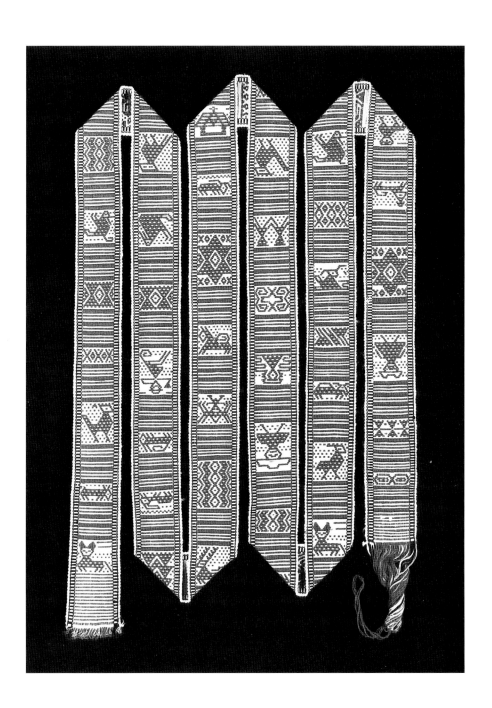

38 Otavalo style wawa chumbi, purchased
in the Otavalo market, Imbabura province.
White cotton plain weave with lavender
acrylic supplementary-warp pickup designs.
3.12 x .05 meters (10 feet 3 inches x 2 inches).
The Textile Museum 1986.19.44, Latin
American Research Fund.

39 *Details of three Otavalo style wawa chumbis, purchased in the Otavalo market, Imbabura province. The belts at center and right, with diamond designs, are called* coco chumbi. *Cotton plain weave with acrylic (left and center) or wool (right) supplementary-warp loom-controlled designs. Widths ranging between 3.8 and 5.5 centimeters (1½ and 2¼ inches). Left to right: The Textile Museum 1986.19.42 (with bars), 1986.19.22, 1986.19.21, Latin American Research Fund.*

The mama chumbi is 8–15 centimeters (3–6 inches) wide and about 1.20–1.30 meters (48–51 inches) long. To put it on, the end is placed in the center front, and it is wrapped straight around from there. Up to the mid-1970s it was possible to find mama chumbis with handspun wool warp yarns, but now acrylic yarn is used instead.

The wawa chumbi is 3.5–5 centimeters (1½–2 inches) wide and 2.75–3.75 meters (8–11 feet) long. The baby belt is wrapped over the mother belt very tightly, again starting center front but winding at a slightly different level each round, and the end is tucked in under the bottom edge. Today, acrylic yarn has replaced wool for the supplementary-warp patterning. In the 1990s, some wawa chumbis had a few supplementary-warp yarns of gilt thread.

Some wawa chumbis have a variety of motifs made by hand-picking selected warp yarns to form the design, called *agllana* (Q., to choose or select) (Figs. 37–38). Motifs include the sun, the planet Venus, animals, plants, people, Inca pots (*Inka manga*), zigzags (*kingu*), diamond-like motifs (*coco*), words such as "Ecuador," etc. If the belt is locally made, the choice of motifs is up to the weaver. The Instituto Otavaleño de Antropología has collected more than 2,000 belt motifs from Imbabura Province (Jaramillo 1981). Other belts with fewer or simpler designs are woven using extra heddle rods to create the designs (Fig. 39).

Another belt that is traditional in Otavalo is the *kanitillu* (Q., cane) *chumbi*, woven on the backstrap loom in the twill-derived weave, with narrow white (cotton) horizontal bars separating wider, colored (wool or acrylic) ones (similar to Fig. 51, center, but wider). The colored bars are usually red on one side of the belt and black, blue, or pink on the other. Some girls and women wear the kanitillu chumbi as their wawa chumbi, and this style of belt is also used to swaddle babies.

Beginning in the mid-1980s some Otavalo women began wearing Cañari men's complementary-warp weave belts (Pl. I). One reason they gave for this preference is that the colors in Cañari belts go well with Otavalo female dress, but women also say that these belts last longer because they can be worn with either side out.

In the early 1990s, two other baby belt styles appeared. One consists of handwoven belts from Bolivia, which are brought back by Otavalos who have traveled there. Bolivian belts (handwoven by a number of different Bolivian ethnic groups) are not as long as Otavalo wawa chumbis, so they usually encircle the waist only once and are fastened with long ties. The second new belt style consists of factory-made acrylic braid imported from Europe, the United States, or Japan, which is sold in long rolls at the Saturday market. This is purchased in three-meter or three-vara lengths and wrapped. The *vara* is an old Spanish unit of measurement, equivalent to about 84 centimeters (33 inches).

Both the headcloth and the shawl are called *fachalina* (Q., to bring cloth, *facha* or *pacha*, onto the body). In the 1940s–60s, the fachalina was generally of cotton, either white or with blue and white stripes, although some shoulder fachalinas were a solid dark color.

In the 1980s and 90s, the shoulder fachalina is a white, blue, black, or occasionally turquoise (solid color) rectangular cloth. The lighter blues are a more recent innovation. The fabric is no longer of cotton, but instead is fine wool (*paño*) from the factories in Quito or commercially manufactured acrylic or velour. The size of The Textile Museum example (1986.19.5) is 1.22 meters (4 feet) long by .68 meters (2 feet 3 inches) wide. The fachalina is worn in one of two basic styles, either covering both shoulders and tied over the chest (Fig. 33) or worn over one shoulder and under the opposite arm and tied near the shoulder (the latter style is called *shalaganana* in Quichua) (Fig. 26).

The headcloth fachalina is usually black or blue, but some woven specifically as headcloths are weft-faced. In this case the warp is white acrylic and the weft consists of a shot of white alternating with three shots of navy blue or black acrylic yarn, with a white border at the top and bottom edges, which are hemmed (Figs. 40–47). This style is called a *suku* (light) *fachalina*, and The Textile Museum example (1986.19.11) is 1.10 meters (3 feet 6 inches) long by .65 meters (2 feet) wide. The weaving of suku fachalinas on the treadle loom is a specialty of the barrio of San Juan, just across the Panamerican highway west of town. These fachalinas are similar to those of the 1940s except that they are woven of acrylic instead of cotton and are no longer used as shoulder wraps.

Formerly, the manner in which the headcloth was worn apparently indicated the woman's village, but today it is purely a matter of personal preference. Juana Arrayán and her daughter Blanca Yolanda Castañeda Arrayán of Ilumán identified and demonstrated four current styles. The first three of these styles were also shown to us by Lucita Fichamba of Peguche.

The most commonly seen style is called *uma watana* (Q., head wrap) (Fig. 33). The fabric is unfolded, with the long side put over the woman's forehead. The two corners framing the side of the face are drawn to the back on top of the draped fabric and tucked under each other. Since the corners are not tied, they gradually loosen and must be periodically readjusted.

Another common style is called *uma tazina* (Q., head nest) (Figs. 40–43). To wear this style, the woman folds the fabric lengthwise, first folding the sides into the middle (Fig. 40), and then in half parallel. The folded fabric is then doubled over crosswise with the ends crossing each other (Fig. 41), and then the ends are tucked under (Fig. 42). This style is especially useful as a sun shade (Fig. 43).

Another way of wearing the fachalina, called *uma watarina tazina* (headwrap nest), involves first putting it on in the uma watana style, then taking the ends that hang down and bringing them back up over the head, crossing them as in the head nest style, and tucking one end under the other (Figs. 44–46). The result looks similar to uma tazina.

A fourth style is called *iskhay fachalina* (Q., two fachalinas). Two separate headcloths are worn. The first is put on in the uma watana style. Then a fachalina is folded in the uma tazina style and worn on top (Fig. 47).

40   41   42

40 Blanca Yolanda Castañeda of Ilumán, Imbabura province, demonstrating how to put on the fachalina in the uma tazina style. First the fabric is folded lengthwise, the ends toward the middle (shown), and then down the middle. Photos by Lynn A. Meisch, 1994.

41 Uma tazina style, step two. The fabric is folded in half at an angle.

42 Uma tazina style, step three. The ends of the fabric are folded under.

The headcloth may also be draped over the head without any folds.

Some young women in Otavalo proper consider the fachalina worn on the head to be old fashioned, especially the uma tazina, and say that only women and girls from the poor communities wear this style (Margaret Goodhart, personal communication). Although this statement is not strictly true, since women from Peguche, Ilumán, and other wealthier villages, wear the uma tazina style, the attitude of these young women does indicate a generational difference in fachalina preferences.

Through the 1960s, women also wore a heavy handmade felt hat, either over or under their fachalinas (Fig. 48). The hats had a broad brim and low crown, the exact shape of which varied from one community to another, and could be either white or reddish brown. They were made principally in Ilumán. Today, however, women wear only the fachalina, describing the hat as "hot and heavy."

For hauling burdens on their backs, women do not use the fachalina, but the *rebozo* (S.), a longer rectangular cloth, about .90 meters (3 feet) wide by 1.52 meters (5 feet) long, which can be deep red (the old style), fuchsia, turquoise, blue, green, black, or white. Turquoise is a common color today, and many rebozos have zigzags machine embroidered along one edge. Fabrics run the gamut from cotton to fine wool to acrylic to velour and fake fur.

Babies are usually tied on their mothers' (or sisters' or brothers') backs with a white cotton cloth, called a *sábana* (S., sheeting), that is 4½ varas long (3.78 meters or 12 feet 4 inches). The mother balances the baby on her back as she leans forward.

43

44

45

43 Uma tazina style, step four. The fabric is placed on the head.

44 Blanca Yolanda Castañeda demonstrating how to put on the fachalina in the uma watana tazina style. The fabric is first put on in the uma watarina style (see Fig. 33), and then the lower ends are brought forward. Photos by Lynn A. Meisch, 1994.

45 Uma watarina tazina style, step two. The ends are crossed.

46 Uma watarina tazina style, step three. The ends are tucked under in front.

47 Blanca Yolanda Castañeda demonstrating the two fachalina style. Photo by Lynn A. Meisch, 1994.

46

47

48 *Old woman wearing the old style of hat at the Otavalo market, Imbabura province. Photo by Lynn A. Meisch, 1984.*

49 *Jairo Castañeda carrying his little cousin Jaime Orlando de la Torre, Ilumán, Imbabura province. Photo by Lynn A. Meisch 1979.*

She covers the baby's back with the cloth, crosses the ends over her chest and then ties them in back beneath the baby's bottom (Fig. 49). The colored rebozo, sometimes with additional light bundles, is wrapped over the mother and baby. The shoulder fachalina is worn under the baby in back but over the tie ends of the carrying cloth.

In recent years, women and girls have added aprons (*delantales* S.) and handknit or factory-made wool, acrylic, or cotton sweaters (*chompas* S.) and vests (*chalecos* S.) to their wardrobes, especially for use around the house or in the fields.

The past forty-five years have seen an enormous increase in the number of

50 *Otavalo women, showing the wrapped hair style, Peguche, Imbabura province. Photo by Lynn A. Meisch, 1993.*

51 *Details of Otavalo style women's hair bands, purchased at the Otavalo market, Imbabura province. Widths 2.8–3 centimeters (1⅛ inches). Left to right: navy blue acrylic plain weave, The Textile Museum 1986.19.12; kanitillu style, white cotton and colored acrylic, float weave based on 2/1 twill, 1986.19.8; white cotton plain weave with acrylic supplementary-warp chevrons 1986.19.41, Latin American Research Fund.*

females wearing shoes or sandals. During the 1940s, no women wore them, but now most indigenous women wear locally made sandals with blue or black vamps (*alpargatas*). These alpargatas have a rubber sole (*suela* S.), velvet toe covering (*manta* S.), and a heel strap (*talonera* S.) with a grommet or loop for attaching a string to tie around the ankle to hold the alpargata to the foot.

Women and girls almost never cut their hair, but wear it pulled back and wrapped with a long band (*cinta* S. or *akcha watarina* Q., hair wrap), which is woven on the treadle or backstrap loom (Figs. 50–51). These bands come in a variety of colors and some have a few gilt threads in the warp. The lengths range from 1.52 meters (60 inches) to 1.72 meters (68 inches). Sometimes the hair is braided into one long braid, but hair worn wrapped is more common.

In the 1990s, teenage girls began to wear their hair pulled back and fastened at the nape of the neck with a puffy bow or a factory-made elastic tie with plastic balls on the ends, rather than wrapped. In addition, a few young women have cut bangs.

Jewelry

In most Otavalo communities women and girls wear bead necklaces (*wallka* Q.) consisting of strands (*sartas* S.) of gilded glass beads (Pl. I). Such beads have been worn in the Otavalo area since at least the 1920s (Gayer 1929, pl. 7). They were manufactured in Czechoslovakia as Christmas tree ornaments. More recently, they have been imported from Japan. In the 1970s and early 1980s, masses of large, gilded glass beads about the size of a grape, up to sixty strands extending from neck to breast, were stylish. Many older women still wear this style. Then, smaller gold beads, about the size of a grain of rice, and flat on the sides, became popular, especially among younger women. The newer style involves wearing smaller beads and fewer strands of them, sometimes only five or six strands. Today, most young women and girls wear necklaces of these newer, smaller, gilded glass beads, although a variety of sizes and styles are sold in the Otavalo market.

Women who can afford it sometimes wear a string of real coral beads or 2.5 centimeter-long (1 inch) coral branches (called *cachas*, S. horns) around their neck in addition to the gilded glass strands. Another variation is to mix just a few coral-colored or red beads in a strand with the gilded glass ones. In some communities, especially around Lake San Pablo, oval or round red or coral-colored beads were worn until recently instead of the gilded ones, a style that appears to predate the use of gilded beads since Hassaurek describes it during the 1860s (1967:162).

Both wrists are wrapped with a long string of red or coral-colored beads, the wrist wrap (*maki watana* Q.) (Pl. I). The kind of beads used, which range from plastic to antique trade beads to glass to real coral, depends on a person's wealth. Some women mix different kinds of beads in their maki watana, and one comadre proudly showed me hers, which had beads of real coral mixed with coral-colored glass beads and brass beads from Cotacachi. Some women and girls are also attaching small, brass hands from Cotacachi, about 2.5 centimeters (1 inch) long, to their maki watanas. (The hand is an ancient Mediterranean symbol that protects against the evil eye.)

A variety of red and coral-colored beads are sold in the Otavalo market along with the gilded glass ones. Women buy the beads for both necklaces and wrist wraps in short strands in the market, then buy nylon or cotton thread and re-string the beads to the desired length. The ends of the necklace strands are braided together at the ends to make ties. For each wrist wrap, a single strand ranging from 1.45 meter (4 feet 9 inches) up to 4 meters (13 feet) long is made with a thread loop at one end. The woman holds the loop with her second or third finger, with the hand vertical, and wraps the strand toward her wrist, tucking the end bead into the loop and adjusting the fit of the beads.

Baby girls have their ears pierced for earrings. In the 1940s, the most common style of earring was long loops of the same red or gold beads used for the necklace, but modern ones of wire and colored glass were coming into use. Today, no single style of earring is considered typical. There are several vendors in the Otavalo market who sell cheap costume jewelry earrings, mestizo-white and indigenous vendors who sell antique silver earrings, as well as hippie vendors who sell earrings made from lapis lazuli, chrysacola (a kind of turquoise), pink quartz, painted clay beads imported from Peru, and amethyst and hematite imported from Brazil. Because many Otavalos travel within Ecuador and abroad, women may also acquire earrings from these trips.

In the 1940s, both men and women wore many finger rings, but few indigenous people wear them any more. Some three-pronged brass rings, with a piece of colored glass set in the prongs, are made by a mestizo-white family in Cotacachi and are sold in the Otavalo market.

In 1978, the sight of an indigenous person wearing eyeglasses was unusual, but today, many of those with poor eyesight, both male and female, are able to afford them.

Men's costume

Otavalos wearing what has been considered traditional dress for the past forty years are easily identified by their white pants and poncho (Fig. 54). Until as recently as the 1960s the white pants were made from handspun and handwoven cotton cloth (*lienzo*), in a style with wide calf-length legs, a large square crotch gusset, and a waistband with ties at one side (called *fundillu calzón*) (Fig. 52). The legs are made of rectangles, approximately 71 centimeters (28 inches) long and 78 centimeters (31 inches) wide, folded in half, often cut horizontally in the fabric so that the selvedge serves as the lower edge. The fabric is pleated into the waistband and a slit is cut at the side of one leg where the ties extend. The gusset can be up to 39 centimeters (15 inches) square. Now only old men wear this style (Fig. 54, right).

The white pants worn today by most men are machine-made and of modern cut: ankle-length with a zippered fly, and a leather belt (*cinturón* S.) that buckles. In the more conservative style, the legs are cut relatively straight and are without cuffs (Fig. 54, left). Boys and young men wear white pants to school and for special occasions, but for daily use all kinds of pants are now worn, from sweat pants to blue jeans.

The older handmade style of shirt (called *tiu camisa*) has tucks next to the front placket, which extends only to the upper chest, and machine embroidery on the placket, collar, and cuffs (Fig. 53). The collar and cuffs are often made of finer fabric than the rest. This style is no longer commonly worn by indigenous men, but has evolved into a tourist item and is sold in the market as the "Otavalo wedding shirt." By 1992, members of traditional music groups, in a revival of the style, were buying and wearing these shirts for performances, but not for daily use. Any kind of shirt or sweater is worn today, although a white shirt is considered traditional (Fig. 55).

The most common old-style Otavalo poncho is red with a group of contrasting stripes near each outer edge. These are rarely seen now, although a few music

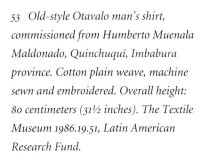

52 Old-style Otavalo pants, commissioned from Humberto Muenala Maldonado, Quinchuquí, Imbabura province. Cotton plain weave, machine sewn. Overall length: 73.5 centimeters (29 inches). The Textile Museum 1986.19.52, Latin American Research Fund.

53 Old-style Otavalo man's shirt, commissioned from Humberto Muenala Maldonado, Quinchuquí, Imbabura province. Cotton plain weave, machine sewn and embroidered. Overall height: 80 centimeters (31½ inches). The Textile Museum 1986.19.51, Latin American Research Fund.

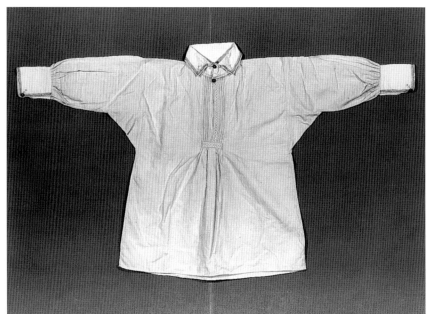

groups wear them for performances. The group in Figure 56 is wearing a modern machine-made style in the old-fashioned red color.

Two basic types of ponchos are currently worn. The older style is a dark blue (indigo-dyed), or a subdued blue-green wool, made from two rectangles woven on the backstrap loom that are sewn together with a slit left open for the head (Figs. 54 and 57, left). The ponchos are large and approximately square, 1.30–1.50 meters (51–59 inches) on a side. Many of these ponchos have an added collar, with a

54 *Otavalo men in formal dress, giving speeches as part of a wedding ritual, Ilumán, Imbabura province. Sr. de la Torre (at right) wears the older style of shorter wider pants and a poncho that is plain on one side, plaid on the other. Daniel de la Torre (at left) wears more modern pants and a solid color poncho. Photo by Lynn A. Meisch, 1993.*

55 *Otavalo men's semi-formal dress, worn on the Day of the Dead. Segundo Santillán, his wife Luz de la Torre, and their sons Humberto, José, and Carlos, of Ilumán, Imbabura province. Photo by Lynn A. Meisch, 1994.*

triangular gusset in the back where the collar is attached to the body of the poncho, and are edged with a navy or black commercial tape. The finest are woven in a complementary-warp weave with a different shade of blue on each face (A. Rowe 1985, fig. 20 and note 59). This style is called *ishkay cara* (*ishkay* Q., two; *cara* S., face), while the monochrome ponchos are called *chulla cara* (*chulla* Q., one of a pair). Fewer and fewer men are weaving the two-sided style, however.

The second, most common poncho style, available since the 1950s, is factory-

made and has a collar, a gusset at the back of the neck, and commercial trim binding the edges. This poncho is navy blue on one side and grey or tan plaid on the other (Figs. 54 and 57, right). It is called a *poncho cuadrada* (S., poncho with squares or blocks, because of the plaid), or a *ruana* or a *poncho jijún* (Jijón). These ponchos are made in a factory in Quito by Otavalos living there. According to Jaramillo (1990:140–41), "Jijón" refers to the name of the factory in Quito, "Chillos Jijón," where these ponchos were first made.

An interesting trend is that many young men are wearing jackets (*sacos* S.) for daily use and ponchos only for special occasions. Some wear white pants and white alpargatas, but say they find ponchos cumbersome for such activities as driving a car or truck, weaving on the treadle loom, or working in their family's artesanías store. (Their fathers manage these activities with ponchos, however.) Most of the young men own a poncho which they wear on special occasions. I attended Otavalo weddings in 1985 and 1993 in which the grooms, from Ilumán and Peguche, respectively, who usually wear a jacket or sweatshirt, wore traditional dress with a dark blue wool poncho for this occasion (Fig. 57, right).

Otavalo men and boys usually wear their hair long and pulled back in a single

57 *Wedding of Rosa de la Torre and Rafael Tituaña, of Ilumán, with Zoila Arrayán and Daniel de la Torre as padrinos, at the church of San Luis in Otavalo, Imbabura province. The bride wears two white anakus and a blouse with white embroidery. Photo by Lynn A. Meisch, 1993.*

braid (*shimba* Q.). Sometimes, a small boy may have a smaller braid that begins just above the center of the forehead or two smaller braids over the temples meeting the main braid in back, which are older styles (Fig. 58).

In 1987, an Otavalo traditional music group, Charijayac, which first attained success in Europe, made a triumphant return to Otavalo and played a series of concerts. The cover of Charijayac's first tape cassette distributed in Ecuador is a photograph of the back of five heads, all with dark, felt fedoras and long, black hair. But instead of being braided, the hair was pulled back and tied in a long pony tail. Charijayac started this hair style, which continues to enjoy a vogue among both young men and women. The Charijayac album cover also inspired woven tapestries showing the back of heads with hats and long hair (which could be braided or just pulled back, the details are not woven in). More recently, a few young, hip, indigenous men began wearing their hair entirely loose, as a sign that they are both progressive and artistic (many are musicians), but it does not look like this fad is spreading beyond a very small group.

The men's handmade felt hats were identical to the women's. However, during the 1940s, some men began to wear broad-brimmed fedoras, and by the 1960s most

58 *Otavalo man's and boy's hairstyles. Carlos Conterón warping a belt, observed by Jaime Orlando de la Torre, Ilumán, Imbabura province. Photo by Lynn A. Meisch, 1986.*

men were wearing this style (Fig. 55). These fedoras (*sombrero* S.) are white, tan, gray, brown, or black felt, with a medium-wide (9 centimeter or 3½ inch) brim and medium-high crown. These hats usually have a braided or simple strip hatband made from the same felt as the hat. One such fedora (called an *ascanta*), which has a slightly wider brim, is considered very fashionable. Many of these hats are made in Ilumán from factory-manufactured felt which is bought in Quito, and cut, molded, and blocked by hand in Ilumán. In the 1970s and 1980s, young men wore their hats backwards to indicate that they were *wambriandu* (Q. with S. suffix) or out looking for (or at) girls, a common occurrence on Friday nights. In recent years the custom of wearing the hat backwards seems to have disappeared (but not the custom of flirting).

White sandals (*alpargatas*) with braided and coiled furcraea fiber soles, have been worn since the colonial period and continue to be worn to the present day (Fig. 59). The cottage industry manufacture of alpargatas by mestizos-whites and by a few indigenous families is a specialty of the communities around Cotacachi, especially La Calera; some are also made in Otavalo. They are hand made (see Jaramillo 1983). The toe piece and the heel strap are interlaced using white cotton string on a cone-shaped block of wood, which allows for the shaping of the toe. The toe piece usually has float patterning in zigzags or diamonds, while the heel is plain weave, with two loops added for the tie. Some examples are now made with rubber instead of furcraea fiber soles (Fig. 59, center). Other kinds of footwear are also worn today, especially by younger men and boys, including sneakers and running shoes. Men also frequently wear a watch.

Male costume in Otavalo is changing faster than female costume. In the early 1990s, it is possible to see three main variations being worn daily by different

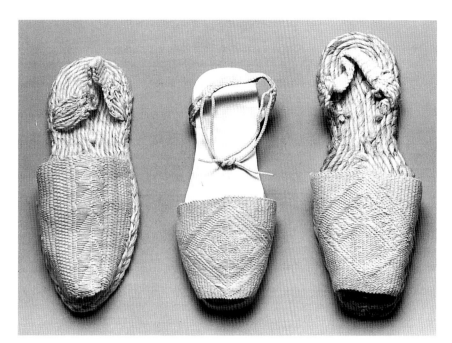

59 *Otavalo men's alpargatas, one from each of three pairs, purchased in the Otavalo market, Imbabura province. Lengths, left to right: 22.5, 24, 28 centimeters (9, 9½, 11 inches). The Textile Museum 1984.46.13, 1986.19.49, 1986.19.10, Latin American Research Fund.*

generations. The huasipungo generation, the *taitas* (Q., fathers, an honorific for elderly men), who are in their fifties and older, tend to wear the oldest style: white shirt, blue poncho, alpargatas, and baggy, midcalf-length, white pants. The *tius* (*tío* S., uncle, also an honorific), the generation in their thirties and forties, still usually wear white alpargatas and white pants, but factory-made, tailored, ankle-length ones with zipper flies, and a leather belt. Some tius wear ponchos daily, but more wear jackets or sweaters and shirts of varying colors.

The *wambras*, the boys and young men through their teens and twenties, particularly those from Quito, Otavalo, and the communities closest to Otavalo (Peguche, Ilumán, Quinchuquí, and Agato), are in the vanguard of change. Some of these young men are bringing back and wearing clothing bought in Europe and the United States during their travels as musicians or merchants: baggy jeans, high-top athletic shoes (sometimes worn with the laces untied like United States hip-hop or rap aficionados), a bandanna around their forehead, baseball caps, T-shirts or sweatshirts with slogans, place names, or athletic team names, down vests, and Gore-Tex™ and denim jackets. For a small group of young men, dark glasses, including Ray-Ban wrap-arounds or ones with designer frames, have become an accessory, a sign that the wearer is a member of the local avant-garde. A few are even sporting one earring.

In buying and wearing clothes bought abroad, the young Otavalos are no different from their American and European counterparts who bring home and wear ponchos, Otavalo wedding shirts, warp-resist dyed vests, and handknit sweaters as trophies from their trips to Ecuador. Other young Otavalo males are buying the latest Euro-American garments in Ecuador in the form of imports or copies.

One young man from Peguche cited "envidia" (S., envy) as a reason for costume change; in other words, peer pressure. Although he began wearing the latest Euro-American fashions several years ago he said it was a "tontería" (S., foolishness, stupidity) to give up traditional dress for daily wear. One of my godsons (and his mother concurred) said that white pants got dirty too fast, especially during the rainy season. There is some truth to this statement in that the old-style pants were shorter, coming to mid-calf or just below the knee, so that a man's legs, rather than his pants, got splattered with mud. But my godson also admitted that he wanted to wear the "la moda de la juventud" (the fashion of the young).

It will be interesting to see if this group of young men reverts to more traditional Otavalo dress as they get older or if they will retain their preference for innovation. Although the long braid, white shirt, white pants, white alpargatas, blue poncho, and felt hat with a medium-wide brim are still the identifying features of Otavalo ethnicity, so many young men are wearing other kinds of clothes that the ascanta and long braid or ponytail (and a certain prosperous air) are now the sine qua non of Otavalo male identity.

Children's costume

Infants are swaddled in cloths secured by wrapping with a wawa chumbi (Fig. 60). As soon as they are toddling, children are dressed like tiny adults, and the godparents' main gift to their godchild at baptism is a complete set of traditional dress. Baptism is the occasion when children "receive their name" and are recognized as members of the group, symbolized by the gift of traditional costume. Many small boys and girls are dressed in sweatsuits or other kinds of Euro-American clothes around the house, but in traditional costume for trips to Otavalo, for school, and for important occasions. This is especially true for little boys, whose mothers despair of keeping the white pants clean if the boys wear them while playing, weaving, or helping in the fields. Clothes are still laboriously washed by hand in concrete washtubs or on rocks in the lakes or streams. I know of no indigenous families who own mechanical washers and dryers.

A sure sign of Otavalo cultural vitality is that the children and young people are wearing traditional dress as they get older and have a choice. Even the hip young men choose to keep their long hair and usually wear their ascanta. Traditional dress is acceptable as a school uniform for indigenous children (since it is a uniform of sorts), while white children must buy a special school uniform (Fig. 61). Many schools require all indigenous students to wear a special school sweater or vest, or for girls, a pinafore, over their regular clothes, so that all the pupils at a school are identifiable by virtue of a special garment. But this is worn over, not in place of, Otavalo costume. Attendance at school, including colegio (high school) and the university is therefore compatible with indigenous ethnic identity because of this custom of allowing indigenous pupils to wear their traditional dress.

60 *Rosalena de la Torre with her grandson Edwin Giovani Teran wrapped in a wawa chumbi woven by her husband Carlos Conterón, Ilumán, Imbabura province. Slide by Ann P. Rowe, 1986.*

61 Otavalo schoolgirls in the Christmas parade, Otavalo, Imbabura province. Photo by Lynn A. Meisch, 1985.

Textile Production

Lynn A. Meisch

The cottage industry production of textiles is the engine that drives the economy of Imbabura province. Agriculture, the manufacture of acrylic yarn in Atuntaqui, and the production of cloth at the San Pedro blanket factory and San Miguel and Pintex cotton jersey factories near Otavalo are also important, but to a lesser extent.

In the Otavalo region virtually every member of an indigenous family participates in textile production, using technology that ranges from backstrap looms to treadle looms to electric looms and from knitting needles to knitting machines. The father of a family usually works full time warping and weaving when he is not involved in agricultural or household chores, while the mother may knot the fringe or otherwise finish textiles when they come off the loom when she is not cooking or taking care of the baby or working with her husband in the fields. Little children often spend a few minutes during the day winding bobbins and carrying them to the weavers. Their older brothers and sisters will spend an hour or two weaving at the loom or sewing labels on goods after school, while an elder brother or sister minds the family's store or takes merchandise to Quito. A disabled relative or a grandparent will card and spin wool, and everyone may help sell at the Saturday Otavalo market. If a family receives a large order they may farm out the work to relatives and neighbors or hire them to come in and help. The possible arrangements are infinite but the point is that textile production is still based in the home and everyone helps in some way.

Tapestries are by no means the only product. Some families specialize in garments worn by other Otavalos. Others make garments designed to imitate those of other indigenous peoples and sell them at local or regional markets in other parts of Ecuador. Other families make acrylic ponchos, shawls, and scarves that are worn by Ecuadorian mestizos and whites, while others make clothing for the tourist market, including acrylic, wool, or cotton jackets, vests, blouses, and purses, or handknit wool sweaters, mittens, hats, and scarves. Some families weave only blankets, while others weave acrylic shawls and dresses for export to other South American countries. This list is in no way exhaustive and is just an example of the kinds of goods produced. Furthermore, products go in and out of fashion and every year new goods show up in the market. Some are invented or copied by local artisans; others are introduced by exporters from abroad.

Because weaving is so important in Otavalo, textile skills, including backstrap loom weaving, are taught in the local public primary schools. Although most textiles are now produced on treadle or electric looms for economic reasons, the old techniques are still considered important. In addition, there is a group of weavers in Agato, of whom Miguel Andrango and members of the Tawantinsuyu Weaving Workshop are especially well known, who specialize in making high quality wool or cotton textiles on the backstrap loom.

Cotacachi Area Communities

Lynn A. Meisch

The Otavalo ethnic group includes the indigenous people of the eastern slopes of Mama Cotacachi. Those people living in Cotacachi and the small towns close to Cotacachi or midway between Otavalo and Cotacachi (Quiroga, La Calera, Gualsaquí, Azama, Cotama, Guanansi, Carabuela, Quichinche, etc.) are also involved in agriculture and the textile industry. Indigenous people high on the slopes of the western cordillera around Mama Cotacachi are primarily agriculturalists.

Although today indigenous men dress in the same basic style as described above for Otavalo, contemporary women's costume is more similar to Otavalo area women's costume of fifty years ago than to today's. For example, women from communities close to Cotacachi often wear plain white fachalinas as headcloths, and older women wear the old-style handmade felt hat (Fig. 62). Women from communities on the eastern slopes of Mama Cotacachi, including such towns as Morlán and Imantag, wear an even more conservative costume. Their fachalinas, both headcloths and shoulder wraps, are red-and-white or blue-and-white striped cotton or acrylic (Fig. 63). Older women wear the old-style felt hats and younger ones may wear narrow-brimmed fedoras. In addition, more of the costume is handmade than is typical of communities closer to Otavalo.

We talked to a woman in the Cotacachi Sunday market, who said she was from Morlán and wore a handspun, handwoven anaku of mottled dark grey wool under her blue anaku, and also had a hand-embroidered blouse (Fig. 63). Another woman, also with a homemade cotton blouse, was not wearing a white anaku, only a dark one with her white cotton slip showing underneath. The slip had one row of turquoise and one of pink rick-rack with 5 centimeters (2 inches) of lace at the hem.

62 Woman in the Cotacachi market, Imbabura province, wearing an old-style handmade hat over a headcloth. Slide by Laura M. Miller, 1992.

63 Woman in the Cotacachi market from Morlán, Imbabura province, wearing a grey handwoven under-anaku and a striped headcloth over her hat. Slide by Laura M. Miller, 1989.

64 Woman from the Cotacachi area wearing an appliqué outer anaku and a fedora, photographed in the Otavalo market, Imbabura province. Slide by Lynn A. Meisch, 1985.

A third woman, spotted in the Otavalo market, with the characteristic white and pink striped fachalina, had several rows of appliqué bands on her blue anaku, worn over her blouse-slip, which in turn had two rows of eyelet ruffles and simple embroidered bands on the hem (Fig. 64). Some women use a baby wrapping cloth that has appliqué along the bottom (Fig. 65).

Natabuela

Ann P. Rowe

The town of Natabuela, located 8 kilometers (5 miles) south of Ibarra, in the cantón of Antonio Ante, is the locus of another substyle of the Otavalo costume. The land formerly was a big hacienda, called Anafo, belonging to the Church.[4] The hacienda land was sold to the indigenous people working on it in 1963. The plots of land are nevertheless too small, and many of the men have left to seek work in the cities, while the women buy and sell produce in the Ibarra and Atuntaqui markets. Quichua is no longer spoken there. Until 1972, the indigenous population formed a majority of the nearly 4,000 inhabitants, but ten years later, because of migration, it formed only about 25 percent of a population of less than 2,300. Mestizos-whites live in the town center and own the local shops.

Though Natabuela has been the parish center since the 1930s, there is a rivalry with the neighboring hamlet of Ovalos, which prefers to manage its own affairs. In the past, mutual hostility was expressed during the fiesta of San Juan, resulting in fighting and injuries. The fiesta is still observed but without the violence.

Little weaving is now done in the area, and we were fortunate to meet a man who wove belts on a vertical loom (Fig. 66).[5] The weaver, José Miguel Limaico, was a grandfather; one of the younger women in the family said she wove belts also. However, belt weavers are so few that in 1986 a man we met in La Compañía near Otavalo, Antonio Cando Camuendo, had been commissioned to weave a Natabuela style belt for a Natabuela resident. People in Natabuela also often had fabric woven for them in the neighboring parish of San Roque. Now most garments are made from purchased fabrics.

Women's costume

The daily women's costume is superficially similar to that of Otavalo proper (Fig. 66). Unlike Otavalo blouses, however, Natabuela examples have a band just above the neck and sleeve ruffles, with a piece of acrylic yarn drawn through an applied ribbon in running stitches, which sticks out in loops every 3 centimeters (1¼ inches). The oldest blouses we saw (Fig. 67), belonging to the weaver's wife, Maria Margarita Potosí, have skirts of handspun and treadle-loom woven white cotton fabric (*lienzo*). The yoke and sleeves are of commercial cotton fabric. Perle cotton in closed double chain stitch (see chapter 5 and Fig. 72) is used for the embroidery, which is similar in design to that of Otavalo blouses. Newer blouses are entirely of commercial cotton fabrics and have acrylic embroidery. The newest blouses are made of synthetic fabrics, some hand embroidered and some machine embroi-

4. The historical information in this section is derived chiefly from Obando 1984, revised 1986, and Tobar Bonilla 1985. Both of these studies are illustrated with line drawings by the authors.

5. Earthwatch volunteer Leslie Grace led the four visits to Natabuela in 1989 and wrote several of the reports. Other volunteers on these visits included Iris Garrelfs, Patt Hill, Liz Drey, and Barbara Borders. I also went on one of the visits. Our contact person, who introduced us to the weaver (his uncle) and his family, was Camilo Gomez, a maker of musical instruments.

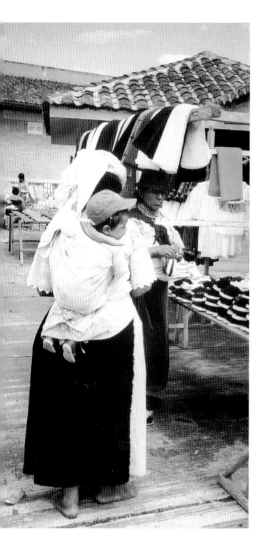

65 *Woman in the Cotacachi market, Imbabura province, with her baby wrapped in a carrying cloth with lavender appliqué points along the lower edge. Slide by Lynn A. Meisch, 1989.*

dered. The designs are relatively uniform over time, but we also saw a few newer blouses with more naturalistic flowers.

Women do not wear a white anaku but only a solid black one over the blouse. The effect is similar to that of Otavalo anakus since the lower part of the white blouse shows a little on the open side of the anaku. The Natabuela anakus have no decoration. The anaku is secured with the local style of handwoven belt. No mama chumbi is worn. The headcloths used are plain white cotton and are generally tied behind the head, now worn without a hat (Fig. 68). The women we saw, who were at home, were not wearing shoulder wraps. One woman had a navy blue wrap, and we saw one that was a yellow-orange synthetic fabric, probably acrylic. The women's gilt glass beads, of the same type as worn in Otavalo, are on the large side. In addition, women wear red beads on their wrists. They wear sandals that are the same as those worn in Otavalo.

The local style of belt is of considerable interest, since it may have supplementary-weft as well as the more usual supplementary-warp decoration (Fig. 69, Pl. p. ii). Some belts have only supplementary-warp decoration. The colors of the supplementary-warp yarns are most commonly hot pink and orange, but a large variety of colors are used for the supplementary-weft patterns. Acrylic is now used for the colored yarns. Both ends of some belts have acrylic tape sewed to them, with the ends crossed. Normally these tapes are worn tucked in, but one of the women said that for fiesta two belts are worn with the tapes hanging down each side.

Also now reserved for special occasions are the enormous old-style felt hats of this area, which have a more upcurving brim than those of Otavalo. Women generally wear the hats with the entire brim up (Fig. 66), over a headcloth draped loosely on the head. Formerly the hats were worn on a daily basis and without any trim. Although the ones we saw were a greyish white, apparently brick-colored ones were also formerly worn.

The baby in the family we visited was wrapped in a piece of pink acrylic fabric coarsely embroidered in floral designs, and with a scalloped lower edge (Fig. 68).

Men's costume

Traditional costume is worn by some old men and by younger ones only for special occasions. The weaver we recorded, José Miguel Limaico, who said he was sixty-eight years old, put on a shirt and pants of lienzo for our photography (Fig. 66). Natabuela style handmade pants have full-cut legs that are ankle length, pleated into the waistband, with a side opening. The closing is secured with ties ending in pink pompoms (see Pl. II). The shirt is not necessarily embroidered, although there is a style of hand embroidered shirt that is worn by some men for fiesta. The weaver also wore a belt similar to the one he was weaving, that had long square-braided ties. A young boy in the family was also dressed up in white pants, an embroidered shirt, and the local style of belt, for our photography (Fig. 66). Otavalo style alpargatas are worn.

66 *José Miguel Limaico and María*
Margarita Potosí with their grandson
Alejandro Miguel Limaico, from Ovalos
(Natabuela), posing for the camera in
fiesta dress. Photo by Patt Hill, 1989.

*67 Detail of a blouse made around 1953
by María Margarita Potosí, of Ovalos
(Natabuela), Imbabura province. Cotton
plain weave, embroidered with red perle
cotton thread in closed double chain stitch.
Overall length: 1.21 meters (47½ inches).
The Textile Museum 1989.22.27, Latin
American Research Fund.*

The handmade hat, worn only for fiestas, is identical to the women's, but is often worn with the brim up in front and down in back (Pl. II). The hat could also be worn the other way around for protection from the sun. The ones we saw in 1989 all were decorated with a blue acrylic ribbon and a pink cord with pompoms. Most Natabuela men now wear their hair short, though we encountered one old man who had long hair pulled back and tied.

The ponchos we saw, also for fiesta use, were made of two pieces of fabric of different colors placed over each other and joined with an edge binding (Fig. 66 and Pl. II). The outside color was red or hot pink with some colored stripes on the sides, and the inside color was solid blue. The fabrics were not handwoven. Obviously, this style of poncho imitates the two-sided weaving of the Otavalo area. The two pieces were fastened together by the edge binding on all the edges and a collar was also attached. One example we saw had a zipper sewn to the seam below the neck slit.

68 María Margarita Potosí with infant wrapped in an embroidered cloth, Ovalos (Natabuela), Imbabura province. Slide by Eileen Hallman, 1989.

Opposite:
69 Belt woven by José Miguel Limaico, Ovalos (Natabuela), Imbabura province. Cotton plain weave with both supplementary-warp and supplementary-weft patterning in acrylic. 3.025 x .045 meters (9 feet 11 inches x 1¾ inches). The Textile Museum 1989.22.28, Latin American Research Fund.

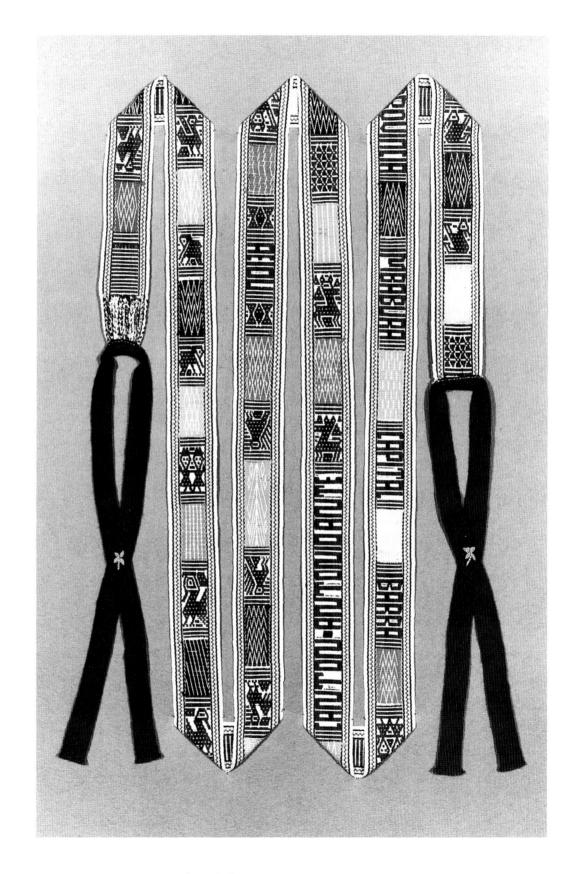

83   *Otavalo, Imbabura Province*

Northeastern Pichincha and Eastern Imbabura Province

Introduction

Lynn A. Meisch

Indigenous people living in the northeastern corner of Pichincha province and in the eastern part of Imbabura wear a costume that is distinct from that of the Otavalo area. These people have no self-descriptive group label, but simply call themselves *gente de* (people from) or *indígenas, runa,* or *naturales de* (indigenous people from) a particular community.[1] We will refer to these people as the N.E. Pichincha–E. Imbabura indigenous group. The costume is similar overall but the women's costume especially differs in detail according to community or parish. Male dress has become increasingly homogenized.

The people in northeastern Pichincha live in a number of small communities in and around Tabacundo and Cayambe, including La Buena Esperanza, San Pablito de Agualongo, Ayora, Olmedo, Pesillo, Paquiestancia, El Prado, Guachalá, Ishigto, San Isidro and San Francisco de Cajas, Monjas, Pisimbilla, Hato, Tupigachi, Chaguarpungo, Juan Montalvo, Cangahua, and a number of others (see map, page xviii). The town of Cayambe, named after the huge snowcapped volcano situated right on the equator and brooding over the town, is the market center for this area.

In Imbabura province, people who share this general costume style live in several communities at the eastern end of Lago San Pablo, including San Pablo del Lago, Cochaloma, El Topo, Ancla, Casco, and González Suárez. People from these communities visit the Otavalo and sometimes the Cayambe market. Others live on the eastern side of Imbabura mountain in such communities as, listed south to north, La Merced, Zuleta, Angochagua, La Rinconada, Magdalena, Las Abras, Paniquindra, La Florida, Chirihuasi, San Clemente, Rumipamba, and La Esperanza. These communities have regular bus service to Ibarra and consequently mainly use the daily food market there, but some people also attend the Otavalo Saturday market. Mariano Acosta, which lies further east, is more isolated.

Most of these people were huasipungeros on the great haciendas of the region, and some still work on these haciendas as wage laborers in the dairy cattle industry and in the new and burgeoning flower export industry. Like many other indigenous people in Ecuador, they are primarily farmers. Some raise dairy cattle on their own land.

---

1. Otavalos refer to the members of this group as "Puendus" or "Puendukuna," terms considered offensive by most members of this group although they are not meant as an insult by Otavalos. Puendu probably derives from the family name (Puento) of a line of native Cayambi lords who were important during the colonial period (Espinoza Soriano 1988 [2]:136–44).

Another source of income is embroidery, based on the fine hand embroidery that typifies the women's blouses. Both men and women embroider, although it is considered primarily women's work. Items made for sale include blouses and dresses adapted to the tourist market as well as napkins, tablecloths, placemats, and towels, which are sold locally, in Otavalo, and in Quito.

Such commercialization was originally promoted for several decades by the Plaza family, owners of the Hacienda Zuleta (Schmit 1991:234–35). It has been continued by local entrepreneurs and representatives of folk art stores in Quito and Ibarra, and has received the backing of the Peace Corps, which has aided in the organization of formal embroidery cooperatives in Angochagua, Mariano Acosta, and Zuleta.

Some young women, highly visible in their traditional dress, work as maids in Quito, a practice that also was begun and promoted by the Plaza family (Schmit 1991:182, 323). Women from the N.E. Pichincha–E. Imbabura area have such a good reputation as maids that they sometimes wear an even more elaborate version of the regional costume than they would wear at home, in order to emphasize their ethnicity. Some men migrate to work in construction in Quito, in agriculture on the coast, or in the oil fields of the Oriente.

A few N.E. Pichincha–E. Imbabura women have stands in the Otavalo market where they sell hand- and machine-embroidered blouses or the embroidered parts of the blouse, and pleated skirts and trim. Some Otavalos also sell such goods, including blouses they have made in what they ascertain is the Zuleta style. Most locally worn blouses, however, are still made within the family or commissioned to local specialists. Most new clothes are made before the fiestas in late June.

Costume

The single most important identifying feature of contemporary N.E. Pichincha–E. Imbabura female dress is the white blouse (*blusa bordada* or *camisa bordada* S.), of cotton or synthetic fabric, which is elaborately embroidered on the yoke (*hombrera* S.) and upper sleeves (*mangas* S.) (Pls. III–IV, Fig. 70). The blouse differs from those worn in the Otavalo area in having a short yoke with a high neckline (without ruffle) with either separate collar pieces (*solapa* S., pronounced "zulapa" in Quichua) or a collar-like design in the same area. The presence of separate collar pieces is the older style (Pl. III), but newer examples are still made occasionally. Contrasting colors of embroidery are normally used for the collar (or collar area) and the yoke. In Otavalo blouses, the embroidery follows a linear path under the ruffle; in N.E. Pichincha–E. Imbabura blouses, the designs are symmetrical around the center front and back seams and over the shoulders. The embroidery often follows the curve of the neck, leaving the corners empty, but sometimes the corners also are filled.

The sleeves have long ruffles (*blondas* S., pronounced "blunda" in Quichua), pleated into the cuff (*puño* S.) of the upper portion. There are two sleeve ruffle

70 *Detail of a blouse from González Suárez, purchased in the Otavalo market, Imbabura province. Plain weave synthetic fabric, embroidered with cotton thread in self couching, orange for the collar area and light blue for the yoke. The Textile Museum 1989.22.37, Latin American Research Fund.*

styles, differing in length. The ruffles are usually made of plain fabric with lace (*encaje* S.) edging and sometimes commercial tape trim (*tira* S.). In many recent blouses, the sleeve ruffles have pressed pleats (Fig. 70). The ruffles are normally white but in the Tabacundo area of N.E. Pichincha a contrasting color such as blue or light aqua may be used. The lace may either be machine-made or hand-crocheted. The body of the blouse (*cuerpo* S., or *ukunchina* Q.) normally extends to the knees and serves as a slip under the skirt. In the Cayambe area, however, some blouses have an elastic waist and a short peplum, which is worn outside the skirt (Fig. 71).

Older blouses are usually hand-embroidered, but some machine embroidery is now also being done that is nevertheless very similar stylistically to the hand work. The embroidery is the most elaborate and beautiful found in Ecuador, and skill at embroidery is a primary definer of womanhood in this area. The general style seems relatively consistent over the whole area. There are some regional variations, but they are not particularly obvious, given the considerable variation that may also be found within an individual community with older and newer designs being simultaneously created.

Usually a blouse has the larger elements worked in one of two stitches. One is a closed double chain stitch that creates a ridge around the edge of the design element, and the other is a self-couching stitch that forms a smooth surface (Fig.

71 *Women from San Isidro, northeastern Pichincha province, in the parade in Cayambe for the fiesta of San Pedro. The woman in the center who is not wearing a shawl has a blouse with a peplum at the waist. The skirts worn for this parade have particularly lavish decoration at the hem. Slide by Lynn A. Meisch, 1989.*

2. The stitch analysis in this paragraph is by Ann Rowe.

72).[2] Apparently the self-couching stitch is a more recent introduction (Schmit 1991:298). The local names of the stitches appear to vary from one community to another. The self-couching stitch is faster (and thus is preferred for embroidery done for sale) than the closed double chain stitch, which is considered more elegant. The closed double chain stitch wastes no thread on the back of the fabric, while in self-couching the stitches on the back are longer. Both stitches may be used in a given community, though one or the other might be favored. Other stitches are used to fill in details, including buttonhole stitch (for the scallops along the edges of the collars), outline stitch and simple chain stitch (for lines), herringbone stitch, and french knots (for dots).

Skirt styles vary, although the differences that once were more striking are now being obscured by the increasing acceptance of a brightly colored skirt of machine-made acrylic fabric with waistband and fine pressed pleats, introduced in the 1970s (Pl. IV, Fig. 71). This style of skirt is usually called a *centro* in Spanish or *sipu anaku*, meaning pleated anaku, in Quichua. More than one skirt may be worn at once,

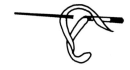

A

B

72 Stitches used in eastern Imbabura embroidery. A: Double chain stitch. B: self-couching. The double chain stitch is shown slightly open so that it is easier to read. Drawings by Kathleen Epstein based on sketches by Ann P. Rowe.

especially for fiestas. A variation sometimes also seen is a centro made of wool fabric in unpressed or pressed wider pleats, either in black (Fig. 73) or in colors, which is an older version of the one with pressed pleats, as documented for example in Zuleta and Pesillo (Obando 1986:262, 291). Women wearing the centro may or may not also wear a handwoven belt.

The decoration on these centros has become much more elaborate in the past ten years. Some have several rows of ribbon trim sewn next to one another at the bottom, forming a decorative band four to six inches wide (Fig. 71). Centros worn in some communities have machine-embroidered designs including zigzags and flowers around the hem and escutcheons above the hem designs. Other centros have a mixture of gilded tape, machine-sewn zigzags, and narrow lace forming a colorful band near the hem about 5 centimeters (2 inches) wide. Centros with all these kinds of hem decoration are sold in the Saturday Otavalo market, and these differences in decoration may reflect personal choice rather than community divisions. In 1989, the more elaborate styles of skirts were most in evidence at the fiesta of San Pedro and Pablo on June 29 in Cayambe (Fig. 71).

In some areas, chiefly in La Rinconada and Angochagua, a dark wrapped anaku, just below the knee to mid-calf in length, shorter than the Otavalo style, is worn instead of a centro. In other areas, for example between La Esperanza and Magdalena, the older women wear an anaku either instead of or over a centro, while younger women wear a centro alone (Fig. 74). The use of the anaku obviously requires a belt, and many belts are similar to those of the Otavalo area and are purchased from Otavalos. Others may be locally woven, though the only village where we recorded belt weaving was Paniquindra (see Fig. 87).

The shawl or shoulder wrap is called by several names throughout the region: *washajatana* (back wrap) or *washa fachalina* in Quichua; *rebozo, chal,* or *chalina* (shawl) in Spanish. The older style was made from handspun and handwoven wool (*bayeta,* pronounced *baita* in Quichua), but now synthetic fabrics are more common. For going to market, a woman uses two wraps, one serving as a shawl and the other as a carrying cloth.

Three basic styles of shawls are worn. One is a rectangle that is about the size of

73 *Women wearing black wool pleated skirts, photographed in the Otavalo market, Imbabura province. The baby-wrapping cloth has appliqué patterns. Slide by Ann P. Rowe, 1988.*

74 *Woman from eastern Imbabura province at the Otavalo market, wearing an anaku over her centro. Slide by Lynn A. Meisch, 1989.*

the Otavalo fachalina. It is invariably worn over one shoulder and under the opposite arm and tied in front. A variety of fabrics are used for this shawl, including velour with stamped patterns. The latter are often trimmed with factory-made gold fringe of the kind that is usually used to trim curtains (Fig. 71). Others have no fringe but are machine embroidered with zigzags around the edge and have small flower-like motifs in each corner.

Another shawl style is a large rectangle of acrylic fabric, probably woven in Otavalo, with long, 20–25 centimeter (8–10 inch) fringe. These shawls are usually worn over both shoulders and tied across the chest. They come in a variety of solid colors, including green, olive, yellow, orange, red, pink, burgundy, navy blue, turquoise, black, and purple. The third kind of shawl is triangular, with fringe, and made from acrylic fabric in a rainbow of solid colors. In addition, a few girls and women wear various acrylic shawls made in Otavalo and sold in the market and in stores there, including square plaid shawls in a variety of colors and longer, rectangular, solid-colored shawls that have a few warp stripes of metallic silver or gold-colored yarn.

In some communities, a woman carries a baby on her back by first wrapping the child in a decorated white fabric that extends below the shawl that actually supports the baby. One style has bands of appliqué, with the upper edges zigzagged (Fig. 73). Another, presumably more modern, style is decorated in simple machine embroidery.

75 *María Dolores Ilis of Paniquindra, eastern Imbabura province, put on her best earrings to be photographed. Slide by Laura M. Miller, 1989.*

Different kinds of footgear are worn, with alpargatas like those worn in Otavalo predominating, but in a variety of colors: black, navy blue, burgundy, olive green, and brown. Sandals (*ushuta*) made from automobile and truck tires are also worn. These sandals have a rubber heel strap and a cloth toe cover, but no ties over the instep. The alpargatas are available in the Otavalo market. We did not see the rubber tire sandals in the markets, but a Chirihuasi woman told Laura Miller that she had gotten hers in La Esperanza and had commissioned another pair in Santa Marianita. Newer styles such as tennis shoes, plastic flats, black leather flats, and rubber boots may also be seen. Most women go barelegged, but some wear knee socks, nylons, or tights.

Women throughout the region wear necklaces (*colgantes* S., *wallka* Q.) composed of numerous strands of red or coral-colored beads (the older style) or gilded glass beads (the newer style). Some women combine strands of red and gold beads or mix a few beads of one color into a strand of the other. Red or coral-colored wrist wraps (*maki watana*) are also traditional, and most women and girls wear them extending a good 7.5 centimeters (3 inches) up their arms. Some women wear silver or brass rings.

Many women, especially older ones, wear large, antique, Spanish style silver earrings (Figs. 74, 75). One kind, called *pepa de zapallo* (S., squash seed), is a hollow 2.5–7.5 centimeters (1–3 inches) long silver teardrop (the seed), with tiny, round discs dangling from the bottom. Another kind, called *palmas* (palm trees), look like silver Christmas trees and range in size from five to thirteen centimeters (2–5 inches) long. The third kind, made from antique Ecuadorian coins or silver circles, are called *candongas* (S., earring). Younger women usually wear smaller earrings.

Hairstyles vary. The oldest style is to wear the hair uncut, parted in the middle, pulled back and wrapped from the nape or just below the nape of the neck down about 30 centimeters (12 inches) with a white tape (*akcha watana* Q., hair wrap) that has long, colored ribbons at the end (Fig. 94). Treadle-loom woven colored tapes bought at the Otavalo market are a more recent style; some of these also have ribbons added at the end. Even more modern variations are to cut bangs and to pull the hair up behind the ears, holding it with a ribbon or commercial elastic band, while the rest of the hair hangs free (Fig. 83). Sometimes several metal or plastic hair clips or barrettes (*vincha* Q.) are also worn. Other variations include one long braid, two braids, or the hair pulled back in a nape-of-the-neck ponytail, held with bows, barrettes, or filmy scarves.

The old felt hat styles of the N.E. Pichincha–E. Imbabura area were variable from one community to another, some resembling Otavalo style hats (e.g.,

76 *Woman wearing a relatively conservative costume of the style worn southeast of Lake San Pablo, Imbabura province. Her blouse has separate collar pieces (and lacks sleeve ruffles); her neck beads are red; she wears a handwoven belt over her skirt; her hat is handmade. Photographed in the Otavalo market. Slide by Lynn A. Meisch, 1990.*

Angochagua), some Natabuela style (e.g., Zuleta), and some of a distinctive shape (e.g., González Suárez). The González Suárez style, also worn in San Pablo del Lago, is tan or gray and has a high, round crown and a narrow, upturned brim (Fig. 76). This style is still made by the Picuasi family in Ilumán. Now, machine-made fedoras with narrow brims are generally worn, and distinguish people of this area from Otavalos.

The most marked distinction between Otavalo men and those of the N.E. Pichincha–E. Imbabura area is that the latter cut their hair. Most men now wear contemporary Euro-American style, machine-made clothes, though they may add a fedora and a poncho.

The poncho styles are somewhat variable and are described in the sections below. Red ones seem to be an older style; blue ones are almost exclusively seen now, but blue ponchos also seem to have a long history in the area. In addition we saw solid green ponchos and striped ponchos in such combinations as red/blue/tan and brown/black/tan. Older ponchos do not have a gusset and collar, but newer examples usually do. Some ponchos have a dark fabric edge-binding, while others have about two inches of warp fringe.

A few ponchos with a different color on each side are still worn, although this style seems to be woven only by Otavalos. Examples noted in the early 1990s include a red and blue one with warp fringe, a green and blue one with edge binding, a blue and white one, and a green and white one.

Hacienda Zuleta

Lynn A. Meisch

The land forming Hacienda Zuleta was originally given to the Jesuits after the Spanish conquest. When the Jesuits were expelled from the Americas in 1767, the hacienda became the property of the Zuleta family. It was sold to the Lasso family in 1898, and the Lasso daughter who inherited the property married General Leonidas Plaza Gutiérrez, who became president of Ecuador on two different occasions (Obando 1986:223). With agrarian reform in 1964, the people on the hacienda were freed from huasipungo, but the property still belonging to the estate is considerable. The estate still belongs to the Plaza family, one of whose members, Galo Plaza Lasso, was president of Ecuador (1948–52) and secretary general of the Organization of American States.

There is a weaving workshop and artesanías store, called Programa Social Hacienda Zuleta, in one of the hacienda buildings. One room has a wall lined with boxes of perle cotton (plied, mercerized) embroidery thread in balls. In July 1993 the brands represented were Perlé, made in Ecuador; Coats Ancla, made in Cuenca (Ecuador); Pearl cotton from Shanghai, China; and DMC Perlé from Paris, France. Another wall is lined with shelves for embroidered textiles, many of which are orders for export to the United States and Europe. The workshop also sells to visitors to the hacienda and to stores in Quito. In another room is a weaving workshop with treadle looms on which men produce the plain-weave white or cream-colored cotton fabric (lienzo) used in the non-clothing items.

Costume

Zuleta blouses are sewn with the back yoke closed and only the front open (Figs. 77–79). The neck has small triangular points projecting from it (*filete* S.). The self-couching stitch is called *llano* in Spanish, *llambu* in Quichua (meaning flat, even, smooth), while the closed double chain stitch is called *bozal* (S., muzzled; pronounced *buzal* in Quichua). The self-couching stitch is used in The Textile Museum's two Zuleta blouses (Figs. 78–79) and is considered appropriate for the wide designs integrating leaves and flowers common in this village (Schmit 1991:106, 209, 342). Unlike other villages, coats-of-arms designs are hand embroidered in Zuleta. Dark or muted colors and threads of shaded colors are common (though not invariable) in the Zuleta style.

Previously, centros made of blue or black handwoven wool with unpressed pleats were worn (McIntyre 1968:277), but now the colorful acrylic centros with pressed pleats prevail.

While formerly women wore a handmade felt hat, similar in shape to those worn in Natabuela, by the 1960s they were wearing fedoras. There has also been a change from necklaces of red or coral-colored beads to the gold-colored type that are also worn in Otavalo.

Many men in Zuleta now wear modern Euro-American style clothing, but some wear dark fedoras and navy blue ponchos, and a few older men also wear white shirts and pants and alpargatas. A few also still wear ponchos that are red on one side and blue on the other, which they say are made by Otavalos.

Textile production

We talked to two families who make blouses. Luis Henrique Quizhpe draws the designs, while his wife María Ramos and their daughters do the embroidery (Fig. 78). In the second family, Estella Albán draws the designs and her mother, Salomé Sánchez de Albán, embroiders them (Fig. 79). After the embroidery is completed, the pieces are assembled by means of a sewing machine.

The same two families also make the pleated centros. The Textile Museum example (1989.22.23) is made of two pieces of fabric 61 centimeters (24 inches, the length of the skirt) by at least 2.70 meters (105 inches). It seems likely that a 1.20-meter-wide (48-inch) piece of fabric is cut in half lengthwise. The two pieces are first sewn together end to end (one seam). Machine-made edging (*varedira* S.) is then sewn to the bottom, followed by a row of machine-made tape about 2.5 centimeters (1 inch) wide that usually has gilt thread (*tira dorada* S.). These bands are made in Colombia and are available in the Ibarra market. Next the fabric is soaked in water and pleated by hand with an electric iron. "It burns the fingers," Estella Albán told us. The ends of the fabric are machine sewn into a tube, with a 10–13 centimeter (4–5 inch) opening below the waist. The pleats are sewn to a waistband that ties on one side. The warp-striped waistbands are usually those made in Cuenca, so are identical to those on the skirts of the Azuay valley.

77 *María Ramos in Zuleta, eastern Imbabura province. She is wearing a dark green skirt, but is holding a lavender skirt. Her blouse has hot pink embroidery in the collar area, dark green below. Slide by Barbara Borders, 1989.*

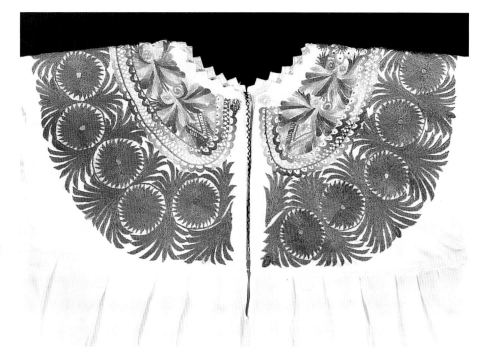

78 Detail of a blouse from Zuleta, eastern Imbabura province. Plain-weave synthetic fabric embroidered with perle cotton thread in self-couching, shaded red at the neck, blue below. Designed by Luis Enrique Quizhpe and embroidered by María Ramos. The Textile Museum 1989.22.22, Latin American Research Fund.

79 Detail of a blouse from Zuleta, eastern Imbabura province. Plain-weave synthetic fabric embroidered with perle cotton thread in self-couching, with green at the neck and hot pink below. Designed by Estella Albán and embroidered by Salomé Sánchez de Albán. The Textile Museum 1989.22.21, Latin American Research Fund.

La Esperanza

Ann P. Rowe

La Esperanza is a village about 4.5 kilometers (3 miles) south of Ibarra, whose 318 houses are located along the main road on the eastern side of Mount Imbabura. It is the seat of a parish that also includes the neighboring non-nucleated communities of Las Abras, San Clemente, La Florida, Paniquindra, Chirihuasi, Rumipamba, Cadena, and San Juan (Obando 1986:183). The total population of the parish in 1980 was 6,600 people.

There are two embroidery cooperatives in the area (ibid.:211). People from La Esperanza, Rumipamba Grande, Chirihuasi, Paniquindra, and La Florida embroider for sale to merchants in Otavalo and Ibarra, and locally to Casa Aida in La Esperanza, which is run by a mestizo-white woman who assembles the blouses.[3]

The La Esperanza blouses in The Textile Museum collection (Pl. III and Fig. 80) are both older than those acquired in Zuleta or Paniquindra. The older of the two (Pl. III) has a separate collar, a lower portion made of fabric that had been woven by a neighbor, and embroidery in the closed double chain stitch. The newer one (Fig. 80) has no separate collar piece, is made of fine machine-made cotton cloth, and is embroidered in the self-couching stitch. Both blouses have the vertical neck opening extending below the yoke in both front and back, with the top corners fastened together with a button and buttonhole, again both front and back. The general style of embroidery is similar to Zuleta (Schmit 1991:106).

In this area, in contrast to Zuleta, the old-style women's costume is a black wrapped anaku, not a pleated skirt, and some older women still wear it. We saw one woman in La Esperanza wearing a four-selvedge anaku that, according to the

3. The information on Casa Aida was recorded by Laura Miller in July 1989. The Earthwatch data that follows was recorded during the same period by a team led by Leslie Grace, assisted by Iris Gerrelfs, Joy Mullett, and Bettye Dennison.

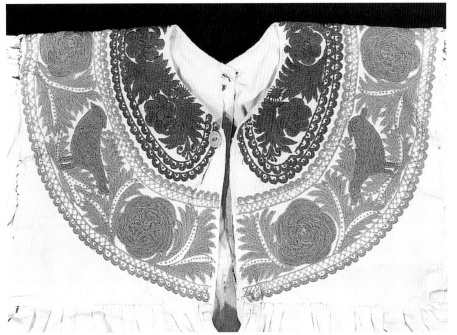

wearer's husband, had been woven in Ilumán by a weaver who died in 1988. This woman also wore a white cotton shoulder wrap. The belt we recorded in La Esperanza (in a different household) has supplementary-warp patterning and is indistinguishable from Otavalo belts. In 1989, most women were wearing the acrylic pleated centro (Fig. 81).

Rumipamba, San Clemente, Chirihuasi, and Magdalena

Ann P. Rowe

4. This text is an amalgam of information from Lynn Meisch, Laura Miller, Mariana Chuquín, Ann Rowe, Breenan Conterón, and Earthwatch volunteers including Joy Mullett, Bettye Dennison, Monique Andre, Eileen Hallman, and Gayle Bauer.

5. We did not see this style of poncho when we visited these communities. The information on its provenience is from Marilyn King, a former Peace Corps volunteer in Angochagua, who showed a photograph of one to people from Angochagua. Jaramillo (1988b:163–65) attributes the style to Rumipamba Grande, Magdalena, and Paniquindra, although the ponchos we saw in Paniquindra had different designs.

The former haciendas of Rumipamba and San Clemente, 2 kilometers (1¼ mile) south of La Esperanza, are small communities of about 1,000 people each.[4] Older women in these communities wear a black or occasionally dark blue anaku over their centro, which has unpressed or broadly pressed pleats, and is worn to nearly ankle length (Fig. 82). Both the centro and the anaku typically have hand or machine embroidery along the lower edge. Some women in Rumipamba were wearing complementary-warp weave belts similar to those we recorded being woven in Paniquindra (q.v.). Younger women in this area wear the newer style of centro with small pressed pleats, slightly below the knee in length (Fig. 83).

In Chirihuasi (Fig. 84), we were told that women wore a white cotton petticoat (called *enagua* or *bajera* S.) over their blouse and under their centro and anaku. A petticoat that had been laundered and laid out on the grass to dry had fabric that was loosely pleated into a waistband and some machine embroidery in colored threads at the bottom. We also saw an older woman in Rumipamba wearing such a garment.

We saw a variety of shawls, some fringed and some unfringed. The women Lynn Meisch talked to called their shawls, which were mostly acrylic twill weaves in various colors, *pañuelo* (which usually means *handkerchief* in Spanish). Virtually all the women were wearing gold-colored necklaces composed of marble-sized beads.

We found one old woman in Rumipamba who was wearing what appeared to be an old-style, handmade, brown felt hat with a narrow, droopy brim, and over it a white cloth of commercial printed cotton (Fig. 82).

The men wear Euro-American style dress except for dark fedoras and navy blue ponchos. Rumipamba Grande, along with Magdalena and Paniquindra, is one of the communities where a pink warp-resist patterned poncho was formerly worn, although we saw no examples there in 1989. Laura Miller talked to an elderly man from Rumipamba Grande who said that he had learned to weave the pink warp-resist dyed poncho from his uncle and had worn it daily as a boy. However, in 1989 he was wearing a navy blue poncho.

The Textile Museum collection includes two pink ponchos with warp-resist dyed decoration, the older one without a collar (Fig. 85) and a newer one with a collar (Pl. p. i). The wider resist-dyed stripes are made by overdyeing yarns of different colors with black, forming designs of diamonds from different colors of small squares. The narrower warp-resist patterned stripes have chevron designs. This style is said to be characteristic of Rumipamba and Magdalena,[5] and is slightly different from that found in Paniquindra described below. La Magdalena is a large hacienda, with the indigenous community of Magdalena dependent on it.

82 *Vitoria Chao and Miguel Maldonado (wife and husband) from Rumipamba, eastern Imbabura province. Her blouse has orange embroidery at the neck, black below. Slide by Joy Mullett, 1989.*

83 *Two young women from Magdalena or La Florida, eastern Imbabura province, in fiesta costume, holding chickens. The woman at right is wearing a hand-embroidered blouse with hot pink embroidery at the neck and blue below. The woman at left wears a machine-embroidered blouse, green at the neck and yellow below. Slide by Joy Mullett.*

84 *Olga Farinanjo (left) and other family members with laundry, Chirihuasi, eastern Imbabura province. Slide by Joy Mullett.*

85 *Warp-resist patterned poncho probably from Magdalena or Rumipamba, eastern Imbabura province. Wool warp-faced plain weave. 1.53 x 1.43 meters (60¼ x 56¼ inches). The Textile Museum 1986.19.92.*

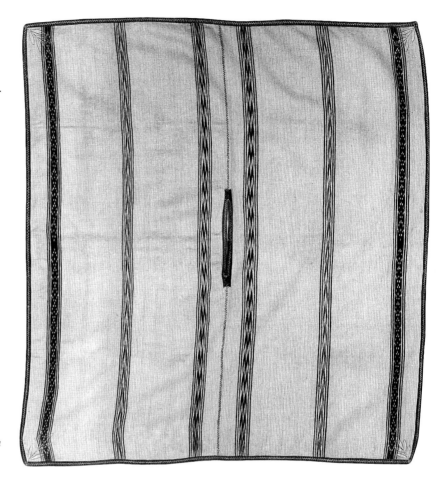

Paniquindra and La Florida

Laura M. Miller

In these communities, 4 kilometers (2½ miles) south of La Esperanza, the old style of women's dress is also a black wrapped anaku, which the older women wear over the colored pleated skirt, while younger women wear only the pleated skirt (Fig. 86). At least two or three pleated skirts are worn at once. The pleated skirt is called either *debajero* or *anaku*. The term *debajero* (S., under) may refer to its sometimes being worn under the wrapped anaku. Women who do not wear a wrapped anaku are most likely to refer to the pleated skirt as *anaku*.

The wrapped anaku is worn with a gap on one side to reveal the pleated skirt underneath and is approximately the same length as the pleated skirt, mid-calf length. The anaku usually has some machine embroidery along the lower edge and part way up the sides.

Some of the pleated skirts we saw had only some machine embroidery at the hem, while others had in addition a gold-colored ribbon applied near the bottom. We were told that this ribbon was imported from Japan and that a Cayambe man

86 *María Dolores Ilis (wearing an anaku over her centro), her husband José Elias Pupiales, and other family members in Paniquindra, eastern Imbabura province. Slide by Laura M. Miller, 1989.*

brought it to Ibarra and Otavalo. One man we talked to in Paniquindra in 1989 said that he still wove wool fabric for pleated skirts on a treadle loom and also assembled the skirts, but most of the women we saw were wearing skirts of machine-made acrylic fabric.

The wrapped anakus are secured with a belt, which can either have supplementary-warp patterns like those of Otavalo belts or have complementary-warp patterning, a style called *chumbi banderilla* (Fig. 87). We recorded the weaving of this latter style of belt in Paniquindra. These belts are woven of acrylic yarn, with a central stripe in red and green or blue and side stripes in yellow and pink or purple. The side edges are red. Three different geometric designs that are heddle-controlled are repeated in each belt. The lengths are variable, ranging from 2.28 to 4.47 meters (90 to 178 inches). Some women who only wear the pleated skirt also wear a belt.

Blouses in Paniquindra are finished the same way in front and in back (Figs. 88–89). The neck opening is extended slightly below the yoke and a rectangular piece of fabric is sewn to the end of the opening to secure it. No trim is attached to the neck opening. The upper corners are secured in front and back with string ties. Although most parts of the blouse have the usual Spanish names, the sleeve ruffle is called *maki punta* (Q., hand; S., point, end) in Paniquindra.

Women embroider blouses for themselves and also to earn money for their families. Some men embroider blouses by machine, both for their families and for sale (Fig. 89).

Women use a shawl, called a *chalina* (S.), similar to the *fachalina* used by Otavalo women, worn under one arm and knotted over the other shoulder. In the

87 Details of three chumbi banderillas from Paniquindra, eastern Imbabura province. Acrylic complementary-warp weave. Widths: 4–4.5 centimeters (1½–1¾ inches). The Textile Museum 1989.22.19, 1989.22.30, 1989.22.31, Latin American Research Fund.

Paniquindra family we visited, several women, including the oldest, were wearing pink or red chalinas, while others wore green.

For jewelry, women wear large, gold, glass-bead necklaces and red wrist wraps on either one or both arms. Although all the women wore earrings, the older woman in Figure 86 got out a pair of her finest earrings with silver filigree work and red and green stones for our photography (Fig. 75).

We saw a variety of hairstyles. The oldest woman was wearing her hair wrapped but with short sidelocks. A few of the younger women (for example, a woman in La Florida who was home visiting her family from her job as a maid in Quito) wore their hair loose.

We saw no one wearing old-style felt hats in this area. While at home, some women do not wear hats, but when outside and at the market, they wear dark-colored felt fedoras.

The oldest women in the community almost always go barefoot. Middle-aged and some younger women wear rubber tire sandals, called *caucho pargate* (*caucho* S., rubber), with toe covers in velveteen, generally wine red, green, brown, or navy

88 *Detail of a child's blouse, from Paniquindra, eastern Imbabura province. Plain-weave synthetic fabric top and cotton skirt, embroidered with perle cotton thread in self-couching in green at the neck and shaded red below. The Textile Museum 1989.22.20, Latin American Research Fund.*

blue. Adolescent girls may wear the same style of alpargatas worn by Otavalo women, called *kwitsa pargates* in Paniquindra (*kwitsa* Q., young girl).

Men's dress in this region is much akin to mestizo-white male dress. Most young men wear zipper jackets, with only a few of the older men wearing ponchos on a daily basis. Most ponchos we saw worn in 1989 were solid blue. One was dark blue on one side and light blue on the other, in a complementary-warp weave, so might have been purchased from an Otavalo weaver.

Pink warp-resist dyed ponchos, locally called *poncho rosado*, are also woven in this area. These ponchos have three warp-resist stripes on each half, which are first dyed bright pink, then resist tied and overdyed in black, creating vinelike designs or lettering. The warp-resist areas are bounded by stripes of the same bright pink. In summer 1989, we saw no one wearing these ponchos on a daily basis. Indeed, it was difficult to find weavers of such ponchos and one man said he stopped weaving this style three years ago because fewer people were wearing it. We were told it is now worn mainly for the fiesta of San Juan in Paniquindra and La Florida, as well as in Rumipamba Grande, Chamuro, and Las Abras.

89 *Detail of a woman's blouse, made by Jorge Gonzálo Pupiales, Paniquindra, eastern Imbabura province. Twill-weave synthetic fabric top and plain-weave skirt, machine embroidered with cotton thread in green at the neck and dark red below. The Textile Museum 1989.22.29, Latin American Research Fund.*

Angochagua and La Rinconada

Ann P. Rowe and

Lynn A. Meisch

6. The 1989 Earthwatch team to Rinconada was led by Breenan Conterón, accompanied by Eileen Hallman and Patt Hill. The team to Angochagua was led by Joy Mullett, accompanied by Gayle Bauer, Elizabeth Drey, and Linda Ruby. Lynn Meisch visited La Rinconada briefly in 1996.

These communities are 7–8 kilometers (4½–5 miles) south of La Esperanza. La Rinconada (the cornered [place]) derives its name from the fact that it is located in a V-shaped cleft between two steep mountains. The houses in both communities are dispersed. The old style of house has a four-sided thatched roof (Gillin 1941: pl. 19). The people of Angochagua were free historically, that is, not bound to a hacienda (Gillin 1941).

Designs on Angochagua and La Rinconada blouses are usually floral motifs with finer leaves and brighter colors than those found on Zuleta and La Esperanza blouses, and the closed double-chain stitch is favored (Schmit 1991:106, 216, 342). Green and orange is a favorite color combination. Like Zuleta blouses, those from La Rinconada and Angochagua appear to be sewn up to the neck in back.

The mid-calf length anaku is still worn by virtually all women and girls in these communities (Fig. 90).[6] It is black or navy blue and worn with two pleats folded in on the front and secured by a belt. The lower part of the blouse shows at the side opening and under the lower edge of the anaku. Although the acrylic pleated skirt is not worn, an old style of pleated skirt, called *kampu anaku*, similar to that mentioned for Zuleta, is worn by some women for fiestas.

One of the women in Figure 90 is wearing an old style of shawl, of handspun and handwoven white cotton, with fine openwork edging and short tassels on the warp

*90 Nieves Pupiales (left) in old-style hat and
handspun cotton wrap, and Filomen Chuquín
of La Rinconada, eastern Imbabura province,
dressed for a relative's visit. Photo by Lynn
A. Meisch, 1996.*

ends. In addition, she wears a pink acrylic fringed shawl (*rebozo*). Both women wear the complementary-warp patterned belt (*chumbi banderilla* or *labor chumbi*), as well as coral-colored bead wrist wraps (*maki watana*), necklaces of large gold-colored beads, and sandals (*alpargatas*) with white toe covers and rubber tire soles and heel straps.

A few old-style hats of white felt, with a relatively high crown and broad slightly upturned brim, are still in evidence worn by older men and women (Fig. 90). One person told us they had been made in Mariano Acosta. Another said they were made in Ilumán. Both places are possible. The hat shown in Figure 90 has a white cotton band around the crown, with the ends extended about five centimeters (2 inches) and pink and blue strings tied over the hatband with 2.5-centimeter-long (1-inch) tassels on each side.

We saw examples of an old style of poncho in Angochagua and La Rinconada in 1989, though we were told they were no longer made. They are finely woven in warp-faced plain weave wool, in red or dark navy, with a band of narrow pink and navy warp stripes near the outside edges. In Angochagua, we also saw a poncho made of a red fabric with stripes near the sides sewn around the edges to a dark blue fabric, similar in concept to those recorded in Natabuela. This poncho was said to be about twenty-five years old and worn for fiestas such as San Juan.

Mariano Acosta

Marilee Schmit Nason

The village of Mariano Acosta is located 45 kilometers (28 miles) southeast of Ibarra across the páramo in a different corner of the valley and reached by a different road than the other eastern Imbabura villages discussed (see map 2).[7] It takes a full three hours to get to Ibarra by truck, so few people go regularly to the market there. The village has a town center with some eighty houses where about 20 percent of the population lives, while the rest are dispersed in six outlying hamlets (*caseríos*). About 80 percent of the population of 2,284 people are indigenous (INEC 1982 [2]:338). The land holdings are small, with an average size of 8.93 hectares (22.07 acres). Those people with more land than they can farm often offer day labor to people with inadequate landholdings.

After the Liberal Revolution of 1895, legal reforms limiting servitude for debt (*concertaje*) were initiated, and the practice of indentured labor was abolished entirely in 1918. Indebted indigenous laborers could leave the large haciendas where they worked in order to occupy open government lands (Walter 1976:15). Mariano Acosta was founded in 1906 by such freed laborers from Zuleta, Angochagua, and La Rinconada, and the haciendas La Magdalena and Cochicaranqui, and gained political recognition as a parish in 1919. The historic ties to the villages of origin are still reflected through kinship, exchange of goods and services, patterns of cooperation manifested in festivals, and in certain cultural forms such as costume and its decoration. There is still a good deal of contact by foot or public transportation with Zuleta, La Rinconada, and Angochagua.

The principal festival of the village is the annual *entrega de gallos*, or ceremonial

7. Data were collected during ten months residence in Mariano Acosta in five field seasons between July 1981 and June 1987. Funding was provided by the Tinker Foundation, the Mellon Foundation, and the Organization of American States. See also Schmit 1991.

91 Blouse bodice panel with wide design, from Mariano Acosta, eastern Imbabura province. Cotton plain weave, embroidered with cotton thread in self-couching in blue at the neck and dark yellow below. 45 x 24 centimeters (17¾ x 9½ inches). Collection of Marilee Schmit Nason, purchased 1981.

handing over of the roosters, which takes place on San Pedro and San Pablo, June 28–29, in Mariano Acosta. The date of the entrega is staggered with Zuleta, where it takes place on San Juan (June 24), and Angochagua, where it takes place on June 30, so that people can take in all three fiestas. The entrega de gallos is a ceremony for the formalized repayment of debts, usually in fowl but also in alcohol, cash, and foodstuffs (Schmit 1991:277). A procession, accompanied by decorated horses, singing, dancing, merriment, and the recitation of *loas* (S., poems of praise), proceeds to the home of the lender where formal repayment is made. The festival is derived from the harvest festivals characteristic of haciendas (such as Zuleta) when payment of goods was made to the hacienda owner or church officials. In Mariano Acosta, certain villagers, called *fundadores* (S., founders) have taken over the role formerly held by the hacienda owner or parish priest, and the fiesta creates a context in which villagers render homage to the saints.

The festival is a context in which traditional values of the village are emphasized (often through inversion of norms of comportment), as is the use of traditional costume. It is a time when new items are integrated into the wardrobes of most Marianos using traditional clothing, as well as a time when innovations in design motifs and materials are introduced in embroidered clothing, and in which open ostentation of lavish materials and designs is deemed acceptable. New outfits premiered at the festival are used during important family rituals and other special occasions for months or even years, until they begin to lose their crispness, novelty, and color, at which point they are integrated into the daily clothing of the owner.

In Mariano Acosta, costume is the most overt symbol of ethnicity indicating group affiliation. The conservation and ostentatious display of traditional costume elements also denote economic well being, since machine-made mestizo clothing is less expensive and its use among the indigenous population indicates economic hardship. A woman may wash as many blouses as possible at once, hanging them out to dry where the public can appreciate both the number and quality of articles. A woman may also wear more than one shawl or anaku to advertise her economic status. Wearing extra clothes also simulates corpulence, considered desirable since it too is an indication of prosperity.

Women's costume

The embroidered blouse is the most important part of the woman's costume. Since the 1950s, and with influences from different villages, the embroidered floral designs have become smaller and more detailed, creating a distinctive Mariano Acosta embroidery style as a variant of the styles identified with the ancestral villages of the Marianos. Designs not based on floral motifs have also been introduced. These include animals such as birds and frogs; letters alluding to the wearer's name; utilitarian and decorative items such as earrings, jugs, and kettles; flags and coats of arms; and architectural elements, especially those taken from the church, such as

92 *Detail of blouse with narrow design, made by Rosa de Juma, of Caserío Puetaquí, Mariano Acosta, eastern Imbabura province. Cotton plain weave, embroidered with cotton thread in the closed double chain stitch, orange on the collar and blue-green below. Collection of Marilee Schmit Nason, purchased 1981.*

doors, towers, altars, crosses, hearts, baptismal fonts, and crowns. Older designs continue to be produced, but innovation is ongoing.

The designs are classified according to whether they are the wider style (Fig. 91), with less complex motifs (*llambu* Q.; *ordinario, ancho, de hoja,* or *de hojita* S.), or whether they are the narrower and more complex style (*jantsi* Q.; *complejo, tupido, menudo,* or *fino* S.) (Fig. 92). The latter style requires more skill and is considered more impressive. In addition, lighter weight fabrics are more difficult to work with, so that well-embroidered blouses on these materials are valued more highly. The self-couching stitch is called the *puntada recta* (S., straight stitch), *larga* or *ordinaria,* and the closed double chain stitch is called the *puntada limeña* (S., Lima stitch), *embozalada* (S., muzzled),[8] or *cadena* (S., chain). The latter stitch is preferred for the small patterns most characteristic of the village. Machine embroidery, done on treadle sewing machines, resembles the effect of the self-couching stitch normally used on wider designs. Despite this fact, more delicate drawings are considered especially apt for machine embroidery and the wide leaf designs are deemed less suitable.

For the two colors of embroidery on each blouse, strong and highly contrasting colors such as fuchsia with turquoise, carrot orange with grass green, or red with teal are considered the best (Pl. IV). Other bright colors are added as accents. Color-coordinated ribbons often are sewn to the sleeves to add both color and

8. The term *bozal* compares this stitch, which crosses over itself, to a halter (e.g., for a horse) made of a single length of rope wrapped around itself (cf. Tobar 1961:49–50).

movement to the overall effect. Despite the above generalizations, however, design style, stitch choice, and color use are also affected by the style of the ancestral village of the woman's family.

Because many women in Mariano Acosta descend from people who migrated from Angochagua and La Rinconada, the anaku is the most common style of skirt (Fig. 93). It is worn to just below the knee in length, which Mariano Acosta women consider more practical for agricultural work than the long anakus worn by Otavalo women. Formerly, it was made of handwoven wool fabric, but now machine-made wool fabric is more common (synthetics are not worn). The ends of the fabric come together on one hip, and one or more small pleats are taken on the opposite hip. The anaku is held in place with a belt (*chumbi*). These are not presently made in Mariano Acosta, and most people buy Otavalo belts in Ibarra or Otavalo, or from Otavalo merchants who travel to the village before the fiesta. Only in very cold weather, especially when working in the higher elevation fields, do the women of Mariano Acosta use an under-anaku. These handwoven white woolen liners, called *ukunchina*, are worn under the long blouse.

Centros are worn by women who descend from Zuleta migrants (Pl. IV). Occasionally in the festivals one sees dark-colored handwoven wool skirts with un-pressed pleats, of the type previously worn in Zuleta or for fiesta in Angochagua and Rinconada. I documented an example made in 1948 in the hamlet of Puetaquí by people from Angochagua.[9] It is called a *follón* and is worn only at the festival of San Pedro and San Pablo. The cloth in the skirt measures 80 centimeters (31½ inches) wide and approximately 9.25 meters (30 feet 4 inches) long.

Outer clothing consists of a shawl (called *fachalina*) and a wrapper (called *baita*). The color of the shawl is often purposely coordinated with the predominant color in the embroidered blouse for aesthetic reasons. Machine-made flannels in different shades of blue, and handwoven woolen lengths dyed in a bright fucshia are most common. The fachalina is used as a shoulder covering and to shield the face from the sun. It is draped over the head, unfolded, forming a small visor over the eyes. The wool baita is used as a body wrapper in cool weather and as a carrying cloth, although a white cotton carrying cloth (*sábana* S.) is also used to carry large, heavy, and dirty loads.

The most common type of jewelry for women is pierced earrings, and women are seldom seen without them. Traditional silver *candongas* (large round earrings), silver filigree earrings, metal earrings with floral designs, those designed with old coins or which sport glass chips in imitation of rubies and emeralds are common. Inexpensive imitations of traditional earrings are available in the markets of Otavalo and Ibarra. This costume jewelry variety is most often worn by younger girls.

Mariano Acosta women also wear necklaces (*wallka*) of multiple strands of gold-tone hollow glass beads, similar to those worn in the Otavalo area, preferring the medium to large sized ones. The number of strands worn for fiesta is double that worn on a daily basis. Some women use a wrapped bead wrist band (*maki watana* or *manilla*) of glass or coral beads on one or both wrists. However, this

93 Sra. Rosa de Juma of Caserío Puetaquí in Mariano Acosta, eastern Imbabura province, wearing an anaku with a blouse in the closed double chain stitch. Photo by Marilee Schmit Nason, 1981.

9. This skirt was collected for the Maxwell Museum of Anthropology, University of New Mexico, Albuquerque (81.35.2b), along with other men's and women's costume items from Mariano Acosta.

94 *Back view of a woman from Mariano Acosta, eastern Imbabura province, showing the manner of wrapping the hair. Photo by Marilee Schmit Nason, 1984.*

practice is falling into disuse in Mariano Acosta and is now most commonly seen in fiesta dress. Silver, tin, and composite metal rings are commonly worn. Older women tend to use more than one ring, in which case they are worn on the ring, index, and little fingers.

Older women most often go barefoot. Young and middle-aged women wear alpargatas like those worn in the Otavalo area. Some women have recently started to wear plastic shoes, especially for going to town or for agricultural work.

The old-style handmade felt hat, which is still made locally by one man, has a broad flat brim similar to those of La Rinconada and Angochagua. It is worn mainly by older villagers and by dancers during festivals. Other women wear machine-made felt fedoras, having either wide or narrow brims.

Hair is an extremely important personal symbol. It is considered a symbol of life, health, and strength and is the only physical attribute that indigenous people of Mariano Acosta value as an index of beauty. Traditional belief suggests that hair grows faster and thicker when it is tied. The fact that most of the adult women wear their hair tied in a *wangu* (pony tail wrapped with a thin white band) may be explained by that belief (Fig. 94). The wrapping differs from that of the Otavalo area in that the wrap is started several inches below the nape of the neck instead of close to the head. Many of the women who wear their hair this way adorn the wangu with bright-colored satin ribbons in pink, turquoise, and light green as a complement to their hairdo. The colors are chosen to coincide with and add to the color combinations in the rest of the costume. Hair held in place by metal barrettes (*vincha*) is also common, especially among women who use hats. When a woman becomes a widow, she may cut the tips of her hair.

Many women purposely coordinate the colors of the different items making up their costume. For example, the woman in Plate IV is wearing a fedora of the same olive green as her centro, while the color of her alpargatas matches the blue of the embroidered bodice of her blouse. At the two extremes of the costume, neck and hemline, there are highlights in orange.

A typical woman's wardrobe consists of eight to ten blouses, four or five anakus, and an equal number of belts. Most women have two or three shawls, one for daily use, one as a change, and a third for festivals. Likewise they have two or three hats, one a work hat, one a dress hat, and the third for festivals. Most women have two multi-strand necklaces, with another in reserve, and three or fewer pairs of earrings. If they have wrist wraps, they usually only own one or two sets. As items become worn with use, they are mended as many times as is feasible. When a blouse body has been mended too many times, but the embroidery is intact, the embroidered part is cut off and attached to a new blouse body.

Men's costume

In Mariano Acosta, the correct aesthetic presentation of women is more important than that of men. Men focus their attention and economic resources on the cos-

95 *Young couple from Mariano Acosta, eastern Imbabura province, with the man in traditional pants, hat, and poncho, during* entrega de gallos *festivities. Photo by Marilee Schmit Nason, 1984.*

tume and adornment of their wives, rather than on their own costume.

Nevertheless, the men's costume is more conservative than in many other East Imbabura communities, and many wear home-sewn white shirts and pants (Fig. 95). Although young and middle-aged men wear pants of machine-made, light-colored fabric, older men continue to use a traditional style of pants of handwoven white fabric (*lienzo*). Usually, these pants have narrower and longer legs than the old style of Otavalo pants, but like them have a side opening secured by ties extending from the waistband (Fig. 96). Some men also use a handwoven belt (*chumbi*). The traditional pants diagrammed in Figure 96 have legs 50 centimeters (20 inches) in circumference (with no tucks into the waistband), and a gusset made from two rectangles of unequal size, creating a 20-centimeter (8-inch) square. The waistband is cut lengthwise in the fabric and measures 124 centimeters (49 inches) long. The legs are not hemmed, but rather are turned up two or more times until they are of a length suitable for the wearer. Shirts are now made of machine-made yardage, though often home sewn. Modern shirts are either white or another light color.

Ponchos are worn most of the time. When working in the fields, men at times take off their ponchos or fold the edges up over their shoulders to allow for more maneuverability. Most use dark blue or red ones, handwoven locally or in Otavalo on backstrap looms. The red ones are worn mainly by older men.

The hats are similar to those worn by the women, but there is more variation in men's fedoras. Large and small brims, and both high and low crowns are common, and the hats may or may not be blocked. Men seem to take less care in coordinating the color of their hat with their costume. They use blue, grey, green, tan, brown, and black hats. Like women, men have everyday work hats and dress hats. Older men more often wear the handmade felt hats.

Many older men go barefoot. Others wear alpargatas with furcraea soles and cotton uppers (the Otavalo style), or with heavy tire soles, a reinforced white muslin upper and heel strap. Both styles are made in Mariano Acosta or are purchased in Ibarra and Otavalo. Rubber boots are also common, especially for agricultural work.

Men usually own five or six examples of both shirts and pants, and two ponchos. They may have one or two pairs of alpargatas, as well as a pair of rubber boots. Like women, they have two or three hats.

Children's costume

Infants in Mariana Acosta are seldom dressed in any way that would indicate sex or ethnicity. Until they are toilet trained, it is common for them to be wrapped in a white cotton cloth fastened in place with a woven belt, in the style of an anaku. Often they wear knit or crocheted sweaters and caps purchased in Mariano Acosta or homemade by women of the family.

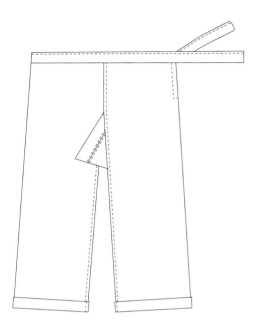

96 *Diagram of the cut of men's pants from Mariano Acosta, eastern Imbabura province. The gusset is made of two rectangles sewn together. Overall length: 84 centimeters (33 inches). Based on pants in the collection of the Maxwell Museum of Anthropology, Albuquerque, 81.35.12. Drawing by Laurie McCarriar based on a sketch by Marilee Schmit Nason.*

97 *Couple with child in print dress, Caserío Guanupamba, Mariano Acosta, eastern Imbabura province. Photo by Marilee Schmit Nason, 1984.*

There is a popular belief that the hair of children is sacred and should not be touched. Boys' hair is not cut until they reach the age of three or four. To cut their hair any sooner would be to invite muteness, or at the very least stuttering.

In the hamlets farthest from the village plaza, the costume of young children is a miniature version of adult costume. Young girls, from the age of eight on, are responsible for embroidering their own blouses, and are taught the appropriate techniques by their female relatives.

In the areas near the village center, children wear mestizo costume (Fig. 97). The shift has been characteristic of male children's clothing since the current grade school was established in the 1960s. Female school-age children continued to wear traditional indigenous costume to class until 1985, when a uniform dress code was enforced.

In general, young adults who have emigrated to work in the cities and those who have left Mariano Acosta to attend high school do not retain any indigenous elements in their costume, either when in the city or upon returning to the village for visits or permanent residence. The one exception to this is the case of young women who have emigrated to the provincial or national capital to work as domestics. In this case, their indigenous style of clothing becomes even more embellished in the city.

Chapter **6**

Cotopaxi Province

Introduction

Mary J. Weismantel

Cotopaxi province is predominantly rural; towns and cities are small, and serve mostly to provide services to the rural hinterlands[1] (see map, page xix). Haciendas long dominated the landscape and remain important today, but most of the population ekes out a living on tiny family farms.

Erosion and depressed prices for agricultural products make most farm families dependent on sources of income outside of agriculture. The most important of these is wage labor in more developed parts of Ecuador, such as Quito or the coastal areas, but artisanal activities, such as making ropes, furniture, grinding-stones, or hats or repairing clothing or radios, are important for families. In some cases, such as painting and mask-making, artistic and craft production oriented primarily toward the tourist market provides this income.

In the cities and towns of the central valley, along the Panamerican highway, factory-made, western-style clothing predominates; only the poorest and least savvy of campesinos wear handwoven clothing in the streets and markets of Latacunga, Pujilí, or Salcedo. In indigenous communities away from the highways and large towns, however, very different dressing styles can be seen. Men and women in these remote areas would be ashamed to appear in public without ponchos or shawls and hats. In this context, mestizos-whites and those who imitate their clothing styles are referred to as *lluchuj* (Q.), naked or skinned, because of their bare heads and form-fitting clothing.

Ethnicity, and the clothing styles that mark it, can best be considered as a kind of sliding scale that operates in several senses: proximity to urban centers, age, gender, and the nature of the occasion all serve to determine what kind of clothing style is appropriate. Older people and women dress more traditionally; so, too, do those who live farther from town. Special occasions such as weddings or baptisms are always marked by western clothing, even among the most traditional. During fiestas, such as Easter, Corpus Christi, or Finados (All Souls'), people wear brand-new, beautiful, traditional clothing. Today, however, not all such clothing is hand-made, as will be discussed below.

1. Field work was conducted in Zumbagua in 1983–84 with the support of a Fulbright-Hayes grant. Return visits were made in 1986 and 1989. See also Weismantel 1988.

Zumbagua

Mary J. Weismantel

98 *House (*chakiwasi*) in Zumbagua, Cotopaxi province. Slide by Mary J. Weismantel, 1989.*

Zumbagua is located in the western cordillera, at the upper reaches of the highway that climbs from Latacunga into the Andes, and then descends steeply toward the western coastal plains. Altitudes range from a few low areas of 3,200–3,400 meters (10,500–11,150 feet) to well above 4,000 meters (13,000 feet), creating cold temperatures and severely limiting the plants and animals that can survive in the parish. The area was probably lightly settled before the colonial period, when Spanish religious orders established enormous haciendas in the zone for the purpose of producing wool to supply the textile obrajes of Latacunga. It remains a predominantly sheep-herding region today, although other agricultural activities are also important. These include growing barley and fava beans, the two major crops, as well as potatoes, onions, quinoa, and lupines, and raising a variety of animals, including llamas, horses, and donkeys.

In this large, mountainous region where foot travel is the primary means of transportation, llamas are highly valued as beasts of burden and a source of meat; their adaptation to this environment makes them healthier and more reliable producers than European imports such as cattle (Fig. 6). Llama herding is far more important in Zumbagua today than is usual in Ecuador, although sheep are more highly valued because of their wool. The high altitudes prevent the growing of crops important elsewhere in the province, including maize and the cabuya plants necessary for making shigras.

Today, household incomes are low, and most younger men are forced to travel outside of the parish in search of wage labor. This fact has depressed textile production in Zumbagua, both because younger men are not weaving and because women, who now have shouldered the entire burden of running the farm on a day-to-day basis, have less time to spin wool. Nevertheless, most men of the parish own at least one handspun and handwoven poncho, made of locally grown wool.

The settlement pattern is extremely dispersed; the only town is on the site of the old hacienda, and even it consists mostly of unoccupied houses, used by their owners only on fiesta and market days. Older houses are large, oval constructions dominated by enormous thatched roofs (Fig. 98); the houses themselves are like a huge textile, constructed of many different kinds of plant materials carefully woven together. Men provide the wood for the armature, which they bring up from the forested western slopes of the parish, while women travel up into the grasslands to bring down the grasses and reeds used for the secondary supports and thatching. These houses are referred to as *chakiwasi* (Q., foothouse), a humorous reference to the fact that the walls are only a few inches high—walls are merely supports ("feet") for the large roofs, which actually serve as both roof and walls.

Today, chakiwasis are only one housing form and, with the exception of temporary shelters for herding, new chakiwasis are not being built (although existing houses are re-roofed). Rectangular, peaked-roof houses are built of a variety of materials, including adobe and cement block walls, thatch and tin roofs. Each building is only a single room, with clusters of buildings around a central patio inhabited by a single, often extended, family. Most tasks take place in the patio,

99 Family in Zumbagua, Cotopaxi province, showing women's costume and infant wrapped in a belt. Photo by Mary J. Weismantel, 1980s.

100 Crocheted acrylic underskirt, purchased in Cochapamba, a community near Zumbagua, Cotopaxi province. 60.5 x 79 meters (23¾ x 31 inches). The Textile Museum 1988.19.59, gift of Roberta Siegal.

with the exception of cooking—and weaving ponchos, which is done on permanent backstrap looms built into the support posts of the chakiwasi. Belts and hair ribbons, however, are woven on a small portable loom and hence can be worked on outside.

Women's costume

Women wear layers of under- and over-skirts (*anaku*), most of which consist of wrapped lengths of cloth, held in place by one or two strong wool belts (*chumbi*) (Fig. 99). These skirts, although consisting of a single rectangular piece of cloth, do not hang straight but rather are bunched to resemble a full, gathered skirt. This is no doubt because of the cold; the quantity of material worn keeps women warm despite their bare legs.

On the upper half of the body, women wear layers of shirts and sweaters, covered by one or two large shawls (called *llijlla, fachalina,* or *paño*). A variety of styles of shirts are worn, from a folkloric style of satin blouse to men's T-shirts and very feminine machine-embroidered sweaters. Aesthetic criteria favor the juxtaposition of several bright, contrasting colors, so that crowds of women create a brilliant and lively picture.

The outer skirt is usually of a dark material, preferably dark blue or black; shawls, however, are brightly colored. The fashions in shawls change rapidly, but favorites in recent years include plaids and monochrome terrycloth or velour. The standard shawl worn on ordinary days is made of acrylic fabric in brilliant colors such as hot pink or chartreuse, with a long fringe of the same color. Women's shawls are long, large, and heavy. The standard shawl is rectangular, whereas other, special occasion styles are often in the form of a large square that is folded either diagonally or straight across. For fiestas, great attention is given to the superimposition of shawls on top of one another, so that contrasting colors and layers of fringe are displayed. Similarly, layers of skirts and petticoats may be arranged to be visible, especially if a woman owns one of the multicolored petticoats described below.

These layers give a woman a stout appearance; it is often a surprise to encounter a woman washing her hair in her own patio on a sunny day, wearing only her innermost slip, and discover a slim, muscular person instead of the familiar rotund figure. The roundness of the female form is enhanced by the fact that women carry everything from babies to food, tools, money, or gifts for friends tucked into the voluminous folds of their clothing. Shawls and skirts give women protection, privacy, and warmth, enabling them to carry on their many, arduous tasks out in the fields and pasturelands. In Zumbagua, women do heavy agricultural work on a daily basis, enduring burning sun, cold rain, sleet, and hail, and strong winds, and their clothing is designed to fit their needs.

Today, neither skirts nor shawls are woven in the parish, although one may occasionally glimpse a very elderly woman wearing the ragged remnants of a handwoven textile. Only one article of clothing is made by women themselves, and this is a multicolored crocheted underskirt made of purchased acrylic yarns (Fig. 100). This craft was taught to local women in the 1970s by Catholic missionaries from Europe. Mestizo-white women in the parish crochet and knit shawls that they prefer to indigenous-style ones, but indigenous women only wear crocheted clothing as undergarments.

There are two kinds of adornment worn by women that are made locally, namely, hair ribbons and belts. Both are woven by men on small backstrap looms, using very thin, but strong, purchased acrylic or cotton yarns in a variety of colors. Yarns with a shiny surface are preferred. Patterns resemble those seen throughout the highlands. Belts are made in a variety of lengths and widths.

Women wear their hair tightly bound into a single, long, thick and stiff tube, created by wrapping a series of hair ribbons or thin belts around a core of hair (Fig. 101). There are several ways to do this, using combinations of thin and thick, long and short belts and ribbons. As with other aspects of clothing, the juxtaposition of bright, contrasting colors is considered most appealing. When completed, the hair is completely covered except for the head itself and a small tuft of hair at the end of the tube. Women pride themselves on having thick, abundant, healthy hair, and worry when it starts to thin with age; they often joke and gossip about adding horsehair to their own, under the ribbons, in order to make it look more abundant than it is.

An older, traditional form of hat made of very thick, stiff felted white wool is still being worn and is made in the nearby town of Pujilí, but this style has been almost completely supplanted by fedoras. Hats may be purchased from outside vendors but are also locally made by one family out of dark-colored felted wool shaped on wooden molds.

Infants are carried in soft, flexible cloths wrapped around the body. I believe that once these would have been the long, cotton, warp-resist dyed shawls with knotted fringe on the ends of the kind made in the Gualaceo area of Azuay province (or possibly in Rumipamba near Salcedo), but here as well economic changes have made these too expensive for indigenous people, who must content themselves with machine-made cloths. Cloths are also used to carry all sorts of other loads, as well as to bind, to store, to pack, and to fasten; for parish residents, textiles are among the most important tools they possess.

Although both men and women dress in distinctively indigenous fashion, women's clothing differs from men's in two critical ways. Little or none of a woman's costume is handmade, and yet because every aspect of her clothing differs from that worn by white women, it is impossible for a woman to "pass" as white.

Men's costume

One cannot visit the parish without being immediately struck by the ubiquity of woven male ponchos (Pl. V). Almost every man wears one, and their brilliant colors—especially the reds and blues—make a crowd of men standing in the plaza

101 *Mother and daughter in Zumbagua, Cotopaxi province, showing the girl's hair wrap. Photo by Mary J. Weismantel, 1980s.*

on market days or fiestas a dazzling picture. Because of the cold climate at this high altitude, the ponchos are very thick and heavy, of a weight that in other areas would only be considered appropriate for blankets. In fact, in Zumbagua blanket weaving is almost identical to poncho production, and ponchos often double as bedding. The older style of Zumbagua poncho is very long, extending below the knees both front and back, with a short fringe at the bottom. Younger men may wear shorter ponchos. Ponchos have a collar, which is woven as a separate piece; usually the selvedge of the collar, as well as the opening for the neck, is covered with a wide piece of bias tape of a matching color.

The weaving is warp-faced plain weave, with decoration taking the form of warp stripes. There are three basic patterns: solid-color ponchos, of either red or dark blue; all over stripes about 2.5 centimeters (1 inch) wide, usually with either whites, browns, and yellows or reds, blues, and greens predominating in a random alternation of colors, producing a rainbow effect; or predominantly solid-color ponchos, of either red or dark blue, with a single wide stripe, usually of the opposite color, approximately 10 centimeters (4 inches) in from the outer edge of the garment. Variations on these patterns are sometimes seen.

Yarns are thick and uniform, and the threads are densely packed, creating a very heavy garment. Washing these ponchos, which weigh perhaps 27 kilograms (60 pounds) or more when wet, is one of the most arduous of female tasks. Like women's shawls and skirts, men's ponchos are utilitarian, serving to keep them warm, to provide privacy (Zumbagua men are extremely modest), and to protect the arms and body when doing agricultural work. Although simple in design, they are also beautiful, and men take great pride in owning them.

The rest of male clothing is machine made with the exception of hats, which are the same as those worn by women, although recently some men have started to wear baseball caps.

In contrast to women's costume, the poncho and hat, which are the two distinctive features of male clothing, have the advantage of being easily removed, revealing an entire western-style outfit underneath. Indigenous men leaving the parish usually carry a small suitcase resembling a bowling ball case with them, into which they stuff their ponchos while in the outside world, putting them back on when they re-enter the parish. While it is not acceptable to be seen in public in the parish in just a shirt and sweater, it is becoming common for men to substitute a machine-made poncho or a short jacket made of nylon or imitation leather, since younger men have a difficult time obtaining handwoven ponchos.

Children's costume

Inside the house, infants wear no clothing, but instead lie on old, soft blankets when they are not being fondled and held by members of the family. When mothers or siblings must go out to work in the fields, however, infants are wrapped up until they resemble little mummies (Fig. 99). The innermost layer is of soft, absorbent cloth very loosely wrapped, but subsequent layers are tougher and more binding; the head is then covered with a cloth; then the outermost layer is added to the entire body. This consists of wool belts that are wrapped around the body in a single continuous strand, additional belts being added by tucking them under the previous one. Only the face is exposed, and even it is surrounded by fabric that juts out, protecting the face from direct sunlight. When completed, the result is a cocoon of cloth as strong as a coat of armor. Watching women working in the fields with their babies on their backs, it becomes apparent why such protection is necessary: even when working with sharp tools or doing work in which pieces of dirt, straw, or sticks are flying up, women know that their infants are safe from injury.

Toddlers are dressed in loose, androgynous tunics, or purchased western clothing such as pants and jackets. Only when they learn to talk are they considered old enough to wear gendered clothing; the ceremony of first haircutting for boys, or ear piercing for girls, marks this occasion. Godparents give a gift of clothing, a full suit of clothes exactly like an adult outfit. Sometimes friends or relatives indicate their willingness to be godparents by giving an article of clothing before the date for the ceremony has been set; especially appropriate is a handwoven poncho for a little boy.

Once this transition has been made, there are no further major transformations in costume. Although younger people might be more willing to experiment with new styles than their elders, and older people are more likely to own handmade and traditional items, there are no generational norms for clothing.

Textile production and acquisition

In Zumbagua, weaving is an exclusively male activity, while spinning is done by women. A finished poncho or blanket represents access to the following: quantities of wool, the contribution of hundreds of hours of spinning by perhaps three different women, and the additional hours of masculine weaving. A handmade poncho worn by a man speaks to everyone around him of hours of loving work performed by the women who contributed the yarn; even if he has woven it himself, others have been involved in its production. Thus, the poncho is one of the most important symbols of a man's participation in the noncash economy of the parish, where family and compadrazgo relationships are the most important form of wealth. As younger men become increasingly involved in wage labor, rather than in the local, agricultural economy, they have less access to this kind of wealth—a fact that their thin, machine-made ponchos demonstrate.

All women learn to spin, and it is very unusual to see a woman walking or tending sheep who is not spinning wool. However, not all men learn to weave. Men who know how pass the skill on to their sons. Older homes are more likely to include the heavy posts of the large backstrap loom used to make ponchos, built into the middle of the house.

Making ponchos is part of an economy based on reciprocity, which is increasingly under attack in Zumbagua today. The principles of giving gifts rather than buying and selling remain strong in some arenas, however, and everything connected with poncho-making is permeated with this way of thinking. In traditional families, sheep, like guinea pigs, are not to be bought or sold, but should only be exchanged as gifts within the family or between compadres. So it is, too, with the labor involved in making a poncho. Making a poncho is a long undertaking, involving the labor of the entire family, and it is only performed either as a gift—in which case the necessary element of surprise adds to the complications of its production—or as a service to someone who can be trusted to fulfill their side of the deal, once all the work has been done. Presenting a finished poncho is an occasion that calls for ceremony, since it represents a substantial economic transaction and symbolizes a strong and enduring social commitment. Clothing is the most significant gift that can be exchanged between people in Zumbagua.

I know of only one man in Zumbagua who makes ponchos in the local style for sale to outsiders, and he is a mestizo who migrated to the parish from elsewhere (although foreigners who buy from him are usually unaware of this fact). There are good quality wool ponchos for sale in the market, but they come from Otavalo or Riobamba. Rather than new ponchos, what one sees most in the marketplace are men with foot-powered treadle sewing machines, who repair torn ponchos, reattaching collars and sewing on new binding tape around the neck. The Zumbagua Saturday market is filled with such curious lacunae (things commonly for sale in other markets but absent here), which reflect the strength of the subsistence and reciprocity economy, and its ethos, in which certain goods and services cannot be sold.

The marketplace is filled with ribbons and belts that are either machine made or made outside of the parish. None of these is sold by local people. Most women must depend upon these market stalls to buy their clothing, for few men make the ribbons and belts; when women or girls are given these locally made items, they prize them as indications of a husband's or father's love and his industriousness. Increasingly, however, as men must spend their weeks away from the parish working for wages, and women must perform all of the farming and household chores, neither sex has time for craft production. Although the plaza is still filled with brightly colored handwoven textiles today, textile production in Zumbagua is clearly an endangered art form.

Nevertheless, married and unmarried, old and young, everyone takes pleasure in wearing new or beautiful clothing, and everyone values finely made textiles. In the storerooms and trunks where people house their most valuable possessions, hats, shawls, ponchos, and other clothing have pride of place; on special occasions, these are carefully taken out and donned with great ceremony and appreciation.

The Valley Bottom

Laura M. Miller

In Cotopaxi province in 1988, we felt we were documenting fast disappearing costume styles. In the valley bottom, only elderly ladies wear traditional-style costume; most younger women wear factory-made pleated skirts, T-shirts, and acrylic cardigans. This trend has obscured much of the regional variation in costume that formerly existed. Greater contact with the cities and more schooling is causing younger people to speak Spanish in place of Quichua and increasingly to identify themselves as white (Stark 1985:461). Yet the changes are often gradual, and some elements of traditional costume, such as beads and handwoven belts, are retained by the younger women.

Women's costume

The oldest style of women's dress in the Cotopaxi valley floor is worn only by a small number of elderly women (Fig. 102). They wear long wrapped skirts (*anaku*) of black or dark-colored wool fabric. We saw a few backstrap-loom woven examples, but most appeared to be made of treadle-loom or machine-woven cloth, including Otavalo-style anakus. This cloth is wrapped on the lower body with side pleats and held in place at the waist with hand-woven belts (*chumbi*). Many women wear two or three belts, usually with fairly simple supplementary-warp designs: alternating bars of color on cotton ground or zigzags (*kingu*) (Figs. 103–104). Wool

102 Old woman with handmade hat and warp-resist dyed shawl, Saquisilí market, Cotopaxi province. Photo by George Crockett, 1988.

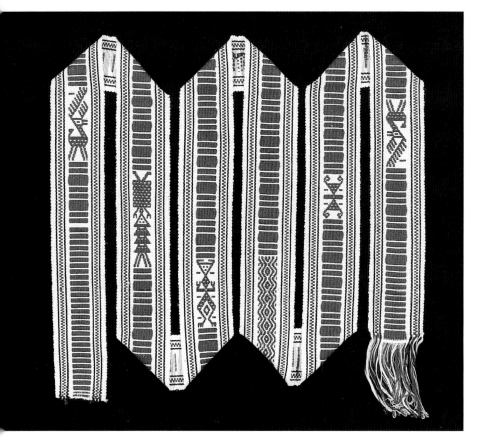

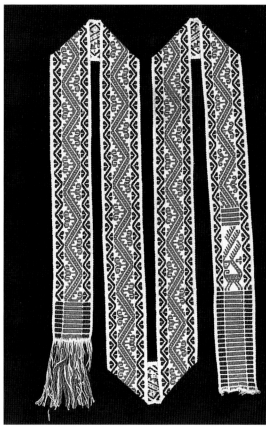

103 Belt from Collana area west of Salcedo, Cotopaxi province. Cotton plain weave, with pink and green acrylic supplementary-warp patterning. 1.36 x .075 meters (53½ x 3 inches). The Textile Museum 1988.19.11, Latin American Research Fund.

104 Belt woven by Pedro Toapanta, from the Quilajaló-Collana-Pilaló de San Andrés area west of Salcedo, Cotopaxi province. Cotton plain weave, with pink acrylic supplementary-warp patterning. 2.98 x .075 meters (9 feet 9 inches x 3 inches). The Textile Museum 1988.19.25, Latin American Research Fund.

belts in the three-color twill-derived weave with bar designs are also worn (Fig. 105); these belts are woven in Chimborazo province, and we saw them sold in the Latacunga and Saquisilí markets. For markets and fiestas, some women wear a leather purse called a *mushapa* tucked into the wraps of their belts.

It was often very difficult to see the blouses that women wear, but we purchased a white cotton blouse with simple hand embroidery on the neckline and cuffs in the Saquisilí market (Fig. 106). Elderly ladies use a shoulder wrap that is often unfringed, worn over the shoulders and held at the neck with a knot or a safety pin. These unfringed shawls are most frequently red. Tupus are not used in Cotopaxi. These women often go barefoot as well.

All the elderly women wear their hair long, wrapped in the back with a backstrap-loom woven tape (*cinta*). Several women used a cotton tape woven with white supplementary-warp patterns, such as triangles and X's, on an indigo ground (Fig. 107). We also saw similar tapes in red and white. Another style of hairband seen in the Salcedo and Saquisilí markets is warp-faced plain weave cotton with larger scale triangle and X designs created using three-span floats (alternating float weave, see Emery 1980:114–15). The weft, also cotton, is much thicker than the warp in the example shown (Fig. 108).

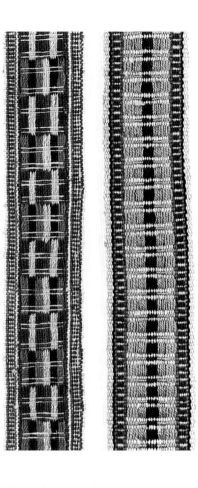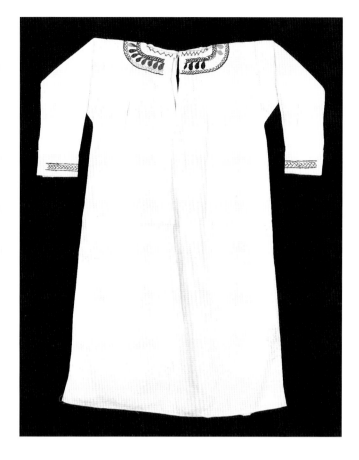

105 *Details of three belts made in central Chimborazo province in the twill-derived weave, purchased from an Otavalo vendor in the Latacunga market (left two examples), and in the Saquisilí market (right), Cotopaxi province. Wool, acrylic, and cotton yarns. Widths: 5.5–8.5 centimeters (2–3⅜ inches). The Textile Museum 1988.19.22, 1988.19.23, and 1988.19.35, Latin American Research Fund.*

106 *Blouse made by the vendor in the Saquisilí market, worn by both indigenous and mestizo women in the Saquisilí area, Cotopaxi province. Cotton plain weave, embroidered with acrylic thread. Length: 1.06 meters (41¾ inches). The Textile Museum 1988.19.17, Latin American Research Fund.*

The traditional costume worn by elderly women includes a handmade white felt hat with little or no added decoration. Women often wore this style of hat with the brim turned down in front and up in the back. Different styles of handmade hats were available in the Saquisilí market. One style, with a low crown, is worn by both men and women. It is finished in the same way, although not as finely, as most hats made in Pomatúg (Tungurahua province), and may be made there. Another style, with a higher crown, worn by women, was said to be made in Latacunga (Textile Museum example 1988.19.34). It was sold without a band around the crown, but women would add a black band there and around the edge of the brim.

Older women also wear beads; heavy red glass or plastic beads predominate. The beads vary in size; the larger ones measure 1–2 centimeters (½–¾ inch) in diameter and the smallest are pea-sized. Individual strands of a necklace contain many different sized beads and the ends of three or four strands are braided together. In many necklaces, one or two of the strands contain an anomalous bead, such as a blue bead with gold decoration, or a white glass bead with pink and gold decoration. Women wear earrings made from old silver coins and sometimes from red seed beads. In addition, many women, often the older women from the countryside, wear large aluminum rings on many fingers.

Older women sometimes use *shigras*, looped bags made by women from agave fiber (Figs. 109–110). Shigras are traditionally used for carrying goods to and from market and for storage of harvested foods, such as corn and potatoes. When used to carry goods by either men or women, the shigra is worn on the back, with the straps around the shoulders and tied in front (Fig. 109). When used for sowing seeds in the fields, two of the straps are tied around the waist or shoulders, with the bag in front.

Cotopaxi shigras have four braided carrying straps. Those made west of Salcedo tend to be made of bright colors, including green, yellow, pink, and orange (Pl. p. viii). Shigras for traditional use are often very simple; the body of the bag is beige, the color of the undyed fiber, with a few orange and pink horizontal stripes. Traditional shigras from the Papaurco area east of the Panamerican highway have bands of two or three geometric designs in red, pink, brown, black, and undyed fiber (Fig. 110). More varied designs are used for shigras made for sale to tourists.

Women also use cloths for carrying things on their backs. Some women use warp-resist patterned carrying cloths, but rarely did we see a woman using the local warp-resist shawl made near Salcedo in Rumipamba (Fig. 111). More commonly, shawls from the Gualaceo (Azuay province) area are used. These shawls have blue designs on a white ground, whereas the Rumipamba *macanas*, as they are called, have white designs on a blue ground. Only four families in Rumipamba were making these shawls in 1988.

It is interesting to note which elements of this traditional dress are retained by younger women. The white felt hat is one of the first elements to be eliminated. A few were available in the Salcedo and Saquisilí markets, but were greatly outnumbered by dark felt fedoras for sale, which is what most women were wearing.

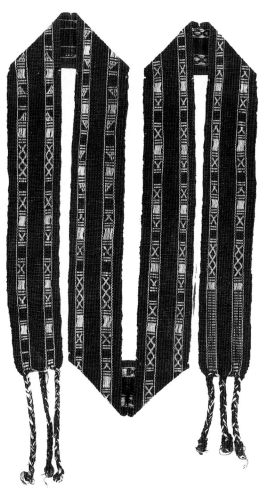

107 *Hairband, worn in the Salcedo and Saquisilí areas, Cotopaxi province. Warp-faced plain weave (indigo) with supplementary-warp patterning (white), cotton. 1.09 x .034 meters (43 x 1⅜ inches). The Textile Museum 1984.46.12, Latin American Research Fund.*

108 *Hairband, worn in the Salcedo and Saquisilí areas, Cotopaxi province. Warp-faced plain weave with alternating float weave patterns, cotton. 88 x 3 centimeters (34⅝ x 1¼ inches). The Textile Museum 1988.19.32, Latin American Research Fund.*

109 *Woman with a shigra on her back, an Otavalo anaku, and a fringed shawl, Saquisilí market, Cotopaxi province. Photo by Lynn A. Meisch, 1988.*

110 *Shigra made by María Ermelinda Lema Maisancho, of Papaurcu, Cotopaxi province. Simple looping with agave fiber yarns. Height: 36 centimeters (14⅛ inches). The Textile Museum 1988.19.47, Latin American Research Fund.*

111 *Warp-resist patterned shawl made in Rumipamba, near Salcedo, Cotopaxi province, with the pata de cabra con mosquito design. Cotton warp-faced plain weave. Slightly more than half of the total 1.78 meters (66 inches) length is shown. Width: 74 centimeters (29 inches). The Textile Museum 1986.19.15, Latin American Research Fund.*

108

109

111

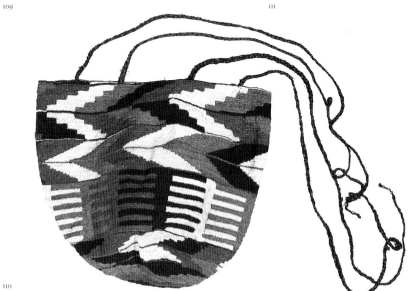

110

121   *Cotopaxi Province*

112 *Woman wearing a handwoven anaku and belt, with her daughter who wears a dress, Salcedo market, Cotopaxi province. Photo by William H. Holmes, 1988.*

113 *Men wearing red ponchos in the Salcedo market, Cotopaxi province, one with a handmade hat. Slide by George Crockett, 1988.*

As an outer wrap, the middle-aged women wear a factory-made acrylic fabric around their shoulders; it is often twill, and sometimes has bold stripes or plaids. Although the fabric is factory made, it still retains the form of the traditional hand-spun and woven shoulder wrap. These women also maintain the anaku, red beads, simple belts, and wrapped hair; however, the anaku is often shorter than that of the older generation (Fig. 112).

A younger woman might wear a factory-made pleated skirt, or an A-line skirt, usually in dark colors. Sometimes they use a hand-woven belt wrapped over the waistband of the skirt. We saw a few younger women wearing an anaku-like cloth wrapped at the waist over a factory-made skirt. These women wear acrylic sweaters or T-shirts and acrylic cardigans. Often some sort of shoulder wrap is used, but often not in the form of the traditional wrap but rather a fringed shawl draped over the shoulders, similar to the way the Hispanic style Cuenca shawls are worn.

Younger women wear red beads and the dark fedora. Though it is often hard to discern, sometimes women in this style of dress wrap their hair with a band or cinta. Other women wear their hair in a loose ponytail, held at the nape of the neck with an elastic.

Some family groups were evident in Cotopaxi markets—the grandmother dressed in the oldest style, the mother wearing the style described for middle-aged women, and the daughter dressed as a replica of her mother or in a sweatsuit or a frilly dress (Fig. 112). In the late 1980s these generational changes were starkly evident.

Beads and belts are the last items of traditional dress to be discarded. In one treadle-loom weaver's family in Cuicuno, all the women of the family—from the grandmother to the little children—wore factory-made garments: shirts, cardigans, pleated and A-line skirts. However, over the waistband of the factory-made skirt, some of the women wore simple, handwoven belts. Also, the baby was swaddled in cloth and wrapped with a handwoven belt.

The eastern side of the valley (divided by the Panamerican highway) has much less traditional costume and artisanry than the western side. All the women in these communities wear factory-made clothing and crocheted acrylic shawls. Whenever we inquired about *tejidos* (S., textiles), we were told of women who knitted and crocheted. These crafts are of European origin, recently introduced, and not a part of traditional indigenous culture.

Men's costume

The poncho is the major element of traditional dress for indigenous rural men of Cotopaxi province (Fig. 113). It is warp-faced and woven on the backstrap loom. It is often fringed and usually has both a gusset at the back of the neck and a collar. Ponchos purchased in the Latacunga market from a local vendor (Textile Museum examples 1988.19.4, 1988.19.14, 1988.19.16) range from 1.32 to 1.63 meters (52–64 inches) long and 1.175 to 1.45 meters (46–57 inches) wide.

Many of the ponchos are either navy blue, red, or dark brown. Often, the brown ponchos have warp stripes of varying gradations of brown, from deep brown to beige. The brown ponchos are currently dyed with walnut, which presumably was the dyestuff used in the past as well. The navy was probably originally indigo dyed and the red cochineal, but now both colors are from synthetic dyes.

Most men wear a dark felt fedora like that described for women. A few of the very oldest men wear a white felt hat, similar to that described for the older women (Fig. 113). Another style is said to be worn by men from Galpón and Cumbilín. It has a wider brim and more contemporary crown shape, with four dents in the top, and is decorated with a blue bow and zigzag stitching around the edge of the brim.

Occasionally, men wear *zamarros*, chaps usually made of unsheared sheep skin, and, indeed, Latacunga has several stores selling chaps, along Calle Guayaquil.

Salamala and Macas

Laura M. Miller

Although very little traditional costume remains among the people of the Cotopaxi Valley bottom, men and women from the communities of Salamala Grande, Salamala Chico, Macas Grande, and Macas Chico wear an elaborate and distinctive costume (Pl. VI, Figs. 114–115). These communities lie in the hills west and southwest of Saquisilí, and people from there frequent the Saquisilí market, which is where we observed this costume.

Salamala women, both young and old, wear their hair in a unique and beautiful fashion (Pl. VI). The hair is divided into two braids with many strands of brightly

114 *Women from Salamala or Macas,*
Cotopaxi province, photographed in the
Saquisilí market. Slide by Laura M. Miller,
1988.

colored ribbon or groups of yarns braided in. Starting at the nape of the neck, a
ribbon is worked into both braids, with some ribbon left free between the two
braids. With each twist of the braid, a new ribbon is worked in. This forms a ribbon
"ladder" between the braids. The end result is a multicolored mass of ribbon at the
nape of the neck that flows into the braids running down a woman's back. Commonly used colors include fuchsia, kelly green, red, yellow, lime green, and blue.
The women of Salamala also wear many multicolored barrettes in their hair.

The oldest women from Salamala and Macas wear handwoven black anakus
held at the waist by a belt, and one woman wore a wine-red anaku. The anaku
fabric is pleated on the woman's left side, with the overlap on her right side. The
older women also wear white felt hats, with a low, rounded crown, and machine
embroidery at the brim edge and on a strip of cloth at the crown base. These two
elements—the white felt hat and anaku—are worn only by the oldest women of the
community.

Younger women wear skirts pleated into a waistband; some skirts have elaborate
embroidery at the hem (Fig. 114). Middle-aged women wear pleated skirts with a
dark cloth wrapped over it and held in place with a belt. It is akin to the anaku, but
only covers three quarters of the body, with the opening on one side. Belts are often
very difficult to see, since women wear many shawls. One belt we saw was very
intricate and looked as if it had supplementary-warp patterning.

115 Woman from Salamala or Macas, Cotopaxi province, photographed in the Saquisilí market. Photo by Lynn A. Meisch, 1988.

The women wear several skirts, and the outer one is usually very elaborate. Some women wear an outermost pleated skirt with gold trim 5 centimeters (2 inches) wide along the hem, while skirts seen on other women are simply embroidered.

It is virtually impossible to see what Salamala women wear as the inner layer over their upper bodies when they are dressed for market, because of all their shawls. Most women wear two or three shawls, mostly of industrial manufacture, with long fringes applied after weaving. For the outermost layer, many women seem to prefer a fuzzy acrylic fake fur or velvet-like fabric, sometimes with a design stamped into it (Pl. VI, Fig. 114), while other women wear a plaid shawl (Fig. 115).

Rather than the red beads common for other women in Cotopaxi province, most women from Salamala wear large gold beads—the same Czechoslovakian Christmas tree ornaments commonly used in Imbabura province. Many women seem to prefer large beads that are almost the size of unshelled peanuts. Other women wear red beads as well.

Salamala women's earrings are made from seed beads. Often these earrings consist of a strip of beads worked in a pattern. At either end of the strip is string, and this is passed through a hole in the ear and then the ends tied to hold the earring in place. Women also wear large aluminum rings on their fingers.

Men from these communities wear ponchos that are red on one side and warp striped in shades of walnut brown on the other. When walking in the market, these men wear the sides of the poncho flipped up over their shoulders, so that both faces are visible. We later learned that these ponchos are made in Carabuela in the Otavalo area.

Salamala men wear dark fedoras and commercially made pants. We saw no old men wearing white hats.

Chapter 7

Tungurahua Province

Salasaca

Laura M. Miller

The Salasaca are a small and distinct ethnic group in Tungurahua province.[1] The community's land lies 14 kilometers (8¾ miles) southeast of Ambato, the provincial capital, and is approximately 14 kilometers (5½ miles) square (see map, page xix), supporting a population of six to eight thousand. On most days, the volcano Tungurahua can be seen from the community, and on clear days, the massive form of Chimborazo can also be seen. The Salasacas refer to Tungurahua as Mama Abuela (S., Grandmother) and to Chimborazo as Taita (Q., Father) Chimba.

Historical references to the Salasaca are scanty. The belief that the Salasacas are mitimas from Bolivia, brought to Ecuador by the Incas as punishment for rebellion, persists in the literature on Salasaca (Scheller 1972:20; Poeschel 1988:32). However, none of these sources cites any historical records in support of this assertion. Moreover, contemporary authors disagree as to whether Salasaca cultural features more logically descend from Bolivian or Ecuadorian (Panzaleo and Puruhá) sources (Peñaherrera and Costales 1959:24, 29; Poeschel 1988:32).

Joseph Casagrande (1977:82) suggests that the belief of both the Salasacas themselves and of local nonindigenous people that they are mitimas, whether true or not, justifies the reputation of the Salasaca as a people who are different and separate. They have lived apart from nonindigenous people and their basic attitude toward outsiders is fundamentally defensive and aggressive (*bravo* S.).

The authors who state that the Salasacas are mitimas imply that all Salasacas assert they are mitimas. However, several Salasacas with whom I spoke fervently denied this. They are in the process of trying to wrest civil rights from the national government and felt that their supposed identification as "Bolivian" had been used against them in their political struggles with the Ecuadorian national government.

Like Casagrande, I can neither confirm nor deny the assertion that the Salasacas are Bolivian mitimas, and like him, believe that this idea helps to justify the Salasacas' resistance to outsiders and to assimilation.

---

1. This text is based on field work in 1983, 1984–85, with return trips in 1988, 1989, and 1992. I am aware of Siles 1983, but have not seen it.

Settlement patterns and subsistence

The community of Salasaca is surrounded on all sides by small towns of mestizo-white farmers and shopkeepers. Pelileo, the cantón capital and largest nearby town, is inhabited only by mestizos-whites, as are El Rosario, Benitez, and Quero, the towns that border Salasaca.

Although now only a twenty-minute bus ride from Ambato, Salasaca was relatively isolated until after the construction of the Ambato-Baños-Puyo-Napo highway by the Shell Petroleum Company in 1934 (Poeschel 1988:36). Salasacas resisted its construction and had a variety of battles with local police. The highway has physically divided the land held by the community and is bitterly resented. Salasacas are frequently killed crossing it, eleven people in 1984 (Poeschel 1988:37).

In 1945, a Colombian order of Catholic nuns, the Hermanas Lauritas, arrived in Salasaca and established an elementary school and high school in the community. The children are allowed to wear indigenous dress to school.

Salasaca is divided into fifteen different areas called *manzanas* (S.), and each one selects a leader or *cabecilla* (S.). Duties of the cabecilla include making sure that people attend communal work parties (*minga* Q.) to do tasks such as cleaning irrigation ditches or cleaning the cemetery before the *Día de los Difuntos* (All Souls' Day) celebration in November. They also organize *la ronda* (S.), nightly patrols to protect the community from robbery and animal theft.

Houses are dispersed, but rarely is there a house that is completely isolated, with no others in view. There are three types of house construction in Salasaca. The oldest type is constructed of low adobe walls with a high peaked thatch roof (Fig. 116). In some cases, the thatch reaches almost to the ground. Older people in Salasaca state that in their youth, all houses in the community were of this type.

More recently, Salasacas have constructed their homes with adobe walls and zinc roofs. Older people complain that the zinc roofs do not insulate the house as well, but younger people say that they prefer the ease of construction and the durability of zinc.

Most recently, people have built their homes from purchased cinder blocks with zinc roofs. Typically, these homes are nearest the highway since it provides greater access to Ambato and facilitates the transport of materials. In contrast, as one walks further into Salasaca, away from the highway, more adobe and thatched houses are visible.

Salasaca lies from 2,500 to 3,000 meters (8,200–9,800 feet) above sea level. Due to its proximity to the volcano Tungurahua, Salasaca's soil is volcanic in origin, fine, dry, and sandy. The area often suffers continued periods of drought, and subsistence agriculture is very difficult. Access to irrigation is essential for the success of crops, and many families try to have land in both irrigated and dry areas.

Unlike the other highland provinces of Ecuador, Tungurahua province has a high percentage of small landholdings—89 percent are under five hectares (12¼ acres) (Poeschel 1988:42). Most of the landholdings within the parish of Salasaca

116 *Salasaca landscape, Tungurahua province, with agave as borders between fields and thatched house in the distance. Photo by Laura M. Miller, 1988.*

are under 5,000 meters (6,000 yards) square (ibid.). Upon arriving in Salasaca, one of the first impressions is of rows of agave and furcraea plants that are used as borders between landholdings (Fig. 116).

The crops grown in Salasaca are barley, maize, beans, potatoes, *chocho* (a kind of bean from lupine), cabbage, lentils, wheat, and squash. Families also cultivate fields of alfalfa to feed to domestic animals like the guinea pig. Almost every family keeps guinea pigs for domestic consumption, as well as for sale within the community or in Ambato, in case of economic crisis, such as the urgent need to purchase medicine or for children's school supplies.

Families also keep a variety of other animals, and wealth is measured both by the amount of land and by the number of animals a person holds. Animals include cattle, pigs, sheep, chickens, donkeys for hauling, goats, and rabbits. Bulls from Salasaca are famed for fierceness and are often taken to nearby towns and sometimes to as far away as Guaranda (in Bolívar province) and Zumbagua (in Cotopaxi province) for use in fiestas and bull fights.

The major market for Salasacas is the large Monday market in Ambato. Purchases include shoes, school supplies, rice, oil, sugar, fruit, and noodles. The dry goods items are available at a few stores within Salasaca but at higher prices than in Ambato so people prefer to purchase these staples in town. Pelileo, which is closer to Salasaca, has a Saturday market but it is much smaller than the Ambato market, with fruit, meat, and dry goods.

Some members of the community get cash income for such purchases by processing furcraea fiber (locally called *cabuya*) and twisting it into rope for sale. Though arduous, rope making was one of the major ways that Salasacas earned money for the cash economy before the advent of tapestry weaving.

Recently, men have begun to migrate out of the community to factory and construction jobs in Ambato, Quito, and in the Galapagos Islands. Those who work in Ambato return to the community in the evening, but men who work farther away may be absent from the community for months at a time. Migration to the Galapagos Islands began in the mid-1970s.

The economic pressure to migrate is strong. During my 1984 field work, the daily wage in Ambato was quoted as s/180 or s/200—at this time, 100 sucres was equivalent to one dollar. The wage in the Galapagos was cited as s/300 or even up to s/450. A Salasaca tapestry weaver at that time said that it would take him at least a day and a half to earn s/200. Men also work day jobs hauling or carting in nearby towns, especially on market days.

Only a small proportion of women work outside the community, but the number is growing. Some women work in Ambato as laundresses or domestic servants. One woman told me of her work in Ambato cleaning chickens for a shop near the market. Other women go as far as Quito for jobs in domestic service. Salasaca women also live in the Galapagos; they have accompanied their husbands or brothers and have found work in hotels or restaurants.

Tapestry weaving was introduced in the 1950s in Salasaca as an alternative source of income. While still an occupation for many Salasaca men, the boom period has passed, and it has not solved the problems of poverty in Salasaca, as originally hoped. The technique was introduced in 1954 by Jan Schreuder, a Dutch artist resident in Ecuador working with the Instituto Ecuatoriano de Antropología y Geografía. Inspired by the rich embroidery designs of Salasaca, Schreuder taught several Salasaca (as well as Otavalo) men (Salinas 1954). The European-origin treadle loom had long been used in Salasaca for weaving clothing, so learning the tapestry technique was not difficult. In 1962, Peace Corps volunteers began to work in Salasaca, organizing a textile cooperative for the marketing of tapestries and other projects.

In 1983, Hans Hoffmeyer, a development worker with the United Nations Food and Agricultural Organization, worked in Salasaca on various economic development projects, including improvement of the tapestry quality and attempts to process and spin tapestry wool within the community (Hoffmeyer 1985). He also introduced silk-screening as an income generating project. Currently, a small group of women print cards with traditional designs inspired by belts and embroidery on fiesta clothing.

Women's daily costume

Most middle-aged and young women in Salasaca were wearing T-shirts or placket front-button shirts in the 1980s (Fig. 117), but some of the older women in the community still wore the traditional black *pichu jerga* about their upper bodies (Fig. 118). *Jerga* is Spanish for a coarse wool twill-weave fabric, and *pichu* is a Quichua-influenced pronunciation of the Spanish word *pecho* or chest. One thirty-five-year-old woman told me that she wore the pichu jerga until she was a teenager (ca. 1965). The pichu jerga is similar to the anaku cloth in length, width, and color. The Textile Museum examples (1987.9.9 anaku, 1988.22.21 pichu jerga) are 1.93 by .76 meters and 2.095 by .70 meters (76 by 30 inches and 82½ by 27½ inches). Despite the name, these fabrics are usually plain weave.

The pichu jerga is wrapped around the upper body, with the weft horizontal, and overlaps at the back so that the outer end of the fabric passes from the woman's right to her left, with the end at the left shoulder. To form the arm hole, the woman brings the edges of the fabric at her back shoulder blade toward the front. She then pulls the fabric at her breast to meet the fabric from her back, with the back lapping over the front. The layers are pinned together with a small straight pin called the *tupullina pichu jerguita,* inserted from front to back. The fabric is pinned in the same way on the other shoulder. The two tupullina are connected to each other with a braided cord or ribbon that crosses the chest so that the pins are not lost from each other.

The arm holes thus formed are very roomy and the folds of the pichu jerga cover most of the body that might be exposed at the sides. Older women in Salasaca comment that it was very easy to nurse their babies while wearing the pichu

117 *Tomasa, Alonso, and María Olimpia Pilla Caiza, Salasaca, Tungurahua province. Photo by Lynn A. Meisch, 1988.*

118 *Yolanda Masaquiza Masaquiza (daughter of Margarita Masaquiza Chango) wearing the pichu jerga, Salasaca, Tungurahua province. Photo by Laura M. Miller, 1988.*

jerga—their breasts were easily accessible through the roomy arm holes.

The *anaku* is wrapped around the body at the waist, on top of the pichu jerga fabric, holding it in place, and hangs to just below the knee or to mid-calf. The ends are lapped at the back, in the same way as the pichu jerga. A woman places the belt (*chumbi*) around her waist, over the anaku fabric, holding the ends in place with her left forearm. With her right hand, she begins to fold pleats into the fabric across her stomach, working from her right side to her left. Depending on the length of the fabric, the woman's size, and the depth of the pleats, there are five to seven neatly folded pleats at the center front of the anaku. When the pleats are in place, the woman continues to wrap the belt about her waist, usually three or four times. The ends of the belt are not tied to each other, but are tucked in under the layers of the belt.

Salasaca belts are among the finest in Ecuador (Fig. 119, Pl. p. iii). Typically, they have borders of plain warp stripes, zigzags (*kingu* Q.), and triangles (*punta* S.). The zigzags are said to represent the irrigation ditches that are the life-blood of the dry Salasaca soil. The central section contains a fascinating array of designs made using pick-up of the supplementary-warp yarns: birds, deer, geometric figures, horses, dancers at the Corpus Christi festival (Fig. 120), monkeys, peacocks, and many more. One common design shows a figure on horseback carrying a rifle (Hoffmeyer

119 Salasaca belt, woven by José Pilla
Curichumbi, Tungurahua province. Cotton
plain weave, with acrylic supplementary-
warp patterning. 2.66 x .07 meters (8 feet 9
inches x 2¾ inches), excluding ties. The
Textile Museum 1988.19.1, Latin American
Research Fund.

120 *Dancers in the Corpus Christi fiesta, Salasaca, Tungurahua province. Slide by Laura M. Miller, 1992.*

1985, fig. 66). These are said to be soldiers of Eloy Alfaro. Prior to his presidency (1906–11), Salasacas had to pay land taxes. However, Salasacas supported Alfaro during the Alfarista Revolution and, in gratitude, Alfaro eliminated the land tax for the community.

Another style of Salasaca belt is called *frutilla* (S., strawberry) and consists of small diamond figures (Fig. 121). It is considered to be harder to warp and weave and therefore is more prestigious. It is the only supplementary-warp patterned belt in Ecuador in which two colors of supplementary-warp yarns are used simultaneously.

The selection of designs is the choice of the weaver, but as one full-time weaver said, a man who is going to weave for others must know how to do everything. Salasacas prefer muted colors for the patterns.

The belt is also used to carry heavy things on the back. For instance, a woman might carry a 50-pound (22.7-kilogram) sack of flour to her home by wrapping the sack in a bayeta and then placing the belt around it. She would use the belt to

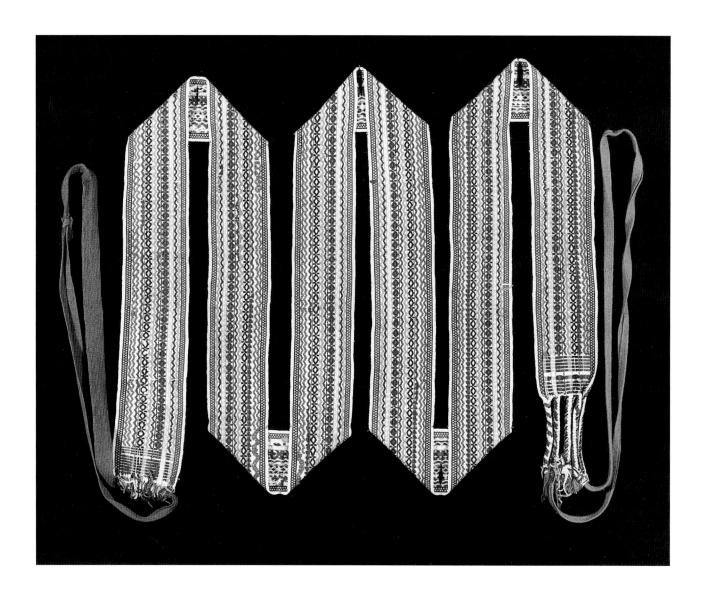

121 *Salasaca belt, Tungurahua province,*
of the frutilla *style. Cotton plain weave,*
with acrylic supplementary-warp pattern-
ing. 2.48 x .06 meters (8 feet 1½ inches x 2⅜
inches), excluding ties. The Textile Museum
1988.19.82, Latin American Research Fund.

support the load, place the sack on her back, and tie the belt at her chest, holding the sack in place.

Over the T-shirt or pichu jerga, Salasaca women wear shoulder wraps (*bayetas*) (Fig. 117). These shawls are plain weave and are slightly longer than wide, The Textile Museum examples (1987.9.10 and 1988.19.138) being 1.025 by .94 meters and 1.16 by .95 meters (40⅜ by 37 inches and 45⅝ by 37½ inches) in size.

Although made predominantly of wool, bayetas have a few narrow warp and weft stripes of white cotton, placed along the edges and down the center. The cut ends of the shawl are reinforced with blocks of stitching alternately in white cotton and in wool. Since cotton does not take dyes as easily as wool, these yarns remain undyed when the shawl is dyed (Figs. 117 and 123, Pl. VII). Bayetas are usually worn with the warp horizontal so that the decorated ends show clearly on the front. For daily work, women wear one or two bayetas, usually of different colors, depending on the weather.

The most common colors in Salasaca bayetas are dark purple, red, olive green, and bright pink. The dark purple and red are most highly prized since these colors are from the natural dye source cochineal. The olive green color was probably originally from natural sources (possibly *chilca* Q., *Baccharis* spp.), but now is from a synthetic dye.

Since spinning is labor intensive, many women now prefer to buy already-dyed acrylic yarn for their bayetas. Many of the bright pink bayetas are also made of acrylic. Cochineal is becoming increasingly scarce and expensive. When synthetic dyes are used (on wool), the dyer tries to replicate the purple and red of cochineal. Acrylic and wool garments are sometimes distinguished from each other by referring to the wool pieces as *runa*, the Quichua term for "people" or "us."

The *bayeta de lishtas* (*lista* S., stripe) is another kind of shoulder wrap frequently worn in Salasaca, and it is locally woven. It is the same size as the bayeta and is worn in the same way. The Textile Museum example (1988.19.62) is 1.18 by 1.08 meters (46½ by 42½ inches). These plain-weave cloths have a white ground, traditionally cotton, and thin red and navy weft stripes placed at regular intervals. In some bayetas de lishtas, the red lines are cochineal-dyed wool, which was usual before the advent of acrylics. Currently, the shawls are often made entirely of acrylic. In either case, they have other colored stripes at the ends as well as stitching on the ends in various colors.

Salasaca women also wear a *rebozo*, which is like the bayeta, but larger. The Textile Museum examples (1988.19.86 and 1993.17.1) are twice as long as they are wide, 2.09 by 1.02 meters and 2.22 by 1.03 meters (82¼ by 40 inches and 87⅜ by 40½ inches). If worn with one or more bayetas, the rebozo is used as the outermost layer. It is folded in half parallel to the weft and worn with the warp stripes vertical down the back (Fig. 123). To carry a baby, a woman may tuck the baby under the rebozo and tie a bayeta underneath the baby and across her chest to support it (as in Fig. 133). Any of the shoulder wraps can be used to carry loads.

For daily use, women use a shawl pin or *tupu* to hold their bayetas in place. The pin is made of silver or steel and often has a multicolored glass bead or other colored stone in the head. It is sometimes marked with the woman's initials and the date that the pin was made. A ribbon (velvet ribbon is most prized and used on special occasions) passes through a loop on the tupu and is placed around the woman's neck so that she does not lose the pin if it works loose from the fabric of her bayetas. One elderly man makes tupus in Salasaca, but young people have not learned the art from him. Consequently, some women now resort to large safety pins to hold their shawls.

Another very important part of women's dress in Salasaca are the beads worn at the neck, called *mullu* (Q.). Each necklace is made up of many strands which vary in length so that when worn, the strands are evenly distributed on the neck. Highly prized within the community are red coral and multicolored Venetian glass beads.

Beads are handed down from generation to generation. Colored beads are scarce now. Several small watch repair shops in Ambato sell beads occasionally, but these are bought quickly by Salasaca women. Actual coral is very rare and often coral-colored glass or plastic beads are substituted. Women from the Chibuleo communities, who also wear coral (or coral-colored) beads, frequent the Ambato market and there is a great deal of competition for these beads.

There is some trade and barter of beads within the community, but women are reluctant to part with their beads. One woman I met during my 1984 field work traded a bayeta for a necklace that was worth s/1,000 (ten dollars). Young girls are given strands of inexpensive red beads when they are young and cannot yet be trusted with expensive beads. Some Salasaca women also wear the gilt glass beads that can be purchased at the Otavalo market.

Salasaca women's earrings are made of loops of string that pass through holes in their ears. Women use coral and multicolored glass beads to make the earrings, called *rinrin wallka* (pronounced *washka*). These earrings usually reach to shoulder level, and rarely pass that point.

Salasaca women are rarely seen without a hat. Most middle-aged and young women now wear dark-colored, machine-made fedoras. Dark olive green, navy blue, and dark brown are favored colors. These fedoras are also worn by little girls, from the age of five or six.

Older women still wear the traditional wide-brimmed white felt hat (*sombrero*) for daily use. These hats are quite thick (at least 1 centimeter, nearly ½ inch) and heavy; young people complain that they are too heavy for daily wear, but wear them for festivals and other special occasions. The traditional hats are made in Barrio Pomatúg near Pelileo, and of the hatmakers in this town, only two brothers (in their sixties) now make the Salasaca style, on a commission basis. Colored string may be tied around the base of the crown.

Salasaca women rarely cut their hair. It is parted in the middle and worn long down the back. They use a backstrap-loom woven ribbon or belt to wrap their hair. This ribbon is called the *akcha watana cinta* or the *uma watana cinta* (Q. and S., hair tying ribbon or head tying ribbon). The Textile Museum example (1988.19.78) is 1.54 by .05 meters (60⅝ by 2 inches), excluding the ties on both ends. Starting at the middle of the hank of hair, the woman wraps downward toward the tip of the hair, then upward to slightly below the nape of the neck, and then back down to the middle point, where she started. Usually the wrap is given a few sharp twists to tighten it before it is tied off. The hairband has braided fringe and sometimes tie cords on both ends, and the fringe or cords are used to tie the wrap in place. Since the wrap begins and ends at the middle of the hair, the fringes (or cords) are tied to each other and then tied around the wrapped hair. During the day, a woman seldom has to rewrap her hair. The wrapped hair lies on top of her shirts, and is hidden below the bayetas.

Traditionally, women wash their hair with furcraea. A frond is cut from the plant and the thorns are taken off with a kitchen knife. Then the frond is heated on the hearth. After it has cooled, it is split lengthwise into strips. The strips are rubbed together and a lather forms. The hair is washed with this soapy substance, which gives a characteristic sheen and stiffness to women's hair. I never noticed this sheen in men's hair.

Men's daily costume

The older men tend to wear white pants, called *calzón* (S.), that are loose and straight-cut and about mid-calf length (Figs. 117, 120). These pants are home sewn from purchased factory-made cotton fabric. Two triangular gusset pieces are cut from the inside top of each leg and then inverted and sewn back on to make a crotch gusset (Fig. 122). The pants have a finished slit at one side seam that allows them to be put on the body. The slit is closed at the top with a cloth loop that hooks over a button or a red bead similar to that used in women's necklaces. Men wrap a handwoven belt (*chumbi*) around their waists as well, over both their pants and their shirt, which is tucked into their pants.

Now younger men often wear modern style white pants purchased in Ambato, and no chumbi. However, unless they are to do heavy labor in the fields, all Salasaca men, young and old, wear white pants.

Older men still wear a traditional shirt called *pijama*, or *camisa de la tela amarilla* (S., shirt of yellow fabric). It is made like a tunic, without any shaping or sleeves, and with a slit for the neck. The sides are simply sewn to create the arm holes. It is made from cotton cloth purchased in Ambato. The Textile Museum example (1988.22.22) is 81 by 77 centimeters (32 by 30¼ inches). Most men now wear T-shirts or front placket buttoned shirts.

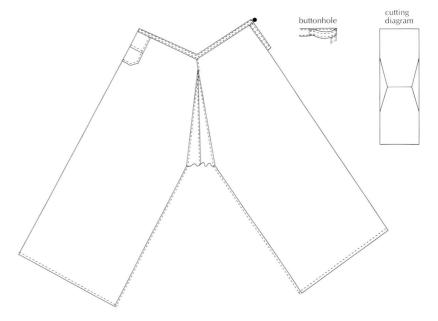

122 Cut of men's pants, Salasaca, Tungurahua province. The side opening is a cut slit with edge binding of the same fabric. The buttonhole is made by folding in an extension of the waistband. The button is spherical and red. The pocket has a side selvedge of the fabric at the top, flush with the edge of the waistband. The legs have a narrow rollup hem. Overall length: 79 centimeters (31 inches). Based on The Textile Museum 1988.22.20, Latin American Research Fund. Drawing by Laurie McCarriar based on a sketch by Ann P. Rowe.

buttonhole

cutting diagram

The most distinguishing piece of clothing for Salasaca men is their poncho. It is black wool, called the *yana poncho*, in 2/2 twill weave, with a thin band of multicolored machine embroidery at the shoulder line, as well as sometimes around the neck slit. The Salasacas say that these colors represent the colors of the rainbow and protect the man wearing them. The poncho is long and narrow. It spans from the mid-upper arm on one side to the same point on the other side. The Textile Museum example (1988.19.79) is 1.875 by .77 meters (73¾ by 30¼ inches). Unlike many other poncho styles in the region, there is no fringe; instead, the ends are finished with an overcast embroidery stitch, often in red, or by machine stitching.

Some ponchos are made of factory produced acrylic fabric, but wool ponchos are most highly prized. One fifty-year-old man commented: "Nosotros ponemos de puro borrego. Algunos ponen de Ambato. Ociosos, pobres, no valen para nada. [We (in his family) wear pure wool ponchos. Some wear (ponchos) from Ambato. Lazy ones, poor (people), they aren't worth anything]" (Miller translation).

Men also sometimes wear a white poncho, called the *yura poncho*, that has no embroidery. On very cold nights, men wear two ponchos, the white poncho underneath the black. Men rarely wear the white poncho alone as their outer layer. When worn together, the white layer shows at the sides, underneath the black poncho. The Textile Museum example (1988.19.91) is 2.10 by .87 meters (82⅝ by 34¼ inches).

On colder days, at night or at fiestas, men also wear a *vara y media* (S.). This is a length of cloth that is a hand-spun, -woven, and -dyed fabric that is one and a half varas long. The Textile Museum examples (1988.19.87, 1987.9.11) are 1.26 by .71 meters and 1.27 by .65 meters (49½ by 28 inches and 50 by 25½ inches). The vara y media is made much like women's bayetas but it has no cotton warp stripes. The colors are also similar to those of bayetas: purple, red, or olive green.

Men carefully fold the vara y media lengthwise into thirds or quarters and drape it about their necks so that both ends hang down their back. Occasionally, a man may wear a rebozo or a poncho in a similar way. In addition, on cold nights, men sometimes wrap a rebozo around their upper bodies, to keep out the cold.

Older men also have a distinctive hair style. Their hair is all of the same length and cut straight below the ear lobes. Their front hair or bangs are long, and these locks are flipped back and tucked under the brim of the traditional wide white hat. This style is called *cebada parba* (S. and Q., barley haystack) because of its resemblance to a haystack. Men wear fedoras on a daily basis, but older men tend to wear the traditional white felt hat more frequently. These hats are identical to those worn by women.

Children's costume

Babies are wrapped in soft cloths (often old bayetas) and carried on their mothers' backs. The chumbi is used to wrap the bayeta around the baby. As one mother stated, "Sueltos se asustan. No pueden dormir con los manos sueltos. [Loose (i.e., not wrapped in cloths) they get scared. With their hands free they cannot sleep]"

Plate II Camilo Gomez, from Ovalos (Natabuela), Imbabura province, in fiesta dress. Slide by Patt Hill, 1989.

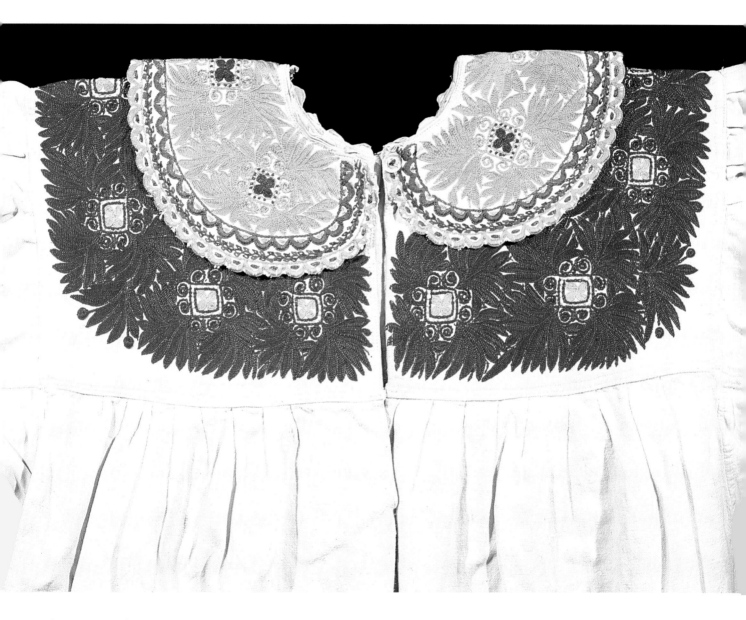

Plate III Detail of a blouse from La
Esperanza, eastern Imbabura province.
Cotton plain weave, embroidered with perle
cotton thread in closed double chain stitch.
The Textile Museum 1989.22.26, Latin
American Research Fund.

Plate IV Blanca Oliva Noques, of Caserío Guanupamba, Mariano Acosta (grand-daughter of a woman born in Zuleta), eastern Imbabura province, wearing a color coordinated outfit, with centro. Slide by Marilee Schmit Nason, 1984.

Plate V Easter Saturday crowds in Zumbagua, Cotopaxi province. Slide by Mary J. Weismantel, 1984.

Plate VI Women's hairstyle from
Salamala or Macas, Cotopaxi province,
photographed in the Saquisilí market.
Photo by Barbara U. Buech, 1992.

Plate VII Margarita Masaquiza Chango in fiesta costume, Salasaca, Tungurahua province. Slide by Laura M. Miller, 1984.

Plate VIIIA Charco family from San Luis Chibuleo, Tungurahua province. Slide by Ann P. Rowe, 1988.

Plate VIIIB Pilahuín schoolchildren in Pucara Grande, Tungurahua province. Slide by Lynn A. Meisch, 1988.

Plate IXA Women from Pulucate, central Chimborazo province, wearing wool baitas and synthetic anakus. The woman at left is wearing a white wool changalli and a millma sumbriru. The woman at right is wearing a pañu sumbriru. Photo by Rebecca Tolen, 1989.

Plate IXB Styles of poncho commonly worn in Pulucate, central Chimborazo province. These men are wearing, from left, a puzu jirga of acrylic, a Cacha poncho, two red acrylic jirgas, a white jirga of wool, and a purple acrylic jirga. The man in the center of the back row is wearing a millma sumbriru with ribbon and tassels. Photo by Rebecca Tolen, 1989.

Plate X Man wearing a warp-resist patterned Cacha poncho at the Cajabamba market, central Chimborazo province. Slide by Ann P. Rowe, 1988.

Plate XI Woman with hairdo characteristic of Chismote, at the Guamote market, Chimborazo province. Slide by Laura M. Miller, 1989.

*Plate XII Woman probably from around
La Merced, southern Chimborazo province,
at the Guamote market. Slide by Lynn A.
Meisch, 1989.*

*Plate XIII Men in the Cañar market.
The one on the left is from eastern Cañar
province. The one on the right is Cañari,
with two kushmas and a warp-resist
patterned poncho. The end of his belt hangs
down in back. Slide by Lynn A. Meisch,
1978.*

Plate XIV Cholo women at the Gualaceo market, Azuay province. Slide by Laura M. Miller, 1988.

Plate XV Indigenous woman, Azuay province. Slide by Lynn A. Meisch, 1977.

Plate XVI Ashuca Losano spinning, with husband Polivio Sarango in indigo-dyed poncho and handmade hat, Tuncarta, Saraguro area, Loja province. Women's beaded necklaces are hanging on the pole in the background. Slide by Lynn A. Meisch, 1981.

123 Manuela Masaquiza Pilla with her daughter Janet wearing a bandanna, Salasaca, Tungurahua province. Photo by Laura M. Miller, 1988.

(Miller translation). Red bandannas are highly prized in Salasaca, and are often used to form a small cap to keep the sun off an infant's head (Fig. 123).

Young children wear traditional dress that is a replica of their parents' clothing from about the age of three or four. For little girls, old anakus are cut down to a smaller size and narrower belts are used. Often, an Otavalo belt is purchased in the Ambato market. The traditional Salasaca belt would be too wide and out of proportion for a child. Little girls have their ears pierced in babyhood and wear tiny loops of coral earrings. Girls are given a few strands of inexpensive red beads when they are small. As they grow older, they are given more beads. For a shawl, they often wear a bayeta folded in half in the manner in which an adult woman wears a rebozo. Young boys wear white pants and cut-down versions of their father's ponchos.

Fiesta costume

Women's fiesta dress in Salasaca is very beautiful (Pl. VII). For the yearly cycle of fiestas, women wear their newest bayetas and finest beads. In fact, before the celebration of Difuntos, or All Souls' Day, there is a flurry of cochineal dyeing in Salasaca. For a fiesta, women also increase the number of anakus and bayetas they wear. Instead of one or two bayetas, they wear four or five, and even in the heat of dancing, they do not remove them. Women carefully layer the cloths so that each color shows at the front opening. Whereas for daily dress women wear one anaku, for fiestas they wear up to three.

Many women also wear a small coin purse tucked into their belts at the waist. Many silver chains hang down about 20–25 centimeters (8–10 inches) from this purse and serve as adornment.

An embroidered shawl is also worn for fiestas, called the *panutzutzu ukufachallina* (Fig. 124). It is a white cotton cloth, with brightly colored animals and geometric designs embroidered along the edges, about 10 centimeters (4 inches) deep. At the very edge there are lines of zigzag, said to represent the irrigation ditches that crisscross Salasaca. Above these lines, there are stylized fruits and plants. *Ramitas* (S., little branches) are a common design. There are also some animal and bird figures above the geometric designs. I saw one example on which the seal of Ecuador was embroidered. There are also pompoms of embroidery floss along the edge. These shawls are made by women for their own use and sometimes rented out to others for fiestas. The panutzutzu ukufachallina is folded on the diagonal, and then rolled, creating a roll of fabric with the embroidery showing richly all along the edge. A woman then places it over her shoulders and ties it in front, on top of all of her other layers of bayetas (Pl. VII).

For fiestas, she wears the traditional white felt hat, if she has one. The hats are whitened by pressing cornstarch and limestone into them with a hot iron. When a hat falls from a person's head, especially at fiesta time after it has been whitened, a flurry of white powder is seen as it hits the ground.

124 *Detail showing the ends of a fiesta shawl,* panutzutzu ukufachallina, *Salasaca, Tungurahua province. Cotton plain weave, embroidered with acrylic yarns. Width: 65 centimeters (25½ inches). The Textile Museum 1988.19.139, Latin American Research Fund.*

125 *Padrinos de la boda (wedding sponsors), wearing wedding costume, and their daughter in regular costume, Salasaca, Tungurahua province. Slide by Laura M. Miller, 1984.*

126 *Detail of wedding pants, Salasaca, Tungurahua province. Slide by Laura M. Miller, 1989.*

Women also wear more beads. Often, a woman has several necklaces in storage that she does not wear on a daily basis but brings out at the time of a fiesta. Usually, the necklaces with the most multicolored beads are put on top, so that they are the most visible.

Men's fiesta dress is not currently distinctive from what has been described for daily dress.

Wedding costume

Wedding costume in Salasaca is flamboyant and beautiful (Fig. 125). There are four central characters in a wedding: the bride and groom and the *padrinos de boda*, or the godparents of the wedding. The padrinos are an older couple who sponsor the couple's marriage. They contribute food to the marriage ceremony and retain a special relationship with the couple after the wedding.

Both the bride and the madrina de boda wear the traditional white felt hats, but around the crown are numerous multicolored ribbons and zigzag trim. The hat also has a large mass of fluffy multicolored feathers at the back. The shawl pins are also more decorated, with many colored ribbons attached to the loops. These ribbons drape colorfully across the back. Otherwise the costume is similar to lavish fiesta dress, although the embroidered shawl is usually worn underneath the other shawls instead of on top, with the colorful ends showing in front.

The costume of the groom and the padrino de boda is also very colorful. Weddings are the only time that the man's poncho is different from the distinctive daily black poncho. Both the groom and the padrino wear a navy blue or black poncho that is wider than the poncho for daily use, and it has narrow bright pink or red warp stripes on either side. They also wear pink and orange embroidered silky handkerchiefs tied over their shoulders and draping across their backs, and pants with figural embroidery in multicolored acrylic on the lower legs (Fig. 126). The embroidery is similar to that of the women's panutzutzu ukufachallina. These ponchos, handkerchiefs, and pants are rented out by various members of the community and provide a small source of income.

Textile production

Textile production in Salasaca can be divided into two distinct classes: textiles for use within the community and textiles for sale to the tourist market. Each has a completely different history, economy, and organization.

Traditional dress in Salasaca is a very strong element of ethnic identity, and the handwork that goes into making these garments is formidable. Traditional garments in Salasaca are made primarily of wool, and families maintain their own small flocks of sheep for this purpose.

Finished products are rarely sold—they are produced within the family for use by that family. Wool for anakus, shawls, and ponchos is spun by a woman and her daughters. When enough wool yarn is spun, the yarn is taken to a treadle loom weaver within the community. Usually, the weaver is a man and known to the family either through kinship or proximity. Small gifts of food are given to the weaver, and a price is arranged for the work to be done. Dyeing of these items is done after weaving, usually by a woman who has specialized knowledge of dyeing. The one who will wear the fabric does the edge finishing.

Young girls are taught to spin at the age of six or seven. At first, they spin weft because weft yarn does not have to be as strong as the warp, since it will not be under tension. When one girl, Yolanda, finished her last spindle of weft and was given wool to prepare to spin warp, she was praised by her mother. An older sister who is not as careful in her spinning was scolded, and Yolanda was presented as an example of a good spinner. Most spinning is with a horizontal spindle, producing an S twist.

Handwoven belts are an important part of both men's and women's costume in Salasaca. Both men and women weave belts on the backstrap loom, but women tend to be the exception rather than the rule. Most men do both treadle-loom weaving and belt weaving, but one man specializes in belt weaving.

The owner of the belt provides the prepared materials. The cotton for the ground weave is purchased in Ambato and rolled into balls. The acrylic for the supplementary warp is purchased in Ambato as well, overspun for strength and then rolled into balls. The owner brings the weaver bread, bananas, and Coca-Cola as goodwill gifts and then negotiates a price for the labor. During my 1984 field work in Salasaca, the woman who taught me to weave did not know how to warp, but her brother came to warp for me. In his honor, we served a dish with rice, a rarity in Salasaca and thus of higher status than soup, which is the daily fare.

Belt weaving is a guarded art. Many believe that the act of teaching will take away the teacher's ability to weave and to remember patterns. Therefore, most people learn from family members. One man, José Pilla, learned from his father. He in turn taught his sister María. Another woman told of her difficulties trying to learn; she watched others weave and then tried on her own, with little help.

Textile technology is passed on from generation to generation. Even though acrylic shawls are becoming more common in Salasaca, young girls still learn to spin, and wool ponchos and shawls are much more highly prized than acrylic garments. It is rarer to see a young man weaving belts. Not many young men express an interest in belt weaving, but there are a few who do carry on their fathers' tradition. Because costume is such an integral part of Salasaca identity, and because the finest parts of the costume are all handmade, those with textile skills are highly respected in the community. The rarer the skill, like cochineal dyeing or belt weaving, the more respected the person who has it.

Commercial weaving

As mentioned above, the tourist trade textiles are mostly tapestries, with designs ranging from traditional Salasaca belt figures or embroidery motifs to other images, such as Navajo-style tapestry designs. Many designs are similar to those used in Otavalo tapestries, including M. C. Escher motifs. There is a great deal of competition in the business and new designs are jealously guarded, lest some competitor within the community or from outside see the design or display it in the market for all to see and copy.

The tapestries consume a large amount of wool—a weaver uses daily much more than a single household could produce in a day. Therefore, wool is purchased from several factories on the northern outskirts of Ambato. Wool prices continually increase, and when they become too high, weavers simply stop buying wool for a time. The wool is dyed with synthetic dyes purchased in Ambato. Hoffmeyer made some attempts to introduce natural dyes into tapestry production, but weavers felt that it was too expensive a procedure. The natural dye sessions took longer and consumed more firewood than synthetic dye sessions.

The tapestries are made in family-centered workshops, and the work is done primarily by men. Often, the master of the workshop has two or three men working for him. Boys as young as nine years old begin to learn to weave, and weaving may be part of their chores, along with hauling water or caring for the family animals. The master is in charge of purchasing and dyeing the wool, as well as selling the finished product. The workers warp their looms and weave.

Salasaca weavers have several networks for marketing their tapestries. Some work for store owners and exporters based in Quito. They turn in their products once a month and pick up orders for more tapestries. Others make tapestries and try to sell them in Quito at various craft stores. They do not have fixed buyers. A few families have stores in Salasaca itself, and get some trade when tourists stop to buy, or when store owners from Quito come on buying trips. These stores carry local tapestries and also items purchased in Otavalo and Cuenca. A number of men also sell their wares in the cooperative store in the main plaza of Salasaca.

On Sunday there is a small market in the plaza in Salasaca along the highway where tourist textiles are sold. Tapestries are the major item sold, but some men have bought shigras to sell and a few have shoulder bags made of two small tapestry squares sewn together. In 1984, most people told me that the market was not as big as it had been in the mid-1970s. On one December Sunday in 1984, I counted ten kiosks set up with goods to sell, and approximately fifty people came by to look at merchandise in eight hours. Compared to the Otavalo market, which thousands of people attend, the Salasaca market is at a great disadvantage. For this reason, several Salasaca men have moved to Otavalo and live and work there, making and selling tapestries. Other Salasacas sell their tapestries to Otavalo buyers who visit Salasaca, or travel to Otavalo where they try their luck in the Saturday market or deliver tapestries to regular Otavalo clients.

Chibuleo

Ann P. Rowe

The ethnic group here referred to as Chibuleo is located to the south of the Río Ambato, southwest of Ambato, in the foothills of Mount Chimborazo. On the road out from Ambato, we saw people in the Chibuleo costume beginning in Santa Rosa and extending out past Pilahuín. After Pilahuín, the road proceeds over the pass toward Guaranda.

Our principal informant, José Manuel Caiza, told us that the Chibuleo were in this same area before the Spanish conquest.[2] He said that originally they were one people, but after the conquest the land and its people were divided among three different Spanish overlords, as a consequence of which people now identify with one of these three groups. The largest of the three is called Pilahuín, for which one of the literacy teachers gave us the figure of about 10,000 people. Besides the community of Pilahuín, Sr. Caiza listed Palogsha, Pucara Grande, Llushcahuaycu, and Apupamba as being Pilahuín communities. The second largest group is the Chibuleo proper, with a population of around 7,500. The Chibuleo communities include Chibuleo de San Francisco, Chibuleo San Luis, Chibuleo San Pedro, and Chibuleo de San Alfonso. The third and smallest group is the Angaguana, who live in the communities of Angaguana Alto, Angaguana Bajo, Apatuc Arriba, and Apatuc Abajo, Santa Rosa, and Milquilli. The Angaguana live in the most easterly area, followed by Chibuleo, and then Pilahuín farther west.

The costumes of all these communities are very similar. The most readily apparent difference is that the Angaguana wear a different shape of hat. The differences between Chibuleo and Pilahuín seem to consist only of such details as the color of the thread around the base of the crown of the hat and the color of the stripes on shigras.

Sr. Caiza said that he was born Angaguana, but his father died when he was six years old and he was brought up by his maternal uncle, who is Chibuleo, so he now considers himself Chibuleo. It thus appears that there is intermarriage among these groups and that, despite this subgroup identification, people still have some sense of their larger ethnic group, even though they have no overarching name for

2. The detailed information in this paragraph was elicited by Lawrence Carpenter and simultaneously recorded in Ann Rowe's notes.

it. Outsiders tend to use the term Chibuleo (or Pilahuín) to refer to all three groups. Because most of our information comes from the specifically Chibuleo community of San Luis, we use this term in the chapter heading. Information on the other groups is included as available.

The Chibuleo communities divide themselves into religious factions that are hostile to each other and consequently it is not comfortable for outsiders to work there. The problems have been exacerbated by infusions of development money from the North American evangelical organization World Vision beginning in the late 1970s (Stoll 1990:266–68, 297, 303–4). There has been little anthropological study of the Chibuleo. All the information presented here was collected by us in 1988.[3]

The main subsistence activity is agriculture. We saw maize, barley, quinoa, fava beans, potatoes, and onions being cultivated on both steep and gentle slopes. There are also some sheep and cows. The land appears to be relatively fertile. The villages have a central plaza with a few stores and other nonresidential buildings and some houses in the center, with other houses dispersed across the fields. The majority of the houses are built of cement blocks, with tin and Eternit A-frame roofs.[4] Some are tile-roofed. The number of houses of this type suggests some degree of prosperity. Other houses are an older style, with adobe walls about 1 to 1.25 meters (3 to 4 feet) high, covered with ichu grass thatch in a hip roof style.

Many Chibuleo or Pilahuín women sell produce in the Ambato market. In addition, the Chibuleo are known throughout Ecuador as garlic and onion growers and vendors and they are a permanent presence in many regional markets, including Otavalo.

Women's costume

The form of the women's costume gives a relatively conservative and spectacular appearance due to the voluminous pleated skirts, embroidered blouses, long earrings, and distinctive hats (Pl. VIIIA, Fig. 127).

Women wear a short-sleeved blouse (*blusa* S.) of white cotton or synthetic fabric, with hand-embroidered floral motifs on the square yoke (Figs. 127, 128). The blouse is relatively short, simply extending long enough to be covered by the skirts. It is cut symmetrically, but there is a vertical opening which is worn in front. The embroidery is now usually acrylic. The designs we saw on contemporary blouses had a remarkable consistency. However, in the Angaguana community of Milquilli, Earthwatch team members recorded a woman wearing a blouse of slightly different design (Fig. 129).[5] Women also wear machine-knitted shirts under their blouses for added warmth.

Women wear multiple wrapped skirts (*anaku*), usually of navy blue but sometimes black fabric. The Angaguana women we saw in the Ambato market seemed to be more often dressed in black, while the Chibuleo and Pilahuín women usually wear blue. Our Chibuleo informants told us that the acrylic fabric had been in use

3. Besides Lawrence Carpenter, Lynn Meisch, and Ann Rowe, Earthwatch volunteers going to San Luis included Maritza Mosquera, Betty Davenport, Sheila Morris, and Helen Evelev. Laura Miller, Sheila Morris, and Helen Evelev also went to Pilahuín.

4. These detailed architectural observations were recorded by Lawrence Carpenter and Earthwatch volunteers Edna and CJ Elfont.

5. The Earthwatch team to the Angaguana communities included María Aguí, and CJ, Edna, and Dayna Elfont.

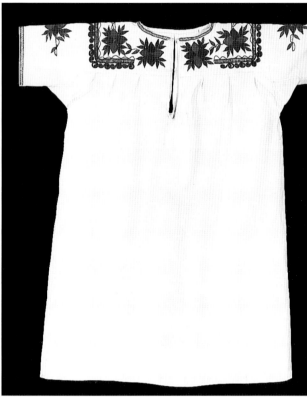

127 *Charco family members in San Luis Chibuleo, Tungurahua province. Photo by Lynn A. Meisch, 1988.*

128 *Blouse from the Chango family, San Luis Chibuleo, Tungurahua province. Synthetic fabric in twill weave, embroidered with acrylic thread. 80 x 71 centimeters (31½ x 28 inches). The Textile Museum 1988.19.70, Latin American Research Fund.*

since 1979, before which treadle-loom woven wool fabric had been used instead. The anaku fabric is 30 inches (76–77 centimeters) wide and is cut into three and a half yard lengths (3.10–3.14 meters as finished), and trimmed with machine embroidery. Most of the skirts we saw had relatively simple decoration in straight stitching, a light blue line, but some anakus had more elaborate zigzag edgings.

Women wear from four to seven anakus simultaneously. To put them on, they fold down the top of each one separately about 5 centimeters (2 inches), so that the finished length is just below the knee or mid-calf. In the demonstration, however, with Lynn Meisch serving as a model, all the anakus were pleated together. One end is placed on the right front, then the length is wrapped around the back, leaving fullness in front and finishing at the left back, so that there is overlap of half the body's circumference. Then a belt is put on with the end at the left and wrapping around the back first. The pleating is started on the right side and progresses toward the left. The first pleats are open to the right. In the middle of the body, the direction of the pleating changes to the left. The exact number of pleats is not important, and we saw some women wearing anakus for which the pleating did not change direction. The pleats are held in place by the right forearm until the belt secures them. The belt wraps around at least twice and the end is tucked in from the bottom. A wider belt is put on first (*jatun chumbi* Q.) (Fig. 130) and then two smaller ones (*uchilla maki chumbi* Q.) (Fig. 131)—or two or even three of each may be worn. One woman was wearing two layers of anakus, each separately secured by belts.

The belts are mostly locally woven, with supplementary-warp patterning. Some of our Chibuleo informants, however, wore belts from the Cacha area in Chimborazo province, which are obtainable in the Ambato market. The Chibuleo belts have relatively wide (2.5 centimeter or 1 inch) plain-weave side borders with a band of supplementary-warp patterning in the center. As elsewhere, the colored threads are acrylic and the white ground threads and borders are cotton, all commercial yarns. The colored threads are often blue, green, and black, though hot pink accents are not uncommon and we also saw brown. The designs are a variety of animal and geometric motifs woven with pickup, separated by bars. All the belts we saw, including used examples, have an unfinished warp loop fringe on both ends. The tightness of the weaving is in the middle range.

The shawls (called *bayeta*) are made of the same fabric as the anakus and are generally navy blue. However, some are white with spaced weft stripes (*fachallina lista*); these were said to be woven in Cotopaxi or Salasaca and brought to the community for sale. One woman had two pink-magenta shawls that she said were for fiesta. A yard and a half (1.27–1.53 meters in The Textile Museum examples) of fabric is used and all four edges are decorated with machine embroidery slightly fancier than that on the anakus. In addition, there are floral sprays embroidered in the corners. When we purchased anakus and bayetas for the Museum, most were sold to us as a set, one anaku matching one bayeta.

Four shawls are commonly worn together, although again the exact number varies. The shawls are put on horizontally so that all the borders show, one above the other. To help achieve this effect, the shawl is folded down at the top, with the short part of the fold inside. If a striped shawl is used, it is usually the bottom layer. The woman with the pink shawls demonstrated wearing one outside, then a blue one, then the other pink one.

Some women pin their shawls with tupus, but since these are no longer obtainable, many women use large safety pins. The tupus have a relatively small head with a large red or green glass ornament in the center (Fig. 132). A woman might wear one, two, or even three tupus simultaneously. A braided band is put through the loop in the tupu. If worn in pairs, they are connected with a braided cord looped through both, with the ends tied together. The cord is wound around the pin and then the loop is thrown back over the left shoulder or it dangles. Multiple tupus are inserted into the shawls parallel, one above the other. One fastens the two underneath shawls, while the other fastens the upper ones.

Small children are carried the same way as in Salasaca, under the outer shawl, with another shawl supporting the child's seat and tied across the chest (Fig. 133).

The women wear both necklaces (*wallka* Q., pronounced *washka*) and earrings (*orejeras* S.). The necklaces are multiple strands of small red beads, with some white beads interspersed. The earrings are spectacular, four long strands of red beads in two loops that hang to below the waist. There are usually some metal

129 *Maria Delfina Isasisa, an Angaguana woman from Milquilli, Tungurahua province. Photo © CJ Elfont/Light Isolates Photography, 1988.*

130 *Woman's belt* (jatun chumbi), *woven by José Francisco Maliza Conceta, San Luis Chibuleo, Tungurahua province. White cotton and colored acrylic plain weave, with acrylic supplementary-warp patterning. 2.97 x .095 meters (9 feet 9 inches x 3¾ inches). The Textile Museum 1988.19.110, Latin American Research Fund.*

131 *Woman's belt* (uchilla maki chumbi), *woven by José Francisco Maliza Conceta, San Luis Chibuleo, Tungurahua province. White cotton and colored acrylic plain weave, with acrylic supplementary-warp patterning. 2.85 x .075 meters (9 feet 4 inches x 3 inches). The Textile Museum 1988.19.112, Latin American Research Fund.*

132 *Pair of shawl pins, San Luis Chibuleo, Tungurahua province. Lengths: 9 and 9.9 centimeters (3½ and 3⅞ inches). The Textile Museum 1988.19.113, Latin American Research Fund.*

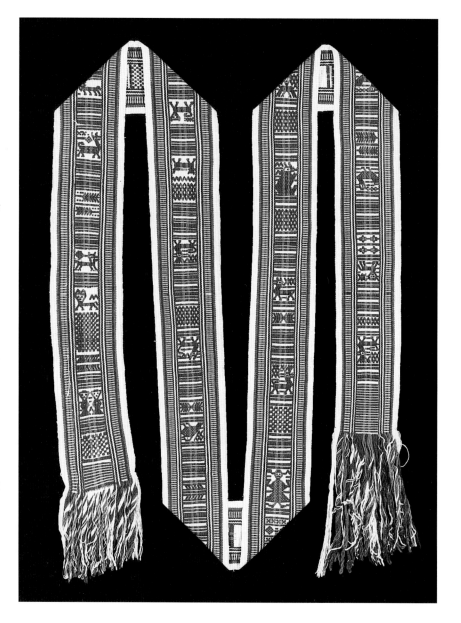

beads at about waist level, and at the tips a small metal pendant, called a *jiga*, which is Spanish for a jig, perhaps because it dances when the women walk. The earrings are worn with the threads at the top looped over the ears, in addition to or instead of piercing the earlobe. This jewelry was said to be purchased from Otavalos who came to the community. The Angaguana women we met in Milquilli were wearing shorter earrings, above waist level.

The hair is parted in the center and wrapped slightly below the nape of the neck with a narrow plain-woven band (*cinta*), usually navy or white. The wrapping is done entirely at the nape of the neck, not down most of the length of the hair as in Otavalo (Fig. 134). Usually the hair in front of the ears is cut short (*rinri*

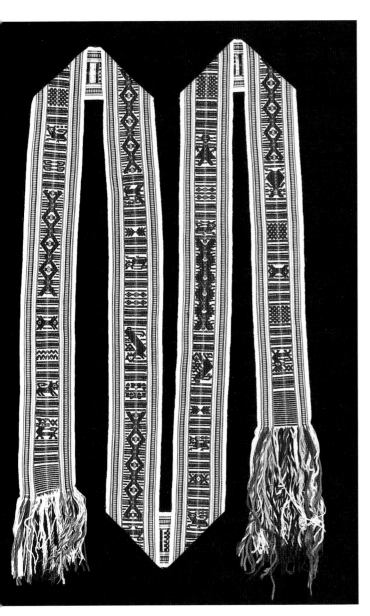

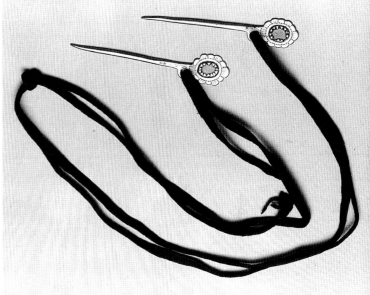

akcha Q., ear hair). Sometimes the hair just behind the ears is secured in place with metal clips.

Men and women wear the same style of hat, which seems to have undergone no recent changes. It is made of felted wool in Pomatúg, near Pelileo, and is obtainable in the Ambato market. Chibuleo and Pilahuín hats have a brim that turns up vertically, giving an effect similar to a sailor's hat (*pinganillu* S., icicle). These hats do not have applied cloth or stitched trim. We were told that Chibuleo wearers tied navy blue thread around the crown of their hats, while the Pilahuín hats have red, purple, or green thread. Some Chibuleo pulled down the front of the brim part way. Angaguana hats have a tall crown and a very narrow brim (*latillu*) (Fig. 134).

133 (left) Chibuleo or Pilahuín woman carrying a child in the Ambato market, Tungurahua province. Slide by Betty Davenport, 1988.

135 (right) Juan José Charco wearing the old style of shirt and pants, San Luis Chibuleo, Tungurahua province (with Lynn Meisch in Chibuleo woman's costume). Photo by Laura M. Miller, 1988.

Some have only colored yarns around the crown as trim, while others have applied cloth trim added around the edge of the brim and the base of the crown (Fig. 129); an informant in Apatuc Arriba told us that the cloth trim was a newer style. Virtually everyone was wearing these handmade hats in 1988; the fedora had not yet made significant inroads.

Most people, both men and women, wear factory-made shoes (*zapatilla* S.). We saw women wearing low tie-up shoes (often without socks) or rubber boots (it being muddy at the time).

Men's costume

There is an old style of man's costume, which was only worn by a few of the oldest men in 1988 (Figs. 135–137). It consists of a white cotton shirt and pants of distinctive cut. The shirt has a high neckband with an opening on the right shoulder (Figs. 135, 136). There is a front placket below the neckband with a hidden opening for the right hand to reach his money pouch (a small shigra). In addition, there is a patch pocket on the right chest. The shirt has a conventional back yoke, long sleeves with cuffs, and square underarm gussets. The pants have wide legs that are ankle length, and a large crotch gusset made of two lens-shaped pieces whose points reach the waistband (Fig. 137). It is cut in a similar way to Salasaca pants but with a rounded instead of straight-sided gusset. The pants we saw in San Luis were undecorated, but a pair shown to us in the Angaguana community of Apatuc Arriba had geometric (probably machine embroidered) decoration around the bottom of the legs.

To hold up the pants, older men wear a plain black (or dark navy blue) wool belt (*ciñidor* S. Fig. 138). The Textile Museum example (1988.22.12) is 9.5 centimeters (3¾ inches) wide and 2.44 meters (8 feet) long including the fringe on each end. It is wound twice around the waist and the ends tied together in front. Our Chibuleo informant told us that Pilahuín men wear red belts, but we were not able to verify this information. In 1988 most men were wearing machine-made shirts and pants in a modern cut. Most men in the Ambato market were wearing white pants, as were our informants in prior-arranged visits to San Luis, but some men wore dark colors such blue or grey, which may be more common for work clothes.

The old-style poncho (called *jirga poncho*), woven of wool, is white with narrow black stripes at even intervals (Fig. 139). The fabric is woven in 2/2 twill weave on treadle looms and is virtually identical to that still used for some everyday ponchos in Chimborazo province. This old-style poncho is longer than contemporary ex-

134 (below) Angaguana woman selling onions in the Pelileo market, Tungurahua province, showing her hair wrap. Photo by Dianne Barske, 1988.

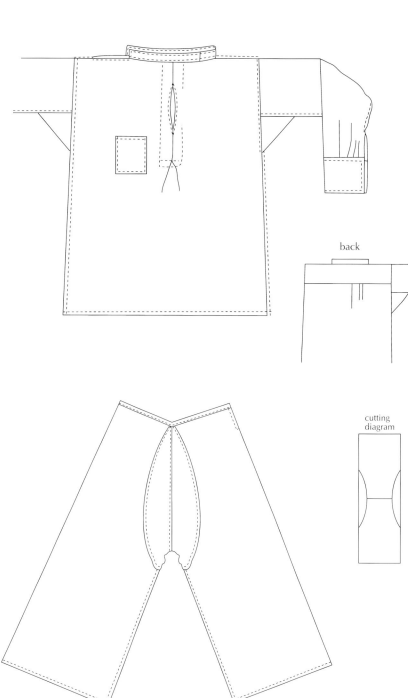

136 *Cut of old-style man's shirt, San Luis Chibuleo, Tungurahua province. The stand-up collar has a side opening. A front slit provides access to a bag carried underneath. The dotted rectangle around the front slit represents the sewing of a rectangle on the inside of the shirt. Overall height: 67.5 centimeters (26½ inches). Based on The Textile Museum 1988.19.115, Latin American Research Fund. Drawing by Laurie McCarriar based on a sketch by Ann P. Rowe.*

137 *Cut of old-style men's pants, San Luis Chibuleo, Tungurahua province. The side opening is a slit with a narrow hem, and no fastening. The legs have a narrow rollup hem. Overall length: 82 centimeters (34¼ inches). Based on The Textile Museum 1988.19.116, Latin American Research Fund. Drawing by Laurie McCarriar based on a sketch by Ann P. Rowe.*

138 *Man wearing the old style of man's shirt and black wool belt, modern poncho, San Luis Chibuleo, Tungurahua province. The pants appear to be locally made, but with a side pocket. Slide by Betty Davenport, 1988.*

139 *Juan José Charco wearing the old style of poncho, San Luis Chibuleo, Tungurahua province (with Lynn Meisch in Chibuleo woman's costume). Photo by Laura M. Miller, 1988.*

amples, covering the torso completely. The Textile Museum example(1988.19.114) is 1.63 by 1.07 meters (64 by 42 inches). It was said to be sometimes worn for weddings now.

The modern poncho is red with two groups of colored warp stripes on each half (Pl. VIII, Fig. 140). It hangs to about waist length (Textile Museum 1988.19.49 is 1.14 by .98 meters or 45 by 38½ inches). The great majority of those that we saw in 1988 were machine woven of acrylic yarns and were being sold in the Ambato market by Otavalos, mestizos-whites, and people from Riobamba. They were available in two shades, a bright red and a darker red. We often saw men wearing two ponchos simultaneously, usually one in each shade. Chibuleo and Angaguana men usually wear these ponchos without any trim, but Pilahuín men often have a blue edge-binding applied in the Ambato market. Exceptions to this distinction could also be found, however.

We saw only a handful of men wearing a poncho of this style that had the end selvedges characteristic of backstrap-loom weaving. Most of these were plain weave and were naturally heavier than the machine-made ones. Although we were told that a few were locally woven, others are marketed by Otavalos in the Ambato market (Textile Museum 1988.19.51, 1.28 by 1.22 meters or 50½ by 48 inches). They do resemble old-style Otavalo ponchos, although the Otavalo style lacks stripes near the center seam. We also saw a small number of men wearing ponchos with a different color on each side. One was red on one side and maroon on the other, and another was red on one side and plaid on the other (Pl. VIIIA). The wearer of the former example said that it had been woven in Otavalo.[6] The latter looks like the prototype for the two-sided machine-made ponchos worn in Otavalo. In general, the red poncho style seems to be a canny Otavalo introduction.

A poncho recorded in the Angaguana community of Apatuc Arriba was dark blue, without stripes or collar, and was said to be locally woven. We also saw an Angaguana man in the Ambato market wearing a blue poncho over a red one; however, blue ponchos did not seem to be a common style.

Some Chibuleo men wear a blue rectangle as a scarf around the neck (*pijurina*). It is made of machine-woven fabric and has machine embroidery on the ends. We saw at least one man with such a scarf worn under his poncho, but most wear it outside the poncho.

Children's costume

Children wear small replicas of adult dress. We saw a group of grade school children, both girls and boys, in Pucara Grande who were all in traditional dress (Pl. VIIIB). Most of the girls were not wearing jewelry, though it is likely that they would wear it for special occasions. Baby-sized red ponchos are available for sale in the Ambato market along with adult-sized ones.

Shigras

Chibuleo shigras are very simple, with the only pattern being stripes in yellow and purple around the top, center, and bottom (Figs. 141, 142). Pilahuín shigras have purple and green stripes and a slightly more elaborate stripe pattern, along with a few embroidered zigzags (Fig. 143). The shigras have four ties. Shigras are not made for sale, and we were able to observe a variety of sizes and shapes locally used for different purposes.

Fine small ones are used by men for carrying money (women tuck money under their blouses or belts). The straps are tied around the neck and the bag tucked under the shirt. Another kind has a drawstring and is used for carrying lunch into the fields (Fig. 142). It is worn with the straps tied over the right shoulder and under the left arm. It is the right size for a roasted guinea pig but evidently other food can be carried as well.

Another shigra was made to fit a gourd bowl. It is also used to carry food. Very large shigras are used to carry potatoes and other crops.

140 Young man in modern poncho, San Luis Chibuleo, Tungurahua province. One way of draping the poncho. Photo by Lynn A. Meisch, 1988.

6. The wearer of the latter claimed to have woven his poncho himself, but some of his other information proved unreliable. In addition, the old-style twill ponchos were certainly not backstrap-loom woven, and we saw no poncho looms in the Chibuleo communities.

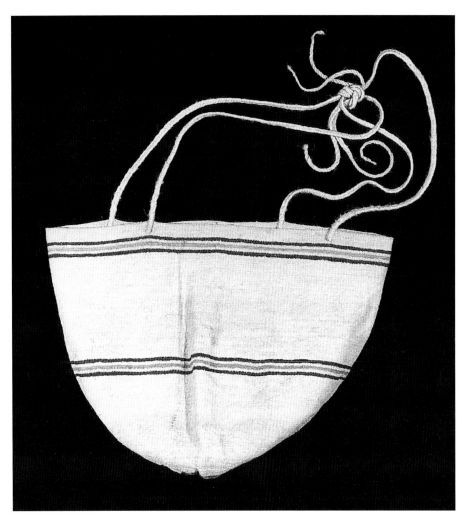

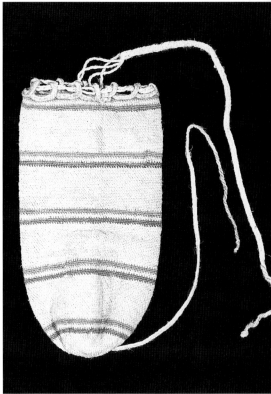

141 Shigra used for carrying bulk foods, San Luis Chibuleo, Tungurahua province. Simple looping with cabuya fiber yarn. Height: 50 cm (19⅝ inches). The Textile Museum 1988.19.127, Latin American Research Fund.

Textile production

Little weaving is now done in these communities except for belts. Even belt weaving does not appear to be a universal skill among the men, so those who do weave make some for sale as well, for women in other families to buy. Chibuleo belts do not seem to be marketed outside the community. Women embroider their own blouses.

Both blue and black acrylic fabric for anakus and shawls is obtainable in the Ambato market, some from Otavalo and some from Riobamba vendors. The embroidery is done by people in the community who specialize in it. We visited a family who proudly showed us their obviously recent-model treadle sewing machine, which was operated by the woman. Although most anakus we saw in use had

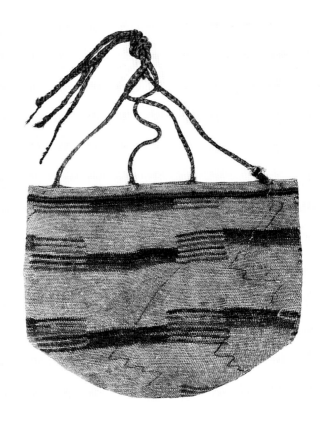

142 *Shigra used for carrying cold lunches to the fields, San Luis Chibuleo, Tungurahua province. Tied over the right shoulder and under the left arm. Simple looping with cabuya fiber yarn. Height: 31 centimeters (12¼ inches), excluding straps. The Textile Museum 1988.19.126, Latin American Research Fund.*

143 *Pilahuín shigra, purchased in San Luis Chibuleo, Tungurahua province. Simple looping with cabuya fiber yarn. Height: 37 centimeters (14½ inches). The Textile Museum 1988.19.72, gift of Maritza Mosquera.*

relatively simple decorative stitching, this family produced elaborate zigzag patterns possible on their new machine, using a variety of different colors. The old-style shirts and pants also were made by community specialists.

Llangahua

Ann P. Rowe

We encountered people who call themselves Llangahua living in the páramo along the road from Ambato to Guaranda, beyond and at higher elevation than the area where the Chibuleo are found.[7] These people are pastoralists and raise sheep with very tight wool and llamas. They also provide horses for expeditions climbing Mount Chimborazo. In addition, we saw donkeys, and people kept chickens, rabbits, cats, and dogs. Most of their houses have adobe walls that are very short and barely visible under the tall thatch roofing. The houses are grouped in small clusters based on extended family groups. There is a plaza in the place called Río Blanco, but few houses nearby.

Women's costume

Women wear several dark blue or black anakus to a length not far below the knee (Fig. 144). Some anakus appeared to be of handwoven fabric and some of commercial fabric. They are pleated in front and in back and secured with at least two belts.

7. The group name was recorded by Lawrence Carpenter, who led several Earthwatch teams into this area. A report written by Edna Elfont includes some information collected by Carpenter. Other Earthwatch volunteers on these trips included CJ and Dayna Elfont, Leonard Evelev, and Marjorie Hirschkind. Lynn Meisch and I also made a trip to Río Blanco. Carpenter noted that the term Llangahua could be a modern-day reflex of at least two earlier Quechua forms: *yanga,* meaning independent, isolated, worthless; or *llanq'a,* meaning to work, working.

144 *Woman in Río Blanco (Llangahua), Tungurahua province. In the foreground is a hand-cranked plying device. Photo by Lynn A. Meisch, 1988.*

The belts we saw in Río Blanco were locally woven, by men for their wives (Fig. 145). They have supplementary-warp patterning in various colors in simple geometric designs on a white ground. Unlike belts of other areas, these are entirely of wool and the colors are not symmetrically arranged. They have four patterned stripes of about equal size, separated by a single colored stripe. The pattern in the central two stripes may be symmetrical and may or may not match the pattern in the side stripes. The weaving is comparatively coarse. Both ends are finished by braiding the warp loop ends in a series of 3-strand braids and putting a short cord loop through the warp loops. The cord is also braided, either a 3-strand braid or a 4-strand square braid. The overall sizes, excluding the end loops, are between 2.27 and 2.92 meters (89¼ and 115 inches) in length and 7 to 9 centimeters (3–3½ inches) wide.

In place of a blouse, or entirely covering a blouse, the women wear one or more commercial sweaters, and over these from one to three rectangular shawls, de-

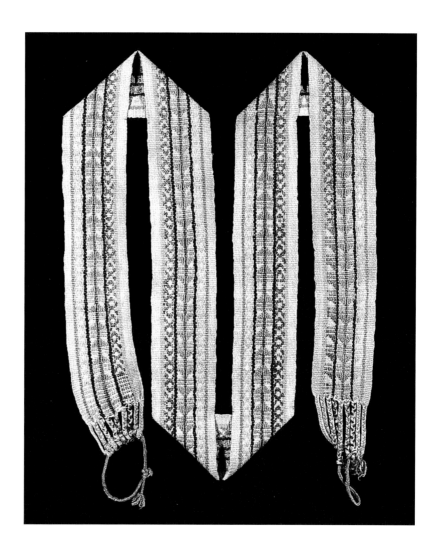

145 *Belt from Río Blanco (Llangahua),*
Tungurahua province. Plain weave with
supplementary-warp patterning, wool. 2.33
x .09 meters (7 feet 7¾ inches x 3½ inches).
The Textile Museum 1988.19.41, Latin
American Research Fund.

pending on the weather. All the shawls seemed to be made of commercial fabrics. Some are fringed on the ends or on the ends and one side, while others are not fringed. Some are fastened on the chest Andean style with a large safety pin, while others are put on overlapping on one shoulder. Both the sweaters and the shawls are in a variety of bright colors. For instance, one woman wore a hot pink shawl over a bright blue one over a maroon one, of which the lower two were fringed, plus a blue sweater. The layering is obviously advantageous in protecting the wearer from the cold of the páramo.

All the women we saw were wearing fedora hats. The hair style was not completely visible, but women use multiple colored plastic barettes over and behind the ears. The forelocks are not cut. Earrings hanging 1–2 centimeters (½–¾ inches) below the ear, of metal with colored stones, are worn. Any necklaces were invisible under the shawls. One woman wore a bracelet of colored beads on each wrist; others wore no bracelets. Some wear a watch. The women we saw were wearing shoes or rubber boots.

Men's costume

Most men wear machine-made clothes including dark pants, a scarf, and a fedora-style hat. However, one man was noted wearing long pants of handwoven undyed wool (Fig. 146). Otherwise, the only handwoven part of the costume is the poncho.

The poncho style is changing, with boys wearing a different one from that of older men. The older style is black, with a 4-centimeter (1½-inch) wide stripe on each side about 8 to 10 centimeters (3–4 inches) from the outside edges, consisting of narrow green, blue, and white stripes (Fig. 146). The Textile Museum examples (1988.19.45 and 1988.19.64a) are 1.64 by 1.52 meters (64½ by 60 inches) and 1.30 by 1.39 meters (51 by 55 inches). They have a warp loop fringe and a collar. Boys and young men were wearing smaller, thicker ponchos mainly in various shades of red, without stripes (Fig. 1). The Textile Museum example (1988.19.77) is 1.20 by 1.21 meters (47–48 inches square). Some were woven of red and black fibers spun together.

Some men also carried whips and wore chaps (*zamarros*). They were barefoot or wore rubber boots.

Shigras

Shigras are made in this area, both for local use and for sale. They have two handles. One we saw in use had a design of only horizontal stripes in brown and black. Another had triangle designs. One made for sale had more colorful stripes and another had innovative designs, including houses, people, airplanes, and trucks. The woman who made the latter said she took shigras to both Latacunga and Ambato to sell.

Textile production

The belts and ponchos are locally woven by men on backstrap looms. The poncho we saw on the loom was undyed, so it appears that the dyeing is often done after the weaving.

The most striking thing about the weaving of these people is that they spin and weave with llama hair as well as with sheep's wool. They said they made the llama hair into blankets, ponchos, and shawls. The thread we were shown was undyed and of mixed natural colors. It seemed quite soft. One old-style poncho we saw was grey (undyed) instead of black and said to have been woven at least partly of llama hair.

146 *A Llangahua man, Manuel Ponina, wearing handmade pants and the old style of poncho, Tungurahua province. Slide © CJ Elfont/Light Isolates Photography, 1988.*

Other Indigenous Peoples

Ann P. Rowe

147 *Woman from Nitón, Tungurahua province, wearing a belt made by Manuel Curay and a pinned upper garment. Slide by Leonard Evelev, 1988.*

8. The first trip to Nitón on July 10, 1988, in which I participated, was led by María Aguí and Gail Felzein, photographs taken by Earthwatch volunteers Leonard Evelev and Carol Mitz, and a report written by Maritza Mosquera. A second trip on July 14 was led by Breenan Conterón, and reported by her and by Leonard Evelev.

9. Discussions with women from this area in the Ambato market were carried out by Breenan Conterón, who also led an Earthwatch team to visit the town. The volunteers visiting Quizapincha and Chachilbana were Betty Davenport, who wrote the report, Adelle Pollock, and Dayna Elfont. Slides of the Ambato market taken by volunteers CJ Elfont and Carol Mitz were also used for this text.

It appears that some indigenous people still inhabit other parts of Tungurahua province, but that, as in central Cotopaxi, they identify primarily by community and not by ethnic group. Also as in central Cotopaxi, the use of a distinctive costume seems to be gradually disappearing.

Nitón

We visited the community of Nitón, located on a ridge on the northeast side of the Salasaca lands.[8] Most people here were wearing commercial clothes and fedoras, but we saw a few women wearing pleated black anakus to below knee length and a few men wearing ponchos. The ponchos did not appear to be of any consistent style, however. We also saw some people wearing a style of handmade white felt hat, with a low rounded crown and a medium wide brim.

When we inquired about weavers, we were told that there was only one active weaver remaining in the community, Manuel Curay, who makes both ponchos and belts. Most of his ponchos are solid color (the one we saw on his loom was solid maroon) and woven on commission. His belts have pink-red, supplementary-warp patterning in geometric designs and he sells them to his neighbors (Fig. 147). His wife, María Teresa Palate, was making a shigra with colored stripes separated by white areas, but using yarn instead of cabuya. She was wearing a backstrap-loom woven anaku and a belt woven by her husband, as well as necklaces of mixed red and white beads. Her sweaters and hat were factory made.

Another woman we met, who was wearing one of Manuel Curay's belts with her two anakus, had in addition to her sweaters, a black wrap over her upper torso secured with shoulder pins, similar to the Salasaca pichu jerga (Fig. 147). She also was wearing a necklace of mixed red and white beads.

The manner of wearing the anaku differs slightly from the practice of other Tungurahua groups discussed. The closing is on the woman's right side, slightly to the front. There are about three pleats on each side of the front, with an unpleated area between them. These anakus are less bulky than the Chibuleo and Llangahua examples.

Quizapincha

A similar style of costume is associated with the area of Quizapincha, a town some 24 kilometers (15 miles) west of Ambato, north of the Chibuleo communities.[9]

We talked to some women from this area in the Ambato market. They wore black anakus pleated in front and not much below the knee in length, which they called *gergueta*. They said that they spun the thread for the anaku and their husbands wove the fabric. The anaku was secured by a handwoven belt (*chumbi*). One of the women, from the village of El Rosario, was wearing two shawls secured with a tupu. The shawls, a red one worn over a green one, were called *wallkarina* (pronounced *washkarina*) and were made from fabrics she described as *cachimira*

148 Woman possibly from the Quizapincha area, at the Ambato market, Tungurahua province. Slide by Carol Mitz, 1988.

(fine wool) and *pañolón*. In general, the shawls worn with this costume are of factory-made fabric.

The woman from El Rosario mentioned above was also wearing necklaces (*wallka*, pronounced *washka*) of various colored beads. The woman who said she was from Quizapincha proper was wearing necklaces predominantly of red beads. A shigra maker we recorded in Quizapincha, who was wearing mostly factory-made clothes, was still wearing her red bead necklaces. The shigras of this area are still looped of cabuya fiber and have brightly colored horizontal stripes, with two handles.

The women recorded by our Earthwatch team in Chachilbana, another community outside of Quizapincha, were wearing anakus of heavy black material that was not obviously pleated. Their belts had simple warp stripe patterning. The older women wore earrings of strands of red and translucent beads that hung down to breast level. Younger girls wore shorter bead earrings or small silver hoops. They wore necklaces of red and white or yellow beads. The costume was completed by factory-made sweaters, shawls pinned with a safety pin, and fedoras.

Some women in this costume were wearing fedoras, but some older people were wearing the same style of handmade hat as we saw in Nitón (Fig. 148). The vendor of this style of hat in the Ambato market said that they were worn in Quizapincha. Adjacent to the hat vendor was a person with a treadle sewing machine who would add a machine-embroidered band around the base of the crown of this hat. The older hats we saw in use often lacked a hatband.

One woman we saw in the Ambato market wearing this handmade hat and the chest length earrings was also wearing a white shawl with embroidery and colored fringe on the ends, somewhat resembling the Salasaca embroidered fiesta shawls (Fig. 149).

Again, there did not seem to be a specific poncho style. One man in the market with the handmade hat style mentioned was wearing a backstrap-loom woven poncho that was red with blue warp and weft stripes. A mestizo-white vendor from Pelileo in the Ambato market had a similar poncho that had been special ordered (Fig. 150). The vendor said that this style is not representative of a specific community or ethnic group.

149 *Woman with embroidered shawl, at the Ambato market, Tungurahua province. Slide © CJ Elfont/Light Isolates Photography, 1988.*

150 *Poncho purchased in the Ambato market, Tungurahua province. Warp-predominant plain weave, red with blue warp and supplementary-weft stripes, wool. 1.45 x 1.38 meters (57 x 54⅜ inches). The Textile Museum 1988.19.50, Latin American Research Fund.*

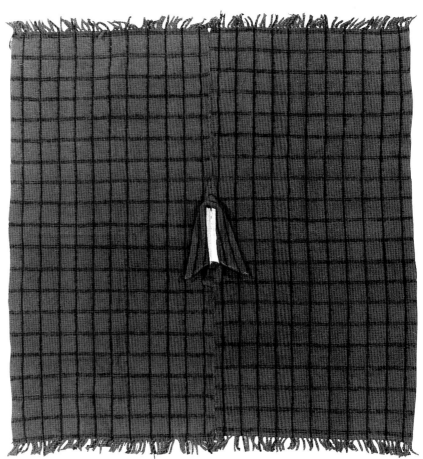

Chapter **8**

Bolivar Province

Laura M. Miller

Guaranda area Guaranda, capital of the province of Bolívar, lies to the west of Chimborazo province, towards the coast, and is separated from Chimborazo by a range of mountains, including Mount Chimborazo (see map, page xx). There is a smaller rise on the western side of the basin, making it a highland valley. The Chimbo river is the major drainage. Indigenous people of the area today do not profess an ethnic group name.

The Saturday Guaranda market (and a secondary market on Wednesday) draws people from the surrounding area including the indigenous communities around the smaller nearby towns of Santa Fe, San Lorenzo, Santiago, La Magdalena, and Guanujo, as well as some people from Simiátug farther north. Unlike the wonderfully confusing diversity of indigenous dress styles seen at the Riobamba or Guamote markets, indigenous people at the Guaranda market, visited in 1988, present a relatively unified appearance.

Women's costume

Women wear several knee-length dark anakus, made of a length of cloth wrapped at the waist and overlapped at the back, either on the left or right side (Fig. 151). The cloth is pleated in front, with as many as twenty or twenty-five folds. The pleated cloth sometimes creates a ridge some four inches thick at the woman's waist. Most of the pleats are made from the woman's right to her left side, pleating the material under. Some women leave a flat panel in the center, and pleat out from that point to either side. Women use the folds of the anaku to hold small items, and several women had leather wallets adorned with silver and gold chains (as in Salasaca) tucked into the pleats across their waists.

Many of the anakus are made from handspun and handwoven wool, which appeared to be treadle-loom woven. One woman wore an undyed anaku made of a mix of both black and white handspun wool (Fig. 152). In addition, some acrylic anaku fabric was for sale in the Guaranda market. According to John Topic, two

162

151 *Women at the Guaranda market,*
Bolívar province. Photo by Ed Healy, 1988.

vendors of treadle-loom woven, wool anaku fabric in the Guaranda market in 1994 said that their cloth was from Otavalo.[1]

The anakus are held in place at the waist with hand-woven belts, including various supplementary-warp patterned belts and the complementary-warp patterned *kawiña chumbi* (see chapter 9, Fig. 161). Most of these belts are woven in central Chimborazo province, particularly Cacha. Some people buy them in Riobamba, but they are also sold in the Guaranda market.

It was difficult to see women's blouses since often a machine-made sweater is worn over them or instead. However, some women do wear white blouses with embroidered cuffs. Prominent embroidery colors are yellow, orange, and green. If these are blouse-slip combinations, they must be shorter than those worn in central Chimborazo since they do not show below the knee-length anakus.

Women wear shoulder wraps called *bayetillas* of factory-made cloth in yellow, royal blue, orange, maroon, or green (Fig. 153). Some of the finer bayetillas are velvet. The bayetillas often have machine embroidery along one long edge (Textile Museum 1988.19.156) or all four edges (TM 1994.20.1), and designs include simple lines and zigzags as well as hearts and flowers. These shawls are a single panel and

1. John Topic is an anthropologist in the Department of Anthropology, Trent University, Peterborough, Ontario.

152 *Woman wearing an undyed anaku, at the Guaranda market, Bolívar province. Slide by Laura M. Miller, 1988.*

153 *Woman wearing a bayetilla, at the Guaranda market, Bolívar province. Photo by Ed Healy, 1988.*

are worn unfolded. The Textile Museum examples are 87.5 by 143 centimeters (34½ by 56¼ inches) and 67 by 132 centimeters (26½ by 52 inches). Of the three vendors of bayetillas in the Guaranda market in 1994, two said theirs were from Otavalo, and one embroidered them locally (John Topic, personal communication). Another style of shawl lacks embroidery, has fringe along the edges, and is worn folded. A woman wears one or two shawls, and if two, they may be the same style or different. These shawls are knotted at the neck or pinned with a large safety pin. There were no tupu-style pins available in the market or in use.

Nearly every indigenous woman uses a warp-resist patterned carrying cloth from Rumipamba in Cotopaxi province to carry goods to and from the market, as well as for carrying their babies. The design called *pata de cabra con mosquito* (S., goat foot with mosquito) in Rumipamba is most commonly used in the Guaranda area (Figs. 111 and 153). In addition, a design consisting of narrow white dashes that we had not seen woven in Rumipamba is popular (Fig. 154). Macanas with unknotted fringes are sold by intermediaries in the market. Shawls in use are finished with six or seven rows of simple overhand knots, which must be done or commissioned by the woman who buys the macana.

Some women wear multiple strands of beads as necklaces, while others wear no necklaces. Gold-colored beads are common, but red, green, yellow, and blue are also worn in various combinations. More traditionally dressed women wear their

154 *Woman with warp-resist patterned shawl, at the Guaranda market, Bolívar province. Photo by Ed Healy, 1988.*

hair pulled back and wrapped with a woven band, but some women wear their hair in two braids.

There is very little generational variation in dress. All females, from the littlest girls to the oldest women, wear the same style of dress.

Both men and women in the Guaranda market wear a distinctive white felt hat with a rounded crown and narrow brim. In shape, the hats are similar to those worn by the older generation in central Cotopaxi province. However, this basic form is embellished by a black band with a line of white in the middle at the base of the crown. There are no streamers. The white felt hat is worn by young and old alike, and few people wear dark-colored fedoras. Some women wear gold or sequined trim along with the black and white hat band. These hats are still being sold in the market.

John Topic, who visited some of the nearby towns in 1993 and 1994, also noted a more modern costume, which seemed to be worn more often by women from south of Guaranda than by women from the north. It includes a fedora and the use of factory-made cloth for skirts. Sometimes these skirts are wrapped and pleated, but sometimes they are tailored. These women usually wear some sort of cardigan sweater instead of a bayetilla, but do use shawls for carrying loads. There is a shop that finishes fedoras in San José de Chimbo.

Men's costume

The poncho is still a major feature of men's dress at the Guaranda market. About half the ponchos are red, a traditional color in the area (Hassaurek 1967:44), some solid red and others with a group of contrasting color stripes near the side edges (Fig. 155). Dark blue ponchos are also common, and some ponchos have stripes in shades of brown. Some ponchos have collars and are trimmed on all four edges with cloth tape. Others with collar and gusset have fringed ends. About half do not have collars.

While a few older men wear white ankle-length pants, which are likely the older style, most wear polyester pants, usually in pine green or royal blue. Men with ponchos also usually wear a hat similar to the women's, but none wore hats with gold trim. Women wearing the distinctive costume far outnumber men with ponchos in the market.

In 1994, Topic observed many men wearing sweaters or jackets rather than ponchos, and fedoras instead of the handmade white hats, including men who accompanied traditionally dressed women. It thus appears that a distinctive men's costume is passing out of use.

Textile production

In 1994, Topic saw a few women spinning wool (two with a vertical spindle in a Z-twist), who said that they took their yarn to weavers who work on commission to have it woven into shawls, ponchos, or blankets. However, neither spinning nor weaving is now common in this area. The only local belt weaver we found was María Margarita Vayes from Cuatro Esquinas (north of Guaranda), who wove ribbed patterns in the twill-derived weave (Fig. 156).[2]

155 *Old man in white pants and red poncho, at the Guaranda market, Bolívar province. Slide by Barbara Buech, 1988.*

156 *María Margarita Vayes, a belt weaver from Cuatro Esquinas, at the Guaranda market, Bolívar province. Slide by Carol Mitz, 1988.*

2. This weaver was encountered by an Earthwatch team, which consisted of Betty Davenport, Carol Mitz, Helen Daly, and Norma Jean Nelson.

Chapter **9**

Central Chimborazo Province

Introduction to

Chimborazo Province

Ann P. Rowe

Chimborazo province is large and culturally diverse, and it was by no means obvious when we started how we could best organize our information. While the Colta area has been studied by a number of anthropologists, other parts of the province have not been studied at all. Since our focus is on costume, the text is organized according to the three different major skirt styles that we found. At this time it is unclear to what degree the skirt styles correlate with other cultural differences, but the areas do seem to reflect separate spheres of cultural interaction, as noted by Rebecca Tolen.

The greater Colta Lake area, defined and described in the following pages by Tolen, lies in the western foothills of the central valley (see map, page xx). It is conventionally designated as "Central Chimborazo" in deference to the fact that farther south the province includes areas on the Pacific side of the Western Cordillera, properly designated "Western Chimborazo," which are outside our range.

The costume is similar throughout Central Chimborazo, characterized by straight, wrapped anakus, until recently full length but now half length, although there are subtle community differences. Costume in Pulucate, Cacha, Majipamba, Troje, and Columbe is all closely related. Since each author has a slightly different approach, however, this text remains in three separate sections. The San Juan area, which lies north of the other communities discussed, is more distinct from them than they are from each other, but since the costume is similar, also employing the straight anaku, we still include it in "Central Chimborazo."

The rest of the province north of Riobamba, the provincial capital, is presently occupied mainly by mestizos-whites. It does, however, have an important industry growing and processing furcraea.

The central valley and the foothills of the Eastern Cordillera are here designated as "Eastern Chimborazo." The anthropological literature is virtually silent on the peoples who wear the striking costumes in this area. We discerned at least three distinct costume zones. Pleated anakus are found in each of them, but the interpretation of this idea and the coordinating elements of the costumes are different in each of the areas we cover.

167

Southern Chimborazo, separated from the north by a desert area between Guamote and Palmira, orients itself south to Cañar province in the gathered skirts of the women's costumes. Lynn Meisch aptly refers to this break as the Great Skirt Divide. In men's costume, old-style pants change from being made of cotton to being made of wool. The cultural break south of Guamote is also noted in Rebecca Tolen's text. Southern Chimborazo was the transition between the Puruhá and Cañar speaking populations before the arrival of the Incas. As in Central Chimborazo, the costumes are similar in this whole area, but there are subtle differences, primarily of hairstyles, jewelry, and hats, from one community to another.

With the help of three Earthwatch teams in 1988 and 1989, we tried to reach as many parts of the province as possible, but we do not claim that our coverage is comprehensive. Nevertheless, as a pioneering effort, we hope that it will prove useful for further work.

Cantón Colta

Rebecca Tolen

Among Ecuadorians, Chimborazo province is probably most associated with popular images of Mount Chimborazo, a massive, snow-capped volcano and Ecuador's tallest mountain (Fig. 157), and with images of indigenous people in tattered, homespun clothing, subservient to and exploited by the province's many haciendas.[1] The hacienda survived as a predominant force in Chimborazo longer than in many other parts of Ecuador and was associated with some of the most extreme forms of social inequality to be found anywhere in the highlands. Over the past several decades, however, central Chimborazo has experienced a period of rapid and thoroughgoing social and cultural transformation, related to the disappearance of haciendas and the increasing participation of rural people in urban markets in labor and goods. In the course of these transformations, both the form of indigenous dress and what it means to be an indigenous person have also changed considerably.

The present discussion deals primarily with Cantón Colta, west of Cantón Riobamba. Other areas, such as San Juan to the north and the Licto-Cebadas area south of the city of Riobamba, belong to rather different zones of social interaction, although they have much in common with communities in Colta. In general, the whole region surrounding Riobamba, or north-central Chimborazo province, constitutes a single social orbit distinct from the part of the province south of Guamote.

The heart of Cantón Colta is a valley between the Western Cordillera and the Yaruquíes hills, a small range of dense, irregular hills lying southwest of Riobamba. This area contains numerous small indigenous communities. The Panamerican highway, the primary artery of transportation through the province, winds along the floor of this valley. In the northern part of the cantón, the town of Cajabamba, the cantonal municipal center, is also the site of an important weekly market on Sundays, devoted to agricultural produce, livestock, and foodstuffs. Although Cacha, in the hills to the east, is in Cantón Riobamba and is in many respects a distinct zone, it has a long history of interaction with communities in Cantón

1. Field work in Chimborazo was conducted in 1988–90, supported by a Fulbright-Hays Doctoral Dissertation Research Abroad Fellowship (U.S. Department of Education) and a Wenner-Gren Foundation for Anthropological Research Student Grant-in-Aid. See also Tolen 1995.

157 *Mount Chimborazo, Chimborazo province, with potato fields at the base. Slide by Lynn A. Meisch, 1989.*

Colta. South of Cajabamba, on a broad plateau, is Colta Lake, a long, narrow lake surrounded by a cluster of indigenous communities, among them Majipamba. This area has been described in several ethnographies (Cornell University 1965; Maynard 1966; Forman 1972; Gellner 1982). The closely spaced, two-story, cement-block houses and churches around the lake give this zone what Bebbington (1990:45) calls its "semi-urbanized" appearance. For several decades, Majipamba has also been the site of an Evangelical Protestant mission complex which is a focal point of the region's indigenous Evangelical movement.

South of the Colta Lake plain, the parish of Columbe begins and hills press more closely on either side of the Panamerican; Troje and Pulucate are in Columbe parish. The small town of Columbe, at the southern extreme of Cantón Colta, has been largely eclipsed in recent years by Riobamba and Cajabamba in its role as political, administrative, and economic center for communities in the parish. South of Cantón Colta, the town of Guamote and the parish of the same name constitute a somewhat distinct social sphere, although Guamote's Thursday market draws many people from communities in southern Cantón Colta. Guamote occupies an intermediary position, in terms of social, political, and economic interaction, between the north-central and southern parts of Chimborazo province.

Central Chimborazo also represents a general region in terms of costume, although there are local variations. Variation, for example, in styles of ponchos, tends to coincide with parish boundaries rather than individual communities (Burgos Guevara 1977:63).

Until relatively recently, rural society in Cantón Colta was organized around the hacienda. Haciendas controlled the largest part of arable land and other key resources, and landowners held a virtual monopoly on social, political, and economic power. The circumstances of particular indigenous communities, even of households within communities, varied, however, from that of *huasipungaje*, in which peasants held usufruct rights to parcels of hacienda land and had significant obligations of labor for the haciendas, to that of "free Indians," who owned some land outright and exchanged limited labor on the haciendas for access to other land and to resources such as pasturage, water, and firewood. Because non-huasipungeros lacked the guarantes of access to land that huasipungeros had and because they had a greater degree of autonomy and mobility, they frequently turned to sources of cash income, including artisanry or small scale commerce (Chiriboga 1986:66). The presence of haciendas, then, had a great effect on modes of livelihood even among those who were not huasipungeros. The image of Colta as an impoverished zone of indigenous people oppressed by white landlords was part of what prompted missionaries, international development programs, and Ecuadorian land reform organizations to make concerted efforts for reform in this zone from the 1960s onward.

Although some large landowners began selling parcels of hacienda land much earlier, in part as a response to trends in national political economy, and in part in attempts to preempt moves for agrarian reform, the agrarian reform laws of 1964 and 1975 had a significant impact on rural Cantón Colta. Indeed, Colta was the part of Chimborazo, and one of the parts of the highlands, most affected by agrarian reform (Bebbington et al. 1992:126). Intense pressure from indigenous groups active in Colta, both through legal claims on land and through protests and land invasions, played an important role in promoting agrarian change (ibid.:122–23).

Despite the redistribution of hacienda lands, most rural families in Colta today find themselves in more precarious circumstances than ever. Parcels of land have been divided through inheritance, and much of the region suffers from severe erosion, crop diseases, and other forms of ecological stress. One of the effects of the decline of haciendas has been a loss of access to pasturage for sheep, since high pastures that were part of haciendas have been parceled and are now used for planting. Consequently, flock sizes have been greatly reduced in Colta, as has wool production.

Households in a few communities that gained high-quality former hacienda lands have been successful in market-oriented farming, raising vegetables for urban markets. Other households have established small-scale family enterprises. Many people from communities near Colta Lake are long-distance merchants in a pattern similar to that found in Otavalo, though not based on a cottage weaving industry, and constitute a small indigenous bourgeoisie, albeit a relatively poor one (Santana 1990:208). This practice has a fairly long history, dating from the hacienda era (Gellner 1982).

The majority of rural families in central Chimborazo, however, have been less fortunate in the face of declining agricultural productivity. Unable to maintain themselves through agriculture alone, most of the rural, indigenous population has responded to this crisis the same way others throughout highland Ecuador have responded, by migrating to cities in search of cash income. Although there has been a significant amount of permanent out-migration, the much more common strategy is that of regular, temporary migration. While migration by married and unmarried women is increasing, the longstanding pattern is one in which men leave for several weeks or a month at a time, leaving the largest part of agricultural labor in the hands of women, children, and the elderly. Most migrants return to the highlands for planting and harvesting and for Carnaval. There are few men under the age of sixty in Colta who have not migrated during a significant part of their lives, and many women have accompanied their husbands for shorter periods. Earlier in this century, coastal plantations were important sites of temporary wage labor, as was the Oriente for a period, but Guayaquil and to a lesser extent highland cities are the more common destinations today. In the city, migrants work as stevedores, street vendors, and construction workers. Income from temporary migration is used to maintain families in the countryside, especially for the expenses of building a house, purchasing food, clothing, and other consumer goods, and paying for children's school expenses. Some of this income is invested in land, but there is relatively little land available for purchase in Colta today.

Despite the prevalence of temporary labor migration, agriculture remains important, and most indigenous people in Colta consider themselves *campesinos*, peasants and rural people. Barley is the most important staple crop, and other grains, tubers, and vegetables are also grown. Most households maintain a few pigs, sheep, and cattle. In most families, agricultural production is oriented toward household consumption, although produce and animals are sold when cash is needed.

The great extent of migration, the continual passage between city and countryside, affects every aspect of life in rural communities in Colta: household organization, gender roles, local political organization, and understandings of what it means to be an indigenous person. Some Colta families have bought market stalls or established other enterprises in Guayaquil, Quito, and elsewhere, and communication between the highlands and communities of Colta migrants in Guayaquil and other parts of the country is rapid and continuous. "Indigenous society," then, has come to comprise both rural and urban components, and the two are not separable: indigenous people do not so much move between two worlds as constitute, through their movement, a world which encompasses both.

Other aspects of the organization of rural society in central Chimborazo have also been transformed in the post-hacienda period. With the disappearance of haciendas, many rural whites, including residents of small towns, have left the countryside, leaving the largest part of rural space under indigenous control (Bebbington 1990:45). The hacienda-centered network of political and economic relations within the rural parish has been transformed, as indigenous communities, now organized as independent *comunas*, have established more direct relations with state and nongovernmental institutions, in relationships no longer mediated by hacienda owners and townspeople. The net effect is one of re-centering political and economic institutions within communities, and bringing these under indigenous control. At the same time, these institutions and their development projects have become important actors in and concerns of political processes within rural communities, creating new forms of dependency upon such institutions (see Lentz 1988). New regional organizations have also emerged that encompass many indigenous communities, with ties to national and international organizations; these include the Indigenous Evangelical Association of Chimborazo and numerous agricultural and artisan cooperatives and associations. Formal education has become a much more important goal for rural people, and many young people have trained to be schoolteachers, a few for other professions such as medicine and law.

The conversion of the majority of the indigenous people of Colta from Catholicism to Evangelical Protestantism represents another important dimension of social change in central Chimborazo in recent decades. Muratorio (1980, 1981) argues that conversion here has been a response to the break-up of the hacienda, a reaction to the Catholic Church's historic support of the hacienda system, and a reaction against racial domination. Much of the appeal of Protestantism for indigenous people lay in the fact that worship was conducted in Quichua, that literacy in Spanish and Quichua was strongly promoted, and that new, more direct and assertive modes of interaction with whites were encouraged; in short, much of the local meaning of Protestantism has to do with how it is used to simultaneously affirm and redefine a distinctively indigenous identity. Conversion has, of course, been associated with the transformation of most aspects of ritual life, which once centered on "fiesta-cargo systems."[2] The latter systems have, however, largely disappeared from Catholic communities as well, suggesting that some aspects of transformation in ritual life have to do with the wider reorganization of rural society, and not only with conversion to Protestantism. Progressive movements for social reform within the Catholic church have also been centered in Chimborazo since the 1960s, although Catholic activists have had relatively little impact in Colta compared to Protestants.

In the course of recent history, "Colta" has also emerged as a distinctive social and cultural space. While only loosely defined in institutional terms, "Colta" as a region has a recognizable social existence, constituted through regional, grassroots, religious, and nonreligious organizations. Marriage between people from different communities within the zone has increased. The generalization of an indigenous style of clothing in synthetic fabrics across this zone is one of the most tangible signs of the creation of new forms of regional indigenous identity, class relations, and social organization.

2. Editor's note: In the fiesta-cargo system, introduced to the Americas by the Spanish, people were forced to spend large sums of money (the *cargo* S.) to sponsor community fiestas, from which they obtained prestige. The system effectively prevented the accumulation of wealth among indigenous people.

Uses of urban and indigenous dress

It has been a commonplace for several decades that the use of indigenous dress was disappearing in central Chimborazo, at least among men (see Cornell 1965; Maynard 1966). Contrary to widespread assumptions about the effect of "modernization" or class and geographic mobility on style of dress in the Andes, however, there has not been a simple linear movement from "indigenous" to "western" styles. What one does find is a situation that is both much more fluid and much more complex than might be expected.

"Western" is, in fact, probably a less useful label than "urban" or "mestizo-white" for describing nonindigenous dress in this context, since the latter terms capture better what is locally most significant, namely, the association of particular garments with cities and/or with white people. Moreover, many garments that were once elements of "urban" dress, such as the fedora, are now so thoroughly incorporated into everyday indigenous dress that they are no longer thought of as "white." A similar process of redefining indigenous-style dress, as well as indigenous identity itself, has gone on continually since the conquest. Many commercially manufactured garments are worn every day and are taken for granted as part of indigenous people's wardrobe today. Nevertheless, it is still a matter of considerable importance within indigenous communities whether, for example, a man ever wears a poncho or a woman wears the anaku, and in what social contexts urban or indigenous styles are worn.

There is some local variation in the extent of use of the poncho in different parts of Cantón Colta. In communities in the northern part of the cantón, most men wear ponchos only around their houses, in the cold of evening and early morning, but usually do not wear them when going about business within the community, in Riobamba or in other towns.[3] In the southern part of the cantón, men wear a poncho much more often around their communities and when traveling within the province, going to Riobamba or other towns to market or do errands. Pulucate seems to represent an extreme of the continuum in the extent to which the poncho continues to be worn: most men in Pulucate continue to wear the poncho most of the time when in the highlands, and only a few men never wear a poncho at all. Although it would be difficult to demonstrate conclusively, it seems to be the case that the poncho is used less in communities that were subject to strong hacienda control, perhaps because in such contexts the poncho carries a stronger stigma of association with a history of submission.

The use of the poncho within the rural community is contrasted, for men, with how they dress when they leave Chimborazo to work. The alternation between wearing a poncho in the countryside and not wearing it in the city is part of the everyday rhythm of labor migration in areas with high rates of temporary migration. The same pattern occurs, for example, in the parish of Flores, south of Riobamba (Farrell, Pachano, and Carrasco 1988:153–54) and in Zumbagua in Cotopaxi province (Weismantel 1988 and this volume). Men returning from the

3. Andrea Allen, personal communication. Allen, of the University of Kentucky, conducted dissertation field work in Gatazo in 1989–90. Miller's comments below also describe this situation.

city, or whole families coming home to the countryside to visit their relatives, are easily identified by their more urban dress. After being away for some time, men may at first resume wearing the poncho only around the house, gradually beginning to wear one when away from the house. This alternation is only partially accounted for by the fact that ponchos, like women's shawls (called *baita*), are too heavy for the heat of Guayaquil, since the same pattern emerges in relation to migration within the highlands.

Among women, by contrast, the use of indigenous dress (anaku, baita, etc.) is virtually universal, whether they are in the rural community or elsewhere. Cantón Colta in general is more homogeneous in this regard than some parts of the highlands, where within a single community some women may wear indigenous dress while others, still identified in some sense as indigenous, wear nonindigenous styles. In Pulucate and, to my knowledge, most of the cantón, all women of all ages wear anaku and baita while in the countryside, and all but a few adult women continue to wear indigenous dress when they migrate. A few adult women who have settled permanently elsewhere (in Guayaquil or in highland cities) have stopped wearing the anaku; this is a sign of their intention not to live in the countryside again and of largely having cut themselves off from their rural kin. Some adolescent girls wear skirts when in the city, but change to anaku when they visit the countryside, and they are likely to use the anaku more once they marry. Young parents who live in the city and/or who do not want their children to be identified as indigenous dress young girls in clothes like those that white children wear, including pants. When these children return to the countryside to visit their grandparents, however, they are dressed in anaku and baita.

In general, men's uses of indigenous and urban modes of dress set up a contrast between city and countryside as ethnically coded spaces, and play upon contrasting and sometimes contradictory aspects of individual social identity. On the other hand, in continuing to use indigenous-style dress when they migrate, women embody and construct the links between the rural and urban dimensions of contemporary indigenous society. It is the dress of migrant women, moreover, that delineates an indigenous space within the city, in and around marketplaces where they work and neighborhoods where they live. A rural/urban distinction does exist within contemporary women's dress of Chimborazo, and this is largely a matter of the contrast between homespun and synthetic indigenous-style garments.

Synthetic indigenous-style clothing

The largest part of indigenous clothing in Cantón Colta today consists of brightly colored and smoothly textured garments, distinctively indigenous in style but made of synthetic, commercially produced fibers and fabrics (Fig. 158). These synthetic garments contrast sharply with the muted colors, highly textured surfaces, weight, and bulk of homespun wool (Pl. IXA). Among indigenous people, wool and synthetics are distinguished in terms of these visual and tactile qualities, but they are

158 *Girls wearing everyday synthetic anakus and baitas, Pulucate, central Chimborazo province. Slide by Rebecca Tolen, 1989.*

distinguished even more in terms of where they come from and where they are worn. Wool clothing is woven within the rural household and is worn in the countryside. Synthetics come from elsewhere, are bought with wages earned in cities, and, while commonly worn in the countryside, are thought of as the clothing of indigenous migration to cities.

Indigenous garments in synthetic fabrics became popular in Chimborazo during the 1970s (Muratorio 1981:513). Synthetics are so taken for granted today that, by 1988, it was hard to elicit detailed accounts of the origin or appearance of this kind of clothing, although people do relate its emergence to the social transformations of recent decades. The most common explanation given, and one that arises in virtually all accounts of this history, is that it was when people began "going to cities," that is, migrating to Guayaquil on a regular basis, that they began wearing these clothes. Otavalo influence is evident in the production and distribution of this kind of clothing, and in the example Otavalos set by their own mode of dress, but people from Chimborazo make no reference to Otavalos in discussing the origins of this style and assert that it was indigenous people from Chimborazo who were the innovators. The use of synthetics may have begun in the communities around Colta Lake and then become more generalized, since people from these communities often appear to be trendsetters today. In local accounts of history, links are also often drawn between conversion to Evangelicalism and the use of synthetics. While synthetics are associated in some way with Protestantism, this seems to be more an expression of historical contemporaneity, and of wider notions of personal comportment, than a statement of causality, and synthetics are used equally among Catholics and Protestants today.

Acrylics and polyesters are the most common synthetic fabrics used for indigenous garments. While synthetic baitas and ponchos may be woven at home using purchased acrylic yarn (and most belts today are woven in acrylic), synthetic garments are spoken of primarily as goods that are purchased rather than made, and are regularly purchased as finished articles in regional markets (Fig. 159). The yarns and fabrics used are produced primarily by the textile industries of Ecuador and Colombia for national markets (see Meisch 1987:59).

Networks of production and distribution of indigenous garments vary depending upon the garment and the kind of fabric, but all indigenous-style synthetic clothing is produced and sold by indigenous people. For example, many anakus, particularly those in elaborately patterned velours, and many ponchos are produced by Otavalos. Otavalos act primarily as wholesalers in Chimborazo markets, while the actual vendors are indigenous people from Chimborazo. Most baitas and simple polyester anakus are produced by people from Chimborazo by cutting lengths of fabric from bolts of commercial cloth and finishing them with machine embroidery.

Synthetic indigenous clothing consists of the same garments, with the same overall form, as homespun wool clothing. For the most part, even the color patterns of wool garments are reproduced, although there are some notable exceptions: fucshia and turquoise are especially popular colors for synthetic baitas and ponchos. The differences between wool and synthetics, then, have little to do with the structure of garments, and have primarily to do with the different contexts of production, consumption, and use of these materials.

The contrast between wool and synthetics is marked in most general terms in everyday speech by the fact that the wool garments are characterized as *runa* (Q., indigenous) in contrast to their synthetic equivalents, giving meaning to otherwise redundant phrases such as *runa baita, runa jirga, runa chumbi*. Wool clothing is also called *maki* (Q., hand[made]), as in *maki baita*, and so forth. Synthetic clothing in general is known as *alli churana*, "good clothing."

Synthetics are valued for being "light" and "soft," while wool is said to be "heavy" and "scratchy." The "strong colors" of synthetics are an important part of their appeal, and are noted approvingly even by people who otherwise prefer wool. On the other hand, synthetics are universally derided as poor protection against cold and rain, while the most valued attribute of wool is that it is warm. Synthetics are valued for being easier to launder, although they also wear out much more quickly than wool garments.

Wool and synthetics also carry racial connotations. Wool clothing is thought of

159 *Synthetic anakus and chumbis for sale in the Riobamba market, central Chimborazo province. Slide by Rebecca Tolen, 1989.*

as in some sense "more indigenous," while using synthetics is spoken of as being "like whites." At first, those who wore synthetics were "scolded" for "dressing like whites." There is a contradiction within such statements, however, because synthetic indigenous clothing is still distinctively indigenous in style and is worn precisely because it identifies the wearer as an indigenous person.

Synthetic indigenous garments are worn most by young people and by people who migrate a great deal. Wool baitas and ponchos are used exclusively in the countryside. Although synthetics are widely used in the countryside, they are still thought of as the kind of clothing one wears to go to cities and, often, to formal public events in the rural community such as weddings, religious meetings, and school events. The local meaning of homespun wool has not remained unchanged. Wool has become more explicitly identified with images of local tradition and indigenous ethnicity. For example, public music performances are held as part of religious revival meetings and for school-related celebrations, such as, during my

160 *Performers in a music contest held during a religious revival meeting, Pulucate, central Chimborazo province. These women are wearing what is locally seen as "traditional" dress: puzu baitas, white wool changallis, kawiña chumbis, and rosarios. Their millma sumbrirus are on the floor in front of them. Slide by Rebecca Tolen, 1989.*

residence, a visit by the wife of the president of Ecuador to inaugurate a child-care center. Performers in such contexts are usually expected to wear wool, rather than synthetic ponchos, baitas, and chumbis (Fig. 160).

The use of homespun wool is by no means limited to such "folkloristic" contexts, however. A few people wear exclusively wool or exclusively synthetics, but most people own several garments of each material. Preferences for one or the other kind of cloth are in general thought of as generational differences, so that, for example, young people are said to prefer acrylic because it is soft, while wool, to which they are "not accustomed," is scratchy. This preference is also considered a matter of generational difference in attitudes toward fashion: young people usually say they prefer synthetics simply because this is the contemporary fashion. In general, young people do in fact use synthetics more, while older people wear wool more often, but there are important qualifications that have to do with the circumstances of particular households as well as with taste and personal preference. For example, widowed women of any age may use synthetics because they lack the resources to have their own wool clothing produced for them. Younger women may wear wool baitas out of preference or because they are warmer for carrying babies. In this case, wearing wool is a sign of the relative well-being of the agricultural component of household economy—that is, the ability to mobilize resources and labor to produce wool baitas.

The use of synthetics is in part a response to the contemporary circumstances of rural households, which make it impossible for people to produce all of their own clothing in wool, even if they wanted to. The popularization of synthetic clothing is not, however, explained by economic necessity alone. Synthetic clothing is also a means of continuing to use some form of indigenous dress in the context of labor migration; in the process, it also embodies new definitions of what it means to be an indigenous person. Homespun wool has been replaced not with "white" or "generic campesino" styles of dress, but through the creation of a new variant of indigenous style. The emergence of this mode of dress, then, goes against the common wisdom that an inevitable process of *cholificación* or *blanqueamiento* (S., whitening), made evident largely through abandonment of indigenous dress, inevitably accompanies changing class positions in the Andes.

Indigenous people feel that in wearing synthetic clothing, they distance themselves from hacienda-era stereotypes of the poor and dirty agricultural laborer who is reticent and submissive in interactions with whites. This style of dress is thus implicated in new modes of personal comportment in which indigenous people may be more direct and assertive in such interactions. Dressed in synthetic baitas, anakus, and ponchos, indigenous people say that they can move more freely in urban spaces (stores, offices, schools); as one woman put it, "when you wear these [synthetic] clothes, you can go into stores and restaurants in the city, and they treat you better." Nevertheless, being publicly identified as indigenous, even wearing synthetic clothing, still makes one subject to many forms of everyday discrimination and coercion. In the context of these everyday relations of power, the use of synthetic indigenous-style clothing represents a kind of insistence upon the maintenance of a distinctively indigenous cultural space.

Distinctions between more "urban" and more "rural" styles exist in women's dress. Besides the broad contrast between baitas of wool and baitas of acrylic, there are also more and less "urban" styles of synthetics. Women who remain in the countryside tend to wear cheaper polyester and acrylic fabrics, while those who spend most of their time in cities may use exclusively expensive synthetics, and dress according to the latest fashion in indigenous dress. New fashions in indigenous dress arise regularly and are brought to the highlands by women who live in Guayaquil. For example, anakus and baitas in patterned velour became popular in 1988–90. While these garments might be everyday dress for women who operated successful market stalls in Guayaquil, they were special-occasion dress for rural women, most often worn for weddings.

The emergence of new styles of indigenous dress in synthetic fabrics has also contributed to homogenizing modes of dress across the region. In general, differences among communities, parishes, or zones have attenuated with the popularization of these garments. As noted above, this regional style in synthetic dress is one of the most tangible expressions of "Colta" as a new kind of social and cultural space.

In short, while the use of synthetic clothing is taken by many outsiders as a sign of deculturation and loss of indigenous tradition (and is viewed with some ambivalence by indigenous people as well), this innovation in indigenous dress is not reducible to any simple distinction between tradition and modernity. Rather, the emergence of this style of dress is bound up with the wider transformation of rural society in complex ways. The single most important point about this style of dress, however, is that it makes it clear that indigenous identity is continually being redefined and recreated by indigenous people themselves, in the context of historical processes.

Elements of Dress in Pulucate

Rebecca Tolen

Pulucate is in the southern part of Cantón Colta, in the parish of Columbe. It has long been known as the most important "free" community (i.e., not part of a hacienda) in the parish. Its status as a free community, and its location in a narrow, steep-sloped valley with relatively poor soils, may account in part for the historic importance of weaving here. As elsewhere in central Chimborazo, people in Pulucate today combine agriculture with regular, temporary migration to Guayaquil.

Contemporary dress in Pulucate is especially striking for two things, compared to some other parts of Cantón Colta. First, it is more homogeneous, both in the fact that the great majority of men and all adult women wear indigenous dress, and in the styles and colors of indigenous garments. Second, wool clothing continues to be produced and worn to a greater extent than in other communities in the region. Pulucate's history as a free community probably contributed to these patterns: modes of dress strongly associated with this local, indigenous sphere appear to have taken on more positive connotations, and played a more important role in the delineation and reproduction of this community, than in other contexts.

Women's costume

Anakus in Pulucate are generally worn long, about ankle length. Adults still speak of their mothers and grandmothers having worn a full-body anaku, presumably the same garment still worn occasionally by older women in the Colta Lake area, but anakus today are half length, or wrap-around skirts. The great majority of anakus worn in Pulucate today are synthetic (polyester or synthetic velour), made by Otavalos, and bought in clothing plazas in Chimborazo markets. Women explain that they are no longer accustomed to wearing wool anakus, which are much heavier, and that synthetics are now the fashion. They also say that they no longer have enough wool to produce anakus even if they wanted to (and black wool is particularly scarce), and choose to use their wool for shawls and ponchos.

Anakus are always blue or black and solid-color, with the exception of recent styles in synthetic velour, which have floral or geometric patterns in the nap (Fig. 159). Most are dark blue, although polyester and velour anakus may range to turquoise-blue and blue-gray. Most anakus have some kind of machine-embroidered border at waist and hem. Everyday anakus are usually embroidered with a few rows of simple multicolored zigzag stitching; more expensive anakus have more elaborate geometric or floral pattern embroidery, often incorporating metallic silver- and gold-colored threads.

The *baita* is a large shawl that is worn wrapped around the shoulders and secured in front with a tupu or large safety pin. *Baita* and *jirga* are both terms borrowed from Spanish and probably dating to the colonial period, when these were names for common obraje products, but both are thought of as Quichua words today. *Baita* is the local rendering of the Spanish word *bayeta;* if any distinction is made between the terms, it is that *bayeta* refers to cloth on the bolt, *baita* to the garment. The term *fachallina,* which elsewhere in highland Ecuador may refer to the shawl itself, is used in Pulucate as the verb for "to put on" or "to wear" a baita.

Handwoven baitas in Pulucate are plain-weave fabrics woven on the treadle loom. Wool baitas are woven with an S-spun (*runa*) warp and a Z-spun (*lluki*) weft. Baitas are solid-color (undyed wool or solid-color acrylic), with the exception of *puzu* (Q., interspersed black and white), a mottled pattern created by using a white warp and black weft. This color pattern, also used in some ponchos, is strongly associated with Pulucate and surrounding communities of Columbe parish. Other common baita colors are white, dark green, and red.

Most baitas in Pulucate are *yanandij* (Q., doubled): woven to double width/length, cut and sewn, and worn folded into a double layer, with the seam worn around the shoulders. Two or more baitas are usually worn at once. Single-layer baitas are called *chulla*, a term that refers to something uneven, unmatched, especially a single element in what should be a pair, such as a single shoe. Chulla baitas are usually synthetic, and it is not clear whether chulla baitas were ever made in wool in Pulucate. While synthetic baitas are very widely used, the baita is the garment that is most often made of handspun wool today, and most of women's spinning is meant for weaving baitas.

The baita is more than an article of adornment. Babies spend the better part of the first years of life on their mothers' backs; likewise, women spend a good part of their lives with children on their backs. The baita creates a space within which babies are nursed and nurtured. Babies and young children are carried inside, secured with a long scarf or with a rolled baita or other cloth that is wrapped, on the outside of the baita, under the child to support its weight and tied around the woman's shoulders. Any kind of object, bundle, or load is carried the same way.

Some tupus used in Pulucate are made of flattened coins (*kullki tupu*), while others are decorated with stones or colored glass or plastic. The tupu or large safety pin that closes the baita is usually worn attached to a long loop of machine-made ribbon (usually bright pink) that hangs loosely around the shoulders over the baita.

The *chumbi* is the only element of indigenous dress today that is by definition handwoven, woven on the backstrap loom. Handwoven belts were once also worn by men, but now only very elderly and very poor men wear them. Most belts today

are woven with acrylic yarn. Although it is fairly rare for anyone to weave a chumbi in wool, wool ones are highly valued by older women when they can be obtained.

Adult women usually wear three belts, a mama chumbi and two wawa chumbis. The mama chumbi is about 9 centimeters (3½ inches) wide and always solid red with narrow blue and/or green borders along the selvedges. Older mama chumbis and the better contemporary examples have a cabuya weft, but many today have a cotton or synthetic weft as well as warp; those made with cabuya are preferred by many women because they are stiffer.

The most common type of wawa chumbi in Pulucate is the *kawiña chumbi* (Fig. 161). This style of belt is apparently worn and woven throughout a good part of northern and central Chimborazo. In the parish of Columbe it is woven much more frequently than any other style. In Pulucate, it is the only pattern known by all men who weave, and it is the only pattern that many men know. The kawiña chumbi carries strong connotations of "tradition" and is essential any time women dress in what is locally seen as the most traditional form of local dress.

The kawiña chumbi is woven entirely of wool or acrylic and always divided into three lengthwise stripes, two in yellow and black or purple with a center stripe in green and red, although in contemporary acrylic belts the exact shades of these colors can vary considerably. The outer edges are red. The designs consist of horizontal bars alternating with small geometric, anthropomorphic, or vaguely animal-shaped motifs. The weave employs complementary sets of warp, so that the colors reverse position on each face of the belt.

Other styles of belt are woven less frequently in Pulucate, for example, that known in Cacha as *esterado*, which has horizontal bars created with the twill-derived weave (Bustos and Pilco 1987:15). These belts are popular, however, as are belts woven in Otavalo, especially among younger women and women who migrate frequently.

Whether the belt is woven at home or purchased, the end loops of the warp yarns are braided until only a tiny loop remains, and then a set of long ties, consisting of commercial ribbons or braided strands of yarn, are slipped through these loops. These are tied together when the belt is wrapped around the waist; many women carry their house keys on the ends of these ties.

The *changalli* (Q., leg- or thigh-wrapping) is a kind of apron, a rectangle of cloth about the length of the anaku and just wide enough to cover the anaku in front (Pl. IXA). If handwoven, the changalli is of the same kind of plain-weave fabric of which baitas are made. Like baitas, wool changallis may be left undyed, they may be puzu, or they may be dyed in the colors also characteristic of baitas. Synthetic changallis are made with fabric and embroidery that match the anaku, and anaku and changalli are frequently sold together. As in the Colta Lake area, the changalli is often worn with the two sides folded inward by a few inches. The changalli is worn today primarily by older women, and it is seen as an "old-fashioned" garment.

Baitas and anakus are worn over a variety of mass-produced, urban-style blouses and cardigan sweaters bought in markets. Most adult women today wear a *camisa*

161 *Kawiña chumbi, complementary-warp weave, wool. This example was worn in Majipamba, central Chimborazo province, but the style is similar throughout the province. 1.33 x .075 meters (52⅜ x 3 inches), excluding ties. The Textile Museum 1988.19.108, Latin American Research Fund.*

bordada (S., embroidered shirt) as an undergarment, a full-length blouse/slip with a slit opening at the neck. It is made of white cotton or synthetic fabric and has embroidery at the neck and cuffs. These garments are purchased in marketplaces. Although they are probably made in various places, people from Troje seem to specialize in making them for sale. In place of the camisa bordada, many women of all ages, but especially younger women, wear full-length, usually brightly colored, factory-produced slips.

Women's hair is worn long, straight, and tightly bound from nape to waist with a *cinta*, or ribbon. A way of wearing the hair popular until a few decades ago involves parting it at the sides, and binding the back while leaving shorter lengths in front hanging loose, on either side of the face. The wrapped ponytail is usually worn tucked inside the baita. Girls and young women who live in cities may wear bangs or perm their hair, but these hairstyles are more popular in the communities around Colta Lake than in Pulucate and Columbe parish. Young women and girls also may secure their hair with urban-style ties, barrettes, etc.; these styles, again, are more popular among young urban women.

The cinta is the simplest textile woven by hand in Pulucate, and is the first textile boys learn to weave when they are growing up. By far the most common pattern for cintas in Pulucate is a simple red, fucshia, or pink band with two narrow, length-wise stripes of blue and white bars. Purchased cintas in other color patterns are sometimes worn. Cintas have a long string or ribbon at the end that is used to tie the hair; the cinta is then wrapped, from about the midway point, up to the nape of the neck and then back down, until just a few inches of hair are showing.

The *lishtu* (*lista* S., stripe) is a kind of carrying cloth worn around the shoulders, over the baitas. It is treadle-loom woven, white, with narrow, closely spaced hori-zontal stripes of red and blue. It is like the changalli in being thought of as a "traditional" garment, but is less commonly used today than the changalli. For carrying cloths, women may use baitas or lengths of commercial cloth stamped in small floral patterns. Unlike the baita, these cloths are treated more like utilitarian objects than like articles of dress.

Most women wear earrings, multiple strands of bead necklaces, and bead wrist wrappings. There is considerable variety in these today, and preferences vary a great deal depending on age and on rural or urban residence. Religious affiliation also plays a role, as some Evangelical churches prohibit women from wearing necklaces and earrings.

For both women and men, and for the majority of people of all ages, hats are an important part of everyday dress in virtually all contexts. Two styles are thought of as distinctively indigenous. The *millma sumbriru* (Q., wool + S., hat) is a round, white hat of hand-felted wool like that worn elsewhere in the province (Pl. IX). In Pulucate, it may be left undecorated or may be decorated with a bit of colored machine embroidery around the crown and brim, and a wide black ribbon wrapped around the base of the crown; the ends of this ribbon hang down and are decorated with yarn tassels. As everyday wear, these hats are most likely to be worn by elderly women and men. They are also often worn by girls and women of all ages as fairly festive dress for going to market or to public events. While these hats are seen as "old-fashioned," they still carry a strong emotional charge in Pulucate; both women and men of all ages may put them on, for example, to pose for a family photograph or in other contexts in which they want to dress up.

The more common and more contemporary style is the *pañu sumbriru* (*paño* S., wool fabric), the small fedora worn by indigenous people throughout central Chimborazo. This style of hat, as recently as the 1960s, was considered a mestizo style, and is still worn by some rural whites or mestizos, but it has become an essential part of indigenous dress. In cities, women may continue to use the fedora, but usually do not wear hats at all.

All but the poorest elderly women wear shoes today, at least when away from their houses. These are primarily soft plastic loafers or slippers in black, brown, or bright colors such as purple and turquoise. Various styles of cloth and canvas slippers are also worn. Young women and women who live in cities may wear a variety of other styles of inexpensive flat or low-heeled shoes and sandals.

Men's costume

Most of indigenous men's clothing is not that different from the dress of non-indigenous men in comparable circumstances: they dress much like nonindigenous farmers, workers, or students. Their wardrobe thus includes mass-produced shirts, pants, sweaters, and jackets in a range of styles, and work boots, tennis shoes, or loafers. The only distinctively indigenous element of men's clothing that is widely worn in Pulucate today is the poncho (Pl. IXB).

Two terms with somewhat different meanings are used in Pulucate to refer to the garment known in English and Spanish as a poncho. *Jirga*, the most common style of poncho woven and worn in Pulucate, is a collarless poncho in a twill weave, woven on the treadle loom. It is either white with thin black stripes spaced about 2.5 centimeters (1 inch) apart, or has black and grey stripes. The latter color pattern is called *puzu* and is the one most identified with Pulucate, although used in neighboring communities of Columbe parish as well. White jirgas may either be left undyed or dyed red or purple. Jirgas are also woven in acrylic in the same color patterns.

Poncho refers to ponchos with collars, such as the Otavalo style, or to ponchos that are bought in the market, such as the Cacha poncho. While *jirga* and *baita* are derived from Spanish words, locally they are considered Quichua terms, so that people may point out that *poncho* means *jirga* in Spanish. But the terms also imply a distinction between a household product and a commodity.

A very popular style of synthetic poncho that is usually purchased, rather than woven at home, is what is called the *Cacha poncho* in Pulucate and elsewhere in Cantón Colta. This style is red (sometimes hot pink or blue) with bands of bright, narrow, multicolored stripes and short looped fringe. It is extremely popular among young men and those who migrate frequently, although it is also almost always worn by male participants in wedding ceremonies. Most "Cacha ponchos" are now produced on electric looms by Otavalos, and the style seems to represent an Otavalo reinterpretation, for a mass market, of the handwoven striped ponchos made in Cacha. While the handwoven prototype was worn primarily for weddings and fiestas, the machine-made version is found over a wider geographic range and in more everyday contexts.

Another prestigious style of poncho is the heavy, dark blue "Otavalo" poncho with a collar, the style that is plaid on one side and machine-woven in Quito for use in Otavalo (see Fig. 54). These ponchos are worn primarily by middle-aged and elderly men as relatively formal dress. A heavy blue poncho machine-woven of acrylic with collar and stripes of bright colors, which is associated with Colta, is also sometimes worn, as is the style of thick red wool poncho woven on the backstrap loom and worn in communities around Guamote.

Now and then, one sees very elderly men in Pulucate wearing the kushma, a garment like a narrow poncho worn over the shirt and under the poncho. The kushma was woven in one panel on the backstrap loom, predominantly of black wool, with red and white stripes along the side edges.

Most men wear the handmade felt hat or the fedora, although some other kinds of hats are also popular and are associated with migration. The most popular is the baseball cap, but men and teenage boys experiment quite a bit with other new styles they find in markets. These more urban styles introduce a gender distinction in headgear, since women do not wear them. Young men who work or study outside the community may stop wearing hats altogether. Their elders see these "students," with their *lluchu umaguna* (Q., naked heads), as "going around naked."

Textile production

Pulucate is known within the region as something of a center of indigenous textile production. While the amount of weaving has decreased greatly in recent years, as it has throughout central Chimborazo, a good deal of household energy is still devoted to it, more so in Pulucate than in many other communities in Cantón Colta. Some weavers regularly or occasionally weave for sale or on a commission basis, but by far the largest part of textile production is for household use, and local views of weaving stress production for household use rather than for sale: weaving is locally seen as an ethnically indigenous "subsistence" activity.

Textile production, ideally, is organized on the basis of a complementarity of men's and women's tasks, and in keeping with cycles of agricultural production and daily activity. Weaving is men's work (although a few women weave for themselves), while spinning is the quintessentially feminine skill (although many older men are adept spinners). Women spin while walking everywhere and in any moments of the day when their hands are not otherwise occupied. Evangelicals do not, however, spin or weave (or plow or do other major agricultural labor) on Sundays or while week-long religious revivals are in progress.

Women also crochet shigras with acrylic yarn. This activity has largely replaced spinning as the favorite pastime and most cultivated skill among young women and girls. Shigras, which are carried by men and women, were formerly made with cabuya fiber in simple looping. Crocheting was introduced to the region by white schoolteachers, probably in the mid- to late 1970s. Some of the most popular designs for shigras incorporate names of people and places.

Most dyeing of cloth is commissioned to specialists who receive and deliver goods in market plazas. These dyers are for the most part mestizos-whites from small towns in other parts of the province. Mending of clothing is done by men on treadle sewing machines at home.

Majipamba, Troje, and Cacha

Laura M. Miller and Ann P. Rowe

Our Colta data is from the community of Majipamba, or Media Colta, as it is also known, which lies near and directly west of the lake.[4] No weaving of traditional garments is now done there, nor do the men know how to weave, although some weaving was still being done in the 1960s and some families still have looms. For example, in the family we talked to, the loom had belonged to the father of the older woman. Troje is a former hacienda, located south of Colta, one valley north of Pulucate.

There are sixteen Cacha communities, with a total of some 6,500 people (Arrieta 1984:113–19), lying in the dry hills southwest of Riobamba beyond the town of Yaruquíes in Cantón Riobamba. It appears that the costume among these communities is similar, but our most detailed data was collected in Cacha Obraje. This village was presumably once the site of a colonial obraje, and still is where the most weaving is done, notably the warp-resist patterned ponchos and belts. Some supplementary information from Cacha Machángara, which is the parish center, is also included.

In all of these areas, three levels of generational change in dress exist, one style worn by people born shortly after the turn of the century, one worn by people born in the 1930s and 1940s, and a third worn by younger people. Of course, people may wear elements from one or more of these basic divisions depending on their taste and means as well as their age. The rate of change also differs slightly from one community to another.

Regional variation in dress in this area is now scarcely apparent, due mainly to the fact that younger people wear purchased machine-made clothing rather than locally handwoven garments. Where we do have data on older styles of dress, a general pattern still seems evident, possibly resulting in part from the fact that many items of dress are/were undecorated, as well as from the fact that weaving was often done on a professional as well as on a domestic basis. Because of the basic similarities in costume styles in the three areas, the description has been consolidated, with regional differences highlighted when they are known.

4. Most field information presented here is from Laura Miller. The descriptions of Textile Museum pieces and some interpretive comments have been added by Ann Rowe. Our informants were friends of the late Sylvia Forman, an anthropologist who had worked in this area in 1968, 1970–71, 1974, and 1988 (1972, 1977). Earthwatch 1988 team 3 volunteers who assisted in gathering data were Kathy Jahnke, Emily Marsland, Ellen McQueary, Robyn Potter, Louise Taylor, and Lorraine O'Neal.

Old-style women's costume

The old style of women's dress in this area is the most conservative in Ecuador, and resembles Inca women's costume to a remarkable degree (Fig. 162). In the Colta area, it is still worn by the very oldest women. We documented the former use of a similar costume in Cacha, Pulucate, and Columbe, and it was probably worn throughout the area.

The key component in this costume is a wrapped dress that covers the body from neck to ankles. In Majipamba, it is now called simply *anaku*, while in Cacha it is called *pichu anaku*. It consists of two lengths of dark navy or black wool backstrap-loom woven cloth, of plied (S-spun, two-plied Z) yarns, sewn together along one side selvedge. In all five examples examined, two collected in Majipamba (Textile Museum 1988.22.2, 1993.18.1) and three purchased in the Riobamba market from Pulucate women (Textile Museum 1989.22.50, 1989.22.53, 1989.22.67), each panel has four selvedges. Two examples have in addition a plain tubular-woven edge binding on the outside edges. In general, the two lengths are the same size. However, one example from Majipamba (1988.22.2) consists of panels that were not originally made to match. In this case, the wider piece was worn on the bottom and the narrower piece on the upper body. The weft direction (height) of the five pieces ranges from 1.30 to 1.42 meters (51–56 inches), and the warp direction (width as worn) from 1.50 to 1.67 meters (59–66 inches).

Sebastiana Chimbolema in Majipamba (born ca. 1920), who wore this costume until 1985 when her daughters convinced her to change to the more modern style, explained to us how the garment was put on, demonstrating it on one of our Earthwatch volunteers (Figs. 163–168). The fabric is wrapped around the body with the warp horizontal. It overlaps at the back, on the right side. The top edges of the cloth are brought over the shoulders with the back overlapping the front. First, the fabric is adjusted over the left shoulder, creating the left armhole, and then it is pinned, first on the right (Fig. 163) and then the left, using straight pins called *wawa tupu* or *rigra tupu* (Q., baby pin or upper arm pin) that are connected to each other by a braided cord (*watu* Q.). The pins are about 7.5 centimeters (3 inches) long, and appear to be made of brass (Fig. 170). The pins are inserted front to back, and the cord connecting them is laced around the pins in a figure eight to secure them.

Once the shoulders are secured, the anaku is folded up at the waist to bring the hem a few inches above the ground (Fig. 164). The woman uses the fold as a pocket for small items. After the fold is in place, belts are wrapped at the waist. The first one is a supplementary-warp patterned belt (*wawa chumbi*) some 7.5 centimeters (3 inches) wide (Fig. 165). Supplementary-warp patterned belts are woven in Cacha, Troje, and probably other nearby places, both for local use and for sale. Women in the Colta area purchase their belts in the Cajabamba or Riobamba markets. They braid the unwoven warp loops at the end of the belt and add long braided loop ties at both ends.

162 Sebastiana Chimbolema of Majipamba, central Chimborazo province, wearing the old-style women's dress except for the hat. Photo by Laura M. Miller, 1988.

163

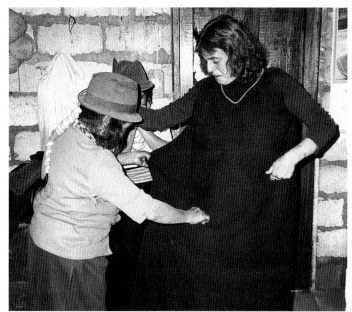

164

165

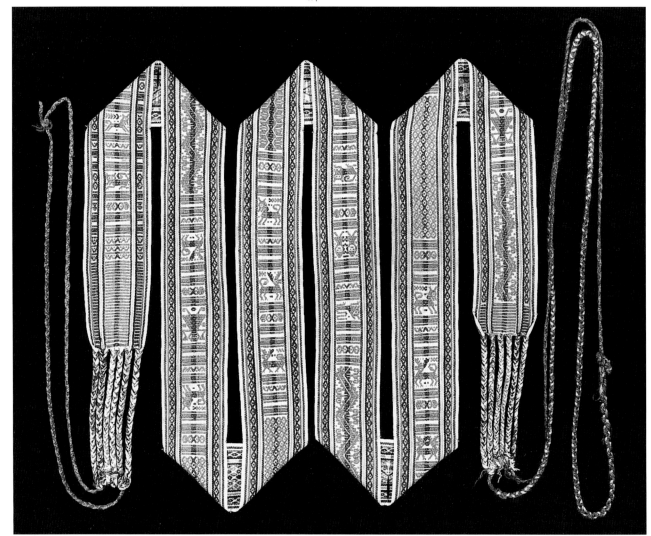

166

167

168

163 *Sebastiana Chimbolema and Manuela Lema dressing Earthwatch volunteer Kathy Jahnke in the old-style Colta women's dress. After checking the amount of fabric needed for the left shoulder, the right shoulder is adjusted and pinned. Majipamba, central Chimborazo province. Photos by Laura M. Miller, 1988.*

164 *A fold is taken at the waist of the dress in order to adjust the length.*

165 *Belt worn in Majipamba, central Chimborazo province. Cotton plain weave, with wool supplementary-warp patterning. 2.88 x .07 meters (9 feet 5⅜ x 2¾ inches), excluding ties. The Textile Museum 1988.22.5, Latin American Research Fund.*

166 *The changalli is added.*

167 *The mama chumbi is put on with its center in front.*

168 *The kawiña chumbi is wrapped and tied over the mama chumbi.*

After the first belt has been wrapped twice around the body, the *changalli* (Q.) or *delantal* (S., apron) is added (Fig. 166). This piece of fabric covers the front of the body from the waist to the ground and in Majipamba is usually dark navy blue or black, matching the anaku. It is secured by the last wraps of the first belt, after which the ties on the belt are tied together. The changalli is made of a single loom panel, 72–75 centimeters (28–29 inches) wide, and ranging from 63 to 93 centimeters (25–36½ inches) long, worn with the warp vertical (Textile Museum 1988.22.6, 1993.18.3 from Majipamba and 1989.22.55). Although it could be of backstrap-loom woven fabric, The Textile Museum examples have hemmed ends, are less strongly warp-faced than the dresses, are woven of S-spun (unplied) yarns, and so are probably treadle-loom woven. One example from Majipamba (TM1993.18.3) has been brushed to raise some nap. Often, both top corners are folded over toward the center front (Fig. 167).

Then the next belt, the mama chumbi, with wool warp and cabuya fiber weft, is added (Fig. 167). The mama chumbi is not as long as the other belts, 98–112 centimeters (38½–44 inches), and has no ties. The example used in the demonstration (Textile Museum 1988.22.4) was 16 centimeters wide (6½ inches) and 1.005 meters long (39½ inches), but other old examples range from 23 centimeters (9 inches) to 9 centimeters wide (3½ inches) and .98 to 1.12 meters long (38½ to 44 inches). It goes around the waist once, with a slight overlap at the back.

On top of the mama chumbi, a kawiña chumbi is wrapped (Fig. 168). A small change purse is affixed to the ties of the kawiña chumbi. Chimborazo province is the only area of Ecuador where the belt ties are actually tied instead of simply being tucked in. Three belts are also worn in Troje, but only the mama chumbi and an

189 *Central Chimborazo Province*

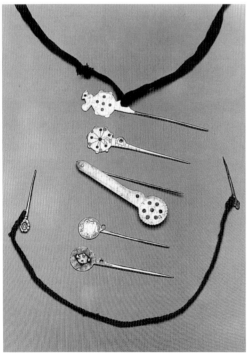

outer belt, called *chumbillina*, are worn in Cacha. The outer belt is either supplementary-warp patterned or the kawiña chumbi.

The shoulder wraps, called *baita*, are worn with the warp horizontal, so that the ends, often finished with contrast color thread, form a decorative edge in front (Fig. 162). More than one shawl may be worn at once. The shawls are wool, of either one loom panel or of two sewn together (called *yanandij baita*).

In Majipamba, dark-colored shawls were worn for everyday use. We were told that red, purple, green, and pink shawls were used at fiestas, and only for fiestas. The old-style Colta shawls we saw had technical features like the changalli and were probably treadle-loom woven. In contrast with Pulucate, the warp and weft are both S-spun. The one-panel shawls are around 1.38 by .74 meters (54 by 29 inches) in size (e.g., TM 1988.22.9). The two-panel shawls are twice the size of the one-panel examples.

In Cacha, shawls are sometimes backstrap-loom woven (Fig. 169). Those we saw are one panel, 68 centimeters (27 inches) wide and 1.26–1.28 meters (49½–50½ inches) long, with a short warp loop fringe on each end (TM 1988.19.135 and 136). They often have some machine-embroidered detail on the ends and are usually dyed after weaving. Shawl colors worn in Cacha are pink, purple, red, and wine.

The shawls are secured with a tupu (Fig. 170). A common style has a shaft about 12.5 centimeters (5 inches) long, and the head has scalloped edges, with small pieces of colored glass set in. Another style has a large piece of colored glass in the center. The tupu has a loop near the head through which a loop of braid or ribbon is passed. This loop is worn around the neck.

The old-style earrings (*orejeras* S.) are made of two loops of red seed beads and fall to below the waist (Fig. 162). A pair from Majipamba measures 70 centimeters (27½ inches) long (TM 1988.22.7a,b), and a pair from Cacha is 54.5 centimeters (21½ inches) long (TM 1988.22.52a,b). Other examples are a full meter (39½ inches) (TM 1988.19.149a,b). Coins are placed at the lowest point in both the Cacha and Colta areas. The earrings are commonly tucked underneath the waist belts to support them and take the weight from the woman's ear lobes.

Women also wear necklaces (*wallka*). In the Colta area, old-style beads are of many colors, while in Cacha, old-style beads are red. In these older necklaces, coins or commemorative religious medallions, strung on edge, are sometimes interspersed with the beads. In the late 1970s most women stopped wearing them, as a result of Evangelical missionaries proselytizing in the province who apparently thought they looked too much like rosaries, which were associated with the Catholic faith and fiestas. Only a few old women now wear this style on special occasions.

Strings of small beads in a variety of colors are also worn on the wrists by older women in the Colta area. Women also wear multiple steel finger rings.

Conservative women leave the front locks of their hair loose at the side in a style called *frente akcha* (S., front or forehead; Q., hair). Some women bleach the unbound forelocks, though this practice is rare today (Pl. X). The rest of the hair is long and wrapped from the nape of the neck down.

In Majipamba, the hair is wrapped first with a cord called *akcha watana cordón* (Fig. 171). The Textile Museum example (1988.22.11b), is made of purple wool, spun, plied, and re-plied twice (S–2Z–4S–2Z) and is a meter (39½ inches) long. This cord is wrapped from the nape of the neck down to the middle of the length of hair. Then the hair is wrapped with a backstrap-loom woven hairband called *akcha watana cinta*. The wrapping begins in the middle of the hank of hair, where the cord left off, and continues down to the bottom; then the hair is wrapped back up to the nape of the neck, and then down to the middle where the wrap started (Fig. 172).

The hairband worn in Majipamba is distinctive (Fig. 173). It has a dark green warp stripe in the center and on each side of the pattern. The pattern is woven with dark red wool and white cotton in complementary-warp weave in a zigzag and dot design. The outer edges have white cotton stripes flanking black wool ones. The size is around 4 centimeters (1½ inches) wide and 1.60 meters (63 inches) long (e.g., TM 1988.22.11a), with braided loops added at both ends like the belts. Similar hairbands are made in Cacha, although plain weave or supplementary-warp patterned hairbands are also used in Cacha.

The old-style hat worn by Colta women is made of felted white wool, with a rounded crown and medium brim (Fig. 184, on Earthwatch volunteer). These hats are brought in from the Ambato area and presumably are made in Pomatúg. The brim is turned down in the front and up in the back. Around the base of the crown is a black ribbon, that continues down into long streamers, the ends of which are embroidered in red and green, and fringed. The streamers are worn hanging down on the side (usually left).

The old-style hats of Troje are similar, with a turned-up brim and a black ribbon, but without streamers. The Cacha hats are smaller. An old woman in

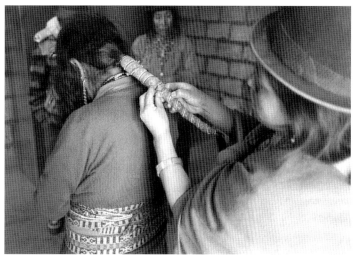

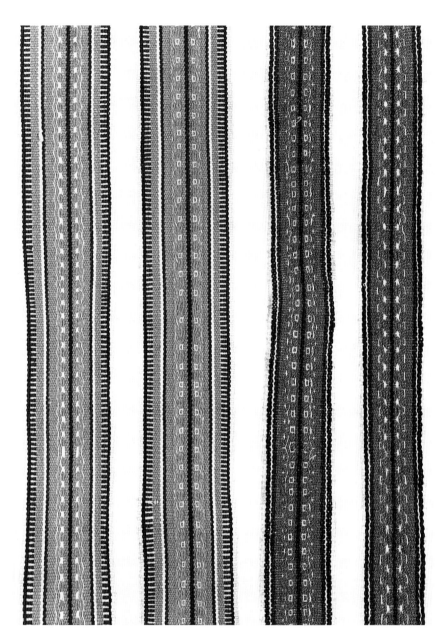

173 *Details of two hair ties in the Majipamba style, central Chimborazo province. Warp-faced plain weave side and center stripes, with the design stripes in complementary-warp weave, dark red (with green accents) acrylic (left) or wool (right) and white cotton. Widths: 6.3 and 4.5 centimeters (2½ and 1¾ inches). The Textile Museum, left: 1989.22.49, right: 1984.46.11, Latin American Research Fund.*

Cacha Obraje was wearing one that lacked any ribbon trim (Fig. 169). However, for fiesta, these hats are currently worn with a light blue ribbon machine embroidered with floral designs around the crown, and with the streamers worn on the side (Fig. 184). We were told that similar hats were formerly worn on a daily basis.

Women formerly went barefoot.

For carrying small items, older women use a looped bag (*shigra*). Looped bags from Chimborazo province have two carrying straps instead of the four found in the Cotopaxi examples (Fig. 174). They have horizontal colored stripes, and usually some linear zigzag patterning embroidered on the outside. Four shigras collected

174 *Shigra from Majipamba, central Chimborazo province, probably made ca. 1970. Simple looping of furcraea fiber yarn. Height: 24 centimeters (9½ inches). The Textile Museum 1993.18.11, gift of Sylvia Helen Forman.*

by anthropologist Sylvia Forman, presumably in Majipamba in 1970–71, have horizontal stripes in purple, pink or orange, and green.

Old-style carrying cloths are of white cotton with dark wool weft stripes at intervals, woven on a treadle loom, with hemmed ends. The loom width is similar to the wool shawls, but they tend to be longer. The Textile Museum examples (1988.19.148 and 1989.22.51) are 1.56 and 1.64 meters (61½, 64½ inches) long.

Contemporary women's costume

Most women today wear an anaku that is only half length, covering the body from the waist down. In the Cacha-Colta-Troje area it is worn ankle length (Figs. 175–177). It is still wrapped with the opening at the back, on the woman's right side. At the front, two folds are made, one on each side of the front, to take up excess fabric at the waist. In Majipamba, both folds are toward the right, while in Troje, both folds face the center. Older women may wear a half-length anaku that is handspun and handwoven and may still wear the changalli. Changallis of machine-made fabric, for example, in Majipamba, may be hemmed on all edges and have simple machine-embroidered motifs at the lower corners.

Younger women mostly wear anakus made of navy blue machine-made acrylic

175 Manuela Lema with baby Elizbeth and Sebastiana Chimbolema in contemporary costume, Majipamba, central Chimborazo province. Sebastiana has unbound forelocks and wears a changalli, while her daughter does not. Photo by Lynn A. Meisch, 1989.

176 A woman and two girls (Ipo-Pilco family) from Cacha Obraje, central Chimborazo province. The woman's shawl is woven on the backstrap loom, her beads are red, and her anaku is fuller than those of the girls, who are wearing shawls and anakus of synthetic fabric. Photo by Laura M. Miller, 1989.

177 María Juany and Rebeca Mullo Yumisaca from Troje, central Chimborazo province, wearing anakus and shawls of synthetic fabric. Photo by Laura M. Miller, 1989.

material with some machine embroidery at the bottom, which are purchased in the market from Otavalos or local indigenous vendors. In Chimborazo anakus, the hem has only a couple of lines of straight stitching or a simple zigzag pattern in machine embroidery. We talked to a young woman in Cacha Obraje who wore an anaku with Otavalo-style floral embroidery at her waist and the local design of a few parallel lines and zigzags placed at the other hem. This embroidery is done by machine in the Riobamba market.

These anakus are still supported by handwoven belts. Modern mama chumbis are narrower than most older ones, have acrylic instead of wool warp, and often have cotton instead of furcraea weft. Acrylic yarn has also been substituted for wool in other styles of belts. Considerable belt weaving is still done in Cacha (Figs. 178–180). In addition to the locally made styles, Otavalo belts may also be worn.

With their half-length anaku, some women wear a full-length blouse-shift combination (*camisa*) (Fig. 181). Modern camisas are embroidered with cotton thread either by hand or machine on machine-made cloth, either cotton or synthetic. They have long sleeves, embroidered on both the cuffs and the mid-forearm. They have a short yoke framing the round neck opening and a vertical slit extending below the yoke. There may be embroidery both around the neck and around the front placket (*pichu*), and on the edges of the underarm gussets. The lower edge is scalloped and often also has some simple embroidery.

In Troje, blouses with this type of scalloped hem are referred to as *camisa chaki picada* (*chaki* Q., foot; *picada* S., chopped or pierced, an interesting mix of Spanish

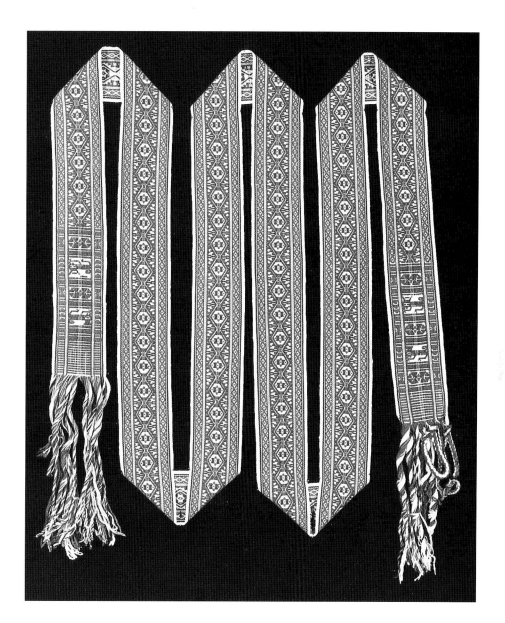

178 *Belt woven by Juan Aurelio Asqui Contero, in Cacha Obraje. The diamond design is called* ladia kingo. *Cotton plain weave, with acrylic supplementary-warp patterning. 3.00 x .055 meters (9 feet 10 inches x 2⅛ inches). The Textile Museum 1989.22.45, Latin American Research Fund.*

and Quichua). In Troje, blouses are hand embroidered in cross stitch in navy blue, pine green, and dark red (Fig. 181). The embroidery on Cacha blouses is similar, but the gussets are not outlined and yellow is added to the palette.

In Cacha, younger women may wear a newer style of blouse-slip combination, often made from floral-printed acrylic fabric and with almost no embroidery. Others wear a factory-made blouse and cardigan. In Majipamba, women usually wear machine-made T-shirts and cardigans, and the same is true in many other areas of Chimborazo, especially for younger women.

Shawls are now often made from factory-made acrylic fabrics in a variety of colors, though some women continue to wear handwoven wool ones. The ready

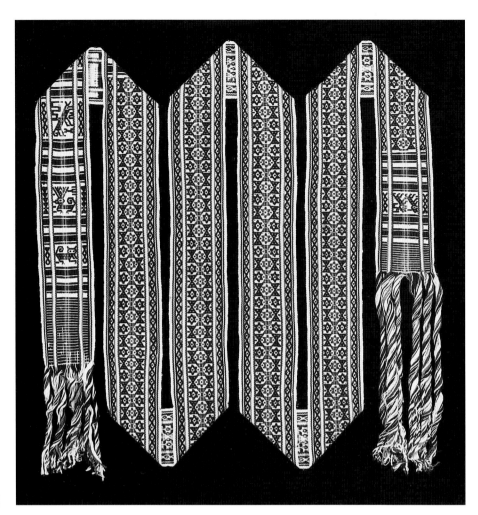

179 Belt purchased in Cacha Machángara, central Chimborazo province. Cotton plain weave, with acrylic supplementary-warp patterning. 3.02 x .065 meters (9 feet 10 inches x 2½ inches). The Textile Museum 1988.19.102, Latin American Research Fund.

availability of many colors of machine-made fabrics has caused the breakdown of some of the traditional color usage. For example, bright colors that were formerly worn only for fiestas in Colta may now be seen in daily use. Red, blue, green, purple, and pink are all common.

Some women still have tupus, but most women, especially for everyday wear, instead use a safety pin, which may or may not also be secured with a braided loop. Most women do not wear the really long earrings, but purchase short ones in the Riobamba market. A typical example has four beaded strands 10 centimeters (4 inches) long (Textile Museum 1988.19.132). Bead necklaces without coins are worn. Currently, Colta women wear beads of a single color while Troje women wear multicolored necklaces. In Cacha, necklaces of middle-aged women are of red, blue, or white beads. Younger women wear a great variety of beads, including clear plastic beads, called *brillantes*. Women in Troje still wear wrist wraps, but only some women in Majipamba wear them.

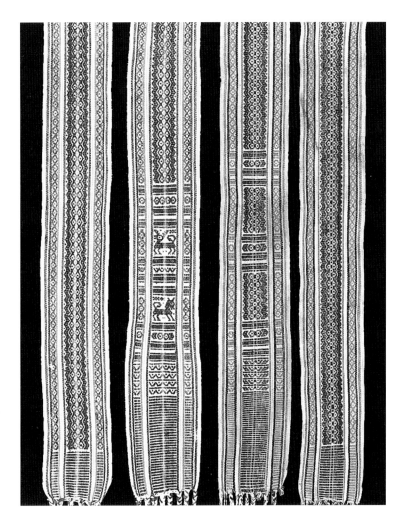

180 Belts in a style made in Cacha, central Chimborazo province. Cotton plain weave, with wool supplementary-warp patterning. 2.685 x .072 meters (8 feet 9¾ inches x 2⅞ inches) and 2.76 x .07 meters (9 feet ⅝ inches x 2¾ inches), excluding ties. The Textile Museum 1989.22.41 and 1986.19.32, Latin American Research Fund.

181 Blouse made in Troje, central Chimborazo province. Slide by Laura M. Miller, 1989.

182 *Girl in Cacha Obraje, central Chimborazo province, with an elaborately crocheted shigra. Photo by Laura M. Miller, 1989.*

Young women may also wear a more modern hairstyle. The hair may be braided rather than wrapped. The forelocks may be held down with barrettes. The handmade felt hats have been replaced by machine-made fedoras, in a variety of dark colors.

Younger women usually wear some sort of machine-made shoes.

While a few older women still make looped shigras of furcraea fiber, younger women make and use shigras crocheted of acrylic yarns, with colorful geometric designs and sometimes lettering as well (Fig. 182). Some young women are using plastic shopping baskets.

A white or printed cotton commercial fabric is used as a carrying cloth for goods slung on the back. A baby is carried under the mother's shawl, while another shawl passes under the baby and over the shoulders outside of the first shawl. The second shawl, called a *sikinchina* (*siki*, Q., rump), is tied on the chest.

Men's costume

Most men in Chimborazo now wear factory-made shirts, pants, and hats, so they identify themselves as indigenous only by wearing the poncho. One thirty-five-year-old man in Majipamba ruefully stated: "Las mujeres conserven más la tradición. Nosotros los jovenes solo ponemos ponchos a veces. [The women maintain the traditions more. We young men only wear ponchos occasionally.]"

Jirga ponchos were formerly made and worn in Majipamba as well as in other communities in the area, and they are still worn in some communities, especially by middle-aged and older men (Fig. 183). They are woven on the treadle loom in a 2/2 twill weave of white wool with narrow black warp stripes at intervals. They are worn either undyed, in which case they are called *yurak poncho* (white poncho), or piece dyed in red, in which case they are called *puka poncho* (red poncho). In Majipamba, we also recorded an all-black twill poncho that was said to be worn for mourning. The size ranges from 1.27 to 1.51 meters in length (50 to 59 inches) by 1.12 to 1.26 meters in width (44 to 49½) inches).

According to one man we talked to in Troje, jirga ponchos are woven and worn in Troje, Pulucate, San Martín, San Bartolo, Cicao, and Miraflores. They are also worn in Cacha and in other parts of Chimborazo province. In Cacha we even found such a poncho (dyed purple) that had been made on the backstrap loom, though this is not the usual method (Fig. 24).

For fiesta, men in all these areas wear another style of poncho that is said to be made specifically in Cacha. These ponchos are backstrap-loom woven in two four-selvedged panels, with a separately made fringe band around the outer edge. In each half of the poncho there are some three groups of narrow stripes separated by some three wider solid-colored stripes. In many (but not all) of these ponchos, the narrow stripes set off a warp-resist patterned stripe (Pl. X). While the oldest examples of this style are all cotton, more recent examples (since at least the late 1960s) have the solid stripes in wool, usually red, sometimes black, and only the

183 *María Rosa Contero Guamán with her husband José Guamán Asqui and baby, Cacha Obraje, central Chimborazo province, all wearing old-style hats. The man is wearing an undyed jirga poncho. The woman is wearing a backstrap-loom woven shawl. Photo by Laura M. Miller 1989.*

resist-dyed stripes, if present, are cotton. The resist-dyed designs are usually simple diamonds. These ponchos are usually of significantly finer yarns and weaving than the other handwoven ponchos in the area. The size is comparable to that of the jirga ponchos.

These ponchos are still woven in Cacha Obraje. We saw relatively few men wearing such ponchos in the market context. Those who were wearing them tended to be young men apparently wishing to make an impression (they did). Passing through Cacha on one occasion, we saw one young man wearing his warp-resist patterned poncho ride by on a motorcycle. These ponchos are more often worn for fiesta, not only in Cacha, but elsewhere in the province as well.

As noted by Tolen, machine-made acrylic imitations of this style, referred to as *Cacha ponchos,* with solid-color stripes (no warp resist), are now being marketed by Otavalos. In Majipamba, a second style of machine-made acrylic poncho, also called *Cacha poncho* but with less justification, is commonly worn (Fig. 184). The ground color is navy blue or red, with some pink and turquoise single stripes on either side. Each side also carries a wide multicolored stripe near the outer edge. These ponchos are made/marketed by Otavalos and are similar to some we also saw being worn in Tungurahua province.

Columbe Area

Lynn A. Meisch

Columbe, Llinllin, and San Bernardo are tiny farming communities about 13 to 19 kilometers (8 to 12 miles) northwest of Guamote. Columbe is closest to the highway, with Llinllin (a former hacienda) and San Bernardo farther off the highway on a dirt road that follows the Llulluccha river upstream.

San Bernardo has a community center with an association that operates a treadle-loom weaving workshop (*taller* S.). When we visited, several older men were teaching a number of teenage boys and girls as well as younger children to weave. One of

184 *Chimbolema and Lema family members in Majipamba, central Chimborazo province, with Earthwatch volunteer Kathy Jahnke in the old-style costume. Photo by Laura M. Miller, 1988.*

5. The Earthwatch team on August 2, 1989, was led by Lynn Meisch and Carlos Moreno A., accompanied by Nancy Tucker, Peggy Jacobs, and Kirby Hall. Nancy Tucker wrote the report. Since Carlos Moreno had taught at the high school (*colegio*) in Llinllin, he was familiar with this community.

the teachers learned to weave in Peguche, outside Otavalo, and had a warp on the loom for acrylic scarves with supplementary-weft patterning, a common Otavalo product. Other looms held warps for shoulder wraps, for shirts or blouses, or for ponchos.

Women's costume

Women and girls in this region wear a costume that is very similar to that described in the preceding section (Figs. 185–188).[5] They wear ankle-length half anakus of factory-made cloth, machine embroidered around the bottom with straight lines and zigzags. Only some older women wear a changalli (we saw one in handspun white wool). A variety of belts are used, including kawiña chumbis, belts in the twill-derived weave, and supplementary-warp patterned belts with pickup motifs

185 *Woman from San Bernardo, near Columbe, central Chimborazo province, wearing an embroidered blouse and a shawl of synthetic fabric. Photo by Lynn A. Meisch, 1989.*

186 *Blouse like that worn by the woman in Fig. 185. Made by Humberto Morocho in Riobamba, central Chimborazo province. The maker told us the style was used in Chuquipogyo. We also saw similar blouses for sale in Licto, in the eastern Chimborazo area. Polyester fabric in plain weave, embroidered with acrylic thread. Overall width (including sleeves): 1.26 meters (49½ inches). The Textile Museum 1988.19.128, Latin American Research Fund.*

woven in Cacha or Otavalo. These smaller belts are called *uchilla chumbi* in this area. *Uchilla* in Quichua means "small" or "child." Some women added pompoms to the ties on their belts. Some women wrapped their belts across a broad area of their midriff, from their navel to their breasts. Some women also wear a mama chumbi, while others do not. Most women and girls wear Euro-American style blouses, sweaters, or T-shirts, but at least one woman was wearing the white cotton embroidered blouse-slip (*camisa*) (Figs. 185–186).

The shoulder wrap is called a *bayeta* or *lliglla* (the Inca term, uncommon in Chimborazo). We saw almost every color: bright blue, rose-pink, red, green, orange, and grey. Women and girls often wear two shawls and use a third as a carrying cloth. The shawls are worn folded in half or turned under at the neck. Most are of factory-made acrylic fabric and some are machine embroidered along the edges with straight lines and zigzags in contrasting colors, but some are made from handspun wool. They are secured with a large safety pin or tupu. The tupu is worn with a bright pink or blue acrylic braided tape around the neck.

The necklaces (*wallka*) consist of six or eight strands of the same color of beads: yellow, white, light blue, red, often with one or two beads of a contrasting color mixed in. Many girls and women wear wrist wraps (*maki watana* or *mullu,* the latter meaning a small, round thing) of tiny seed beads, the colors of which were also varied. Costume jewelry earrings (*sarcillus,* from Spanish *zarcillos,* or *rinrin* Q. ear) predominate. Most females wear plastic shoes; black, light blue, brown, and turquoise are popular.

187 *People from San Bernardo, near Columbe, central Chimborazo province. The young girl wears the handmade hat. Photo by Lynn A. Meisch, 1989.*

188 *Men and women from San Bernardo, near Columbe, central Chimborazo province. The man at left wears a red jirga poncho, the one at right a machine-made poncho similar to those also worn in Majipamba. Photo by Lynn A. Meisch, 1989.*

The most distinctive feature of the female costume in this area is that many women and girls still wear the handfelted white hat (Fig. 187). These hats have a medium-width brim, about 4.5 centimeters (2 inches), and flat. The brim is edged with a black grosgrain ribbon machine embroidered in straight lines and zigzags in bright colors such as red and green. A black satin ribbon 5 centimeters (2 inches) wide goes around the crown, meets, and hangs down in two streamers each about a foot long. The ends of the ribbons are machine embroidered in the same colors as the brim with rectangles, zigzags and trefoils. Then multicolored fringe (purple, blue, green, red) is sewn to the ends. The streamers hang down on either side or in back of the head. Some women also tie a braided white string around the crown with the ends hanging down ending in a pompom (*sisa*). Some pompoms were white, others were bright pink or yellow and pink. These were considered optional, a matter of personal preference. Some women and girls do wear a dark fedora, with narrow brim turned down in front. The hairstyle is parted in the middle, pulled back and held with a barrette, wrapped tape, or ribbon (*cinta*).

Men's costume

Most of the men and boys now wear Euro-American style shirts, pants, sweaters, shoes or rubber boots, and a fedora. Kushmas, of black and white wool, are only worn by old men. A few men wear sheepskin zamarros.

We saw many different styles of poncho in this area (Figs. 187–189). Many men and boys wear the red or white twill-weave poncho, with narrow black stripes, woven on treadle looms of handspun wool (Fig. 188). The Cacha style striped poncho (without warp-resist patterns) is also common, both in the handwoven form and the machine-made acrylic imitation (Fig. 187). The machine-made style with colored stripes at the outside edge and individual contrast stripes at wide intervals is also worn (Fig. 188). Another style has stripes about 5 centimeters (2 inches) wide, red and white or red and black. Some men wear ponchos in solid red or blue, woven of handspun wool on the backstrap loom (Fig. 189). This style often has a gusset and collar. In Llinllin most of the men and boys were wearing handspun backstrap-loom woven red ponchos.

San Juan Area

Lynn A. Meisch and

Ann P. Rowe

The town of San Juan lies some 13 kilometers (8 miles) west of Riobamba on the road to Guaranda. There is a small Sunday market there, with produce sold by mestizo-white women. Ropes and ponchos are also sold. A statue of the Virgin Mary in the yard of the church is dressed in traditional women's attire, including a tiny felt hat with black streamers.

A regional style of dress characteristic of the surrounding area is identifiable, just north of the area described above, under the southern side of Mount Chimborazo. The towns of Nitiluisa and San Vicente de Luisa, some 5 kilometers (3 miles) north of San Juan, and Chanchahuán, 3 kilometers (2 miles) southeast of San Juan, are also in this sphere. The costume is worn as far east as Tuntatacto, some 7 kilometers (4⅓ miles) northeast of Nitiluisa on the other side of the Panamerican highway.

Farming is the main occupation in this area. We also found women from San Juan selling the Pomatúg-made hats of various Chimborazo styles in many of the markets of the province, including Riobamba and Guamote.

While we were told that women formerly wore an anaku that fell from the shoulders, without either a blouse or shoes, we saw no one wearing this style.[6] Many women now wear an embroidered camisa with a half-length anaku (Figs. 190–191). We were told that the camisas were purchased in San Juan and that the embroidery was done by both men and women. The anakus of this area are shorter than for the Cacha-Colta-Columbe area. Women wear them between just below the knee and mid-calf length. Sometimes the decorated hem of the camisa is just visible. Factory-made sweaters are worn also, so the upper part of the camisa is often not visible.

Although anakus are navy blue or black, as elsewhere, the changalli, if worn, is often a contrasting color. The most common color is green (Fig. 191), although in the Riobamba market we also saw some women wearing a red or purple changalli. The same range of colors is found in the shawls, with the addition of blue and undyed. The younger women do not wear the changalli, however (Fig. 192). Some women wear backstrap-loom woven anakus, and some wear machine-made ones.

6. The following description, in addition to being based on observations by Lynn Meisch, Laura Miller, and Ann Rowe, also employs Earthwatch reports and photographs from 1989 team 3. The Earthwatch reports for San Juan were written by Cindy M. Ferguson, Louise Hainline, and Peggy Jacobs, those for Nitiluisa by Patricia Meloy and Kate Beamer.

189 *Boy in San Bernardo, central Chimborazo province, wearing a plain backstraploom woven poncho with collar. In the background a man is wearing a Cacha poncho. Photo by Lynn A. Meisch, 1989.*

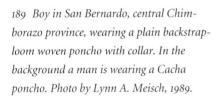

190 *Maria Juana Mollo (center) and a neighbor in San Juan, central Chimborazo province, with Earthwatch volunteer holding a blouse. Slide by Mary C. Shook, 1989.*

Belts include the same kinds seen elsewhere, with supplementary-warp patterning, the kawiña chumbi, and Otavalo styles. One man in Nitiluisa, Santiago Sulasisa, weaves multi-colored striped belts in the twill-derived weave (Fig. 193), which local women buy. He also knows how to weave the kawiña chumbi. The belts have narrow ties added that are used to secure them. At least some women were wearing two belts. The mama chumbi, however, is not worn.

The shoulder wrap (called *bayeta*) is variable in both fabric and color. We saw navy blue, bright blue, red, bright pink, emerald green: no one color was typical. Some are handspun wool, woven on the backstrap loom or on the treadle loom in either plain or twill weave. Some are handwoven of acrylic yarn. Santiago Sulasisa of Nitiluisa, the belt weaver, brought out a bright rose-pink acrylic bayeta, with its cabuya fiber dovetail cord still in, indicating that it had just been taken off the backstrap loom. He said that the ends would not be left as loops, but would be cut, and he pointed out a young girl who was wearing such a bayeta. Other bayetas are made of commercially manufactured acrylic fabric, some brushed so that they had

191 Woman in San Juan, central Chimborazo province, wearing a green changalli over her anaku. The embroidered lower edge of her blouse is also visible. Slide by Mary C. Shook, 1989.

192 Family in Nitiluisa, San Juan area of central Chimborazo province. Photo by Lynn A. Meisch, 1989.

a thick, fuzzy nap (Fig. 192). The bayetas vary in length from quite long, to the wearer's knees, to ones that only reach the waist. Many are folded in half when worn. Either a tupu like those seen elsewhere (nickel inset with five or six tiny pieces of colored glass) or a safety pin is used to secure the fabric. The carrying cloth is sometimes a Rumipamba warp-resist dyed macana or a low quality Gualaceo area (Azuay) warp-resist dyed shawl, or else a piece of machine-made fabric. Both acrylic and cabuya fiber shigras are made in the region.

Most women we saw still wear handmade felt hats. The hats are similar in shape to the Colta ones, and like them have a black ribbon around the crown. The distinction is that the ribbon does not pass completely around the crown, but there is a gap about 3 centimeters (1 inch) wide. The streamers have no tassels and hang down on the right side. This hat is called a *sombrero, zhutu,* or *panza de burro* (S., donkey's belly). A few women wore these handmade felt hats with only the black band around the crown and no streamers or with only the white band that comes with the hat. A few women do wear the modern dark felt fedora with narrow brim.

The traditional hairstyle is parted in the middle, pulled back behind the ears and wrapped with a tape beginning at the nape of the neck. Different kinds of tapes and ribbons are used including ones woven in Otavalo that are sold in local markets.

193 *Our recording of Santiago Sula Sisa's belt weaving technique draws a large crowd of neighbors in Nitiluisa, San Juan area, central Chimborazo province. Photo by Lynn A. Meisch, 1989.*

No sidelocks are worn. Some women and girls use elastic bands with little plastic balls on the end, or barrettes, instead of a tape.

Women wear bead necklaces (*wallka*). The older style seems to be for strands of red or coral-colored beads or of blue or white beads in various combinations. Strands of white mixed with strands combining yellow, white, and green beads are also worn. A few young women are now wearing the type of small gold glass beads seen in Otavalo. Women wear a variety of short earring styles (*aretes* S.).

For work in the countryside, women and girls wear rubber boots, plastic shoes, or go barefoot. Some women wear acrylic knee socks and tennis shoes, and in the Riobamba market we saw a few young women wearing even knee-high stockings and heeled leather shoes.

Men were wearing mostly factory-made clothes. However, ponchos are commonly backstrap-loom woven of handspun wool, with a short warp fringe (Figs. 192–193). Some ponchos are bright red, either with or without a gusset and collar. Another style has blue and white stripes (Fig. 193). Neither the twill nor the Cacha-style ponchos were seen in this area. A few old men were wearing handmade hats, but most now wear fedoras. We also saw a few men wearing sheepskin chaps.

Chapter 10

Eastern Chimborazo Province

In the central valley of Chimborazo province a costume is worn that contrasts with dress on the western foothills, the chief difference being that here the women's anakus are pleated and may be tubular rather than rectangular. Within this area, we have been able to distinguish at least three substyles: one in the northern part of this area, which we documented in the most detail in Licto; one in the eastern part, which we recorded in Chambo; and another in the southern part around Palmira Dávalos.

Licto Area

Lynn A. Meisch

Licto is a small town, the capital of its parish, located 23.3 kilometers (14½ miles) south and slightly east of Riobamba (see map, page xx). The people of the area are small farmers and artisans, including cabuya spinners, belt and poncho weavers, and shigra makers. They grow the usual highland crops, including maize, potatoes, wheat, barley, quinoa, and lupine. The local indigenous federation, Federación de Cabildos de Licto (FEDECAL), comprises thirty small communities, including Susul San Francisco, Guesech, Cecel Grande, Tunshi San Javier, Tunshi San Miguel, Tunshi Grande, Huancatúz, Molobóg, Flores, Santa Ana, San Antonio, and Licto proper, all of which have populations wearing traditional dress.

The region encompassing people who wear Licto style dress extends from Molobóg, a tiny community just north of Licto, to Flores, 8 kilometers (5 miles) over the ridge to the west, to Pungalá, a few kilometers southeast across the Chambo river from Licto, to Cebadas, 16 kilometers (10 miles) south of Licto. Cebadas is closer to Guamote (9.5 kilometers or 6 miles) than to Licto, so some people wearing Licto style dress from Cebadas and the southern communities attend the Sunday market in Guamote, while others from the northern communities attend the Saturday market in Riobamba.

The small Licto market takes place on Sundays. Besides local people, there are vendors from Cacha selling belts, hair wraps, and acrylic ponchos woven in the Cacha communities. Other vendors sell the Rumipamba and Gualaceo area warp-

194 *Women from the Licto area of Chimborazo province in the Guamote market. Slide by Lynn A. Meisch, 1989.*

195 *Old woman from the Licto area of Chimborazo province in the Guamote market, wearing a shawl over her head. Photo by Naeda Robinson, 1989.*

resist dyed shawls that are used as carrying cloths, and others sell the ribbons and tapes that are used to wrap hair or to hold tupus.

Old-style women's costume

The old-style anaku is made from handspun, handwoven black wool and covers the entire body (Figs. 194–195). Some women around Licto still wear this garment pinned on the shoulders with small tupus and wrapped at the waist with a belt (see also Saenz 1933:89). The garment is called an *anaku* or *chakillilla* (pronounced "chakizhizha"). *Chaki* means foot or leg below the knee; *lli* or *li* and *lla* are suffixes that indicate reflexivity, or "onto the body," and restriction, respectively, so the sense of the word is "only to the foot" or "onto the foot."

Most are made from S-spun wool and woven on a treadle-loom in a plain (most common) or twill weave. In addition, some of these chakillillas are sewn together into a tube, which is folded into pleats in the front, pinned on the shoulders, and belted. Others are identical, but not sewn into a tube, and are also pleated when the belt is wrapped.

196 Group in the Licto market, Chimbo-razo province. The woman in the center wears a black shawl over a bright pink one. The man at left wears a navy blue poncho. The boy at right has a navy poncho with red stripes. Slide by Dianne Barske, 1988.

The wrap is called *fachallina* (pronounced "fachazhina"). The old-style fachallina is a large, black, handspun (S-spun singles) wool treadle-loom or backstrap-loom woven rectangle; some are almost as big as a blanket. The larger ones are folded in half or a third of the way down, then wrapped over the shoulders and pinned with a tupu. Even so, many of these fachallinas come down to the woman's knees. Frequently, women wear two fachallinas, with a third one for a carrying cloth (called a *rebozo*). Although many women wear all-black garments, we saw a num-ber of women in the old-style anaku, hat, and fachallina with a colored fachallina worn under the black one (Fig. 196). The colors are deep red, fucshia, pink, ma-roon, navy blue, or purple.

The tupus used to fasten the shawls are varied and include types seen elsewhere in the province. They include nickel ones with a round head inset with pieces of colored glass, examples similar to the preceding but with an octagonal head and a little bird on top, examples with an old coin used for a head, and others that are a flat spade shape with a quadrangular head inset with glass. As elsewhere, the tupus have a ribbon loop that is passed around the wearer's neck. A vara and a half of factory-made braided acrylic ribbon is the usual kind.

The mama chumbi is not worn in this area. The local belts have supplementary-warp patterning in a variety of pick-up designs, in pink, orange, or black (Fig. 197). In the Licto market, we met a belt weaving family from Molobóg, Manuel Pilatacsi Minta and his wife, María Quizhpe, who were selling belts similar to those we saw people wearing. A mestizo-white belt vendor said that her belts, which were similar

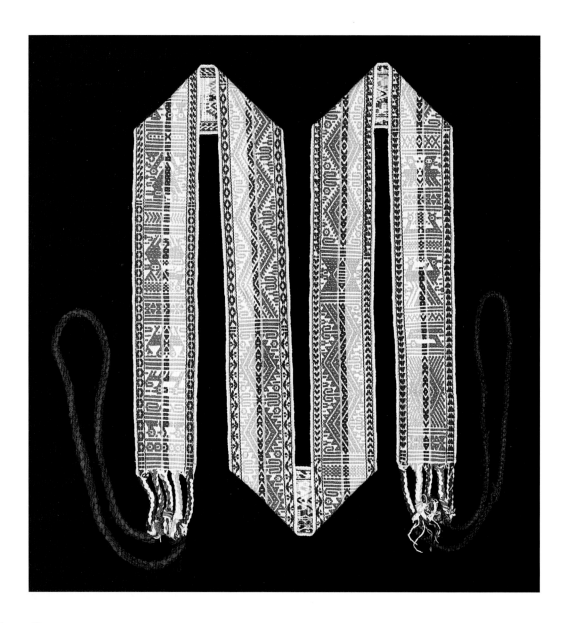

197 *Belt purchased from a Licto woman in the Riobamba market, Chimborazo province. Cotton plain weave, with acrylic supplementary-warp patterning. 2.34 x .08 meters (7 feet 8 inches x 3⅛ inches), excluding ties. The Textile Museum 1988.19.157, Latin American Research Fund.*

to those from Molobóg, were woven in Cachatón (Fig. 198). The general format of these belts is similar to Cacha belts, but relatively elaborate zigzag designs seem to be characteristic, with other designs less emphasized. The belts are usually sold with warp loop fringe at both ends. The buyer makes the fringe into a number of small braids, then joins them with a cord loop. The belt is wrapped and tied with the loops.

The older style Licto hat is a white, handmade felt hat, with a low, round crown and narrow, flat brim (Figs. 194, 196). A white cotton cord (*piolita* S.) about the thickness of a pencil, or a little thinner, is tied around the crown. A bow is tied at the side with the tasselled ends hanging down ten to fifteen centimeters (4–6 inches) over the side of the brim. String and cord for the piolita as well as the

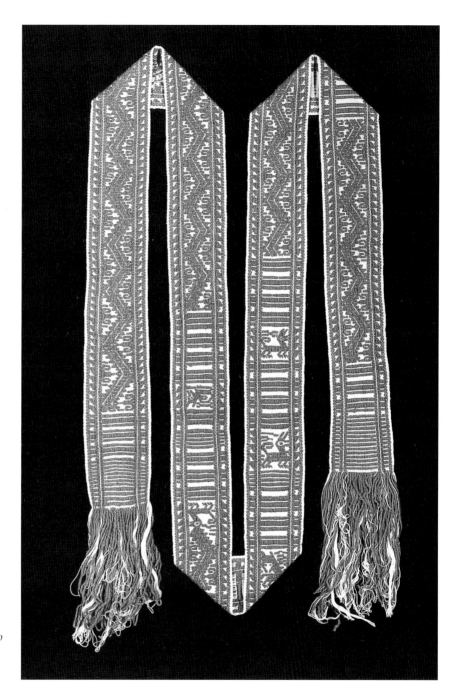

198 *Belt purchased in the Licto market and said to be from Cachatón, Chimborazo province. Cotton plain weave, with acrylic supplementary-warp patterning. 3.12 x .09 meters (10 feet 3 inches x 3½ inches). The Textile Museum 1988.19.158, Latin American Research Fund.*

hats are sold in the Licto Sunday market. Some of the hats are from Pomatúg, Tungurahua; others are less finely finished and may be made in the area. The purchaser of a Pomatúg hat removes the ready-made trim and puts on the piolita instead.

Some people in Tunshi Grande wear a variation of the Licto hat that has a 5 centimeter-wide (2 inch) black ribbon around the crown, with very short streamers that hang down to the ears (Fig. 195). Other people in the same town wear the Licto style described above.

The hair is worn parted in the middle, pulled back behind the ears and wrapped with a tape beginning at the nape of the neck. No sidelocks are worn. The colors of the hair wraps vary and seem to reflect personal preference.

The necklace (*wallka*, pronounced "washka") consists of multiple strands of large (pea- to marble-sized), red or coral-colored beads. One woman had a large silver or nickel crucifix attached to the front of her necklaces. Earrings worn by older women are loops of red beads 30 centimeters (12 inches) long. Some women also wear wrist wraps. Women not wearing factory-made shoes were barefoot.

In addition to the locally woven rebozos mentioned above, women use warp-resist dyed shawls as carrying cloths, either from Rumipamba in Cotopaxi province or the low-quality ones from the Gualaceo area in Azuay. Other women use shigras.

199 *Dyer Marlene Cabezas demonstrates how the Licto anaku is put on, Chimborazo province. Photo by Lynn A. Meisch, 1988.*

Contemporary women's costume

The more recent style of anaku is half length (Fig. 199) and worn over an embroidered blouse and slip combination or with separate blouses or sweaters and slips of various kinds. The locally sewn blouse and slip combination (*camisa*) is made from machine-made white or cream-colored cotton or cotton-synthetic blends. It has a front and back yoke, no collar, square gussets under the arms, and long sleeves ending in cuffs, similar to the newer style camisas of central Chimborazo (cf. Fig. 186). It is hand embroidered with acrylic yarn in a variety of colors on the cuffs, yoke, and sometimes the yoke opening and/or the sleeve below the elbow with floral motifs inside lines of zigzags or x's. Some are hand or machine embroidered around the hem, and a few have scalloped hems with machine embroidery.

The most common half-anaku is a smaller version of the anakus described above made of black handspun wool and woven on the treadle loom. Older women wear them to their ankle, younger women wear them slightly shorter (Fig. 196). One old woman we saw had a black, handspun wool anaku with fringe on the bottom, as well as a fringed fachallina. These anakus are wrapped with the closing in the back and four or five pleats across the stomach (Fig. 199). The most recent anaku style is of factory-made acrylic fabric, dark blue or black, either from Otavalo or locally produced. Nevertheless, we saw more handspun, handwoven dress worn in the small Sunday Licto market than we did anywhere else in Chimborazo province.

Colored fachallinas are much more common among younger women who also wear commercially made anakus and fedoras; this seems to be the newer fashion. Safety pins may be used to fasten them.

The Textile Museum anaku (1988.22.16) is made of black fabric with a 75 centimeter (29½ inch) loom width, which is the length of the garment, and 1.84 meter (72½ inch) length sewn into a tube. It is a treadle-loom woven twill fabric. The fachallina (1988.22.15) is backstrap-loom woven with four selvedges of black wool; it is 1.28 by .945 meters (50½ by 37¼ inches) in size (one panel). The rebozo (1988.22.14) is a treadle-loom woven plain-weave fabric of dark red wool, made of two panels sewn together, 1.32 by 1.305 meters (52 by 51¼ inches) in overall size. All of these pieces are woven of S-spun yarns.

Many of the wool garments are woven first, and then dyed by professional dyers, who make the rounds of the local markets, picking up orders one week, dyeing them, and then returning them to their owners the next market day. The garments often have a small skein of yarn looped through one end, which people use for making joins or edging, or for mending. We met one such dyer in the Licto market, Marlene Cabezas of San Geraldo, on the outskirts of Riobamba, and visited her at home as well (Fig. 200). She uses enormous (1 meter or 3 feet in diameter, 45 centimeters or 18 inches deep) copper tubs (*pailas* S.) over open wood fires, together with German synthetic dyes and sulfuric acid as an assistant.

Besides necklaces of red beads, some women were wearing necklaces of predominantly red with a few blue and green beads mixed in, or entirely of bright blue beads. Earrings include fine old silver examples with coins and colored glass and inexpensive modern costume jewelry pieces. Younger women most often wear plastic flats.

200 Dyer Marlene Cabezas in San Geraldo, on the outskirts of Riobamba, Chimborazo province. Photo by Lynn A. Meisch, 1988.

Men's costume

We noted one elderly man wearing the same white hat as the women, white pants, sheepskin zamarros, and a red wool backstrap-loom woven poncho without a collar. This costume undoubtedly represents the older style in this region. We also saw two teenage boys at the Licto market wearing white pants, short red ponchos, and green fedoras. However, most males wear Euro-American style trousers, shirts, jackets, sweaters, dark fedoras, and shoes or rubber boots (Fig. 196).

Solid color red, navy blue, or black ponchos predominate. Some are acrylic, others wool. Some have gussets and collars, while others do not. Some have warp fringe, others have a cotton or acrylic edging. Some are woven on the backstrap loom, others on the treadle loom. One variation is a cherry-red poncho with one contrasting 5–13 centimeter (2–5 inch) wide stripe near the outer edge of each half, for example, green or yellow. We also saw men wearing white or red twill-weave ponchos with black stripes like those in central Chimborazo. Other ponchos have black and white large windowpane checks. Cacha style striped ponchos, usually of acrylic yarn, also are worn in this area.

In Pungalá we visited mestizo-white weavers who specialized in weaving ponchos and warp-resist dyed blankets on the backstrap loom. While we were there, one of the weavers had half of a handspun wool navy blue adult's poncho on the loom, and another was warping a handspun wool red child's poncho that had a blue stripe on each half. The choice of color is up to the person ordering the poncho. Cherry red or navy blue are frequent choices, but people also ask for green, fucsia, or yellow (all dyed with synthetic dyes).

Opposite:

201 Women from Alao visiting the Chambo feria, eastern Chimborazo province. The woman at left is wearing an embroidered blouse and a handsome belt. The girl at center is wearing a blue shawl, but the other shawls are red. Slide by Naeda Robinson, 1989.

202 Women from Alao, eastern Chimborazo province, visiting the Chambo feria, showing the hairstyle. Slide by Naeda Robinson, 1989.

203 Men, women, and children from Alao visiting the Chambo feria, eastern Chimborazo province. The men are wearing black (left) and navy (right) ponchos. Slide by Laura M. Miller, 1989.

Chambo and Alao

Lynn A. Meisch and
Ann P. Rowe

The town of Chambo, which is the capital of the cantón of Chambo, is 10.5 kilometers (6½ miles) southeast of Riobamba on the east side of the Chambo River (see map, page 000). It is famous for its shrine to the Virgen de la fuente de Carmelo de Catequilla, whose fiesta is on July 16. People from all over northern Chimborazo and from as far away as Peru attend this fiesta, including families from the San Juan, Licto, and Cacha areas, though very few from Colta, probably because Colta is now primarily evangelical Protestant.

We met a number of women and girls at this fiesta who wore a distinct costume and who told us they were from Alao, near Pungalá (Figs. 201–203).[1] They were wearing pleated anakus that just cover the knee in length, over an embroidered blouse-slip combination (Fig. 201). Some of the anakus are plain black wool, but others are a factory-made plush fabric and have blue or silvery rickrack trim along the lower edge. The pleats are more numerous and prominent than in the Licto costume. In some cases the pleats seem to be pressed. A few women were wearing this anaku over long (factory-made) pants. Many were wearing shawls of machine-made pink, red (most common), or blue plain or plush fabric, fastened across the chest either with a knot or with a tupu.

---

1. Photographs taken in 1989 by Earthwatch volunteers Naeda Robinson, Celia Foss, and Carol Siegal were used in writing the following descriptions.

Their hairstyle is also distinctive, consisting of a single long braid with colored tape braided into it which ends in several brightly colored pompoms (Fig. 202). Their hats have either a plain white band around the crown or a black band with short streamers on the side. A few women were wearing a hat with a slightly taller crown with no decoration except a colored string around the crown.

The men accompanying these women were wearing navy blue or black ponchos with collars (Fig. 203).

Palmira Dávalos Area

Lynn A. Meisch

Palmira Dávalos is located on the páramo at 3,207 meters (10,523 feet) above sea level, approximately 46.5 kilometers (29 miles) south of Guamote (and slightly north of Palmira proper) and just south of the ridge of Tiocajas (see map, page 000). There are 180 families or about 900 persons in the community. Almost everyone, down to tiny girls barely able to walk, wears the local version of traditional dress.

Women and girls wear ankle-length half-anakus with machine embroidery along the bottom consisting of straight lines enclosing zigzags, with a few flowers above the lines (Fig. 204). Some of these anakus are sewn shut to form a tube. One such half-anaku was made from black acrylic fabric with a red edging sewn on the bottom. In one home we visited, the family was making anakus from navy blue acrylic fabric. They sewed these into a tube and edged them at the top and bottom with bright pink factory-made acrylic tape, which is sold in stores and markets throughout Ecuador. The tubular half-anakus have a few big back-over-front folds at each side. The use of tubular anakus with folds places this area within the eastern Chimborazo nexus, though the use of machine-made fabrics now makes the costume confusingly similar to central Chimborazo. Some women, though not all, wear a changalli, which usually is in a contrasting color, for example, green.

The shoulder wraps (called *bayeta*, pronounced "bayita") are typically red or pink, but sometimes green, and machine embroidered on all four edges with zigzags enclosed in lines and a small branch in each corner (Fig. 204). The use of embroidery on all edges distinguishes these wraps from those of the central Chimborazo area. Usually at least two wraps are worn at once, and a third similar fabric serves as a carrying cloth.

Belts are varied. Some women wear a kawiña chumbi, which is perhaps an older style. One woman was wearing a blue acrylic belt with shots of gilt thread. Various kinds of blouses, sweaters, and T-shirts are worn. These are mostly machine made, but one woman had a green blouse with embroidery on the cuffs.

Women usually wear bead necklaces, but not all women wear wrist wraps. The necklaces are red and clear or red and white beads mixed. One woman had yellow bead wrist wraps.

Women wear their hair parted in the middle, pulled back, and wrapped at the base of the neck with a tape or ribbon. Some women use a band like those woven in Cacha. Many women wear machine-made fedoras, but two young girls were wear-

204 *Woman in Palmira Dávalos, Chimborazo province, weaving on a treadle loom, wearing a blue anaku with black changalli and a red shawl. Slide by Lynn A. Meisch, 1989.*

ing handmade white felt hats from Pomatúg which were unaltered from the state in which they are sold, so had only a white cloth button on top with six cotton strings from the button to the hatband, a white cotton band around the crown, and white cotton edging around the brim.

Men wear factory-made shirts, sweaters, and pants, as well as green or brown fedoras. Most wear ponchos, however. One man was wearing a red, handspun, and backstrap-loom woven poncho, with a gusset, collar, and looped-warp fringe at the bottom. Another man was wearing an acrylic treadle-loom woven poncho with red and black houndstooth checks (Fig. 205). In another house, where the man and his wife weave women's wraps to sell, he showed us a white, acrylic, balanced-twill weave poncho with narrow black warp stripes that he had woven.

The community's Asociación de Palmira Dávalos has a large weaving workshop (*taller*), started in 1984, with eleven looms, including countermarch four-shaft looms and a Jacquard loom, where some of the clothes worn in the community are made. The four-shaft looms were being used to weave women's wraps in plain weave or twill, in yellow, bright pink, or kelly green. At other times, twill-weave ponchos are woven like those described above. The association also weaves wool fabric that is exported to Venezuela for use as upholstery. Both individual families and the association sell their products to a store on the main street of Palmira Dávalos.

Regional variations

A similar costume is worn in several nearby communities that we were not able to visit but saw in the Guamote market. That is, women from these communities wear ankle-length anakus of factory-made fabric with machine embroidery on the bottom, often belted with a kawiña chumbi, with or without a changalli, and up to five shoulder wraps with machine embroidery, often on all edges. The hair style is wrapped, although many of these women also wear side locks. A blouse-slip purchased in the Guamote market (Fig. 206) represents a style worn in this area.

The main distinguishing feature of these communities seems to be the hats. A hat with a low crown and narrow brim with a broad pink or red ribbon around the crown ending in streamers was said to be worn in Galte and Tiocajas, both communities near Palmira Dávalos (Fig. 207). These hats were being sold by a San Juan woman who had added the trim and confirmed that they were made in the Ambato area (probably Pomatúg). A variation on this hat, also said to be worn in Galte, has machine embroidery over the ribbon and yarn tassels (Fig. 208).

A more crudely made hat with a higher crown worn with a red and blue string tied around it was said to be worn in Chismote (east of the Panamerican highway), as well as in Santa Lucia, Pachamama, San Carlos, San José, Tipín, Galte, and García Moreno (Fig. 209). Laura Miller's pass through San Carlos, San José, Tipín, and Garcia Moreno, communities west of the Panamerican highway between Tixan and Palmira, confirms this information. The Chismote women were distinguished by masses of ribbons of various colors tying their hair in back (Pl. XI).

205 *Man in Palmira Dávalos, Chimborazo province, weaving on a treadle loom. Slide by Lynn A. Meisch, 1989.*

206 Blouse purchased in the Guamote market, said to have been made in San José de Chacaza, Chimborazo province. Cotton plain weave, embroidered with acrylic thread. Overall size: 1.26 x 1.395 meters (49½ x 55 inches), including sleeves. The Textile Museum 1988.19.129, Latin American Research Fund.

207 Woman wearing a Galte-Tiocajas hat in the Guamote market, Chimborazo province. She wears a blue changalli over a black anaku and two red shawls over a pink one. Slide by Lynn A. Meisch, 1989.

208 Woman wearing a red shawl and a hat with machine embroidery on the pink ribbon, at the Guamote market, Chimborazo province. Slide by Lynn A. Meisch, 1989.

Opposite:
209 Woman with high crown hat worn in San Carlos, San José, Tipin, and Garcia Moreno, at the Guamote market, Chimborazo province. She has a green changalli, a kawiña chumbi, and gold color, over red, black, and pink shawls. Slide by Lynn A. Meisch, 1989.

210 *Group of women wearing red changallis and shawls, at the Guamote market, Chimborazo province. Slide by Ed Healy, 1988.*

Opposite:

211 *Man in a red poncho and zamarros on horseback, at the Guamote market, Chimborazo province. Slide by Laura M. Miller, 1989.*

212 *Man in undyed poncho and zamarros and a warp-resist patterned scarf, at the Guamote market, Chimborazo province. Slide by Lynn A. Meisch, 1989.*

The multiplicity of hats ascribed to a single area, such as Galte, may be because women from small hamlets give as their residence the nearest larger community. In any case, this summary does not exhaust the variety of hats seen in the Guamote market. For example, we saw a group of women in similar costumes, all with red changallis and shawls, each wearing a hat with a wide ribbon and red strings over the top similar to a style also worn in southern Chimborazo (Fig. 210).

Men's Costume in the Guamote Area
Laura M. Miller

Most indigenous men in the Guamote market were wearing a costume that seems general for southern Chimborazo (see chapter 11). Virtually all were wearing ponchos, the vast majority of which are red, with no fringe and falling to just below the waist (Fig. 211). They have triangular gussets in the back and collars, and some also have edge binding.

Many men wear chaps (*zamarros*). Some chaps are made in Riobamba and sold there or brought to Guamote for sale. In addition, chaps are made and worn in Galte and Tipín. Men who wear the chaps are also said to be from Palmira and from as far away as Osogochi to the southwest. The chaps are made of unsheared sheepskin, and the wool goes all the way around the leg, even in the inseam. Most of the chaps seen in Guamote were of white sheep's wool, but a few were dark wool.

Interestingly, many of the men wear warp-resist patterned shawls around their necks like scarves (Fig. 212). Both the macanas from Rumipamba, in Cotopaxi province, and low-quality shawls called *pacotillas* from the Gualaceo area in Azuay province are used.

Most men wear dark-colored fedora hats, but we saw a few elderly men with white felt hats.

Many men carry whips with them to market. They usually wear these diagonally across the chest, with the wooden handle at their backs and the leather part of the whip across their chests. Several of the whip handles are decorated with brass.

The Guamote Market

Lynn A. Meisch and

Laura M. Miller

Guamote is the capital of its cantón and is situated at 3,026 meters (9,928 feet)—and it feels like it, windy and cold. Although the towns of Guamote and Palmira are predominantly mestizo-white, the surrounding countryside is overwhelmingly indigenous. Even after agrarian reform, however, most of the land in the cantón has remained in the hands of large landowners (see Iturralde 1977:79).

We saw more different kinds of costume worn at the Thursday Guamote market than anywhere else in Ecuador. Rural people come from all over southern Chimborazo, representing each of the major costume divisions, that is, with a straight wrapped anaku from the southern portion of central Chimborazo, with a pleated anaku from the southern portion of eastern Chimborazo, and with Spanish-style gathered skirts with a waistband (*pollera*) from the northern part of southern Chimborazo.

Guamote is perhaps the market with the greatest percentage of indigenous people. Only some 5 percent of the people present were mestizo-white, and the sellers (many of them mestizo-white) knew sufficient Quichua to call out to clients and to bargain.

A central market area is filled with grains and potatoes. There are very few stalls with processed foods, such as Quaker oats and noodles. There is also a large animal market with cattle, horses, sheep, llamas, and pigs. All kinds of costume items are also sold in the Guamote market: embroidered blouses, anakus, polleras, handwoven and synthetic shoulder wraps, tupus, beads, hand-felted white hats, fedoras, ponchos, carrying cloths, rubber boots, and leather and plastic shoes.

Chapter 11

Southern Chimborazo Province

Introduction

Lynn A. Meisch

Today the region south of Guamote near Palmira and Tixan (see map, page xx) constitutes the Great Skirt Divide. Women south of this line wear pollera skirts instead of anakus, a custom that extends through southern Chimborazo and all of Cañar, Azuay, and Loja provinces. We saw some polleras for sale in a store on the main street of Palmira Dávalos, which as noted is an anaku-wearing community. We were told that the polleras were bought by women from the nearby community of Moyacancha, where polleras are worn.

The skirts and shawls within southern Chimborazo are all basically similar, so the costume from one community to another is differentiated mainly by the hats, hairstyles, and jewelry. People identify themselves by community in this area.

Sanganao Area

Ann P. Rowe and

Laura M. Miller

On the west side of the Panamerican highway, anakus are worn as far south as the area between Cochapamba (a mestizo-white town) and Sanganao.[1] In Sanganao and in nearby Yauti Alto, a costume with pollera is worn (Fig. 213). The polleras (also called *centro*), in contrast to those discussed below, are made of machine-made cotton or synthetic fabric in blue or black and have no embroidered trim. They were said to be made in Sanganao or in Tixan. They are worn belted, often with a kawiña chumbi, which can be purchased in Guamote. This costume appears to be transitional from an anaku style to mestizo-white dress.

Over their machine-made turtleneck sweaters, women wear up to three shawls (*bayeta*), which may be handwoven, often red, but we also saw green, blue, and yellow. These fabrics usually have a hem on each end in a contrasting color of thread. The women we met pinned their shawls with large safety pins. Most wear fedoras, but one had a plain white felt hat. One woman from Yauti Alto and one from Sanganao wore their hair in two braids, but others we saw wore their hair wrapped. The latter were also wearing colored-bead necklaces (*wallka*, pronounced "washka"). The beads are purchased in Guamote.

There are several weavers in Sanganao who make blankets, ponchos, and scarves. Ponchos are woven white and taken to Tixan for dyeing.

---

1. This section was written by Ann Rowe, based on notes and photographs by Laura Miller.

213 Group of women in Yauti Alto, near Sanganao, southern Chimborazo province. Slide by Laura M. Miller, 1989.

La Merced,
Zúlac, and Cocán

Ann P. Rowe

Women wearing wool or acrylic polleras in the Guamote market are said to be from the communities of La Merced and Zúlac (Pl. XII, Figs. 214–217).[2] Although this area is primarily agricultural, there is a marble quarry in Zúlac, now belonging to the community. Some people around Cocán keep llamas. The following information has mostly been gathered by talking to and observing people in the Guamote market, though Laura Miller also passed through Zúlac and Cocán. These communities are east of the Panamerican highway between Palmira and Achupallas. We also saw some women in this same costume in the Alausí market.

The women visiting the market were wearing several polleras at the same time. These skirts are just below the knee in length, with 2.5-centimeter-wide (1 inch)—pleats (unpressed) sewn into the waistband. They are machine embroidered along the lower edge and there is a wide strip of printed cotton fabric on the opposite face. Some women wear the outermost skirt so that the embroidery shows, others wear it reversed so that the lining strip shows. Some of the polleras are embroidered with flowers in the same style as Cuenca polleras (Fig. 214), and others have simpler zigzag embroidery (Fig. 215). Red, hot pink, and red-orange skirts are most common, but we also saw blue and green. Many of these women wear the kawiña chumbi wrapped at their waists, over the waistband of their pollera (Figs. 214–215), and others wear supplementary-warp patterned belts.

They wear two or three bayeta shoulder wraps, often with simple machine embroidery at the edge. The shawls are most often large, are worn folded horizontally, and have hemmed ends, but some women wear a fringed wool or acrylic shawl under a shawl with hemmed ends (Fig. 216). The colors of the shawls are similar to those of the skirts. Women also use low-quality, warp-resist patterned shawls from

2. This text is based on information from Laura Miller, Lynn Meisch, and Breenan Conterón, and slides taken by Earthwatch volunteers Carol Siegel, Ken Henisey, and Nancy Tucker.

214

215

216

217

214 *Woman from southern Chimborazo province at the Guamote market wearing a Cuenca style pollera with a kawiña chumbi. Photo by Naeda Robinson, 1989.*

215 *Woman from southern Chimborazo province, at the Guamote market, wearing a locally made blue pollera, a kawiña chumbi, red and hot pink shawls, white beads, and hat with red strings. Slide by Nancy Tucker, 1989.*

216 *Young couple probably from the Zúlac area, southern Chimborazo province, at the Guamote market. Photo by Laura M. Miller, 1989.*

217 *Woman at the Alausí market, southern Chimborazo province, showing her hat with red ribbon and strings, braided hair with colored tassels at the ends, and masses of red beads. Slide by Laura M. Miller, 1988.*

the Gualaceo area of Azuay for carrying things on their backs or supporting a baby carried inside the outer shawl.

Women wear many strands of pea-sized, glass-bead necklaces, most often white, but sometimes red or blue (Fig. 217). Women seen in Cocán wore white beads, while those in Zúlac wore orange beads. Many women at the markets with this style of dress wear their hair in two thick braids at the back, augmented with dark yarn. Most are barefoot.

Many women wear handmade white felt hats, made in Pomatúg. These hats have a low, round crown and a flat relatively narrow brim. Several women were wearing hats with a wide pink or red ribbon around the crown and red strings running from the button to the hatband. In some cases, the pink ribbon extends into long streamers. Some women have several colors of ribbon overlapping around the crown of their hats in place of the pink alone (Fig. 217). A number of women were wearing hats with a white cotton band around the crown, and the red strings, which seems to be the Zúlac style (Figs. 214–215).

Men in Zúlac and Cocán wear red ponchos with collar and gusset, and without edge binding or fringe. Some also wear sheepskin chaps.

Alausí Market and Nizag

Ann P. Rowe

218 *Girl with Nizag hairdo with red yarn, and a blue shawl, in the Alausí market, southern Chimborazo province. Slide by Laura M. Miller, 1988.*

3. The Earthwatch team to Alausí July 31, 1988, led by Laura Miller and Fernando Moreno, included Judith Kelly, Jean Hayden, and Emily Marsland.

4. The information on Nizag is from an August 1989 Earthwatch team led by Julio Chérrez S., accompanied by Jacquelyn Engle, Patricia Meloy, and Sandra Baker.

The Sunday Alausí market is the major market for its area. In the plaza by the church are clothing vendors from whom one could purchase the skirts and warp-resist dyed shawls from Cuenca, the white hats to which one would have to add the colored bands, streamers, and cords, embroidered blouses, and bayeta shawls like those that women were wearing.[3] Nearby streets wind around and down to a produce vending area. Rope vendors are located at a higher overlook. Down near the railroad station, men were stacking sheep and goat hides and vendors were moving bags of potatoes and grain.

The most distinctive indigenous group attending this market is from Nizag, a community in the mountains 3.5 kilometers (2 miles) south of Alausí as the crow flies. Women from this area have an unusual hairstyle, in which the hair is wrapped at the nape of the neck with a large ball of loose yarn in solid bright colors: pink, red, or green (Fig. 218). The sides of the hair are held with metallic barrettes. Some women with this hairstyle wore no hats, others wore the white felt hats with a white hatband and white strings over the crown, and perhaps a single strand of colored yarn around the crown.

Nizag women wear polleras in pink, green, blue, or purple and shoulder wraps in solid pink, dark red, or orange, secured with a tupu. Some women also wear handwoven belts wrapped over their polleras. They use low-quality, warp-resist patterned shawls from the Gualaceo area as carrying cloths. They wear multicolored bead necklaces, and some wear wrist wraps of green beads. Many women wear plastic bird- or chicken-shaped earrings, but some have silver earrings. They are barefoot.

We also visited this community.[4] It seems that the fancy hairstyle is worn only on special occasions, since at home the women we met simply wrapped their hair in a hot pink braided acrylic ribbon. Also, these women were not wearing wrist wraps.

Although most women in Nizag were wearing polleras, one old woman was wearing pleated half-anakus (Fig. 219). The anakus were coarsely woven, the top one dark brown and the bottom one cream-colored. They were secured with a kawiña chumbi. Her cotton blouse had embroidered cuffs and neck area, in a style also worn by other women in the community. The blouse style is more similar to that worn in Saraguro than to the blouses of central Chimborazo. This same woman had a handwoven wool hot pink shawl. Her hat, hairstyle, and jewelry were like those already described. It is possible that in the not too distant past, the Great Skirt Divide was slightly further south than it now is, as suggested also by the fact

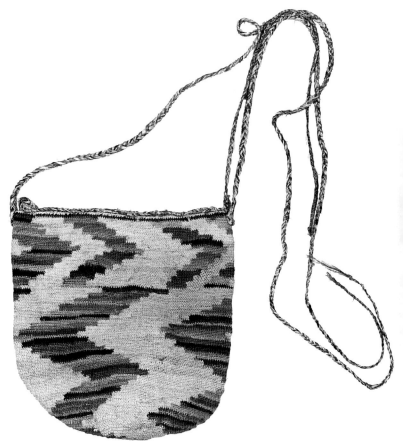

219 *María Agustina Tenemasa, Nizag, southern Chimborazo province, wearing a pleated anaku, as well as a handwoven shawl and handmade hat. Girl wearing a pollera. Photo by Patricia Meloy, 1989.*

220 *Shigra made by María Agustina Tenemasa, from Nizag, southern Chimborazo province. Simple looping of furcraea fiber yarn. Height: 32 centimeters (12½ inches). The Textile Museum 1989.22.64, Latin American Research Fund.*

that handwoven belts are still worn with the pollera in this area as well as in the Sanganao and La Merced areas.

A conservatively dressed man was wearing a handwoven red poncho with black edge binding and a hat similar to the women's, while a younger man was wearing a machine-woven red poncho with stripes and a fedora. The rest of the men's clothes were factory made.

In Nizag we found women making shigras with vertical zigzag designs (Fig. 220). They said they purchased the colored threads, and that the undyed thread they used was furcraea. The bag has two braided handles plus another braid stitched to the rim at intervals with its end hanging free. They said that this size shigra took a month to make.

Achupallas Area

Laura M. Miller

Achupallas is a small town approximately 19.3 kilometers (12 miles) on an unpaved road southeast of Alausí. Before the construction of the Panamerican highway, Achupallas was on the main road from Cuenca to Riobamba. People from Riobamba, Palmira, and Achupallas used to take fava beans, peas, lentils, and potatoes to Cuenca, and they brought back products of Azuay, such as palm leaf "Panama" hats, pears, and apples. The old road is still used for transport of contraband goods, including liquor.

221 Woman in Mapahuiña, near Achupallas, southern Chimborazo province, wearing two polleras, a blue fringed shawl, and a handmade hat. Photo by Laura M. Miller, 1989.

Other nearby communities with a costume similar to Achupallas include Mapahuiña, a 15-minute walk from the center of Achupallas; Letrapungu, 2 kilometers (1¼ mile) east of Achupallas; and Pumallacta, 5 kilometers (3 miles) northwest of Achupallas.[5]

Women's costume

Women wear polleras (also called *follón* or *centro*) similar to those described for other communities in southern Chimborazo province (Fig. 221). At least two polleras are worn at once. Some polleras are brought to the area from Cuenca and are identical to those worn in Azuay province. Others are made in town, by several mestizo-white women with sewing machines, with embroidery of either simple geometric designs or flowers. The edge of the skirt is sometimes scalloped (*orejeado* S.). Local seamstresses also make skirts similar to those of Cañari women, with appliqué designs, as well as skirts decorated with a series of horizontal pleats called *festones* (S.) instead of embroidery, like the *bolsicón* skirts of Cuenca.

The women with sewing machines in Achupallas also embroider the shawls (*rebozo*) with very simple designs such as zigzags or curved lines around the edges. The shawls may also be embellished with floral designs in the corners. Some rebozos are commercially made, but others are woven in the community on the backstrap loom or on the treadle loom. A woman may wear two shawls at once. Some women use a shawl pin (*tupu*) to hold the rebozo about their shoulders (Fig. 222). Others knot the ends together.

Many women in the Achupallas area wear a blouse (*camisa* S.) that is embroidered at the yoke (*hombrera* S.) and cuffs (*puño* S.) (Fig. 223). Several town women who own small stores do this embroidery, and rural women around Achupallas also embroider their own blouses. Designs for the embroidery include a leaflike design called *realce* (S.) and scallop work called *filete* (S.). The blouses are similar to those worn in Nizag.

A woman in town who embroiders and sells these blouses, Rosa viuda de Zea, lamented that the younger women no longer wear them but use factory-made T-shirts and acrylic cardigans instead. The same vendor also sells baby bonnets (*gorra* S.) for indigenous use.

Women wear their hair in a single braid at the back, often with many different colors of yarn braided in. Some younger girls wear their hair in two braids, similar to the style of rural Azuay. No one in this area wore their hair wrapped.

Many older women wear white felt hats, while younger women and girls wear dark-colored fedoras. The white hats, called *sombreros de lana de lado de Ambato*, are probably made in the hat-making workshops in the Pelileo barrio of Pomatúg. The Achupallas style hats have little embellishment: just a few white strings across the crown, a strip of white cloth at the base of the crown, and simple diamonds machine embroidered on the white cloth covering the edge of the brim.

Women wear beads (*wallka* Q.) at their necks. The necklaces are only a few

5. The Earthwatch team to Pumallacta in August 1989 was led by Julio Chérrez S., accompanied by Sandra Baker and Patricia Meloy.

strands in this area, and the beads are usually fairly small, about the size of peas. Red beads predominate in this area.

Many women of the Achupallas area wear earrings (*zarcillos* S.) like those common in both the Cuenca and Cañar regions. One style, also found in Cañar, is decorated with a small molded bird. Often a woman wears a colored ribbon that connects both earrings and rests on the nape of her neck. Presumably this keeps her from losing one earring and ruining the pair.

The simplest kind of cotton warp-resist patterned shawls made in the Gualaceo area (Azuay province) are used as carrying cloths. We did not see belts in this area.

Men's costume

Common poncho colors are red or blue, often with stripes, though red predominates. The ponchos usually have no collar or gusset in the back and have no edge tape, either. Men also wear chaps (*zamarros*) of sheep skin on cold rainy days when outside working in the fields. Most wear fedoras. Very few men wear the simple white felt hats the older women still wear.

Textile production

A woman wanting a pollera brings the cloth (*bayeta*)—often a treadle-loom woven balanced twill—to one of the local seamstresses and pays her to sew the skirt and embroider the hem. There are also dyers in Achupallas who specialize in dyeing fabric for the polleras. One seamstress with whom we spoke, María Luisa Ortega, had only one pollera to show, since the rest of her work had been picked up by the owners. When embroidering a pollera, she first places a strip of cloth, called *guarda polvo* (S., dust protector), on the back of the fabric and then machine embroiders the designs.

Many men in the Achupallas area know how to weave, both on backstrap looms and treadle looms. One weaver we talked to in Mapahuiña in August 1989, Simón Cachipulla Auqui, was weaving an orange and red warp-striped poncho for his nine-year-old grandson on the backstrap loom. He told us that many men in the area use the backstrap loom to weave ponchos for themselves and shawls for women in their families. This weaver is well known and receives commissions (*obras*) from other rural people and from "gente blanca" from town.

We encountered several women spinning Z-twist thread with a vertical spindle (Fig. 221).

222 *Woman in Letrapungo, near Achupallas, southern Chimborazo province, wearing two red shawls fastened with a tupu and a handmade hat. Photo by Laura M. Miller, 1989.*

223 Blouse made by Berta Álvarez,
Achupallas, southern Chimborazo province.
Cotton plain weave (unbleached muslin),
embroidered with dark red and green
acrylic yarns. .76 x 1.28 meters (30 x 50⅜
inches), including sleeves. The Textile
Museum 1989.22.59, Latin American
Research Fund.

Chapter **12**

Cañar Province

Central Cañar

Lynn A. Meisch

Indigenous people who identify themselves as Cañaris now occupy the higher portions of modern Cañar province (see map, page xxi). In 1973 there were an estimated 70,000 Quichua speakers in Cañar Province, 60 percent of whom were monolingual (Stark 1985:470). Today, with increased education and contact with outsiders, many Quichua speakers also speak Spanish. A 1977 map of the ethnic groups of Ecuador, published by the Summer Institute of Linguistics (Wycliffe Bible Translators), put the Cañari population at 40,000.

Indigenous people divide highland Cañar into two parts: *jatun* (Q., great) *Cañar*, comprising the town of Cañar, Sisid, Hierba Buena, Manzanapata, Honorato Vásquez, El Tambo, Quilluag, Ingapirca, and Juncal; and *uru llacta* (Q.) or *zona baja* (S., lower land) to the west, comprising the area around Suscal, Chontamarca, Socarte (also known as General Morales), Zhud, Gun Grande and Gun Chico, Gullandel, and Cercapata, to list the major communities. This area is in fact of lower elevation and has a warmer climate than jatun Cañar. Costume description in this section is of central highland Cañar, jatun Cañar.[1]

The town of Cañar, at 3,100 meters (10,150 feet), is the market and commercial center, but most indigenous people live at yet higher elevations on the cold, wet, treeless páramo of the western and eastern cordilleras of the Andes. Most Cañaris are farmers, raising corn, beans, potatoes and other tubers, quinoa, barley, and wheat, but some are cattle and sheep herders. Some are seasonal migrants, who work in the sugarcane fields and processing factories in the coastal lowlands or in construction in the highland and coastal cities.

The Cañaris have a reputation in Ecuador for being *bravo* (S.), or fierce. Because many white landowners resisted the 1964 reforms, violent land takeovers have occurred in Cañar and elsewhere. Some land was redistributed to individuals or to cooperatives, but many large haciendas remain. In Cañar, as elsewhere in the sierra, land redistribution is high on the indigenous peoples' political agenda.

1. This information was collected in 1977–79, with return visits in 1989 and 1993, in the communities of Cañar, Sisid, Manzanapata, Hierba Buena, El Tambo, and Ingapirca. See also Meisch 1980a–b.

230

Women's costume

Women and girls wear two different kinds of locally made blouses. One is a white cotton pullover long-sleeved blouse (*camisa* S.) with hand or machine embroidery on the yoke and cuffs (Figs. 224–225). The other, often made of a cotton print or of shiny, synthetic fabric, is either a pullover or has buttons up the back and is trimmed with lace and rickrack at the cuffs, neckline, lower hem, and sometimes on the bodice (Fig. 226). Both kinds of blouse can be bought in the market or in shops on Calle Guayaquil in Cañar, but women with treadle sewing machines make their own. In addition to the blouse, or sometimes instead of it, women and girls may wear commercially manufactured acrylic sweaters.

Women and girls wear a gathered pollera skirt, just below the knee in length (Figs. 224, 227). Some polleras are made locally from handwoven wool fabric (*bayeta*) and gathered into a handwoven waistband (*reata* S.). They are finished around the hem with appliqué (Fig. 227), machine embroidered with flowers, and finished with edging or scallops. A 15-to-20 centimeter (6–8 inch) piece of cotton fabric is sewn to the inside of the skirt to form a backing for the embroidery. Some

224 Girls in Manzanapata, Cañar province. Slide by Lynn A. Meisch, 1981.

225 *Woman's blouse, purchased at the Cañar market. Cotton-polyester blend in plain weave, embroidered with acrylic yarns. 61 x 149 centimeters (24 x 58⅝ inches), including sleeves. The Textile Museum 1986.19.83, Latin American Research Fund.*

skirts have sequins or metallic-thread embroidery. The use of appliqué distinguishes the Cañari style from similar skirts made in the Cuenca area. Also, Cañari polleras are made in a variety of bright solid colors, while Cuenca ones occur only in pink, red, orange, and yellow. Two or three polleras are worn at once on special occasions, and the front of the top skirt may be tucked up into the waistband to reveal the decorations on the skirt (or skirts) below. Polleras are often worn inside out around the house to protect the "right" side (Fig. 228).

Some Cañari women wear skirts made in Cuenca from cotton, wool, or synthetic velour fabric commercially manufactured in Quito. There are two Cuenca skirt styles (see chapter 13). The first is the pollera or centro, which is machine embroidered with flowers around the hem. The second style is the bolsicón, which has numerous horizontal tucks near the hem and is made in green, blue, or purple. While all Cañari females wear one or more polleras, not everyone wears the bolsicón; this seems to be a matter of personal preference. The skirts are sold in the Cuenca, Cañar, Paute, Azogues, Gualaceo, and other regional markets.

226 Presentación Duy Tenesaca in complete traditional dress, Manzanapata, Cañar province. Photo by Lynn A. Meisch, 1979.

227 Cañari woman wearing a yellow appliquéd pollera and a warp-resist patterned carrying cloth made in Azuay, in the Cañar market. Slide by Lynn A. Meisch, 1979.

228 Etelvina Zaruma with baby wrapped in appliqué patterned cloth, Manzanapata, Cañar province. She is wearing her skirt inside out. Photo by Lynn A. Meisch, 1979.

If the skirt is homemade, it is gathered into a handwoven band made of wool or of fine commercial acrylic yarn. The waistband is woven in warp-faced plain weave with lengthwise stripes and crosswise bars, which result from warping alternate colors of yarn. If the pollera or bolsicón is made in Cuenca, the waistband is a striped cotton commercial band from the PASA (Pasamanería Sociedad Anónima) factory. Cañari women sometimes wrap a handmade band over a Cuenca-made pollera.

The woman's rectangular shoulder wrap is called a *wallkarina* or *tupullina* in Cañar (Figs. 224, 227). Some are woven in one panel in a plain weave from handspun wool on the backstrap loom, then dyed black, blue, purple, or dark green. A Textile Museum example (1986.19.67), decorated with a single narrow blue stripe near one edge, is 1.18 by .60 meters (46½ by 23½ inches). Some wallkarinas have warp-resist dyed stripes; the example in Figure 229 has blue warp-resist bands overdyed with black. Treadle-loom woven bayeta or factory-made acrylic velour or wool cloth from Quito (*paño* S.) is also used. The wallkarina is edged with commercial cloth tape and machine embroidered. It is wrapped around the shoulders and fastened with a shawl pin (*tupu*) or safety pin (Fig. 230). In fact, *tupullina* means to bring the tupu onto the body, while *wallkarina* means to bring the *wallka* (necklace) onto the body.

229 *Wallkarina with warp-resist dyed pattern, from Sisid, Cañar province. Warp-faced plain weave, with blue acrylic plain areas, and wool warp-resist stripes. 84 x 43 centimeters (33 x 17 inches). The Textile Museum 1994.15.3, Latin American Research Fund.*

The tupus commonly worn today are made of nickel, nickel washed in silver, or low-grade silver. One style is silver or brass with a disk-shaped head, similar to Inca examples. Two other styles have more ornamentation, including one with pronounced protrusions, like the petals of a daisy, with a piece of colored glass set in the center (Fig. 230). The third tupu style is flat and six-sided, inlaid with small, round pieces of colored glass. The fourth style has a head made from old silver coin. A fifth style, quite common, is silver, in the form of a round ball with a thin, pointed shaft. There is a very rare tupu, which is made of brass in the form of the head and bust of an indigenous woman. All contemporary tupus are about 10 to 13 centimeters (4 or 5 inches) long and have a metal loop. A ribbon is passed through the loop, and when the tupu is pinned through the wallkarina, the ribbon is wrapped around both ends of the tupu to keep it from falling out.

There are several white jewelers in the town of Cañar who make and sell tupus and earrings. One of these jewelers is actually from Gualaceo, where he has a jewelry store and workshop, but he comes to Cañar on market days, where he has a store in the main market building (Karen O. Bruhns, personal communication, 1992).

Earrings (*zarcillos*) are today considered essential for women and girls (Fig. 230). Baby girls have their ears pierced soon after birth. Cheap metal costume jewelry earrings are sold in the market, but finer silver and gold earrings are available in shops in Cañar and Cuenca. Fine earrings are sometimes connected by a silver chain (*cadena*) or ribbon worn around the woman's neck to keep the earrings from getting lost if they slip out. Two popular styles are little birds and hearts and hands of Fatima.

Cañari women and girls wear many strands (*sartas* S.) of beads as necklaces (*wallka* Q.), which are worn as chokers rather than as long strands. The beads range from antique European glass trade beads to more modern glass and plastic ones. No single color or style predominates and usually there are several colors combined in a strand. Some strands are also strung with old coins. In the 1990s some Cañari women began wearing kingu wallkas from Saraguro (chapter 14).

Cañari women and girls wear their hair long, either braided in a single braid or pulled back and wrapped or tied with a ribbon.

Most Cañari men and women wear a handmade white felt hat with a narrow brim that is sometimes turned up in front. There were a few local hatmakers in the 1970s, but most hats are from Pomatúg, outside Pelileo, Tungurahua. In 1988 in Cacha Machángara, Chimborazo, we met two local hatmakers, the Guapi brothers, who had learned in Pomatúg and, in turn, were teaching three Cañaris (two men and a woman) from Cuchucún so that they could return to their communities and make Cañari style hats (Fig. 231). The Pomatúg hats are adapted to Cañari style by having the brim molded, commercial cotton edging (*ribete* S.) sewn on the edge of the brim, and tassels (*sisa* Q., flower) tied around the crown. Some Cañaris are now wearing factory-made dark brown fedoras.

Footwear for women includes rubber boots, sandals made from old car or truck tires, and plastic shoes from the market.

Women carry bundles in their wallkarinas, but they also buy low-quality, warp-resist patterned shawls (*paños pacotillos*), which are made around Gualaceo in Azuay, to use as carrying cloths (Fig. 227).

Men's costume

Some men and boys wear a white cotton pullover shirt (*camisa*) with long, full sleeves, cuffs, collar, front placket, and diamond-shaped gussets under the arm (Figs. 231–232). The shirt is hand or machine embroidered on the collar, sleeves, and cuffs. Like women's blouses, these shirts are sold in the Sunday Cañar market and in stores in Cañar along Calle Guayaquil. Factory-made shirts, sweaters, sweatshirts, and jackets are also worn.

Men and boys wear a black wool tunic (*kushma*) over the shirt (Fig. 231). Cañari kushmas are never sewn up the sides, but are lapped back-over-front (or more rarely, front-over-back) and wrapped with a belt. As many as three kushmas are sometimes worn at once. Kushmas are always made from fine, handspun wool. They are woven in one piece on the backstrap loom, with the slit for the neck woven in. The Textile Museum example (1986.19.71) is 1.56 by .755 meters (61½ by 29¾ inches). Kushmas are dyed after they are woven. Then the kushma is taken to a local woman who owns a treadle sewing machine, who edges it around the outside and the neck with cotton or velvet tape (*ribete* S.). Some kushmas are even

230 Shawl pin and earrings, purchased in Cañar. Length of tupu: 14 centimeters (5½ inches). Length of earrings: 6.5 centimeters (2½ inches). The Textile Museum 1986.19.82 and 1986.19.81a,b, Latin American Research Fund.

231 *Rafael Pichisaca, of Cuchucún, Cañar province, with his sister, photographed in Cacha Machángara. Photo by Lynn A. Meisch, 1988.*

edged with homemade rickrack. Little rows of zigzags are machine embroidered on or near the edge binding, and all four corners are embroidered with little flowers. This edging, which is not at all necessary on a four-selvedge textile, is a distinctive feature of Cañari costume, distinguishing Cañari kushmas from similar ones that were worn until recently in such Chimborazo communities as Pulucate.

The Cañari kushma is wrapped with a belt (*chumbi*), which has intricate pick-up motifs (Figs. 233–234). The weave structure is a complementary-warp weave with 3-span floats in alternating alignment (Figs. 19–20). The traditional colors are wine-red (*lacre* S., sealing wax) and white or black and white. Today as many as six colors are used, in stripes, three on each side. The belts are woven from extremely fine handspun wool or from Singer cotton sewing thread. Occasionally acrylic yarn is used, especially in the border. The belt is wrapped with the ends tucked in and left hanging in back (Pl. XIII). Sometimes the looped fringe at the end of the belt is left hanging, but it is also finished in an eight-strand braid (*tocumado*). The belt can

232 *Man's shirt, purchased in the Cañar market. Cotton in twill weave and plain weave, embroidered with acrylic thread. 71 x 154 centimeters (28 x 61½ inches), including sleeves. The Textile Museum 1986.19.84, Latin American Research Fund.*

also be decorated with commercially made ribbons, which are sewn to the end loops and to the finished edge of the beginning of the belt.

The men's belts are sometimes used to swaddle babies, and on two occasions I have seen a woman wearing one. In 1992 I saw a Cañari man with a traditional belt made into a modern-style belt, complete with metal buckle and grommets. Similar belts are made in artesanías shops in Cuenca for sale to tourists.

While a weaver can include designs of his own invention, a number of motifs appear on almost all belts. These include such animals as llamas, goats, cows, horses, deer, foxes, doves, and ducks engaged in various activities including fighting and copulating; such religious symbols as angels, chalices, and crosses; the sun, flowers, plants, numerals, people, mountains, the ruins of Ingapirca, Inca pots and skeletons, the train that runs through Cañar, local buses; exotic figures from calendars and books, including horses and elephants; and, ironically, the Cañaris' old enemy Atau Huallpa and his general Rumi Ñahui. One belt has Atau Huallpa with

233 *Belt woven by Rafael Pichisaca, of Cuchucún, Cañar province (cf. Fig. 231). Complementary-warp weave, in black and white cotton sewing thread. 2.75 x .041 meters (9 feet ¼ inches x 1⅝ inches), excluding tie. The Textile Museum 1988.19.99, Latin American Research Fund.*

a sword and Rumi Ñahui with a necktie. Sometimes the weaver's name, the date, and his village are woven in. Various writers (Fock and Krener 1978, Meisch 1980a, Fock 1981, Salomon 1987) have commented on the irony of the contemporary Cañaris' identification with the Incas, given the horrendous treatment they suffered at Inca hands.

Some older men wear ankle-length black pants, made from handspun wool fabric (*bayeta* S. or *walutu* Q.) woven in a balanced twill weave on the treadle loom (Fig. 231). The pants are sometimes machine embroidered with flowers around the cuffs. Cañaris rarely waste anything, so some pants are pieced together from more than twenty small pieces of fabric. Often two pairs are worn at once. Commercially manufactured black or navy blue pants are also used, especially by younger men.

There are three grades or qualities of ponchos worn in Cañar for everyday use. In

Cañar, the term *wanaku* (guanaco) refers to any coarsely spun, plain-weave poncho. *Pacha* (Q., cloth) refers to any plain-weave poncho with fine spinning.

Walutu (or *waluto*) in Cañar refers to twill-weave handspun wool fabric (*bayeta*), woven on the treadle loom. A common style has red and black checks. It is made from black and white bayeta overdyed with red synthetic dye. These ponchos are similar to the jirga ponchos worn in Chimborazo province, and probably were produced originally in colonial obrajes.

Besides grades of ponchos there are a bewildering variety of ponchos worn for daily use in Cañar province. The ponchos vary in size from small ones covering only the upper chest to ponchos that come to mid-thigh (Fig. 235 shows a typical short one). Among the varieties are solid black ponchos, solid red ones, or ponchos that are predominantly red, burgundy, blue, or black with contrasting narrower groups of stripes; for example, black with blue stripes, red with blue and white stripes, red with green, maroon with white, black, and green, etc. Ponchos are usually backstrap-loom woven from 2-ply handspun wool yarn, but fine acrylic yarn is also employed. Karen Bruhns (personal communication, 1992) observed Cañari men near Rivera (locally called Zhoray) wearing ponchos made from commercially produced acrylic knit fabric.

Warp-resist patterned ponchos (*poncho amarrado* S.), finely woven on the backstrap loom, are worn for fiestas and weddings and on market day (Pl. XIII).

234 Belt made outside of the Cañar/ Quilluag/Manzanapata area, Cañar province. Complementary-warp weave, of red and white wool. 2.85 x .05 meters (9 feet 4 inches x 2 inches). The Textile Museum 1986.19.64, Latin American Research Fund.

235 Man in the Cañar market wearing a short poncho. Photo by Lynn A. Meisch, 1981.

There are two main color combinations, one predominantly blue or black and the other predominantly red. The choice of color seems to be personal, rather than indicative of the wearer's community. For example, both red and blue warp-resist ponchos are worn by males from the community of Sisid. The warp-resist patterned stripes are usually red overdyed with black. A common motif is a rough diamond shape, called *cruz churuku* (S., cross; Q., a small snail). Narrower warp-resist dyed bands bordering the main ones have small blocks or dots called *puntos* (S., dots). Some warp-resist patterned ponchos now contain acrylic yarn in the main, nonpatterned part of the poncho, with the patterned stripes made from handspun wool.

Like kushmas, all Cañari ponchos are trimmed with cloth edge binding and usually with machine embroidery. As many as three ponchos in any combination of styles may be worn at once. Except for walutu ponchos, Cañari ponchos are woven in two separate halves on the backstrap loom and joined by hand when they come off the loom.

Contemporary Cañari males employ the concept of layering for warmth, frequently wearing a shirt, then two pairs of wool pants, two or three kushmas, topped by two or three ponchos. They are the only ethnic group in Ecuador whose men wear so many layers, including several kushmas at once.

The Cañaris are one of three ethnic groups (with Otavalo and Saraguro) in Ecuador whose males traditionally never cut their hair, but wear it in a long braid. In Cañar, the braid is often wrapped for an inch or two with a tape or ribbon and tied at the end with colored yarn or tassels. The braid is called a *jimba* or *wangu* (Q.). (*Wangu* is an insult when used by whites.) *Wangu* is the term used for the distaff, and is probably applied to the braid because of its resemblance to a long, straight stick or pole. Some Cañari males cut their hair, especially if they are migrating to the cities or the coast to look for work. The hat style is the same as that described for women.

Males occasionally wear a cotton warp-resist patterned scarf (*bufanda* S.), made around Gualaceo, Azuay. Alternatively, they wear wool or acrylic scarves, some from Otavalo, others handmade. The warp-resist dyed scarves are of the same quality as the pacotillo (lower grade) paños, with relatively simple motifs. The statue of San Antonio (St. Anthony), patron saint of Cañar, in the church of San Antonio on the main plaza in Cañar, has been dressed in a tiny Cañari hat, miniature poncho, and four scarves, both to keep him warm and to indicate his relationship to the community.

Footwear (*ushuta* Q.) varies. Most common are tire-tread sandals made locally and sold in the market or rubber boots manufactured in Guayaquil and also sold in the market and in local stores.

Some men also wear riding chaps made of sheepskin, called *shagshu zamarro*, with the wool still on the hide. They are useful when herding, but they are also worn into Cañar on market day as a status symbol. Several shops on Calle Bolívar in Cañar make and sell zamarros, bridles, whips, and other riding gear. One Cañari told me that brown zamarros are better than white ones because brown wool is better for one's health, a belief also encountered in Gualaceo, Azuay, and Saraguro, Loja (see also note 5).

A mounted Cañari man will carry a whip (*chicote* S.). The handle is usually a round, foot-long piece of wood, often chonta palm, banded with strips of brass. The lash is braided leather, about a yard long. Such whips are useful in sheep and cattle herding, but unmounted Cañaris also use them for protection against packs of dogs and in fights. The chicote is worn slung over one shoulder and under the opposite arm, with the handle in front and the lash in back.

Children's costume

Babies are tightly swaddled in layers of wool and wrapped with a belt or waistband until they are five or six months old. Some of the swaddling cloths are elaborately embroidered and appliquéd, like the bottom of polleras (Fig. 228). Children from about six months to two years are wrapped in a rectangular cloth instead of wearing pants or a pollera, until they are toilet trained. Beginning at about age two children are dressed like miniature replicas of their parents (Fig. 226). I have even seen young boys in the Cañar market wearing fine, small-size, warp-resist patterned ponchos.

Textile production

Most families living in the country in Cañar own at least a few sheep for their own use, but fleece can also be bought or traded among neighbors or at the market. Spinning (with vertical spindle, Z-twist) is considered to be the work of females, but plying (with horizontal spindle, S-twist), warping, and weaving are done by males. These tasks are learned at an early age. A woman is not considered to be marriagable until she can spin well.

Solid-color pieces such as kushmas, ponchos, and wallkarinas are dyed after they are woven. The yarn for belts and for ponchos with stripes is dyed after it is plied and before it is woven. Both men and women dye, although only men do warp resist. The earlier material for wrapping the resist was probably cabuya, but I saw cut-up plastic bags being used. Synthetic dyes are imported from Peru and sold in the Cañar market.

Virtually every household has a backstrap loom, sometimes several. Most Cañari men can weave the complex, complementary-warp patterned men's belt.

Commercial weaving

Traditionally, prisoners serving time in the Cañar jail have woven ponchos, waistbands, and belts to support themselves. In the mid-1980s, the complementary-warp weave belts began to be marketed in Otavalo. To meet the demand, jail weavers began to weave two belts on the same warp, leaving a space for fringe between them, and cutting them apart. Jail weavers also increased the number of horizontal bars separating the motifs from two to six or eight, thus saving time. Cañari weavers occasionally make the trip to Otavalo to sell these belts and Otavalo merchants also stop by the Cañar jail to buy them. Other Cañari weavers are weaving reatas to sell in Azogues as hatbands for palm-leaf hats exported to Germany.

In the 1970s Cañari weavers began to make small wall hangings (about 30 centimeters [12 inches] long by 13 centimeters [5 inches] wide) for sale to the tourist trade in Cuenca and Quito, using traditional belt materials, colors, and motifs. In the late 1980s Cañari weavers began using colored cotton sewing thread to make plain-weave scarves, napkins, placemats, and ponchos, which are sometimes decorated with warp stripes and have a thick weft that gives them a ribbed appearance. These items are woven on the backstrap loom for sale, primarily to non-Cañaris.

Western Highland Cañar

Lynn A. Meisch and

Laura M. Miller

There are several variations on both the female and male costume that are typical of this region.[2] Young women from the Suscal region wear a square, silky, colorful polyester print scarf over their backs and shoulders and knotted across the chest, instead of a wool shawl (Fig. 236). The scarves are too light for warmth or for use as carrying cloths and are worn solely for adornment. In the warmer climate, a wool shawl is not needed. A few old women in the Suscal area wear white handmade felt hats with red strings across the brim, like those worn by indigenous women in southern Chimborazo province. Other similarities to Chimborazo female costume include the use of small bead earrings made into a loop and multicolored bead wrist wraps. The Suscal market also has a larger supply of the simple warp-resist patterned Gualaceo area paños for sale than do other Cañar markets.

The majority of males and females wear green, brown, olive, or dark blue fedoras with narrow brims, but some older people, and politically conscious younger people, wear Cañari hats with minimal trim that includes gold and multicolored braid (imported from Japan) around the crown. Some of these hats are decorated with bird pompoms—yarn pompoms that have a small, paper beak attached—that are sold in the Suscal market.

More males have short hair, although most men do wear their hair in a braid. Many who wear a braid insert yellow, blue, and red strings about halfway through the braiding and plait them with the hair.

2. The text was written by Meisch using information from Miller, who did extensive research on costume and weaving in Suscal between 1985 and 1986, as well as on tuberculosis in 1992.

236 *Filomena Lema Yupangui peeling potatoes, Quilloloma, near Suscal, western Cañar province. Photo by Laura M. Miller, 1992.*

Eastern Cañar

Lynn Hirschkind

3. The author resides at a hacienda near Colepato. Bibliographic references consulted were Brown-rigg 1972, Cordero 1981 [1920], Correa and Pacheco 1992, Einzmann and Almeida 1991, Espinoza and Achig 1981, Espinoza 1989, Iglesias 1985, Muñoz 1986, and Oberem 1981. See also Hirschkind 1995, written subsequent to the present volume.

The Quichua-speaking population in eastern Cañar province inhabits the agricultural cooperatives of Huairapungo, Colepato, and Queseras and environs. These people consider themselves to be distinct from other indigenous people in Cañar, and interrelated among themselves by kinship ties. The origins and history of this population have yet to be thoroughly researched. Therefore, the data upon which this work is based come from contemporary observations and conversations as well as from locally available published sources.[3]

It may be briefly noted that the subjects of this essay are not the only indigenous people in eastern Cañar. Other people of indigenous ancestry, identifiable by their surnames or by kinship with others having indigenous surnames, live throughout the canton of Azogues, especially in Taday and Pindilig parishes. Taday and Pindilig were important prehispanic settlements, the populations of which were only peripherally incorporated into the Inca and Spanish colonial empires. Today, only a few old people in this population speak Quichua; most of them are monolingual Spanish speakers. Their dress conforms to standard Ecuadorian peasant wear, mostly of machine manufacture, and they do not use ethnicity to define their communities.

Until about 1950, the present-day cooperatives of Huairapungo, Colepato, and Queseras were a single, vast, private hacienda. The hacienda was bequeathed to the Catholic Church in about 1950 and thereafter passed into the hands of the state. When the agrarian reform laws were passed in 1964, Huairapungo became a cooperative owned by its workers. Queseras separated from Huairapungo after the 1964 Agrarian Reform legislation was in place and Huairapungo had already become a cooperative. Although Quesereños share the same surnames as Huairapungos and Colepatos, they are geographically isolated from central Huairapungo and felt they could manage their affairs better, and more to their advantage, as a separate, autonomous organization.

At present, each member family holds title to a plot of land on the former hacienda, and the rest is held by the cooperative and worked by its members communally. Huairapungo has about 270 families and a total population of 1,000. Colepato has about 50 families and a population of 250. Queseras is the smallest of the three cooperatives and sits on the poorest agricultural land. It has about 35 member families.

Subsistence and settlement patterns

Huairapungo was considered to be the finest state hacienda (Brownrigg 1972:321). With over 12,000 hectares (46⅓ square miles), it encompasses the upper Huairapungo River watershed and large areas of river plain. The higher region consists of páramo grasslands at up to 4,200 meters (13,775 feet) above sea level and is used for extensive cattle and sheep grazing and some potato cultivation. The lower region, at an average altitude of 3,500 meters (11,480 feet), is used mainly for pasturing dairy cattle. Potatoes, beans, and grains are also grown in this area. Both the cooperative and its individual member families own dairy cows, whose milk is sold daily to a local processing plant. Milk provides a substantial cash income, making Huairapungos "rich" by local peasant standards (Correa and Pacheco 1992.).

Subsistence agriculture is practiced on the individual holdings, providing staple foods and a seasonal surplus that is sold locally or in the Ingapirca or Cañar markets. Each September, Huairapungos take horses loaded with potatoes over the páramo to Colepato where they trade for corn. Cooperative members also have preferential access to the produce cultivated on communal lands. Cooperative produce may be given out in equal shares to member families, sold at below-market prices to members, or sold wholesale at the Cañar market.

Agricultural production on Queseras' 1,500 hectares (3706.5 acres) is similarly based on extensive cattle raising in the páramos and intensive animal husbandry on pasturelands. Milk is sold daily to an itinerant buyer who resells it to the processing plant. Potatoes and other tubers, fava beans, and grains are the principal crops, produced both by the cooperative for commercial sale and by individual members for private consumption and sale of surpluses. Milk and crop sales are facilitated by an all-season road connecting Queseras with Azogues. A second road links the cooperative center with central Huairapungo and from there to Cañar.

Colepato is more isolated than Huairapungo and Queseras. The road linking the Colepato cooperative center with Rivera (Zhoray), the parish town, is passable only in dry weather and often not even then, since broken log bridges and landslides frequently block the route. Colepatos rely on horses to transport themselves and their produce to Rivera or to Huairapungo.

Colepato cooperative owns about 5,000 hectares (12,355 acres) of páramo grasslands, native cloud forest, and cleared agricultural land. From 4,000 meters (13,120 feet) altitude in the páramo, these lands descend steeply to 2,600 meters (8,525 feet) at the cooperative's lower border. The lower region is used for mixed dairy and crop production, while the páramo is used sporadically for cattle grazing. Colepato's milk is made into fresh cheese and sold at the weekly market in Rivera. Corn is the principal crop. It is the dietary staple, consumed as boiled kernels, and surpluses are also sold at harvest or traded to Huairapungos for potatoes. Commercial crops of peas and wheat are grown, with small amounts consumed locally. Each family cultivates small plots of broad beans, potatoes, onions, and other vegetables for its own use.

Small numbers of sheep, pigs, chickens, guinea pigs, and horses are raised by each household. These animals provide food for the family and cash when needed. The sheep provide wool for family needs: ponchos, pants, shawls, blankets, and horse blankets. Huairapungo maintains a much larger sheep herd than the other two cooperatives because it has much more available pasture land. Horses are necessary for transportation within the cooperatives which lack internal road networks. Men, women, and children are adept riders and take pride in their ability.

Settlement patterns in each of the cooperatives are dispersed: each family lives on its private holding. Horse trails connect houses with one another and with the cooperative administrative center. Administration buildings occupy the sites of former hacienda establishments. Each cooperative has a chapel and a volleyball court next to the *casa comunal* or community center. Weekly meetings are held here to discuss cooperative business and internal affairs. Property belonging to the cooperative, such as stored grains, potatoes, tools, agricultural supplies, cooking equipment, and so on, is also stored here. A small dry goods store operates in the community center, supplying basic groceries and household supplies.

Most homes consist of at least two separate buildings, and sometimes three. The larger one, usually a 4 by 6 meter (13 by 19.5 feet) rectangle, is used for sleeping and storage. The smaller structure, usually 3 by 4 meters (10 by 13 feet), is used for cooking, eating, and storing cooking supplies and utensils. Most of these buildings are made of wattle-and-daub walls with sheet-metal roofing and dirt floors. In

Queseras, straw roofs are more common because the grass needed, *Stipa ichu,* is readily available in great abundance. In Colepato, there are a few wooden houses, made with boards hewn from hardwoods taken from the cooperative's forest. Queseras and Huairapungo own no significant forests, and members of these cooperatives will seek to buy or trade wooden implements such as yokes for oxen, plows, feed troughs, and carved bowls made by Colepatos.

In Huairapungo there are adobe houses as well as the usual wattle-and-daub constructions, and recently some cement block and brick houses with corrugated asbestos roofing have been built. The use of these new materials is indicative of the comfortable economic position of some Huairapungo households.

The basic house plan is the same in all three cooperatives. The houses are one story (though two-story houses also exist and are considered very high class), with one room, one door, and one window with a wooden shutter. Outside the door but under the roof overhang is a *corredor* (S.), a sheltered area in which to receive guests, to sit, and to weave. Inside the house are one or two beds, a trunk or cabinet, and a small table with a bench or a few chairs. The walls have many nooks where small things are stored, and pegs from which clothes hang. There is usually a half attic made from bamboo-like canes fixed at ceiling level. Grain and large things are stored in the attic. The outside walls also have pegs or hooks from which to hang saddles, bridles, and plowing tools.

Population

The population of the three cooperatives appears to be stable. A small number of young men and women leave each year to seek work or to marry outsiders. From Colepato, many go to Biblián canton where Colepatos have established a small community. A number of young men have married into the local population. For many of them, the establishment of affinal, compadrazgo, and friendship ties has provided them with the knowledge and the means to migrate to the United States. Nevertheless, out-migration from the cooperatives is minimal, and all three are presently dealing with the problem of allotting communal lands to new nuclear families.[4] So long as the cooperative economies continue to thrive, this pattern of population stability should be expected to continue. Cooperative members are more secure and comfortable economically than many of their mestizo neighbors, so the attractions of out-migration are attenuated. The strong ethic of ethnic superiority professed by many respected group members also discourages migration. They claim to be of "better quality" than the indigenous people who live around Cañar. Huairapungos interviewed by Correa and Pacheco claimed superiority to their braid-wearing neighbors, with whom they said they were unable to get along (1992:166). White and mestizo peasants are referred to as *chazos,* a term that emphasizes the lowly origins and humble circumstances of its objects.

4. This text reflects the situation in 1993 when it was written. By 1997, however, international migration has become a growing trend, the ultimate effects of which remain to be seen. Cash remittances sent by migrants more than compensate for the loss of their labor and are reinvested in part in the subsistence farming they left behind.

Relations with outsiders

Because of the large distances separating the core areas of each cooperative, as well as the existing roads and available means of transportation, members of each cooperative attend separate markets and fiestas. Huairapungos go to Ingapirca or Cañar to sell and to shop. Cañar is the capital of their canton, so they must go there to deal with government officials. Colepatos go to Rivera for market and to Azogues for official business. Quesereños go to Pindilig for market and Azogues for business.

Each cooperative celebrates its own patron saint's day, San Carlos in Colepato and Santa Teresa in Huairapungo. These fiestas are four or five days long and include a Mass and public entertainment consisting of bull fights, horse races, pole climbing, foot races, rooster grabbing, pot bashing, music, and dancing, as well as much eating and drinking. Aside from their own fiestas, members of each cooperative attend others' fiestas and the San Andrés fiesta in Taday, the Virgen de la Nube fiesta in Biblián, the Virgen del Cisne in Loja, and Nuestro Señor de Andacocha in Guachapala.

Huairapungo has earned a reputation for its rejection of outsiders and their interests. In 1987 when the Intercultural Bilingual Educational program was initiated, Huairapungo declined to take part in it. The cooperative decided that, since its members already spoke Quichua, they did not need instruction in their first language and would benefit more from classes in Spanish. If a second language were to be taught, then English would be a useful choice (Correa and Pacheco 1992:42). As this example indicates, Huairapungos are developing their own criteria for accepting or rejecting external influences and do not necessarily follow the advice or example of other indigenous groups and leaders.

All three cooperatives consider themselves private domains: outsiders are not permitted free entry and will be interrogated and escorted off the property unless they can justify their presence. No missionaries, Peace Corps volunteers, or development organizations operate within cooperative boundaries. The only acceptable outsiders are school teachers, land reform agency workers, Ministry of Agriculture employees, and the priest. Recognized local cattle dealers, milk and cheese buyers, and crop merchants also may enter without challenge, since their activities are considered to be in the interests of cooperative members. There are itinerant traders who appear infrequently but are welcomed and provided with room and board for a night. These traders travel on foot carrying huge packs of pots, pans, cloth, clothing, and other small items which they barter for sheepskins or sell for cash. They speak Quichua and apparently come from the Riobamba area.

Traditional dress and contemporary fashion

The sense of distinction that the indigenous people of eastern Cañar feel from their indigenous neighbors is based, in part, on their manner of dress and grooming. Among the men, a short hair cut (Fig. 237) is taken as a sign of being civilized (not

237 *Man with short hair, wearing two ponchos with relatively wide embroidery, from eastern Cañar province, in the Cañar market. Photo by Lynn A. Meisch, 1981.*

238 *Woman with baby, and man, Colepato, eastern Cañar province. The baby's wrapper and the woman's pollera have appliqué designs. The man is wearing handmade pants and a poncho. Photo by Claire Hirschkind, 1993.*

acculturated), while a long braid betrays crudeness. Ironically, outside observers often take Huairapungos to be the quintessence of tradition with the rejection of ideas of Christian civilization that this term usually implies (Correa and Pacheco 1992:159–60; Brownrigg 1972:332). Whatever the historical foundations for their sense of separateness, having lived within the confines of hacienda social organization since the colonial period probably has contributed to eastern Cañar indigenous people's maintenance of an ethnic boundary.

Other details of dress, accessories, and grooming distinguish the eastern indigenous population. Men do not wear the kushmas used in central Cañar or the complementary-warp patterned belts. The older men wear black, homespun, twill-weave woolen pants, often with machine embroidery around the cuffs and down the side seams (Fig. 238). They use thick, short, plain-weave ponchos, often dyed red, some with machine embroidery in floral motifs around the edges (Fig. 237). This floral embroidery is more elaborate than that found on ponchos in central Cañar. The older style ponchos have no collar and are worn with the seam running along the shoulders and down the arms. This is a distinctive characteristic of old-fashioned dress. Men wear commercial sweaters under their ponchos and cotton

239 *Old woman spinning, Colepato, eastern Cañar province. Photo by Claire Hirschkind, 1993.*

240 *Man and woman, Colepato, eastern Cañar province. The woman is wearing a Cuenca cholo style blouse and pollera. Photo by Claire Hirschkind, 1993.*

shirts with embroidered cuffs bought in the Cañar market and identical to those used in central Cañar. They also buy the round white felt hats used in central Cañar, under which they wear a square scarf folded into a triangle with the three points tied at the back of the neck. Against the cold they use long woolen scarves wrapped several times around the neck and sheepskin zamarros or chaps. They use Spanish-style spurs strapped to their rubber boots for riding.

They often wear a whip (*chicote*) as a standard accessory. Whips have a 60-centimeter (2-foot) long chonta palm handle wrapped in brass or other metal rings held with studs, and a 90-centimeter (3-foot) rawhide lash. The lash is sometimes a twisted strip, or it may be an intricate multiple-strand braid. Whips are worn with the handle diagonally across the back and the lash across the chest and tied to the handle at the waist in a quick release knot. A tug on the knot allows the wearer to grasp either the handle to use the whip as a herding tool or the lash to use it as a fighting weapon.

Younger men prefer a modified version of this outfit. The wool pants are considered too heavy and are replaced with commercial slacks. The ponchos may be any color, though dark colors predominate, have a sewn-in collar, are worn with the seam running front to back, and usually have warp stripes of commercial yarn of contrasting color (Fig. 238). They prefer fedora hats and mass-produced shirts and aviator-style jackets. Although rubber boots are the standard footwear for everyone, if weather conditions permit, the young men like canvas shoes and leather boots. The head scarf is seldom used now among this younger generation. Large digital watches are common, and most adults wear several steel finger rings. These rings protect against bewitchment.

Older women wear homespun twill-weave skirts (*pollera*), full and gathered at the waist, with a sewn-on woven waistband (*watu* Q.). These skirts may be any color, but red, yellow, pink, blue, and green are favorites. They are machine embroidered around the hem (Figs. 238–239). They are longer than the skirts worn in central Cañar, generally covering to mid-calf. Eastern indigenous people find the knee-length skirts favored by central Cañar women somewhat scandalous. They prefer to cover as much skin as possible, perhaps as a precaution against dangerous airs and winds.

They wear homespun rectangular shawls (*wallkarina*) with floral-patterned machine embroidery and ribbon sewn to the edges (Fig. 239). As with ponchos, the floral embroidery is more elaborate than that found on shawls worn in central Cañar. These shawls are dyed red or black. Women also wear commercial sweaters and blouses purchased in the Cañar market with the buttons down the back and embroidery on the cuffs. They use the round white felt hat and arrange their hair in a single braid down the back, tied at the end with a piece of yarn braided in. They wear rubber boots or plastic shoes to go to market. For riding they add a large, heavy shawl with long fringes, usually in a solid dark color or a two-color plaid. These shawls are purchased from market clothing dealers or in shops.

Younger women wear a modified version of this costume. Many styles of commercial skirts are available in synthetic materials that are cheaper than the homespun and lighter. Commercial shawls are also replacing the homespun ones. Especially popular are the thin wool or synthetic shawls (*chalinas*) produced and sold by Otavalos. Younger women prefer mass-produced blouses with buttons down the front in print materials, or the short chola cuencana blouse with an elastic waistband, gathering across the front, lace on the sleeves and at the neck, and perhaps some sequins or plastic pearls sewn on top of the front gathering (Fig. 240).

Women sometimes wear small whips. All women have pierced ears and wear a wide variety of earrings, from elaborate pearl and silver figurine combinations to a few beads on a string. Most women and girls wear necklaces of red beads with a few contrasting colored beads and charms or crucifixes attached. Many women wear watches. The fedora hats are also replacing the round white ones, but more women than men continue to use the typical Cañar hat.

Children are dressed exactly like adults after they are toilet trained (Fig. 241). Before then they wear a shirt and a cloth wrapped around the waist secured with a wool belt in warp-faced plain weave with warp stripes.

Textile production

The availability and lower cost of mass-produced clothing, together with the status value of some purchased goods, is clearly contributing to the abandonment of homespun and woven textiles. While most older and middle-aged men know how to weave and all women know how to spin, and the clothing and blankets produced at home are considered warmer and much more durable than their commercial counterparts, nevertheless, the costs incurred in their production make the cheaper alternatives much more attractive. Thus, ironically, it is the wealthier sector of the population that continues to produce and use homespun items and this same sector that purchases the latest market fashions (expensive watches with lots of functions, velvet skirts, Colombian fedoras, gold jewelry). Poor people wear the cheapest synthetic skirts, pants, shawls, and ponchos.

Most women own or keep in their care at least a few sheep. In Huairapungo there are large herds of several hundred sheep belonging to single families. In Colepato and Queseras, four to ten sheep is the norm. Sheep are sheared twice a year with scissors. The vast majority of sheep are of Creole ancestry, a very hardy, small breed with medium-length staple and medium-diameter fiber. An average fleece weighs .90–1.35 kilograms (2–3 pounds), including belly wool and leg wool (*chakimillma* Q.). Of this clip, about two-thirds is clothing quality fleece. The poorer quality fleece is used for blankets. At this level of production, most families do not produce enough fleece for family needs. Additional fleeces may be obtained

241 Two girls with cow's head, Colepato, eastern Cañar province. Photo by Claire Hirschkind, 1993.

through barter or purchase from neighbors, but there is little extra fleece available and market clothing must be used instead.

By the time they are twelve or thirteen, most girls are able to spin blanket yarn, a thick, uneven strand that will be plied to even it out somewhat. By the age of fifteen they can spin a fine thread, and their skill continues to improve as they get to be adults. No emphasis is placed on starting young or on becoming especially accomplished. Only girls and women spin, and they also weave belts on a small backstrap loom. Men weave cloth (*bayeta*) and blankets on both the treadle loom and the backstrap loom but do not spin. Spinning is done primarily for personal and family needs, though some women will accept jobs for others. Such spinning is often done in exchange for fleece or other bartered goods.

There is no commerce in textiles. They are not produced for sale. If a family member weaves, he will do so for his immediate family. Otherwise weaving is done on order by a few older men who specialize in this craft. Women take their yarn and a gift (e.g., a guinea pig) to the weaver and ask that specific yardage be made for them. They pay the weaver by the vara, or by the job if short lengths are desired. In Huairapungo, weaving may be paid for in return for labor in agriculture or with agricultural produce (e.g., potatoes, barley, beans).

There are only two active specialist weavers in Colepato, and probably not many more in Huairapungo and Queseras. Young men are generally not interested in weaving as a trade, though they continue to learn the basic skills from their fathers, grandfathers, and uncles. Spinning is taught by mothers to daughters. Weaving and spinning are considered old fashioned subsistence activities, and so do not attract young people who have progressive plans for their futures. Nevertheless, these are considered basic skills and useful for everyone to know.

After yardage is woven, if it is to be made into pants, poncho, skirt, or shawl, it must be taken to the town of Cañar, to one of the many workshops of seamstresses who make indigenous clothing. These workshops cater to all the indigenous people of Cañar province, but are staffed by mestizo and white women. Thus, the cut of the pants, the style of the poncho collar, and the machine-embroidered edging are the same for all the indigenous communities of Cañar. Embroidered edges are about 5 centimeters (2 inches) wide and serve to hold the edges of clothing firmly in place and protect against unravelling. Often, a narrow ribbon is sewn around the extreme edge of a poncho or shawl to make it even more secure. The embroidery is usually designs of flowers, zigzag lines, S-lines, or leaves. These workshops charge substantial fees for cutting, sewing, and embroidering, and represent the biggest expense in the production of homespun clothing.

While pants are always black, ponchos and skirts may be any color, as described above. Yarn is dyed with purchased synthetic powders used in a boiling dye bath. No mordant is used. In the past, natural dyes were used made from local plants and tree bark. In the 1990s this practice is nearly abandoned, though people still know which plants are good for dyeing. I have seen wild blackberries mixed with red synthetic dye used to provide a longer lasting dye. Even black fleece may be overdyed with black synthetic dye to give it a uniform color. The long lasting blackness of clothing made from naturally colored fleece is appreciated because people often find that the synthetic dyes quickly wash out, leaving them with prematurely faded clothing. However, black fleece has a number of drawbacks in local reckoning and people prefer not to raise black sheep. Black wool is considered hot, in the hot/cold scheme of things, and its hotness can cause headaches and even severe illness to susceptible women.[5] Some women are especially sensitive to the dangerous properties of black fleece, while others can handle and spin it without any ill effects. Still other women can work with black fleece when they are well, but succumb to its malignant potency when they are weak or sick.

Both shearing and washing of fleece is considered highly unwise during the five-day period known as *luna tierna* (S.) or new moon. This period begins at the dark of the moon and continues for the five following days. Fleece sheared or washed during this time is said to rot or be infested with moths in a very short time. Planting, weeding, felling trees, and a long list of other activities are also prohibited during the new moon.

The indigenous people of eastern Cañar live in fairly close contact with white and mestizo neighbors. The cooperatives provide an institutional boundary between their members and outsiders, but they do not define this group. Indigenous people who consider themselves, and are considered, members of this group are not affiliated with any cooperative or formal organization, but live as independent peasants in the area, interspersed among nonindigenous neighbors. Indigenous people, whites, and mestizos share a significant common culture, including religious beliefs, medicinal knowledge, agricultural practices, and understandings about the properties of colored fleece and new moons. Dress remains one of the few markers of ethnic identity and is used proudly as such by indigenous people in eastern Cañar.

5. Editor's note: The "hot/cold scheme of things" refers to the medical theory of classical antiquity, according to which illnesses and foods are classified as metaphorically hot or cold, with cold foods used to treat hot diseases and vice versa. It continued to be the basis for European medical practice until modern anatomical studies and was taught in Latin American medical schools until well into the nineteenth century (see Foster 1993).

Chapter **13**

Azuay Province

Lynn A. Meisch

The Spanish city of Cuenca was founded on the site of the Inca city of Tumi Pampa (Plain of the Knife), the capital of the Inca province that included what is now the southern highlands of Ecuador[1] (see map, page xxi). Fine mortarless stonework remains of Inca buildings can be seen along the Tomebamba river in the heart of the modern city. Cuenca is now Ecuador's third largest city, with a population of approximately 250,000. The city has light industry and universities and also serves as the market center for agricultural products and craftwork (*artesanías*) that are produced both in the city and in the surrounding region. Certain small towns are known for their crafts. For example, fine warp-resist dyed shawls (*paños amarrados*) are made in the suburban Gualaceo villages of Bulcay and Bulzhun, pottery and gold and silver jewelry in Chordeleg. Paute is a center for handspun yarn, and many small towns throughout the region, including Azogues and Biblián in Cañar, are centers for the production of the misnamed Panama hats (*sombreros de paja toquilla*).

Although the original population of the Azuay valley before the arrival of the Incas was Cañar, people here no longer identify themselves as such. The valley suffered particularly severe depopulation in the aftermath of the Inca civil war and the Spanish conquest, and new peoples were moved in both under the Incas and under the Spanish administration of the area. Today, two groups of people wear a distinctive costume, one group identifying themselves simply as indigenous, and another group identifying themselves as cholo.

Cholos

In many parts of the Andes, *cholo* is an insult and means an indigenous person who is attempting to present himself or herself as white (the equivalent insult in Cañar and Azuay is *chazo*). In Cañar and Azuay the term *cholo*, which is used by outsiders and by cholos themselves, is not derogatory and refers to a group that is defined by dress and lifestyle, rather than by race. Most cholos now live in the countryside or in small towns, although some live in Cuenca. Called *cholos cuencanos*—no matter where they live—they are farmers, market vendors, and artisans who fall between

1. Lynn A. Meisch lived in Cuenca and did research in the Cuenca valley at intervals during 2½ years in 1977–79, with short return visits in 1981, 1986, 1988, 1992, 1993, and 1994.

whites and indigenous people in the social-economic hierarchy. They constitute a true intermediate group, and are an exception to the usual bipolar split into indigenous people and whites. By now, most cholos are Spanish monolinguals although some older people speak Quichua or are bilingual.

Azuay is a conservative region for the most part and its inhabitants continue to maintain many customs, including the use of distinct cholo and indigenous costumes. Since I first visited the region in 1973, however, fewer people are wearing these costumes. Some young people are choosing to wear Euro-American style dress for a number of reasons, including the stigma attached to being seen as a country hick and considerable (usually temporary), mostly illegal immigration to the United States to work. Still, there are thousands of people in the region who wear cholo costume and some who wear indigenous costume. For women there is still considerable prestige attached to the use of an especially elegant chola cuencana outfit.

Women's costume

Although cholo women wear a variety of commercially manufactured blouses and pullover and cardigan sweaters (Fig. 242), two blouse (*blusa* S.) styles are more traditional.

The older blouse style, seen as early as photographs from the 1920s, buttons up the back. It is a solid light color or striped, has no collar, a yoke that opens in front, with the bodice of the blouse gathered into the yoke front and back, and long sleeves that end in cuffs. Modern examples are frequently decorated with rickrack on the cuffs and down the front.

The newer blouse style pulls on over the head (Fig. 243). It has short sleeves gathered into a band or cuff, a collar, and a gathered waist. A plain, everyday variety is made of cotton. Fancier versions of this same blouse are made from shiny, synthetic fabric in a variety of solid colors (white, pink, blue, lavender) and sometimes prints. They are smocked from below the bust to the waist and decorated on the collar, cuffs, and bodice with lace, sequins, fake pearls, and sometimes embroidery and a rosette at the neck.

Cholo women wear a pollera skirt alone or a pollera with a bolsicón over it (Pl. XIV). Modern polleras worn in Azuay province can be homemade from wool bayeta, but they are most commonly made in little shops, particularly in Cuenca around the 10 de Agosto and San Francisco markets (Fig. 243). These polleras are made from solid color, commercially woven wool, cotton, or acrylic cloth, and come to mid-calf. They are gathered at the top into two waistbands that tie at the sides, which are made from cotton tape manufactured at the PASA factory in Cuenca. Polleras are lined at the bottom with a cotton backing, then machine embroidered with flowers and sequins, with scallops along the lower edge. The skirts are sometimes worn inside out to protect the right side. Traditional pollera colors are gold, orange, red, burgundy, and rose-pink, with the red tones the most

242 *The Calle family, Chicticay, Azuay province. Most members of this family died in the La Josephina landslide of March 1993, and the town of Chicticay disappeared. Photo by Lynn A. Meisch, 1978.*

243 *Blouses and skirts for sale in the Cuenca market, Azuay province. The skirts are hung inside out. Slide by Lynn A. Meisch, 1988.*

popular. As is true in many places, subtle details within the overall style indicate a woman's community. For example, women and girls from Gualaceo wear polleras with one horizontal tuck near the bottom of the skirt above the embroidery (Fig. 244).

Bolsicón skirts come to mid-calf, and are also gathered at the waist into one or two tie waistbands, or they have an opening on one side with a hook and eye. They are made in the same shops that make polleras and from the same fabrics, although fine, commercially made wool fabric (*paño* S., a use of the term different from the paño shawl) is most popular. The bolsicón has a number of small, horizontal tucks parallel to the hem, usually six to ten, which are faced on the inside with shiny black fabric. The bolsicón is worn over the pollera and is sometimes tucked up in front into the waistband so that the decoration on the pollera shows. The bolsicón is also one solid, dark color and is meant to contrast with the pollera. The most popular bolsicón colors are purple, navy blue, sky blue, bright green, or dark green.

Generally, if a woman is wearing an apron (*delantal* S.) in public it means she is a market vendor (Fig. 245). The typical vendor's apron is made of red, blue, or yellow-and-white gingham. One kind, a half-apron, ties at the waist and has two large pockets. The pockets, hem, and sides of the apron are trimmed with lace (*encaje* S.) or gingham ruffles. The other style apron, made from the same kind of fabric, is more like a smock or pinafore. It pulls over the head and has a yoke trimmed with lace or ruffles, and lace or ruffles on the pockets, at the neck and armholes, and at the hem.

The warp-resist dyed shawl (*paño*) with its elaborate knotted fringe (*fleco* S.) is the pièce de résistance of cholo women's costume (Pl. XIV, Pl. p. iv, Figs. 242, 244, 246). Fine shawls with starched fringe are usually worn on Sundays, market days, and for other special occasions, although some women wear them daily. They are usually worn with both ends draped over the left shoulder, with one or both ends arranged so that the fringe is prominently displayed—for example, over the back of the left shoulder if the woman is using her arms, or over the left forearm if not (Fig. 246). Occasionally, the shawl is worn folded into a square and wrapped around the shoulders like the indigenous *lliglla* (with the fringe inside and not showing), sometimes pinned with a safety pin (not a tupu), in which case it may be called a *lliglla*.

Paños are made in the Gualaceo area, especially in the communities of Bulzhun and Bulcay el Carmen. They are warped, wrapped, and dyed, usually by women, and woven on the backstrap loom, usually by men, then given to another woman, often a fruit vendor in the Gualaceo market, who knots the fringe (Fig. 245) (see Meisch 1981a; Penley 1988; L. Miller 1989, 1991, for technical information). The overall size is 2.50 to 3.00 by around .75 meters (98 to 118 by 30 inches).

The older style is made of cotton with indigo blue or synthetic black resist designs, with a white fringe (Pl. XIV, Figs. 244, 246). The resist designs are small repeated birds, flowers, or geometric forms, either without borders or with dark borders next to the fringe, or sometimes with side borders. The fringe is often 60 to 90 centimeters (2–3 feet) long and contains designs made in an overhand knot using the warp ends. Designs include birds, flowers, the great seal of Ecuador, and sometimes folk sayings, the date, or the wearer's name.

In recent years, however, both cotton yarn and indigo dye have become so expensive that the majority of contemporary shawls are made of wool and dyed with synthetic dyes. Usually the yarn is first dyed rose-pink (or bright red), then wrapped and overdyed black (Fig. 242, Pl. p. iv). This style is called *paño cachemira*, literally, "cashmere" but actually just referring to fine wool. The resist motifs used are similar to the cotton examples but the format usually includes several solid-color vertical stripes near the sides. Although fine knotting is sometimes done on these shawls as well, another common finish is to make a relatively simple diamond mesh with knotting and then embroider over it with floral designs or sometimes the great seal of Ecuador, with sequins added to the embroidery.

An undecorated shawl of imported wool fabric (called *bayeta de Castilla*, Castillian baize) may be worn over the paño on important religious occasions (Penley 1988:89–90). According to Margaret Young-Sánchez (personal communication, 1988), this shawl is called a *rebozo* and is usually dark blue or turquoise, of twill woven fabric with one surface brushed and the long edges machine sewn.[2] A typical example is 174 by 55 centimeters (68½ by 21½ inches) in size. Such

244 The woman at right wears a Gualaceo style burgundy pollera, a yellow satin blouse, and fine cotton shawl, at the Gualaceo market, Azuay province. Slide by Lynn A. Meisch, 1978.

2. Margaret Young-Sánchez lived in Gualaceo, Azuay province, from November 1985 through July 1986, doing research on cholos and cholo costume as a graduate student project in art history at Columbia University.

245 *Maria Juana Yansa, a market vendor in the Gualaceo market, Azuay province, wearing an apron and a pollera. She has arranged a shawl for knotting at her stall. Photo by Lynn A. Meisch, 1978.*

shawls are worn for marriages, baptisms, and religious processions.

Women frequently wear a factory-made or Otavalo-made wool or acrylic shawl (*chal* S.), or a handspun and handwoven one, instead of their paños, especially for everyday activities. These shawls come in plaids or solid colors and are rectangular or triangular in shape, with added fringe.

Shawls, warp-resist dyed paños, and simple rectangular navy blue or purple-and-white-striped cotton cloths are also used as carrying cloths to haul bundles and babies. For this purpose, they are tied in a knot across the chest. For wrapping a baby, sometimes a wool or acrylic fabric is used, with the lower edge decorated with machine embroidery similar to that on the pollera (Fig. 247).

Cholo women wear their hair in two braids tied with a tape or ribbon. This distinguishes them from indigenous women who wear one braid or their hair pulled back and wrapped with a tape. Two kinds of hats are worn. One is the cream colored paja toquilla (palm leaf) hat with a dark hatband. Women from around Paute wear hats with higher crowns than those worn elsewhere in the Cuenca region. The other kind of hat is the factory-made dark felt fedora now worn throughout Ecuador.

The paja toquilla hats are made from the leaves of the *Carludovica palmata,* a shrubby relative of the palm that grows on the coast, and are made by interlacing the strands from the center of the crown outwards (Aguilar de Tamariz 1988). The hat industry got started on the coast and was introduced into the highlands during the nineteenth century. People bring the hats they make to the Saturday Azogues market and sell them to middlemen who in turn sell them to factories in Cuenca where the hats are finished, softened, bleached, and sold locally or shipped abroad (see also T. Miller 1986).

Cholo women do not wear beads. All kinds of costume jewelry or high-quality gold or silver earrings are worn. The traditional earrings (*aretes* S.) are silver or gold and shaped like a half-moon or canoe (and called *canoas*), an obviously Spanish style (compare Anderson 1951:200, 220, 261). Various styles of earrings are made in Chordeleg.

Footwear varies from nothing to tennis shoes or truck tire sandals to plastic or leather flats and even high heels for special occasions. Many women go barelegged, but some wear stockings (*medias* S.), including colored tights, nylon pantyhose, and wool or acrylic knee socks. Simple cotton or synthetic slips, underpants, and bras are sold in local markets and stores and are commonly worn as underwear by most women, cholo and white.

Men's costume

For those who still wear ponchos the most common current everyday style is dark red or burgundy, sometimes one solid color and sometimes with a few white, black, gray, or mixed stripes on each poncho half (Fig. 248). Another common style is multicolored stripes about 5 centimeters (2 inches) in width across the entire

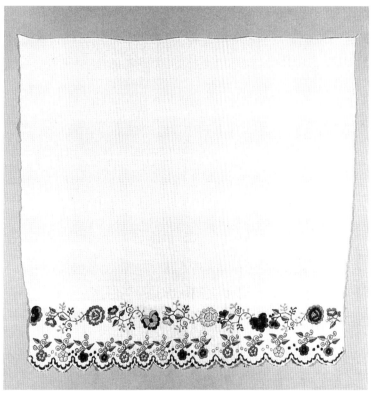

247 *Cholo style baby wrapping cloth, Azuay province. Acrylic plain weave, machine embroidered in cotton thread. 78 x 81 centimeters (30¾ x 32 inches). The Textile Museum 1986.19.78, Latin American Research Fund.*

246 *Cristina Pérez of Bulcay, photographed in Gualaceo, Azuay province, wearing a cotton warp-resist patterned paño. Photo by Lynn A. Meisch, 1993.*

poncho, or alternating tan and brown stripes. Most ponchos have a triangular gusset at the back of the neck, a collar, and warp fringe. They are made locally on the backstrap loom, sometimes by the wearer himself, but more frequently by a male weaving specialist. A few such ponchos are sold in local markets. The poncho is sometimes called a *wachuku* (Q., little furrow or line) in Azuay.

The traditional Sunday and fiesta poncho has warp-resist dyed stripes (Fig. 249). These warp-resist patterned ponchos (*ponchos amarrados*) cannot be bought in the local markets, but must be ordered directly from the weaver (see Meisch 1981b). There are fewer and fewer resist poncho weavers as the older generation dies,

248 Cholo man in a red poncho with mottled brown stripes, and carrying a wool alforja, buying sugar at the Gualaceo market, Azuay province. Slide by Laura M. Miller, 1988.

249 Cholo man in a red poncho with warp-resist patterned stripes, at the Gualaceo market, Azuay province. Slide by Lynn A. Meisch, 1978.

mainly because weaving is a poorly paid occupation. Most young men are turning to other work, including jewelry making and shoe making locally, and emigration abroad or within Ecuador to work in factories, on coastal plantations, and in construction.

There are two main kinds of warp-resist ponchos worn in the Cuenca area. One is red or burgundy with resist-patterned stripes and sometimes with resist lettering (the name of the wearer and his community). The resist-patterned band is usually bordered by narrow warp stripes in white, black, blue, yellow, and rust. The second warp-resist style is a brown poncho dyed with walnut bark and sometimes over-dyed with synthetic dye if the dyer is not satisfied with the color. A common, multicolored resist motif on both kinds of ponchos looks like a series of inverted Vs and is called *plumilla* (S., feather). Older men in Sigsig wear warp-resist dyed ponchos with a background color of dark red, dark brown, or navy blue.

The remainder of the costume now consists of factory-made shirts, pants, etc. Shoes range from truck-tire sandals to modern, western-style leather loafers and tie-shoes to running shoes and black rubber boots.

Saddlebags (*alforjas* S.) of handspun wool, locally woven on the backstrap loom, are commonly used by men and sometimes by women to carry things (Fig. 248). The handspun wool saddlebags usually have a white background with a few narrow red or blue warp stripes, and are made throughout Azuay. Alforjas are often woven for people as specific orders (*obras* S.), like the warp-resist patterned ponchos. Occasionally country people will use cotton alforjas that are woven in southern Loja Province (see chapter 14).

Throughout Azuay, male dress increasingly conforms to general Euro-American fashions. This seems especially true of young men who emigrate (often illegally) to the United States to work for a while and then return to Azuay. Very few younger men in Azuay are wearing the poncho or the palm-leaf hat.

Indigenous People

By the late 1970s, people identifying themselves as indigenous lived in only the more remote areas of Azuay province. Solís (1992:79) notes that currently the presence of a hacienda is the best marker of indigenous communities in Azuay and Cañar. Indigenous communities supplying labor to haciendas are located on the less accessible and desirable mountainous slopes above the hacienda lands.

The main indigenous areas today are around Tarqui near Cuenca, Nabón in the southern part of Azuay and Sigsig and Quingeo east of Cuenca. Some indigenous people from the latter region come into Gualaceo for the Sunday market. These people call themselves *naturales* (S., native), a term also used by indigenous people in other parts of Ecuador including the Otavalos. Stark estimated that in the mid-1980s there were approximately 80,000 indigenous people in Azuay, of whom only half spoke Quichua (1985:471).

There are several distinguishing features of Azuay indigenous dress. Not unexpectedly, a main feature is the hat, which is a hand-felted white hat with no band or decoration, rather than a palm-leaf hat or factory-made dark, felt fedora (Pl. XV and Figs. 250–251). The handmade felt hat, which is worn by both males and females, is similar in form to the palm-leaf hats, with a crown that is higher in the front than in the back and a medium-sized round brim.

Indigenous women wear their hair in one braid or long and tied at the nape of the neck. Two braids are considered to be a cholo style and therefore inappropriate for an indigenous woman or girl.

The other main distinguishing feature of indigenous dress is the *lliglla*, a rectangular shoulder wrap woven on the backstrap or treadle loom and pinned across the chest with a tupu or safety pin, worn instead of the warp-resist dyed shawl (Pl. XV, Fig. 250). I have seen lligllas in a variety of colors, most often red or black, less often blue or green. The lligllas usually have a contrast color edge binding and are

250 *Indigenous woman at the Gualaceo market, Azuay province, wearing red polleras with the top one tucked up. Slide by Lynn A. Meisch, 1979.*

251 *Indigenous couple at the Gualaceo market, Azuay province. Photo by Fernando Sánchez, 1985–1986.*

frequently machine embroidered with birds and flowers about three-quarters of the way around the edge, leaving the top and front of the garment (when worn) unadorned.

The rest of the indigenous women's costume is similar to that of cholo women. However, indigenous women seldom wear a bolsicón, often wearing two polleras instead, with sometimes the upper pollera tucked up into the waistband in front (Pl. XV). Their polleras are more often made of handwoven fabric, and red or black are the predominant colors. They also wear a blouse or sweater, earrings, and shoes or sandals of various kinds.

Indigenous men also wear the hand-felted white hat that resembles in its shape the local palm-leaf hats and short hair (Fig. 251). They also wear a poncho, usually red, sometimes with stripes on each half, like those described for cholos, but they seldom wear warp-resist patterned ponchos. Some men wear pants of handwoven black bayeta. Otherwise their dress resembles that of cholos in every respect.

Chapter 14

Loja Province

Lynn A. Meisch

Saraguro

The indigenous people of Saraguro, called Saraguros or Saragureños, are the main indigenous group in Loja Province.[1] They live in small settlements, called *barrios* (S.), consisting of houses which are surrounded by corn fields and scattered along the footpaths and roads in the green, misty Andes within a 20-kilometer (12-mile) radius of the town of Saraguro in the parishes of Saraguro and San Lucas (see map, page xxii). One Saraguro friend identified eighteen named barrios. The current, Quichua-speaking indigenous population numbers about 30,000 people (Stark 1985:472). Saraguro itself is set at 2,500 meters (8,240 feet) in the eastern cordillera of the Andes, 160 kilometers (100 miles) south of Cuenca and 68 kilometers (42 miles) north of Loja via the winding, precipitous Panamerican highway alternate route. The town of Saraguro has a population of about 1,600 people, mainly mestizos-whites, and serves as the political, commercial, and religious center of the area, with a Sunday market attended by Saraguros from throughout the region. This market is not a tourist market and fewer than twenty foreign travelers visit Saraguro each year, most of whom stay in the town proper.

Modern Saraguros hold that their ancestors were Inca mitimas, a notion not contradicted by the available very meager historical information. While it is common in Ecuador for groups to claim Inca ancestry, including the Cañaris and the Otavalos, for whom documentation exists to prove this is not the case, it is possible that the Saraguros' claims are true. In several small communities around Saraguro, such as Cañaro, the inhabitants wear a different costume. The Saraguros say these are "other runa," and they may be descendants of the pre-Inca inhabitants (e.g., Cañar or Palta), of mitima from other areas, or of more recent immigrants.

After the Spanish conquest, the Saraguros managed to retain their lands and never became part of the hacienda system. This independence, coupled with their isolation—the road connecting Cuenca, Saraguro, and Loja was not constructed until after World War II—has resulted in a prosperous, tightly knit and proud community. Jim and Linda Belote, who did research in Saraguro between 1962 and 1972, note that "it is unlikely that many basic elements of Saraguro settlement have changed appreciably over the last two centuries" (Stewart et al. 1976:377).

1. Field research in Saraguro was conducted at intervals (separated by work in Azuay, Cañar, and Imbabura) during two years between December 1977 and December 1979; with shorter return visits in 1981, 1986, 1988, 1992, 1993, and 1994. See also Meisch 1982 and 1991. I am grateful to Jim and Linda Belote for providing a critical reading of this chapter.

Saraguro today

Farming and cattle herding are central to Saraguro life. Nuclear families generally form separate households, which average fifteen hectares (thirty-seven acres) of decent agricultural and pasture land (Belote and Belote 1977:106). Ownership of land is extremely important to Saraguros and a person without land is considered truly poor. Because land is divided evenly among all children, a married couple tends to have land in scattered areas. Saraguros primarily grow corn, fava beans, quinoa, potatoes, squash, peas, and wheat. Families also have household gardens where they grow vegetables and herbs used for spices and for healing.

Most Saraguro houses are made of adobe, packed clay, or concrete blocks, with red-tiled roofs, and are surrounded by gardens and corn fields. When I arrived in Saraguro at Christmas in 1977, no indigenous barrio had electricity, but in the 1980s electrification was being extended to the barrios closest to town.

Every family keeps guinea pigs in the kitchen, and most families have a few chickens scratching around outside and perhaps a pig staked out in the yard. More important are horses, cattle, and sheep. Sheep are essential for clothing, since most Saraguro clothing is handspun and handwoven and there are no camelids in the region. Horses are handy for transportation, especially in barrios lacking roads (the majority), and are also a sign of wealth and status.

Cattle, however, are the basis of the Saraguros' prosperity, with families averaging about ten head (Stewart et al. 1976:384). A yoke of oxen is frequently used to plow fields for planting, and milk and cheese are consumed at home and sold in the market, but the Saraguros are also the main suppliers of beef in southern Ecuador. While some barrios have grazing lands on the hilltops, the number of cattle far outstrip the available pastures. Since before the turn of the century the Saraguros have practiced transhumance, driving their cattle east across the páramo, over the continental divide, and down into the jungle around Yacuambi (also known as 28 de Mayo). The cattle are fattened up and driven back over the Andes for sale in the Saraguro market (*ibid.*:384).

Saraguros place great emphasis on education. Every barrio has a grade school, some staffed by Saraguro teachers, and there are several high schools (*colégios*) in town. In addition, Saraguros in increasing numbers are attending the universities in Quito, Cuenca, and Guayaquil, and there are now a number of school teachers and several indigenous nurses, physicians, and veterinarians in the area. The best thing about electricity, many Saraguros told me, was that their children could now do their homework after dark.

Both boys and girls are educated up to the university level, consistent with the relative equality of the sexes in indigenous society. Indigenous women also speak up at community meetings; one was recently elected president of Las Lagunas barrio.

Ideally, a newly married man and woman will build their own house, but they may live with either the woman's or man's family until they are able to construct their own house, depending on which family has more resources.

Both Spanish and Quichua are spoken in Saraguro, with Spanish tending to be the predominant language in barrios closer to Saraguro and Quichua predominating in more distant barrios. Many people are bilingual and some are monolingual in one language or the other. A creole language called *chaupi shimi* (middle language), with a Spanish lexicon and Quichua grammar, is also spoken by some people in the Saraguro area (Muysken 1975–76).

Population growth and a scarcity of land and jobs in the past decade have resulted in the migration of young people out of Saraguro, a fact lamented by the elders and by many of the migrants themselves, who feel that prolonged residence away from Saraguro will mean a loss of their culture and community cohesion. Young men (sometimes accompanied by their wives and children) work in construction and similar kinds of jobs in Loja, Cuenca, and Guayaquil. A number of Saraguros work in the gold mines of Nambija in the Oriente southeast of Saraguro or live permanently around Yacuambi in the jungle.

Costume

At first sight, Saraguro dress is predominantly black or dark blue with a white hat—but a closer look reveals brightly colored poncho joins, embroidery around the hems of pants, and flashes of red, yellow, or bright pink blouses (Pl. XVI, Fig. 252). While Saraguros are identifiable generically by their dark dress, braids, and hats, the details of the costume indicate the wearer's particular community.

Traditional Saraguro dress has been dark-colored for as long as people can remember. Saraguros offered several reasons why they always wear black. One reason is to protect against the rays of the full moon and against rainbows, which are considered maleficent. (Rainbows cause pregnant women to give birth to malformed children.) The other main reason given is in mourning for the death of the Inca Atau Huallpa. Saraguros also attach significance to other colors. Red is considered to be the color of people in love with each other, and green is the color of hope.

Saraguros have many words to describe the various colors of dark, undyed, plain-weave sheep's wool cloth. *Yurak* refers to white bayeta, with white warp and weft. *Yana* refers to black warp and weft. *Suku* (light) refers to dark brown cloth with flecks of white in both the warp and weft. *Zhiru* refers to one white and one black yarn plied together and woven into cloth which appears mottled gray. *Shanu* refers to cloth woven with a white warp and black or mixed black and white weft, which gives it a mottled or tiny checkboard appearance. *Uki* (from the Inca and Aymara word *u'qi*, meaning gray) refers to solid dark brown (not gray) cloth. *Pukailo*, from *puka hilo* (Q., S.), means brown yarn. In addition, the late Ashuca Losano said there were four different Quichua words (which I did not learn) for the shades of brown obtained with walnut. The point is that the large number of terms for dark wool cloth indicates the importance of these distinctions.

252 *Two girls and a man, Gunudel, Saraguro area, Loja province. Photo by Lynn A. Meisch, 1979.*

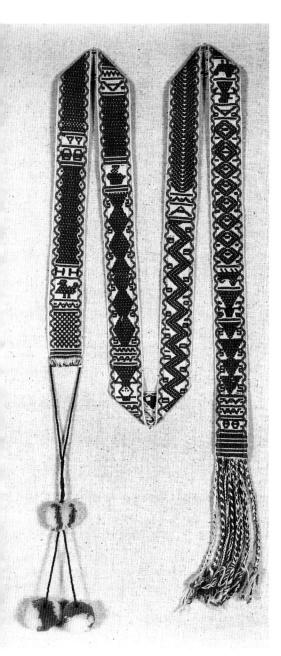

253 *Woman's belt, woven by María Asuncion Quizhpe, Gunudel, Saraguro area, Loja province. Cotton plain weave, with blue acrylic supplementary-warp patterning. 1.48 x .035 meters (4 feet 10¼ inches x 1⅜ inches), excluding ties. The Textile Museum 1979.2.1, gift of Lynn Ann Meisch.*

There has been a color shift since the 1940s from undyed, dark sheep's wool to black or navy blue (*yana*). According to Ashuca Losano, the older generation wore only uki or suku clothing. She recounted a saying that "undyed wool is warmer," but added that now (1978) there was social pressure to wear dyed clothing. Many Saraguros confirmed that the older style was to wear dark, undyed clothing, and this is still true for the barrio of Jera.

The favored dye for the newer style was originally indigo imported from El Salvador. When it became difficult, if not impossible, to obtain indigo in the late 1970s, synthetic dyes were used instead, particularly *azul marino* (S., navy blue). Garments were also sometimes dyed with indigo and then overdyed with a synthetic dye to get the right shade.

Women's costume

Women now wear a tailored embroidered blouse (*camisa bordada*) (Pl. XVI), although before about 1920 they wore a wrapped upper garment perhaps similar to the Salasaca pichu jerga. The Saraguro blouses are made from commercial cotton, velvet, velour, or rayon cloth, which is sold in stores on the plaza in Saraguro. Some indigenous women sew and embroider their blouses, but most people buy them from mestizo-white women in town, who make and sell them in their homes. The road to Quisquinchir and the western barrios is lined with blouse makers. The blouses are simply cut with a yoke front and back, long sleeves, and gussets under the arms. They are hand embroidered in a contrasting color on the sleeve cuffs and in the form of a false collar at the neck.

Blouses made from plain colors (red, wine, white, yellow, orange, green, blue) are usually worn by women from Las Lagunas and the other eastern barrios, while blouses made from patterned fabric (often small flower prints) are worn in the western barrios of Sauce, Tinta, Selva Alegre, Jera, and possibly Quisquinchir, although there are exceptions to this rule that seem to be personal idiosyncrasies.

Women and girls wear both polleras and anakus, one under the other. The Quichua name for the pollera is *uku churana,* meaning inside or interior garment. The pollera is made from handspun, twill-weave wool fabric (bayeta), woven on the treadle loom, sewn into a tube, and gathered into a waistband (*reata*) that ties. The waistband is frequently a striped cotton band manufactured in the PASA factory in Cuenca, but some are woven on the backstrap loom in plain-weave wool stripes. As with blouses, mestizo-white families in town make polleras to sell. These have a 15-to-20-centimeter (6–8-inch) cotton lining near the hem, machine embroidery, and sometimes sequins at the hem. Some polleras, especially for little girls, are now made of acrylic.

A belt about 4 centimeters (1½ inches) wide, called a *ñajcha chumbi* (Q., comb belt), is wrapped over the pollera. It is woven on the backstrap loom in the twill-derived float weave, with a design of horizontal bars. Some ñachja chumbis are made of acrylic and cotton; others are of handspun wool, and most have round pompoms (*sisa* Q., flower) at the ends. Ñachja chumbis are usually bright colors: green and red, purple and red, or red and white. In some communities pregnant women wear a wider version of this belt, called *mama chumbi.*

An anaku is always wrapped over the pollera (Pl. XVI, Fig. 252). Saraguro women wear an unusual version of this garment. Anakus are usually woven on the backstrap loom, then gathered into a waistband (*watu* Q.), and made into hundreds of tiny pressed pleats. The Textile Museum anaku (1989.22.5) is made from a fabric 4.90 by .69 meters (16 feet by 27 inches). The watu is longer than the reata used to tie the pollera, and is often handspun and handwoven with warp bars (*esparábul*) that result from warping alternate colors. The ends are finished in a four-strand braid (*tucumar*). Anakus usually open on the right side, although this is a personal preference.

The origin of the pleated anaku is a mystery, but it was probably copied from European fashions. Pleated polleras were worn in the first half of the nineteenth century in Quito (Hallo 1981:68) and perhaps Cuenca as well. Similar long, black, finely pleated skirts were worn through the mid-twentieth century in such places as Montehermoso in Extremadura and some towns in Navarra, Spain (Anderson 1951:156; Ortiz Echagüe 1957:35–39, 206–9).

Yet another belt is wrapped over the anaku, called a *de la china* (S., of the female) *chumbi* (Fig. 253). The de la china belt is woven on the backstrap loom with a white cotton, acrylic, or handspun wool ground warp, and acrylic or wool supplementary-warp motifs in a contrasting color. Typical motifs include people, roosters, dogs, goats, deer, birds, the weaver's initials, zigzags, baskets, eucalyptus trees, leaves of the bean plant, and stars. The belt is often finished with a four-strand braid, then pompoms (*sisa*) are added. The de la china belt is wrapped so that the pompoms hang down the woman's side or back. While the reata and watu are tied, belts are not tied, but wrapped several times around the wearer's waist, with the end tucked under the wraps.

A rectangular shoulder wrap (*lliglla*) is an essential part of female dress, held closed with a stick pin (*tupu*) (Fig. 252). Most lligllas are handspun and made from bayeta, but a few are woven on the backstrap loom. An example of the latter in The Textile Museum collection is a single panel (1994.15.2), 1.19 by .58 meters (47 by 23 inches). A treadle-loom woven one (1989.22.8) is the same length, but wider, 70 centimeters (27½ inches). Some lligllas have narrow blue, rose, or purple stripes (*listas*) at one side selvedge, which becomes the bottom of the garment when it is worn. Others have an embroidered straight line or zigzag (*kingu*) instead of a woven stripe. Lligllas, anakus, and polleras are all black or dark blue. Some anakus and lligllas are now woven from commercial acrylic yarn. The lliglla not only serves as a shawl but as a carrying cloth for hauling bundles and babies.

Hats are the same for both sexes and there are three styles. The oldest is the wide-brimmed, flat-crowned white felt wool (*sombrero de lana*) (Pl. XVI, Fig. 252). The black spots under the brim are a result of the felting and ironing process and are considered an integral part of the design. In 1977–79 these were handmade by one old mestizo-white man in town, Manuel Armijos. The two young men who knew the tedious felting process had sold their tools because the trade was not lucrative. However, in 1994 an indigenous man from Tuncarta was learning how to make the hats so that the tradition will not die out. The old-style hats are carefully guarded by families and brought out mainly for mass, fiestas, and markets, although a few old people wear them regularly.

Hats from Jera, Gurudel, and Oñacapac have a rose, green, or yellow piece of yarn tied around the crown, while hats from Tambopamba, Ñamarin, Las Lagunas, and Gunudel have a black yarn or horsehair tie. While most of these hats are of similar shape, hats with small, stiff brims are worn in San Lucas, and with drooping brims (an older style) in Oñacapac.

Two other, more modern, hats are worn by both sexes. One kind is a palm-leaf hat from the Cuenca area, which is colored white. The other is a brown, black, dark gray, tan, or olive-green felt fedora, manufactured in Ambato. The latter two styles are sold in shops around the Saraguro market and in dry goods stores in the center of town. There are also hat repair shops near the market where all three kinds of hats are cleaned and reblocked and the old-style hats are whitened with maize flour or talcum powder.

Women and girls never cut their hair, but wear it in a long braid. Hair is braided in three, four, or six strands or wrapped in two strands in a figure eight, and tied with a string, yarn, or commercial ponytail twist. Occasionally I saw a woman with two braids, but most women said "two braids make us look like chola cuencanas."

If women or girls wear shoes, they are usually black plastic shoes or tennis shoes that are manufactured in Ecuador and sold in the Saraguro market, although beginning around 1990 some started wearing blue or black alpargatas made in Otavalo.

Women dress more casually for daily activities than they do for fiestas. The blouse, lliglla, tupu, pollera, and anaku are worn daily, although a woman may substitute a T-shirt for the blouse and a sweater for the lliglla around the house. For fiestas families haul their finest clothing out of trunks and down off the walls and house beams. On special occasions, heirloom jewelry, the newest anakus, and the old-style hats make an appearance.

Jewelry

Jewelry is an integral part of female dress in Saraguro. In 1978–80 jewelry-making was a specialty of three mestizo-white men who live in Saraguro proper. The oldest and finest tupus and earrings now extant are made from old Peruvian silver sol coins (*soles blancos,* or white soles), which were 900 per 1,000 parts silver (925 is sterling), and called *nueve décimos* (S., nine-tenths). These coins have not been minted since the turn of the century, so a second, more common and less expensive, tupu is made from Ecuadorian sucres minted in 1937 and 1946, which have a high nickel content. Some tupus are also made of nickel washed (*bañado* S.) with silver. Fine silver or silver-washed tupus and earrings are considered family heirlooms and are passed down from mother to daughter.

Metal tupus come in a variety of sizes, from 10 centimeters (4 inches) long for a little girl to 20–23 centimeters (8–9 inches) long for an adult. The protrusions are called *cachos* (S., horns) and represent alternating male and female heads. A small hand, sometimes holding a rose, is molded where the head (*broche* S.) joins the shaft (*vara*) of the tupu. The hand is an ancient Mediterranean symbol to protect against the evil eye, and it has the same meaning, of protection and good luck, in Saraguro. To keep the tupu from getting lost, a silver or nickel chain (*cadena* S.) or a piece of ribbon or acrylic braided tape (sold in the market) is tied through a loop in the back of the tupu and hung around the wearer's neck.

Women also wear bead necklaces (*collar* in Spanish, *wallka* in Quichua) of which there are two basic kinds often worn together. One kind consists of several strands (*sartas*) of glass or plastic beads. The second kind, called *tejido* (S. woven), is made from tiny glass or plastic seed beads (*mullu* Q.) imported from Czechoslovakia, the United States, and possibly elsewhere. The beads are joined in zigzag rows (*kingu*), and the number of rows and color combinations indicate the wearer's barrio (Pl. XVI, Fig. 254). The largest necklaces are worn by women from Gurudel and sometimes by women from Tuncarta. Smaller ones with only eleven kingus and strands with just two different colors are typical of Las Lagunas. One family I knew in Tuncarta specialized in making necklaces to sell to other indigenous women.

A third style of necklace, called *colgante* (S., pendant), appeared in the 1990s. It has an inverted triangle of beads hanging down the breast for about 12–15 centimeters (5–6 inches) and usually ends with a fringe of tear-drop shaped false pearls in a single solid color.

Saraguro is unusual among Ecuadorian indigenous communities in that specific kinds of earrings (*zarcillos* S.) are worn by women and girls, rather than just any style. Two styles are worn today. One, with half moons, is called (logically) *media luna* (S., half moon) *con piedra atachi* (S., with fastened or attached stones) (Fig. 254). The stones are small pieces of cut, colored glass. Sometimes these earrings have a hand, which, like the hand on the tupu, symbolizes good luck. Any earring with the half moon is called a *media luna,* regardless of size (2.5–12.5 centimeters, 1–5 inches long) or other ornamentation. The other filigree style is called *kurimolde* (a mixture of Quichua and Spanish meaning *gold mold*), although no one can remember when these earrings were actually made of gold (Fig. 255). A nickel or silver chain (*cadena*) or a ribbon is attached to the top near the hook or to a loop on the earring and worn around the wearer's neck to keep the earrings from getting lost if they slip out.

Although the kurimolde and media luna earrings are most common, some families own other fine, old silver earrings, of styles I have seen worn throughout the Ecuadorian highlands. These seem to be general Spanish-style earrings. One style worn in Saraguro and elsewhere has a flower or bird near the hook. Sus-

254 *Young woman wearing media luna earrings, Gunudel, Saraguro area, Loja province. Photo by Lynn A. Meisch, 1993.*

255 *Rosa Angelita Cango wearing kurimolde earrings, Gunudel, Saraguro area, Loja province. Photo by Lynn A. Meisch, 1988.*

pended from that is an ornate pendant, often with birds, leaves, and flowers ending in round, teardrop-shaped pieces of colored glass mounted in a silver cone. These earrings range in size from four to ten centimeters (1½–4 inches) long. Traditionally, only married women in Saraguro wear rings (*anillos* S.), which are usually made of silver.

Men's costume

The Saraguro male dress, like the feminine costume, is a mixture of the ancient, old, and modern.

Men wear a *kushma* that is sewn up the sides (Fig. 256). It is woven in a plain weave on the backstrap loom and is made in one of two ways. The first is to weave two separate rectangular fabrics which are joined together with a slit left open for the head. The second style is to weave just one piece, with the neck slit woven-in using discontinuous-weft yarns. When this second style is made, the neck slit is frequently embroidered at the front and back to reinforce it. A typical kushma in finished form looks almost square and measures approximately 80 centimeters (31½ inches) on a side. The kushma, like the poncho and pants, is always of dark-colored wool, either natural or dyed.

Kushma joins are done in a decorative embroidery stitch with colored yarn, and indicate community affiliation. For example, the barrio of Gurudel uses three or four different colors in the join, Oñacapac and Tambopamba use three colors, while Las Lagunas, Ilincho, Gunudel, and Gulacpamba use just one color, either red, green, or blue. The same is true for poncho joins. Saraguros emphasized that the joins are important, especially the small crosses that are often embroidered on the join just below the neck opening.

Today many men and boys wear factory-made shirts, sweaters, and T-shirts under or instead of their kushmas around the house and while working in the fields, but the kushma is still worn on such formal occasions as weddings, funerals, and fiestas, and to Sunday mass and the market.

A generation earlier the kushma was belted with a handwoven wool belt called a *mama chumbi* or *ñajcha chumbi*, similar to the woman's belt of the same name but wider. A few old men still use this style, but most men now wear a leather belt (*cinturon* S.). One style is made in town, with three to six buckles (*tres* or *seis billas* S.) and decorated with hammered, old Ecuadorian brass sucre coins (Fig. 257). Some of these belts also come with a similarly decorated machete sheath and money pouch (*kullki wakaychina* Q., money guarder).

Another distinctive feature of Saraguro male dress is short, knee-length pants (*pantalones cortos* S.). A likely inspiration for these pants is Spanish colonial knee breeches, of the style common in the eighteenth century. Details of the pants indicate the barrio. Pants from Las Lagunas are made from extremely fine, backstrap-loom woven fabric (*pacha* Q.) and from treadle-loom woven, balanced twill-weave fabric (*bayeta*) and have no embroidery or woven decorations at the lower hems or up the sides. Men from Gañil are known for their thick bayeta pants, which are embroidered around the leg hems and along the outside seams with flowers. Pants worn in Mater also have embroidery around the leg hems and up the outside seams. Pants from Jera have multicolored embroidery around the hem. Pants worn in Tuncarta, Tambopamba, Oñacapac, Gurudel, San Isidro, and Jera have stripes of white, red, purple, or some other color woven in so that they appear as a vertical stripe along the outside side seams when the pants are worn. Pants worn by men from Jera and Oñacapac have multicolored embroidery or a three-colored braid (*jimba* or *togliado*) sewn along the leg hem.

Homemade versions of the pants have a waistband made from the same fabric as the pants, or they may be tied shut with a band (*watu*) that is woven separately on the backstrap loom and then sewn on. These watus are identical to ones that are attached to women's and girls' anakus. Pants are also made from commercially manufactured fabric, which is bought in the stores around the Saraguro plaza and sewn at home on treadle or electric sewing machines. In some cases, purchased long pants are cut off at the knee and hemmed.

It is unusual for cloth woven on the backstrap loom to be cut and tailored, but this occurs in Saraguro for both pants and cloth chaps (*zamarro*) (Fig. 258). Unlike the heavy, sheepskin chaps worn by horseback riders for cattle and sheep herding in Chimborazo and Cañar provinces, Saraguro zamarro are woven from finely spun, white wool and are now associated more with special occasions than with daily use. Zamarro are woven in one piece on the backstrap loom, then cut in half crosswise. The panels in The Textile Museum example (1988.17.5) are 67 by 35.5 centimeters (26¼ by 14 inches). The cut ends are overcast by hand, then sewn to a handwoven band (*watu*), which is tied low around the waist, so that the zamarro resembles an apron with two overlapping pieces. Each piece is joined to itself at the bottom hem, so forming a "pants leg" that is open in back.

The most common poncho is a dark blue or black (*yana*), undecorated, woolen plain-weave garment, woven in two sections on the backstrap loom and joined with a hole left for the head (Pl. XVI, Figs. 252, 256). These ponchos are dyed after they come off the loom. One variation is called the *poncho listado* (S., striped poncho), which has a narrow purple or blue stripe bordered by narrower white stripes near each outer selvedge (Fig. 259). According to people from Tuncarta, the wool for the stripes is dyed as fleece and then spun.

256 *Taita Raimundo Cango wearing a kushma and a plain poncho, Gunudel, Saraguro area, Loja province. Photo by Lynn A. Meisch, 1988.*

257 *Leather belt, Saraguro, Loja province. 1.25 x .09 meters (4 feet 1 inch x 3½ inches). The Textile Museum 1988.17.15, Latin American Research Fund.*

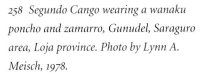

258 *Segundo Cango wearing a wanaku poncho and zamarro, Gunudel, Saraguro area, Loja province. Photo by Lynn A. Meisch, 1978.*

259 *Taita Vicente Andrade wearing a poncho listado, Gunudel, Saraguro area, Loja province. Photo by Lynn A. Meisch, 1986.*

In Saraguro, *wanaku poncho* refers to a two-color striped poncho that is worn in at least four barrios: Ñamarin, Tuncarta, Gunudel, and Las Lagunas (Fig. 258). The garment has the same name as the wild camelid, guanaco, now surviving only in Tierra del Fuego, and was possibly once made from its fiber or named after the animal since guanacos and vicuñas are bi-colored, mostly tan but with lighter-colored hair on the front of their necks and chests. The original undyed version of this poncho was the color of these animals, tan with groups of white stripes. Modern examples are navy blue or black with red, magenta, pink, or purple stripes, probably originally cochineal, but now synthetic dye.

In the late 1970s, when I first began to do research in Saraguro, several new poncho variations appeared. These were made of black or navy blue acrylic fiber and were woven on treadle looms in one workshop in Ilincho and one in Quisquinchir for sale to other Saraguros. They included ponchos listados, wanaku ponchos, and regular ponchos with colored, acrylic fringe sewn on. The fringed ponchos enjoyed a brief vogue, but I have not seen a poncho with added acrylic fringe since 1983. In addition, Otavalo vendors sold (and sell) dark-colored acrylic ponchos at the Saraguro Sunday market. Families with lots of boys often buy the Otavalo or locally made acrylic ponchos for their sons, but many families handspin and handweave ponchos for even their youngest male offspring.

260 *Rosa Angelita Cango fixing her husband's hair in a figure-eight wrap, Gunudel, Saraguro area, Loja province. Photo by Lynn A. Meisch, 1978.*

Like the males of Otavalo and Cañar, Saraguros traditionally never cut their hair, but wear it pulled back in a loose braid (*jimba*) and tied with string or yarn. The Saraguros make a three-strand or six-strand braid, or wrap the hair around long, core strands in a figure eight (Fig. 260). Men's hats are the same as the women's.

Footwear in general is called by its Quichua name, *ushuta*. It includes rubber boots (*botas* S.) manufactured in Guayaquil and shoes. In the latter case, socks (*medias* S.) are also worn.

Both men and women carry *alforjas* (saddlebags) over their shoulders. These items are not usually locally woven, but are sold in stores around the plaza and market place in Saraguro. Several kinds are available. The more expensive ones are made from commercial cotton thread, in a warp-faced plain weave with alternating float weave motifs (Fig. 261), in the southern Loja towns of Gonzanamá, Cariamanga, Quilanga, Yamana, and Catacocha, and in Oña, to the north, just over the provincial line in Azuay. A less expensive kind of cotton alforja has warp stripes, predominantly black and white, and no pickup motifs (Fig. 262). Wool alforjas, without pickup motifs, are also available (Fig. 263).

Some Saraguros make large knotted net carry-all bags, called *linchi* or *shigra*, from furcraea fiber (locally called *penko wadarín*) (Fig. 264). People harvest the leaves, process the fiber and knot the bags themselves. According to Ashuca Losano, linchis were used before the Saraguros obtained alforjas.

Children's costume

Babies are swaddled until they are five or six months old (Fig. 265). Gender is indicated by pierced ears on baby girls. Toddlers of both sexes wear wrapped skirts made from discarded, cut-up pieces of adult clothing until they are toilet trained. Then they are dressed as miniature versions of the adults. Until about age two, both boys and girls have their heads wrapped with a kerchief (*pañuelo*). American cowboy bandannas are popular and foreign visitors are frequently asked if they have any to sell (Fig. 266). Because older children are already wearing what amounts to a uniform they are allowed to wear traditional dress to school, while mestizo-white children must buy a school uniform.

Blankets and food sacks

Indigenous people (and mestizos-whites in the countryside) weave blankets (*cobijas* S.) and large storage sacks (*costales* S.) for grain or potatoes on the backstrap loom. The yarn for blankets is generally coarsely spun and plied, and the blanket is woven in two separate halves which are sewn together. Blanket styles vary; some are undyed, others are dyed, and most have stripes of some kind.

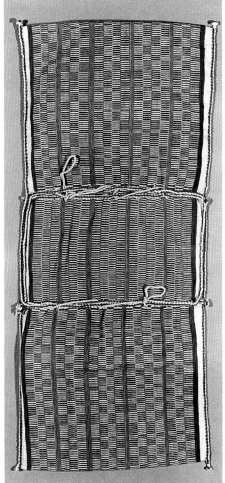

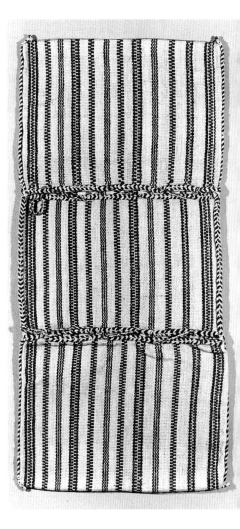

261 Cotton alforja with alternating float weave designs, probably woven in 1977, Feliz Navidad (Merry Christmas) on one side, Feliz Año 1978 (Happy 1978) on the other side, Loja province. 98 x 47.5 centimeters (38½ x 18¾ inches). The Textile Museum 1988.19.38, Latin American Research Fund.

262 Alforja in warp-faced plain weave, in natural brown and white cotton, Cariamanga, Loja province. 94 x 41 centimeters (37 x 16 inches). The Textile Museum 1989.22.3, Latin American Research Fund.

263 Wool alforja, warp-faced plain weave, made in Saraguro, Loja province, in 1978–79. 1.08 x .515 meters (42½ x 20¼ inches). The Textile Museum 1988.17.7, Latin American Research Fund.

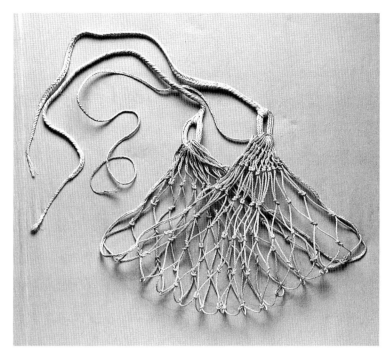

264 Linchi, furcraea fiber yarn with square knots, Saraguro area, Loja province. 2.56 meters (8 feet 4¾ inches), including ties, x .72 meters (28¼ inches), opened out. The Textile Museum 1988.17.9, Latin American Research Fund.

265 Baby wrapped in a belt, with parents Francisco Cango and Dolores Quizhpe of Gunudel, Saraguro area, Loja province. Photo by Lynn A. Meisch, 1981.

266 Two children at a baptismal party, Las Lagunas, Saraguro area, Loja province. Photo by Lynn A. Meisch, 1993.

Textile production

More so than anywhere else in Ecuador, Saraguro costume is handmade locally. Except for shoes, some hats, and occasional exceptions such as shirts and some ponchos from Otavalo, garments are handspun and handwoven by the family, occasionally by neighbors, or by mestizo-white specialists in Saraguro.

Because so much of the clothing is still handmade, virtually every little girl learns how to spin well by age seven or eight. Most men and boys also know how to spin, and I watched a four-year-old boy practice spinning with a tiny distaff and spindle, but spinning is basically females' work. Throughout the countryside around Saraguro women and girls spin as they walk along the road or sit outside the house.

For backstrap-loom woven garments, extremely fine S-spun wool yarn is used, often finer than commercial sewing thread. Saraguro textiles differ from those of the rest of the highlands today in being woven with paired, rather than plied, warp yarns. This configuration is, however, common in what we know of the pre-Inca cotton textile tradition of Ecuador and northern Peru.

Most Saraguro households have a shelf attached to an inside wall with a series of holes drilled in it where empty and full spindles are set. Many households also have a couple of wooden pegs sunk in the wall indoors to hold the backstrap loom bars and weaving tools.

Saraguros may wash and dye raw fleece and then spin it, or dye yarn, which is then warped and woven; but most commonly they dye garments or garment halves (*hojas* S., leaves) after they are woven. The reason I was given was that dyeing yarn tangled it up.

Men predominate as weavers, especially for the larger garments, but women weave watus and belts. Almost every family has a backstrap loom set up under the eaves of the porch, but only a few weavers have treadle looms on which they make both plain-weave bayeta (called *llano* S., plain) and a balanced twill weave bayeta (called *estameñado* S., serge).

Weavers with treadle looms weave for their neighbors, who bring the spun and plied yarn and pay the weaver to make it into yardage. In 1978 the cost was 10 sucres (U.S. $.40) per vara, and most people felt it was not worth having less than four varas of cloth made at a time. The barrio of Ñamarin is known as a weaving barrio; men weave for others using either the backstrap or treadle loom. In addition, there is a weaving workshop in Ilincho run by Incarnación Quizhpe, which makes acrylic ponchos for men and boys, as well as cotton tablecoths and napkins in a variety of patterns, which are sold in Cuenca and Quito.

Care of clothing

Clothing is taken down and washed in the stream or washed at home if the family has piped water. Traditionally, furcraea leaves are used to make soap for washing textiles. The leaf is slapped against rocks or beaten with a rock and the foamy sap

267 *Pleating an anaku, Chalán household, Las Lagunas, Saraguro area, Loja province. Photo by Lynn A. Meisch, 1978.*

added to a pot of hot water. The textile is washed in the furcraea soap, then rinsed in fresh water. Now Deja brand commercial powdered detergent is often used instead of furcraea.

There are various customs connected with the care of clothing. According to Ashuca Losano, if clothing is washed during the new moon it does not last. No clothing is washed during the last three days of the waning moon or the first five days of the new moon.

Because the pleats on the anaku eventually come out they have to be redone on a regular basis. The anaku is washed and then painstakingly re-pleated. Every family has a rectangular wooden platform in the yard for this task (Fig. 267). The wet anaku is laid on the platform and the pleats are re-formed one by one, often with the shaft of a shawl pin. Poles and stones are used to hold the pleats in place until the anaku dries. Anakus are stored rolled up tight, wrapped with the watu and or yarn to preserve the pleats, and hung on a nail in the wall.

Because so much time and energy is invested in the production of textiles, they are mended, recycled, and cut up, ultimately ending up as baby diapers or swaddling cloths.

Other Ethnic Groups and Textiles

There are other indigenous people in Loja Province. Some live around Las Juntas, near Loja, in such villages as Jimbilla and Capur. Until about the 1950s the males of Jimbilla wore their hair long, and a few old men still do. The men of Capur wear short pants, either uki or black, short hair, and a poncho with orange, brown, and brick-colored stripes. I have no information on the women's costume. One Saraguro woman friend referred to the indigenous people from Jimbilla and Capur as "Lojanos," with "different customs."

Cañaro

People from the town of Cañaro, especially the barrio of Paquishapa, are also considered by Saraguros to be "other indígenas, not Saguareños." The name Cañaro suggests that the town once might have been occupied by Cañaris.

Some Saraguros specialize in weaving wool ponchos for the men of Cañaro. These ponchos differ from Saraguro ones in a number of ways. First, the yarn is always plied, and the ponchos are dark red or maroon, with a group of narrow, multicolored stripes (for example, white, rose-pink, yellow) on each half near the outside selvedge (Fig. 268). Cañaro ponchos weigh about three pounds. According to Polivio Sarango and his wife, Ashuca Losano, who made Cañaro ponchos for sale, the yarn is first dyed with walnut, then over-dyed with three ounces of *sangre de toro* (S., bull's blood) synthetic dye. The side stripes are now made from commercial acrylic yarn because it is too expensive to buy packages of synthetic dye for such a small amount of yarn. Also, the rose-pink synthetic dye is not firm and the dye from the stripe runs onto the other colors. In the 1950s, before acrylic yarn was available, *semi-seda* (S., artifical silk, probably rayon or nylon) was used for the colored stripes. Cañaro ponchos traditionally have three or four colors in the join.

268 Cañaro poncho, barrio of Paquishapa, Loja province. The poncho is warp-faced plain weave in dark red wool, consisting of walnut overdyed with synthetic dye, and acrylic accent stripes. 1.41 x 1.31 meters (55½ x 51½ inches). The Textile Museum 1988.17.6, Latin American Research Fund.

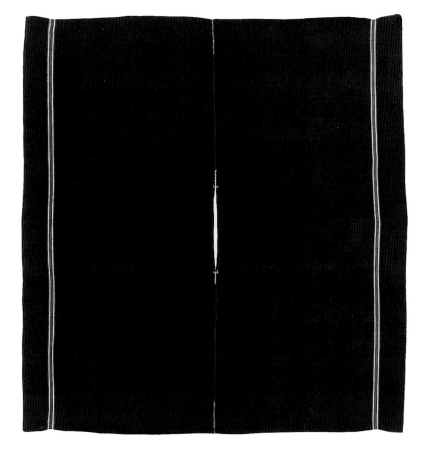

Alforjas

We have not visited the towns where the alforjas, mentioned in connection with the Saraguro male costume, are made. According to Edward Mittenberger (personal communication), a Peace Corps volunteer working in Quilanga in 1988, weaving in this town is a mestizo-white occupation done mainly by women on the Ecuadorian style loom with a circular, dovetailed warp. Weavers make cotton alforjas in various sizes, including the *alforja escolar* (scholar's alforja, for school books), and *alforjas medianos* and *grandes* (medium and large). They also make bags (*bolsas* S.), and one woman weaves cotton horse blankets with designs made using alternate colors of warp, like the ones woven from wool in Azuay.

There has been a recent move, abetted by the Peace Corps, to use natural colors of cotton for some of these alforjas (Fig. 262).

Horse blankets

The town of Oña, north of Saraguro on the road to Cuenca, is a mestizo-white community, but some wool textiles, especially ponchos, blankets, and horse blankets are woven in the area. The horse blankets are about 162.5 centimeters (64 inches) long and 71 centimeters (28 inches) wide and are usually woven in a pattern of warp bars, which result from warping in alternate colors. One horse blanket I saw from Moras Loma (near Oña), however, had supplementary weft yarns at the top and bottom. Two thicknesses of two-ply brown or yellow yarn were laid in under groups of two or three warp yarns to make little blocks of color about 7.5 centimeters (3 inches) wide.

Warp-resist dyeing

Very little warp-resist dyeing is done in Loja Province, but the technique does exist. In 1979 I saw a mestizo-white man in Saraguro on the road to Quisquinchir wearing a wool warp-resist patterned poncho. This poncho had a wine body, with one patterned stripe on each side. The resist designs looked like a series of "M"s, one above the other, bright pink against a purple background. I also saw an indigenous man in Saraguro with a Cañaro warp-resist patterned poncho. This poncho was also wine colored, with a resist-patterned band on each side. In this case, narrow stripes of orange, white, and lime-green bordered the resist-patterned band, which consisted of a series of vertically stacked "Y" designs in lime-green against a wine background.

Conclusions

Ann P. Rowe

Regional variation in dress is a complex phenomenon, often difficult to interpret on account of gaps in the historical record. Such gaps exist in Ecuador as well, but enough is known to make some general observations worthwhile.

To begin, it may be noted that some factors operating in regional costume variation elsewhere hardly exist in Ecuador. For example, there is comparatively little survival of unmixed pre-empire cultural or ethnic groups. Population movements during the Inca and Spanish empires have thoroughly scrambled the original ethnic boundaries. Many cultural features, including such key markers as language and costume, can be traced to Inca or Spanish rather than local precedent. In terms of costume, the tunic (with sides sewn), full-length anaku, and pinned shawl are probably from Inca sources, at least in northern Ecuador (A. Rowe ms), while the shirt, pants, embroidered blouse, pollera, and felted hat are Spanish. Moreover, many of the features that cannot be traced to these colonial sources and may be aboriginal, such as the loom style, the hand-supported spinning technique, a preference for coral-colored beads, wrist wraps, and braided hair for men and wrapped hair for women, are found widely in highland Ecuador.

In addition, there is little variation in woven or embroidered design, such as occurs for example in Guatemala or Bolivia. In fact, as noted, the supplementary-warp patterned belts have remarkably similar designs throughout highland Ecuador and can only be distinguished by relatively subtle clues. Most other garments are unpatterned, whether made from treadle-loom or machine-made yardage or laboriously woven on the backstrap loom. Even ponchos are not particularly distinctive; most of the variations (solid color, or with warp stripes in one of about three arrangements, or with some warp-resist dyed patterns) are found in many areas.

The regional variation that does exist today has partly to do with the extent to which a costume recognizable as indigenous is retained. Earlier in this century, as Casagrande (1974) observed, those groups that maintained the most distinctive costume were those that were the most free of domination by the hacienda system, such as Salasaca, Saraguro, and Otavalo. Today, however, the use of a distinctively indigenous dress has more to do with the degree of political or ethnic consciousness felt by each indigenous group. Land reform, however limited, and population pressure have led to large-scale periodic migration to cities for jobs, resulting both in a shortage of time for spinning and weaving and in access to cash. The wearing of inexpensive factory-made clothes becomes economically necessary under these circumstances and it is certainly occurring in many parts of highland Ecuador.

What is interesting in Ecuador is that some groups are adapting factory-made cloth or yarn into indigenous forms, as obraje fabrics had been adapted at an earlier period. For Otavalos, with their long tradition of commercial weaving supporting a sense of their self worth, commercialization of their costume (so that all parts can be purchased in the market) was a natural step. Groups using factory cloth for indigenous-style dress, however, include not only the Otavalos but also the Chibuleos and the people of central Chimborazo who have a history of hacienda oppression, but whose political consciousness has been raised in recent years in part by Evangelical Protestantism and Roman Catholic liberation theology and in part by local indigenous federations and such national indigenous organizations as CONAIE. While it is certainly no accident that the Otavalos are responsible for purveying cloth to these groups, it is also true that without some desire on the recipients' part for a distinctive indigenous dress, this marketing tactic would not succeed.

Saraguros and Salasacas have seen less change in their social situation, which was more independent to start with, and are still self-sufficient enough to be able to produce much of their clothing. However, they are not without cash income either, so their continuing costume production reflects the importance of handwoven clothing to their political or ethnic sense of self. Elsewhere, machine-made fabrics increasingly predominate. Although the use of machine-made materials has reduced regional variation on the local level, broad distinctions remain discernible.

The main focus of these distinctions is the women's skirts, whether pollera or anaku, and if the latter, how many are worn together, how long they are and with how many pleats. The key to these variations appears to be historical, and thus only partly discernible. There are three main variations. The clearest case is the long and narrow anaku, known to derive from the Inca or provincial Inca full-length wrapped dress (A. Rowe ms). We also know that the pollera is eighteenth-century Spanish in origin. The severe displacement of the original indigenous population of Cañar and Azuay may have made these areas more susceptible to Spanish influence in costume. Unfortunately, for the pleated, shorter anakus found in Cotopaxi, Tungurahua, Bolivar, and eastern Chimborazo, we have little historical information. Possibly they are the result of a combination of the indigenous concept of a rectangular wrapped skirt with the visual effect of the Spanish pollera.

All these factors do tend to point in the same direction. It appears that regional variations in the indigenous costume of highland Ecuador derive as much from historical colonial policies as from local ethnic differences. What is remarkable is that despite the increasing use of machine-made clothing items, indigenous costume remains a core cultural value and for some even a form of political expression.

Glossary

S. = Spanish
Q. = Quichua, modern Ecuadorian dialects of the Inca language

acrylic synthetic fiber that mimics the appearance of wool.

agave plant genus originating in Mexico. Species *Agave americana* introduced into Ecuador during the colonial period. It has long fleshy leaves from which fibers are extracted.

akcha watana or **watarina** (Q., hair wrap) tape used for wrapping women's hair.

alforja (S.,) double bag or saddlebags, made by folding each end of a rectangle toward the center. Form introduced by the Spanish during the colonial period, but often backstrap-loom woven.

alpargatas (S.,) sandals. In Ecuador, usually made with braided furcraea fiber soles, or rubber soles, and cloth uppers.

anaku (Q.) originally referred to the Inca style woman's full-length rectangular dress, pinned at the shoulders and belted, still worn in several areas of Ecuador until recent memory. Today, the term usually refers to a wrapped skirt (half-length) made of a rectangle and secured with a belt. There may be many (e.g., Chibuleo, Llangahua) or few (e.g., Otavalo, central Chimborazo) tucks taken. In Saraguro, the anaku has pressed pleats sewn into a waistband. The length of the skirt is variable from one area to another, ranging from just below the knee to the ankle.

backstrap loom indigenous loom in which tension is maintained by a strap passing around the weaver's back or hips.

baita (pronounced "bay-ta") common Quichua pronunciation of the Spanish word *bayeta* (q.v.), used for example in central Chimborazo and in eastern Imbabura. In Quichua it refers to the woman's rectangular shawl, worn pinned on the chest.

bayeta (S.) 1. coarse treadle-loom woven wool fabric. The equivalent English fabric name is *baize*. 2. woman's rectangular shawl pinned on the chest, made from bayeta fabric. May be pronounced *baita* (see above) or *bayita* (e.g., in Palmira Dávalos in Chimborazo province) in Quichua.

bayetilla (S.) 1. fabric similar to but finer than bayeta. 2. woman's rectangular shawl pinned on the chest, made from bayetilla fabric. Term used in the Guaranda area of Bolivar province.

bolsicón (S.) Spanish style skirt gathered into a waistband, with a series of horizontal pleats near the lower edge.

cabuya (Taino) fiber from the leaves of either furcraea or agave.

cachimira (S., cashmere) any fine wool fabric.

calzón (S.) Spanish style men's pants.

camisa (S.) Spanish style woman's blouse or man's shirt. Some women's blouses are long enough to serve as slips under their skirts.

centro (S.) Spanish style gathered or pleated skirt with waistband. Term used in eastern Imbabura and northeastern Pichincha, as well as in southern Chimborazo.

chalina (S.) woman's shawl, term sometimes used in eastern Imbabura. In eastern Cañar, it refers to a type of thin shawl produced and sold by Otavalos.

changalli (Q., leg or thigh wrapping) an apron-like rectangular panel worn in central Chimborazo province over the front of a wrapped dress or skirt.

cholo (S.) term used in Cañar and Azuay for a group of people with a distinctive costume intermediate between mestizos-whites and indigenous people in the social-economic hierarchy.

chumbi (Q.) handwoven belt.

cinta (S.) tape used for wrapping women's hair.

cochineal red or purple dye from an insect (*Dactylopius* spp.), indigenous to the Americas, that is parasitic on the prickly pear cactus.

complementary-warp weave weave with two sets of warp, each of a different color, that are co-equal in the fabric. See Figs. 19–20 in chapter 2 for the variation most common in Ecuador.

CONAIE (Confederación de Nacionalidades Indígenas del Ecuador) Confederation of the Indigenous Nations of Ecuador, founded in 1986 to promote indigenous causes on the national level.

concertaje (S.) debt peonage.

fachalina (Q., to bring cloth, *facha* or *pacha*, onto the body) woman's shawl and headcloth in the Otavalo area. Term also sometimes used in Zumbagua in Cotopaxi province for women's shawls.

fachallina (may be pronounced *fachazhina*) variant pronunciation of *fachalina*, used in Licto (eastern Chimborazo) for the woman's shawl and in the Chibuleo area for the striped shawl.

furcraea plant genus originating in tropical America. Species *Furcraea andina* common in Ecuador. Has long fleshy leaves from which fibers are extracted, for use in making shigras, braided sandal soles, woven food sacks, etc.

hacienda (S.) large estate, consisting of agricultural and grazing land.

huasipungo (Q.) a plot of land belonging to a hacienda, worked by an indigenous family and the produce kept in exchange for their labor on other hacienda lands. This form of serfdom was abolished by the 1964 Law of Agrarian Reform.

indígena (S.) indigenous person.

indigo blue dye. The dye compound (indigotin) is produced by various plants, of which the most important one native to the Americas is *Indigofera suffruticosa*. The same compound is now also produced synthetically.

jerga (S.) coarse twill-weave wool cloth, woven on the treadle loom.

jirga poncho (S. with Q. pronunciation) poncho made from *jerga* fabric. The style worn in several areas of central Ecuador is white (sometimes overdyed red or purple) with narrow black warp stripes at about 2.5 centimeter (1 inch) intervals.

kawiña chumbi (Q.) belt woven of wool or acrylic in a complementary-warp weave (see Fig. 161). It has a central stripe in green and red, side stripes in yellow and black or purple, and has red edges. Woven mainly in central Chimborazo, but worn all over the province and in Bolivar province also.

kingu (Q.) zigzag design.

kushma (Q.) tunic, sometimes sewn up the sides (Saraguro) and sometimes not (Cañar). Often made from one panel with a neck slit woven with discontinuous-weft yarns, but occasionally with two panels. In Saraguro and Cañar it is worn belted.

liencillo (S.) fine handwoven plain cotton cloth.

lienzo (S.) handwoven plain-weave cotton cloth.

lista (S.) stripe. May be pronounced *lishta* (in Salasaca) or *lishtu* (in the Colta area) in Quichua.

llama (Q.) domesticated Andean camelid (Fig. 6), still raised in small numbers in central Ecuador primarily as a pack animal and for meat. In the Llangahua area the hair is also spun and woven.

lliglla (Q.) woman's rectangular shawl, worn pinned on the chest. The term is Inca but is used in only a few areas, including Saraguro and the indigenous parts of Azuay.

looping fabric structure formed by a single element, the free end of which has been drawn through an opening in the fabric and then crossed over itself (Fig. 5). It is of prehispanic origin in Ecuador and is still used to make bags (shigras) of furcraea or agave fibers in some areas.

macana (S.) warp-resist patterned shawl with fringed ends. Term commonly used for the shawls made in Rumipamba in Cotopaxi province, occasionally for the shawls in Azuay.

maki watana (Q., hand wrap) beaded wrist wrap.

mama chumbi (Q., mother belt) wide underbelt. Those worn in Otavalo and central Chimborazo are red with green borders, have four selvedges, and a heavy cabuya (sometimes cotton) weft.

mestizo (S.) literally, a person of mixed European and indigenous ancestry, but in Ecuador the term implies a social class, somewhere between the top and the bottom, rather than race.

mestizo-white general reference to nonindigenous people.

mitima (Inca word in Spanish spelling) people moved by the Incas from previously conquered areas to newly conquered ones as part of the pacification process.

obraje (S.) Spanish-run factories common during the colonial period, which produced textile yardage on Spanish style equipment.

paño (S.) 1. wool treadle-loom or machine-woven fabric, finer than bayeta. 2. rectangular warp-resist patterned shawl with fringed ends made and worn in Azuay province.

pichu anaku (*pecho* S., chest, with Q. pronunciation) term used in Cacha (central Chimborazo) for the full-length anaku, to distinguish it from the half-length one.

pichu jerga (S.) rectangular wrapped upper body garment pinned on the shoulders formerly worn by Salasaca women and still worn by some older women.

pollera (S.) Spanish style gathered skirt sewn into a waistband. The lower edge may be embroidered, usually by machine.

poncho (S.) man's overgarment consisting of a square or rectangle with a neck slit in the center. In Ecuador, ponchos are usually made of two loom panels sewn together, except in Salasaca where they are a single panel.

puzu (Q.) interspersed black-and-white effect created by using a white warp and a black weft, a color scheme particularly common in Pulucate (central Chimborazo).

rebozo (S.) woman's rectangular shawl. In Ecuador, the term often refers to a woman's carrying cloth (e.g., Otavalo, Licto). In Salasaca it refers to a larger size of shawl. In the Achupallas area of South Chimborazo it refers to the regular shawl. In Azuay it refers to a ceremonial shawl.

ruana (S.) term for the poncho (q.v.) used in northern Ecuador and Colombia.

runa (Q., person) indigenous person.

shigra (indigenous non-Inca word) looped bag, made of agave or furcraea fiber.

sisa (Q.) flower, a common design on textiles; or may refer to a pompom or tassel.

sombrero (S.) Spanish style hat. May be pronounced *sumbriru* in Quichua (for example, in the Colta area of Chimborazo province).

supplementary warp set of warp yarns added between the ground warp yarns and floated either on the front of a fabric to create patterns or the back between pattern areas. See Fig. 16 and discussion in chapter 2.

treadle loom Spanish style loom, in which the threads are separated for the passage of the weft by depressing foot pedals or treadles.

tupu (Q.) straight-pin used to secure women's wrapped dresses and shawls.

tupullina (Q., bring the tupu onto the body) term used for the woman's shawl in Cañar province.

twill-derived weave in this book, the weave referenced is woven warp-faced using three colors, of which one is white, and forms a design of horizontal bars. See Figs. 17–18 and further explanation in chapter 2.

ushuta (Q.) sandals, usually with leather or rubber soles.

vara (S.) old Spanish unit of measurement, equivalent to about 84 centimeters (33 inches).

vincha (Q.) Inca term for the woman's headband or hair fastener. In contemporary highland Ecuador, it refers to commercially manufactured hairclips.

wallka (Q., sometimes pronounced *washka*) necklace.

wallkarina (Q., sometimes pronounced *washkarina*; literally, to bring the necklace onto the body) term used for the woman's shawl in Quizapincha (Tungurahua prov.) and Cañar.

warp-faced the warp elements outnumber and hide the weft elements.

warp-resist dyeing groups of selected warp yarns are partially wrapped and bound and then dyed before weaving, in order to create designs in the finished fabric.

washajatana (Q., back wrap) a term sometimes used for the woman's shawl or carrying cloth in eastern Imbabura and northeastern Pichincha.

watu (Q.) a narrow handwoven band, such as a waistband for a skirt.

wawa chumbi (Q., baby belt) long narrow belt worn over the mama chumbi.

yana (Q.) black.

yurak (Q., pronounced *yura* in Salasaca) white.

zamarro or **zamarros** (S.) chaps, usually made of sheepskin with the fleece left on, but in Saraguro made of cloth.

References Cited

Aguilar de Tamariz, María Leonor

1988   *Tejiendo la vida . . . : Las artesanías de la paja toquilla en el Ecuador.* Centro Interamericano de Artesanías y Artes Populares (CIDAP), Cuenca.

Alchon, Suzanne Austin

1991   *Native Society and Disease in Colonial Ecuador.* Cambridge University Press, Cambridge and New York.

Alvarez, Silvia G.

1987   "Artesanías y tradición étnica en la Península de Santa Elena," *Artesanías de América,* no. 25, pp. 45–119. Centro Interamericano de Artesanías y Artes Populares (CIDAP), Cuenca.

Anderson, Ruth Matilda

1951   *Spanish Costume: Extremadura.* The Hispanic Society of America, New York.

Arrieta Ch., Modesto

1984   *Cacha: Raíz de la nacionalidad ecuatoriana.* Banco Central del Ecuador, Quito.

Barrett, Samuel A.

1925   *The Cayapa Indians of Ecuador.* 2 vols. Indian Notes and Monographs no. 40. Museum of the American Indian, Heye Foundation, New York.

Barthes, Roland

1977   "Rhetoric of the Image," *Image/Music/Text,* trans. by Stephen Heath, pp. 32–52. Hill and Wang, New York.

1983   *The Fashion System.* Translated by Mathew Ward and Richard Howard. Hill and Wang, New York.

Bebbington, Anthony J.

1990   Indigenous Agriculture in the Central Ecuadorian Andes: The Cultural Ecology and Institutional Conditions of Its Construction and Change. Ph.D. dissertation, Geography, Clark University, Worcester, Massachussetts. University Microfilms International, Ann Arbor, Michigan.

Bebbington, Anthony, Galo Ramón (coordinator), Hernán Carrasco, Victor Hugo
    Torres, Lourdes Peralvo, and Jorge Trujillo
1992   *Actores de una década ganada: Tribus, comunidades, y campesinos en la
        modernidad.* COMUNIDEC, Quito.

Belote, Jim, and Linda Smith Belote
1977   "The Limitation of Obligation in Saraguro Kinship," in *Andean Kinship
        and Marriage,* ed. Ralph Bolton and Enrique Mayer, pp. 106–16. Ameri-
        can Anthropological Association Special Publication 7. Washington, D.C.

Bianchi, César
1982   *Artesanías y técnicas shuar.* Ediciones Mundo Shuar, Quito.

Bogatyrev, Petr
1971   *The Functions of Folk Costume in Moravian Slovakia.* Translated by Rich-
        ard G. Crum. Mouton, The Hague. Originally published in 1937.

Brownrigg, Leslie A.
1972   The *Nobles* of Cuenca: The Agrarian Elite of Southern Ecuador. Ph.D.
        dissertation, Political Science, Columbia University, New York. Univer-
        sity Microfilms International, Ann Arbor, Michigan.

Bruhns, Karen Olsen
ms   "Costume in Ecuador Before the Incas." Manuscript submitted for publi-
        cation in *History of Indigenous Costume in Highland Ecuador,* edited by
        Ann P. Rowe.

Burgos Guevara, Hugo
1977   *Relaciones interétnicas en Riobamba.* Instituto Indigenista Interamericano,
        México.

Bustos M., Gonzalo, and Magdalena Pilco J.
1987   *Chumbi: Diseños de fajas.* Ediciones Abya-Yala, Quito.

Caillavet, Chantal
1982   "Caciques de Otavalo en el siglo XVI: Don Alonso Maldonado y su
        esposa," *Miscelánea Antropológica Ecuatoriana,* no. 2, pp. 38–55. Museos
        del Banco Central del Ecuador, Cuenca, Guayaquil, Quito.

Cardale Schrimpff, Marianne
1977   "Weaving and Other Indigenous Textile Techniques in Colombia," in
        Ethnographic Textiles of the Western Hemisphere, ed. Irene Emery and
        Patricia Fiske, Irene Emery Roundtable on Museum Textiles, 1976 Pro-
        ceedings, pp. 44–60. The Textile Museum, Washington, D.C.

Carpenter, Lawrence K.
1982   Ecuadorian Quichua: Descriptive Sketch and Variation. Ph.D. disserta-
        tion, Linguistics and Anthropology, University of Florida, Gainesville.
        University Microfilms International, Ann Arbor, Michigan.

Carrillo y Gariel, Abelardo
1959   *El traje en Nueva España.* Instituto Nacional de Antropología e Historia,
        México.

Casagrande, Joseph B.

1974   "Strategies for Survival: The Indians of Highland Ecuador," in *Contemporary Cultures and Societies of Latin America*, 2nd ed., ed. Dwight Heath, pp. 93–107. Random House, New York. Reprinted in Whitten 1981, pp. 260–77.

1977   "Estrategias para sobrevivir: Los indígenas de la Sierra," in *Temas sobre continuidad y adaptación cultural ecuatoriana*, ed. Marcelo F. Naranjo, José L. Pereira V., and Norman E. Whitten, Jr., pp. 71–96. Ediciones de la Universidad Católica, Quito.

Castelló Yturbide, Teresa, and Marita Martínez del Río del Redo

1971   *El rebozo.* Artes de México, año 18, no. 142. México.

Chiriboga, Manuel

1986   "Formas tradicionales de organización social y actividad económica en el medio indígena," *Del indigenismo a las organizaciones indígenas*, pp. 29–90. Ediciones Abya-Yala, Quito.

Collier, Jr., John, and Aníbal Buitrón

1944   *The Awakening Valley.* University of Chicago Press, Chicago.

CONAIE (Confederación de Nacionalidades Indígenas del Ecuador)

1988   *Derechos humanos y solidaridad de los pueblos indígenas.* Quito.

1989   *Las nacionalidades indígenas en el Ecuador: Nuestro proceso organizativo.* Second ed. CONAIE and Ediciones Abya-Yala, Quito.

Cordero, Octavio Palacios

1981   *El Azuay histórico: Los Cañaris y los Inco-Cañaris.* Consejo Provincial del Azuay, Cuenca. Originally published in 1920.

Corkill, David, and David Cubitt

1988   *Ecuador: Fragile Democracy.* Latin America Bureau, London.

Cornell University

1965   *Indians in Misery: A Preliminary Report on the Colta Lake Zone, Chimborazo, Ecuador.* Department of Anthropology, Cornell University and the Ecuadorian Institute of Agrarian Reform and Colonization.

Correa, Wilson Castillo, and Carlos Pacheco Narváez

1992   Estudio etnográfico de la vestimenta en dos comunidades indígenas de Cañar: Quilloac y Huairapungo. Tesis de Licenciatura en Historia y Geografía, Universidad de Cuenca.

Cushner, Nicholas P.

1982   *Farm and Factory: The Jesuits and the Development of Agrarian Capitalism in Colonial Quito, 1600–1767.* State University of New York Press, Albany.

Doyon-Bernard, Suzette

1994   "La Florida's Mortuary Textiles: The Oldest Extant Textiles from Ecuador," *The Textile Museum Journal*, vols. 32–33, 1993–94, pp. 82–102. Washington, D.C.

Einzmann, Harald

1985   "Artesanía indígena del Ecuador: Los Chachis (Cayapas)," *Artesanías de*

América, no. 19, pp. 13–78. Centro Interamericano de Artesanías y Artes Populares (CIDAP), Cuenca.

Einzmann, Harald, and Napoleon Almeida

1991   *La cultura popular en el Ecuador: Tomo VI: Cañar.* Centro Interamericano de Artesanías y Artes Populares (CIDAP), Cuenca.

Emery, Irene

1980   *The Primary Structures of Fabrics: an Illustrated Classification.* The Textile Museum, Washington, D.C. Originally published in 1966.

Espinosa, Leonardo

1989   *La sociedad azuayo-cañari, pasado y presente.* Editorial El Conejo, Quito.

Espinosa, Leonardo, and Lucas Achig

1981   *Proceso de desarrollo de las provincias de Azuay, Cañar y Morona Santiago.* Editorial Don Bosco y Centro de Reconversion Económica del Azuay, Cañar y Morona Santiago, Cuenca.

Espinosa Soriano, Waldemar

1988   *Los Cayambes y Carangues, siglos XV–XVI: El testimonio de la etnohistoria.* 3 vols. Instituto Otavaleño de Antropología, Otavalo.

Farrell, Gilda, Simón Pachano, and Hernán Carrasco

1988   *Caminantes y retornos.* Instituto de Estudios Ecuatorianos, Quito.

Fock, Niels

1981   "Ethnicity and Alternative Identification: An Example from Cañar," in *Cultural Transformations and Ethnicity in Modern Ecuador,* ed. Norman Whitten, pp. 402–419. University of Illinois Press, Urbana and Chicago.

Fock, Niels, and Eva Krener

1978   "Los Cañaris del Ecuador y sus conceptos etnohistóricos sobre los Incas," in *Amerikanistische Studien: Festschrift für Hermann Trimborn,* 2 vols., ed. Roswith Hartmann and Udo Oberem, vol. 1, pp. 170–81. Haus Völker und Kulturen, Anthropos-Institut, St. Augustin.

Forman, Sylvia Helen

1972   Law and Conflict in Rural Highland Ecuador. Ph.D. dissertation, Anthropology, University of California, Berkeley. University Microfilms International, Ann Arbor, Michigan.

1977   "The Totora in Colta Lake: An Object Lesson on Rapid Cultural Change," *Ñawpa Pacha* 15, pp. 111–16. Institute of Andean Studies, Berkeley, California.

Foster, George M.

1993   *Hippocrates' Latin American Legacy: Humoral Medicine in the New World.* Gordon and Breach, Langhorne, Pennsylvania.

Franck, Harry A.

1917   *Vagabonding Down the Andes.* The Century Co., New York.

Franquemont, Edward M.

1986a   "Cloth Production Rates in Chinchero, Peru," in *The Junius B. Bird Con-*

ference on Andean Textiles, April 7 and 8, 1984, ed. Ann Pollard Rowe, pp. 309–30. The Textile Museum, Washington, D.C.

1986b   "Threads of Time: Andean Cloth and Costume," in *Costume as Communication,* ed. Margot Blum Schevill, pp. 81–92. Haffenreffer Museum of Anthropology, Brown University, Bristol, Rhode Island.

Gardner, Joan S.

1979   "Pre-Columbian Textiles from Ecuador: Conservation Procedures and Preliminary Study," *Technology and Conservation,* vol. 4, no. 1, pp. 24–30. The Technology Organization, Boston.

1982   "Textiles precolombinos del Ecuador," *Miscelánea Antropológica Ecuatoriana,* no. 2, pp. 24–30. Museo del Banco Central, Cuenca, Guayaquil, Quito. Translation of Gardner 1979, but with some different illustrations.

1985   "Pre-Columbian Textiles, Los Ríos Province, Ecuador," *National Geographic Society Research Reports,* vol. 18 (grants in the year 1977), ed. Winfield Swanson, pp. 327–42. Washington, D.C.

Gayer, Jacob

1929   "Among the Highlands of the Equator Republic," *The National Geographic Magazine,* vol. 55, no. 1, pp. 69–76. National Geographic Society, Washington, D.C.

Gellner, Bernhard

1982   Colta Entrepreneurship in Ecuador. Ph.D. dissertation, Anthropology, University of Wisconsin, Madison. University Microfilms International, Ann Arbor, Michigan.

Gentry, Howard Scott

1982   *Agaves of Continental North America.* University of Arizona Press, Tucson.

Gillin, John

1941   "Quichua-speaking Indians of the Province of Imbabura (Ecuador)," *Bulletin* no. 128, *Anthropological Paper* no. 16. Bureau of American Ethnology, Smithsonian Institution, Washington, D.C.

Gómez de Vidaurre, Felipe

1889   *Historia geográfica, natural y civil del Reino de Chile . . .* Ed. J.T. Medina. Colección de Historiadores de Chile y Documentos Relativos a la Historia Nacional, vols. 14–15. Imprenta Ercilla, Santiago. Written in 1789.

Guaman Poma de Ayala, Felipe

1936   *Nueva Corónica y Buen Gobierno* (Codex péruvien illustré). Travaux et Mémoires de l'Institut d'Ethnologie, 23. Université de Paris, Paris. Written in 1615.

Hagino, Jane Parker, and Karen E. Stothert

1984   "Weaving a Cotton Saddlebag on the Santa Elena Peninsula of Ecuador," *The Textile Museum Journal,* vol. 22, 1983, pp. 19–32. Washington, D.C.

Hallo, Wilson

1981   *Imágines del Ecuador del siglo XIX: Juan Agustín Guerrero.* Ediciones del Sol, Quito and Espasa-Calpe, Madrid.

Handweaver and Craftsman

1959   "Indian Textiles from Ecuador," *Handweaver and Craftsman,* vol. 10, no. 1, pp. 19–21, 56. New York.

Hassaurek, Friedrich

1967   *Four Years Among the Ecuadorians.* Southern Illinois University Press, Carbondale. Originally published in 1867.

Hendricks, Janet Wall

1991   "Symbolic Counterhegemony among the Ecuadorian Shuar," in *Nation-States and Indians in Latin America,* ed. Greg Urban and Joel Sherzer, pp. 53–71. University of Texas Press, Austin.

Hirschkind, Lynn

1981   On Conforming in Cuenca. Ph.D. dissertation, Anthropology, University of Wisconsin, Madison. University Microfilms International, Ann Arbor, Michigan.

1995   "History of the Indian Population of Cañar," *Colonial Latin American Historical Review,* vol. 4, no.3, pp. 311–42. Spanish Colonial Research Center, University of New Mexico, Albuquerque.

Hoffman, Marta

1979   "Old European Looms," in *Looms and Their Products,* Irene Emery Roundtable on Museum Textiles, 1977 Proceedings, ed. Irene Emery and Patricia Fiske, pp. 19–24. The Textile Museum, Washington, D.C.

Hoffmeyer, Hans

1985   "Diseños salasacas," *Cultura,* vol. 7, no. 21a, pp. 339–355. Banco Central del Ecuador, Quito.

Iglesias, Angel María

1985   *Los Cañaris: Aspectos históricos y culturales.* Consejo Provincial del Cañar, Cañar.

INEC (Instituto Nacional de Estadística y Censos)

1982   *IV Censo de población 1982: Resultados definitivos, Imbabura.* 2 vols. Quito.

Iturralde, Diego A.

1977   *Guamote: campesinos y comunas.* Colección Pendoneros, no. 28. Instituto Otavaleño de Antropología, Otavalo.

Jaramillo Cisneros, Hernán

1981   *Inventario de diseños en tejidos indígenas de la provincia de Imbabura.* 2 vols. Colección Pendoneros 48 and 49. Instituto Otavaleño de Antropología, Otavalo.

1983   "Los alpargateros de Quiroga," *Artesenías de América,* no. 14, pp. 39–46. Centro Interamericano de Artesanías y Artes Populares (CIDAP), Cuenca.

1988a   *Textiles y tintes.* Centro Interamericano de Artesanías y Artes Populares (CIDAP), Cuenca.

1988b   "La técnica ikat en Imbabura: Un aporte para su conocimiento," *Sarance,* no. 12, pp. 151–74. Instituto Otavaleño de Antropología, Otavalo. Also published in *Ecuador indígena: Estudios arqueológicos y etnográficos de la*

Sierra Norte, pp. 151–74. Instituto Otavaleño de Antropología, Otavalo, and Ediciones Abya-Yala, Quito.

1990   "Indumentaria indígena de Otavalo," in *Ecuador indígena: Antropología y relaciones interétnicas,* pp. 127–44. Ediciones Abya-Yala, Quito, and Instituto Otavaleño de Antropología, Otavalo.

Juan, Jorge, and Antonio de Ulloa

1748   *Relación histórica del viaje a la América Meridional.* 2 vols. Antonio Marin, Madrid. Facsimile: Fundación Universitaria Española, Madrid, 1978.

Kleymeyer, Carlos David

1990   *¡Imashi! ¡Imashi! Adivinanzas poéticas de los campesinos indígenas de la sierra andina ecuatoriana/peruana.* Ediciones Abya-Yala, Quito.

Klumpp, Kathleen M.

1983   "Una tejedora en Manabí," *Miscelánea Antropológica Ecuatoriana,* no. 3, pp. 77–88. Museos del Banco Central del Ecuador, Cuenca, Guayaquil, Quito.

Lentz, Carola

1988   "Why the Most Incompetent Are on the Village Council: Development Projects in an Indian Village in Ecuador," *Sociologia Ruralis,* vol. 28, nos. 2–3, pp. 199–215. European Society for Rural Sociology, Assen, Netherlands.

Macas, Luis

1991   *El levantamiento indígena visto por sus protagonistas.* ICCI, Quito.

Males, Antonio

1993   "El levantamiento del general . . . del pueblo indio," in *Sismo étnico en el Ecuador: Varias perspectivas,* pp. 145–68. CEDIME and Ediciones Abya-Yala, Quito.

Maynard, Eileen, ed.

1966   *The Indians of Colta: Essays on the Colta Lake Zone, Chimborazo (Ecuador).* Department of Anthropology, Cornell University, Ithaca, New York.

McCracken, Grant

1987   "Clothing as Language: An Object Lesson in the Study of the Expressive Properties of Material Culture," in *Material Anthropology: Contemporary Approaches to Material Culture,* ed. Barrie Reynolds and Margaret A. Stott, pp. 103–28. University Press of America, Lanham, Maryland.

McIntyre, Loren

1968   "Ecuador—Low and Lofty Land Astride the Equator." *National Geographic,* vol. 133, no. 2, pp. 259–98. Washington, D.C.

Meisch, Lynn A.

1980a   "The Cañari People: Their Costume and Weaving," *El Palacio,* vol. 86, no. 3, pp. 15–26. Museum of New Mexico, Santa Fe.

1980b   "Spinning in Ecuador," *Spin-Off,* vol. 4, pp. 24–29. Interweave Press, Loveland, Colorado.

1980c   "The Weavers of Otavalo," *Pacific Discovery,* vol. 33, no. 6, pp. 21–29. California Academy of Sciences, San Francisco.

1981a   "Panos: Ikat Shawls of the Cuenca Valley," *Interweave White Paper,* vol. 1, no. 2. Loveland, Colorado.

1981b   "Abel Rodas: The Last Ikat Poncho Weaver in Chordeleg," *El Palacio,* vol. 87, no. 4, pp. 27–32. The Museum of New Mexico, Santa Fe.

1982   "Costume and Weaving in Saraguro, Ecuador," *The Textile Museum Journal,* vols. 19–20, 1980–81, pp. 55–64. Washington, D.C.

1986   "Spinning in Bolivia," *Spin-Off,* vol. 10, no. 1, pp. 25–29. Interweave Press, Loveland, Colorado.

1987   *Otavalo: Weaving, Costume and the Market.* Ediciones Libri Mundi, Quito.

1991   "We Are Sons of Atahualpa and We Will Win: Traditional Dress in Otavalo and Saraguro, Ecuador," in *Textile Traditions of Mesoamerica and the Andes: An Anthology,* ed. Margot Blum Schevill, Janet Catherine Berlo, and Edward B. Dwyer, pp. 145–77. Garland Publishing, New York.

ms   "Northern Peru and Southern Ecuador as a Textile Region: Loom and Spinning Styles and Pre-Inca Populations." Paper presented at the 21st Annual Meeting of the Institute of Andean Studies, Berkeley, California, January 10–11, 1981.

MICH (Movimiento Indígena de Chimborazo)

1989   "Movimiento Indígena de Chimborazo (MICH)," in *Las nacionalidades indígenas en el Ecuador: Nuestro proceso organizativo,* ed. CONAIE, 2nd ed., pp. 173–78. Tincui-CONAIE and Ediciones Abya-Yala, Quito.

Miller, George R., and Anne L. Gill

1990   "Zooarchaeology at Pirincay, a Formative Period Site in Highland Ecuador," *Journal of Field Archaeology,* vol. 17, no. 1, pp. 49–68. Association for Field Archaeology, Boston University.

Miller, Laura M.

1989   "Tradiciones de los paños de ikat en el norte del Perú y el sur del Ecuador," *Artesanías de América,* no. 28, pp. 15–41. Centro Interamericano de Artesanías y Artes Populares (CIDAP), Cuenca.

1991   "The Ikat Shawl Traditions of Northern Peru and Southern Ecuador," in *Textile Traditions of Mesoamerica and the Andes: An Anthology,* ed. Margot Blum Schevill, Janet Catherine Berlo, and Edward B. Dwyer, pp. 337–58. Garland Publishing, New York and London. English version of Miller 1989.

Miller, Tom

1986   *The Panama Hat Trail: A Journey from South America.* William Morrow and Co., New York.

Montell, Gösta

1929   *Dress and Ornament in Ancient Peru: Archaeological and Historical Studies.* Elanders Boktryckeri Aktiebolag, Göteborg, Sweden.

Moreno Yánez, Segundo E.

1985   *Sublevaciones indígenas en la audiencia de Quito: Desde comienzos del siglo*

XVIII hasta finales de la Colonia. 3rd ed. Ediciones de la Universidad Católica, Quito.

Mörner, Magnus

1985   *The Andean Past: Land, Societies and Conflicts.* Columbia University Press, New York.

Muñoz Bernand, Carmen

1986   *Enfermedad, daño e ideología: Antropología médica de los renacientes de Pindilig.* Ediciones Abya-Yala, Quito.

Muratorio, Blanca

1980   "Protestantism and Capitalism Revisited in the Rural Highlands of Ecuador," *Journal of Peasant Studies,* vol. 8, pp. 37–61. Frank Cass and Co., London.

1981   "Protestantism, Ethnicity, and Class in Chimborazo," in *Cultural Transformations and Ethnicity in Modern Ecuador,* ed. Norman Whitten, pp. 506–34. University of Illinois Press, Urbana and Chicago.

Muysken, Pieter C.

1975–76 *La media lengua: I. II. III.* Instituto Inter-Andino de Desarrollo, Salcedo, and University of Amsterdam.

Obando A., Segundo

1986   *Tradiciones de Imbabura.* 2nd ed. Ediciones Abya-Yala, Quito.

Oberem, Udo

1981   "Los Cañaris y la conquista española de la sierra ecuatoriana. Otro capítulo de las relaciones interétnicas en el siglo XVI," in *Contribución a la etnohistoria ecuatoriana,* ed. Segundo Moreno Y. and Udo Oberem, pp. 129–52. Instituto Otavaleño de Antropología, Otavalo.

Ortiz Echagüe, José

1957   *España: Tipos y trajes.* 10th ed. Publicaciones Ortiz Echagüe, Madrid.

Parsons, Elsie Clews

1945   *Peguche, Canton of Otavalo, Province of Imbabura, Ecuador: A Study of Andean Indians.* University of Chicago Press, Chicago.

Paz y Miño, Isabel

1994   "Two Tongues Are Better Than One," *Q: Ecuador's English Language Newspaper,* no. 9, April, p. 13. Quito.

Peñaherrera de Costales, Piedad, and Alfredo Costales Samaniego

1959   *Los Salasacas.* Llacta, no. 8. Instituto Ecuatoriano de Antropología, Quito.

Penley, Dennis

1988   *Paños de Gualaceo.* Bilingual ed. English translation by Lynn Hirschkind. Centro Interamericano de Artesanías y Artes Populares (CIDAP), Cuenca.

Poeschel Rees, Ursula

1988   *La mujer salasaca: Su situación en una época de reestructuración económico-cultural.* 2nd ed. Ediciones Abya-Yala, Quito.

Robinson, Natalie V.

1987   "Mantones de Manila: Their Role in China's Silk Trade," *Arts of Asia*, vol. 17, no. 1, pp. 65–75. Hong Kong.

Rowe, Ann Pollard

1977   *Warp-Patterned Weaves of the Andes.* The Textile Museum, Washington, D.C.

1985   "After Emery: Further Considerations of Fabric Classification and Terminology," *The Textile Museum Journal*, vol. 23, 1984, pp. 53–71. Washington, D.C.

1997   "Inca Weaving and Costume," *The Textile Museum Journal*, vols. 34–35, 1995–96, pp. 4–53. Washington, D.C.

ms   "Costume in Ecuador under the Inca Empire." Manuscript written for publication in *History of Indigenous Costume in Highland Ecuador*, edited by Ann P. Rowe.

Rowe, John Howland

1946   "Inca Culture at the Time of the Spanish Conquest," in *Handbook of South American Indians*, ed. Julian H. Steward, vol. 2: *The Andean Civilizations*, pp. 183–330. Bureau of American Ethnology, Bulletin 143. Smithsonian Institution, Washington, D.C.

Saenz, Moisés

1933   *Sobre el indio ecuatoriano y su incorporación al medio nacional.* Publicaciones de la Secretaria de Educación Pública, México.

Salazar, Ernesto

1981   "The Federación Shuar and the Colonization Frontier," in *Cultural Transformations and Ethnicity in Modern Ecuador*, ed. Norman Whitten, pp. 589–613. University of Illinois Press, Urbana and Chicago.

Salinas, Raúl

1954   "Manual Arts in Ecuador," *América Indígena*, vol. 16, no. 4. Instituto Indigenista Interamericano, México.

Salomon, Frank

1973   "Weavers of Otavalo," in *Peoples and Cultures of Native South America*, ed. Daniel R. Gross, pp. 463–92. The Natural History Press, Garden City, New York. Reprinted in Whitten 1981, pp. 420–49.

1986   *Native Lords of Quito in the Age of the Incas: The Political Economy of North Andean Chiefdoms.* Cambridge Studies in Social Anthropology 59. Cambridge University Press, Cambridge and New York.

1987   "Ancestors, Grave Robbers and the Possible Antecedents of Cañari 'Incaism,'" in *Natives and Neighbors in South America: Anthropological Essays*, ed. Harald O. Skar and Frank Salomon, pp. 207–232. Etnologiska Studier 38. Göteborgs Etnografiska Museum, Göteborg.

Santana, Roberto

1990   "El protestantismo en las comunidades indígenas del Chimborazo en

Ecuador," in *Etnia, poder y diferencia en los Andes Septentrionales,* ed. José Sánchez-Parga, pp. 197–215. Ediciones Abya-Yala, Quito.

Saussure, Ferdinand de

1960   *Course of General Linguistics.* Translated by W. Baskin. Philosophical Library, New York. Originally published in 1949.

Scheller, Ulf

1972   *El mundo de los Salasacas.* Fundación Antropológica Ecuatoriana, Guayaquil.

Schmit, Marilee

1991   Costume as a Means of Group- and Self-Identification in the Ecuadorian Sierra. Ph.D. dissertation, Anthropology, University of New Mexico, Albuquerque. University Microfilms International, Ann Arbor, Michigan.

Siles C., Ligia

1983   *La indumentaria en Salasaca.* Instituto Andino de Artes Populares (IADAP), Quito.

Solís, María, ed.

1992   *Azuay: 500 años. Ubicación del problema indígena-campesino.* CPOCA-CECCA, Cuenca.

Stark, Louisa R.

1985   "Ecuadorian Highland Quechua: History and Current Status," in *South American Indian Languages: Retrospect and Prospect,* ed. Harriet E. Manelis Klein and Louisa R. Stark, pp. 443–80. University of Texas Press, Austin.

Steele, Valerie

1989   "Appearance and Identity," in *Men and Women: Dressing the Part,* ed. Claudia Brush Kidwell and Valerie Steele, pp. 6–21. Smithsonian Institution Press, Washington, D.C.

Stevenson, William Bennett

1825   *Historical and Descriptive Narrative of Twenty Years Residence in South America.* 3 vols. Hurst, Robinson, and Co., London.

Stewart, Norman R., Jim Belote, and Linda Smith Belote

1976   "Transhumance in the Central Andes," *Annals, Association of American Geographers,* vol. 66, no. 3, pp. 377–97. Washington, D.C.

Stoll, David

1990   *Is Latin America Turning Protestant?: The Politics of Evangelical Growth.* University of California Press, Berkeley and Los Angeles.

Stutzman, Ronald

1981   "El Mestizaje: An All-Inclusive Ideology of Exclusion," in *Cultural Transformations and Ethnicity in Modern Ecuador,* ed. Norman Whitten, pp. 45–94. University of Illinois Press, Urbana and Chicago.

Tobar Bonilla, Guadalupe

1985   "Natabuela: Un caso de resistencia y adaptación cultural de la indumentaria indígena," *Cultura,* vol. 7, no. 21a, pp. 243–81. Banco Central del Ecuador, Quito.

Tobar Donoso, Julio

1961   *El lenguaje rural de la región interandina del Ecuador: Lo que falta y lo que sobra.* La Unión Católica, Quito.

Tolen, Rebecca Jane

1995   Wool and Synthetics, Countryside and City: Dress, Race and History in Chimborazo, Highland Ecuador. Ph.D. dissertation, Anthropology, University of Chicago. University Microfilms International, Ann Arbor, Michigan.

Towle, Margaret

1961   *The Ethnobotany of Pre-Columbian Peru.* Viking Fund Publications in Anthropology, no. 30. Wenner-Gren Foundation for Anthropological Research, New York.

Turner, Terence

1980   "The Social Skin," in *Not Work Alone: A Cross-Cultural View of Activities Superfluous to Survival,* ed. Jeremy Cherfas and Roger Lewin, pp. 112–40. Sage Publications, Beverly Hills, California.

Tyrer, Robson Brines

1976   The Demographic and Economic History of the Audiencia of Quito: Indian Population and the Textile Industry, 1600–1800. Ph.D. dissertation, History, University of California, Berkeley. University Microfilms International, Ann Arbor, Michigan.

Vicens, Francesc (text), Joaquim Gomis (photos), and J. Prats Vallès (selection and sequence)

1968   *Artesanía/Craftsmanship/Art populaire/Volkskunst.* Ediciones Polígrafa, Barcelona.

Vreeland, Jr., James M.

1978   "Algodón 'país': Un cultivo milenario olvidado," *Boletín de la Sociedad Geográfica de Lima,* vol. 97, pp. 19–26. Lima.

1986   "Cotton Spinning and Processing on the Peruvian North Coast," in *The Junius B. Bird Conference on Andean Textiles,* April 7 and 8, 1984, ed. Ann Pollard Rowe, pp. 363–83. The Textile Museum, Washington, D.C.

Walter, Lynn Ellen

1976   Interaction and Organization in an Ecuadorian Indian Highland Community. Ph.D. dissertation, Anthropology, University of Wisconsin, Madison. University Microfilms International, Ann Arbor, Michigan.

Weismantel, Mary J.

1988   *Food, Gender, and Poverty in the Ecuadorian Andes.* University of Pennsylvania Press, Philadelphia.

Whitten, Jr., Norman E.

1976   *Sacha Runa: Ethnicity and Adaptation of Ecuadorian Jungle Quichua.* University of Illinois Press, Urbana.

1985   *Sicuanga Runa: The Other Side of Development in Amazonian Ecuador.* University of Illinois Press, Urbana and Chicago.

Whitten, Jr., Norman E. ed.

1981   *Cultural Transformations and Ethnicity in Modern Ecuador.* University of
        Illinois Press, Urbana and Chicago.

Whitten, Jr., Norman E., with Kathleen Fine

1981   "Introduction," in *Cultural Transformations and Ethnicity in Modern Ec-
        uador*, ed. Norman Whitten, pp. 1–41, University of Illinois Press, Urbana
        and Chicago.

Wobst, H. Martin

1977   "Stylistic Behavior and Information Exchange," in *For the Director: Re-
        search Essays in Honor of James B. Griffin*, ed. Charles E. Cleland, pp. 317–
        42. Anthropological Papers no. 61. Museum of Anthropology, University
        of Michigan, Ann Arbor.

Wolf, Bernard

1969   *The Little Weaver of Agato: A visit with an Indian boy living in the Andes
        Mountains of Ecuador.* Cowles Book Company, New York; General Pub-
        lishing Company, Toronto.

Yacovleff, Eugenio, and Fortunato L. Herrera

1934–35 "El mundo vegetal de los antiguos peruanos," *Revista del Museo Nacional,*
        vol. 3, no. 3, pp. 241–322; vol. 4, no. 1, pp. 29–102. Lima.

Index

Achuar (formerly Jivaro) people, 7, 13
Achupallas area, 226–28
Acrylic fibers, 19–20
Agato, 51, 73, 76
Agave americana, 16–17, 120
Agrarian reform effects, 12–15, 51, 169–72, 244
Agricultural cooperatives, 12, 244–47
Agustín Guerrero, Juan, 47
Akcha watana cinta (hair tying ribbon), 136, 191
Akcha watana cordón, 191
Alao area costume, 214–16
Alausí marketplace, 225
Alforjas (saddlebags), 260-61, 273-74, 279
Algodón criollo (cotton), 18
Alpargatas (sandals): Angochagua–La Rinconada communities, 103; Hacienda Zuleta, 92; historical influences, 49; Mariano Acosta community, 107, 108; Natabuela community, 79; N.E. Pichincha–E. Imbabura, 90; Otavalo ethnic group, 64–65, 72, 73; Paniquindra–La Florida communities, 100; Saraguro ethnic group, 268
Anaku styles: Angochagua–La Rinconada communities, 101; Chambo-Alao area, 214; Chibuleo area, 145–46; Columbe area, 200; Cotopaxi valley floor, 117, 122; Guaranda area, 162–63; historical origins, 45, 280, 281; La Esperanza community, 94–95; Licto area, 208, 212–13; Llangahua ethnic group, 155; Majipamba-Troje-Cacha communities, 187–89, 193–94; Mariano Acosta community, 106; N.E. Pichincha–E. Imbabura, 87–88; Natabuela community, 79; Nitón community, 159, 160; Quizapincha communities, 159, 160; Nizag community, 225; Otavalo ethnic group, 56–57, 76, 78; Palmira Dávalos area, 216, 217; Paniquindra–La Florida communities, 97–98; Pulucate community, 174, 180–81; Rumipamba/San Clemente communities, 95; Salamala-Macas communities, 124;

Salasaca ethnic group, 131, 139; San Juan area, 203; Saraguro ethnic group, 266, 267; Zumbagua community, 112. *See also* Bolsicón styles; *Centros* (skirts); Pollera styles
Angaguana ethnic group, 144; children's costume, 153; men's costume, 149–53; women's costume, 145–50
Angochagua costume, 88, 101–3
Aniline dye, 20
Aprons: Azuay valley cholo, 256–57; Majipamba-Cacha communities, 189; Otavalo ethnic group, 64; Pulucate community, 182. *See also Changallis* (aprons)
Araucanian (now Mapuche) people, 49
Arrayán, Juana, 61
Ascanta (fedora), 72
Asociación de Palmira Dávalos, 217
Azuay Province indigenous people, 254-61

Backstrap looms: plain weaving process, 26–31
Bags. *See Shigras* (looped bags)
Baitas: Majipamba-Troje-Cacha communities, 190; Mariano Acosta community, 106; Pulucate community, 174, 181. *See also* Shawl styles
Bayeta de lishtas, 135
Bayeta fabric, 36
Bayetas (shawls): Columbe area, 201; La Merced-Zúlac-Cocán communities, 223–24; Palmira Dávalos area, 216; Salasaca ethnic group, 133–35; San Juan area, 204–5; Sanganao area, 222. *See also* Shawl styles
Bayetillas (shawls), 163–64. *See also* Shawl styles
Beads (jewelry): Achupallas area, 227–28; Angochagua–La Rinconada communities, 103; Cañar Province, 235, 242, 250; Columbe area, 201; Cotopaxi valley floor, 117, 119, 122, 123; Guaranda area, 164; La Merced-Zúlac-Cocán communities, 224; Licto area, 212, 213; Majipamba-Troje-

Cacha communities, 190, 196; Mariano Acosta community, 106; Natabuela community, 79; N.E. Pichincha–E. Imbabura, 90; Nitón community, 159; Quizapincha communities, 159; Nizag community, 225; Otavalo ethnic group, 66; Palmira Dávalos area, 216; Paniquindra–La Florida communities, 99; Pulucate community, 183; Rumipamba/San Clemente communities, 95; Salamala-Macas communities, 125; Salasaca ethnic group, 135–36, 141; San Juan area, 206; Sanganao area, 222; Saraguro ethnic group, 269
Belote, Jim, 263
Belote, Linda, 263
Belt looms, 27–29, 31
Belts, handwoven *(chumbis):* Angochagua–La Rinconada communities, 103; Cañar Province, 236–38; Chibuleo area, 146–47, 150; Columbe area, 200–201; Cotopaxi valley floor, 117–18, 122, 123; decorative techniques, 31–33; Guaranda area, 163, 166; historical influences, 47; La Esperanza community, 95; La Merced-Zúlac-Cocán communities, 223; Licto area, 209–10; Llangahua ethnic group, 156; Majipamba-Troje-Cacha communities, 187–89, 194; Mariano Acosta community, 106, 108; N.E. Pichincha-E. Imbabura, 88; Natabuela community, 78, 79; Nitón community, 159, 160; Quizapincha communities, 159, 160; Nizag community, 225, 226; Otavalo ethnic group, 57–60; Palmira Dávalos area, 216, 217; Paniquindra–La Florida communities, 98; Pulucate community, 181–82; Rumipamba/San Clemente communities, 95; Salamala-Macas communities, 124; Salasaca ethnic group, 131–34, 137, 142–43; San Juan area, 204; Sanganao area, 222; Saraguro ethnic group, 266–67, 270; Troje community, 189; Zumbagua community, 112, 113

Belts, leather, 67, 73, 270-71
Blankets, 114-15, 273, 279
Blouse styles: Achupallas area, 227; Angochagua–La Rinconada communities, 101; Azuay Province, 262; Azuay valley cholo, 255; Cañar Province, 231, 250; Chambo-Alao area, 214; Chibuleo area, 145; Columbe area, 201; Cotopaxi valley floor, 118; Guaranda area, 163; historical influences, 47, 280; La Esperanza community, 94; Licto area, 212; Majipamba-Troje-Cacha communities, 194–95; Mariano Acosta community, 104–6; Natabuela community, 78–79; N.E. Pichincha–E. Imbabura, 85–87; Nizag community, 225; Otavalo ethnic group, 55–56, 76, 78; Palmira Dávalos area, 216, 217; Paniquindra–La Florida communities, 98; Pulucate community, 182–83; San Juan area, 203; Saraguro ethnic group, 265, 266; Zuleta community, 92
Blouse-slip combinations. See Blouse styles
Bolivar Province. See Guaranda area (Bolivar Province)
Bolivian belts, 60
Bolsicón styles: Azuay valley cholo, 255, 256; Cañar Province, 232–33; historical origins, 45. See also Anaku styles; Centros (skirts); Pollera styles
Bulcay el Carmen, 254, 257, 259
Bulzhun, 254, 257

Cacha communities: contemporary women's costume, 193–98; factory-made clothing, 186; men's costume, 36-37, 198–99; old-style women's costume, 187–93
Cacha ponchos, 184–85, 199
Cajabamba, 168, 169
Camelid hair, 18–19, 22
Cañar Province, 242; children's costume, 241; men's costume, 235–41, 242, 247–50; socio-economics, 230, 243–47; textile production, 235, 241–42, 251–53; women's costume, 228, 231–35, 242, 250
Cañar ethnic group, 41
Cañaro poncho styles, 278
Canelos Quichua people, 7
Cantón Colta: costume trends, 173–79; rural versus urban fabric choice, 173–74; socio-economics, 168–72; wool versus synthetic fabric, 174–80. See also Columbe area; Majipamba community
Capur costume, 277
Carabuela, 55, 76
Care of clothing, 276–77
Cariamanga, 274
Carrying cloths: Achupallas area, 228; Azuay valley cholo, 258; Cañar Province, 235; Chibuleo area, 147; Columbe area, 201; Cotopaxi valley floor, 120; Guaranda area,

164, 165; La Merced-Zúlac-Cocán communities, 223–24; Licto area, 209, 212; Majipamba-Troje-Cacha communities, 193, 198; Nizag community, 225; Otavalo ethnic group, 62, 64; Palmira Dávalos area, 216; Pulucate community, 181, 183; Salasaca ethnic group, 133–34; San Juan area, 205; Saraguro ethnic group, 267; Zumbagua community, 113
Casa de la Cultura Ecuatoriana, 51
Casagrande, Joseph, 126
Caucho pargate (sandals), 99–100
Cayapa (now Chachis) people, 4
Cebadas, 207
Cebada parba hairstyle, 138
Centros (skirts): La Esperanza community, 95; Mariano Acosta community, 106; N.E. Pichincha–E. Imbabura, 87–88; Rumipamba/San Clemente communities, 95; Zuleta community, 92. See also Anaku styles; Bolsicón styles; Pollera styles
Ceremonial clothing, 42–44, 74, 116, 257–58
Chachilbana, 160
Chachis (formerly Cayapa) people, 4
Chakiwasi (foothouse, Q.), 111–12
Chalina. See Shawl styles
Chambo area costume, 214–16
Changallis (aprons): Columbe area, 200; Guamote area, 220; Majipamba-Troje-Cacha communities, 188, 193–94; Palmira Dávalos area, 216, 217; Pulucate community, 182; San Juan area, 203
Chaps: Cañar Province, 240–41, 249; Chimborazo Province, 202, 206, 214, 220, 225, 228; Cotopaxi valley floor, 123; Llangahua ethnic group, 158; Saraguro ethnic group, 271
Charijayac music group, 71
Chibuleo ethnic group: children's costume, 153; men's costume, 149–53; socio-economics, 144–45; women's costume, 46, 145–50
Chicticay, 37, 242
Chillu (cotton), 18
Chirihuasi costume, 95
Chismote, 217
Cholos cuencanos: defined, 254–55; men's costume, 258–61; women's costume, 255–58
Chordeleg, 254, 258
Chulla cara ponchos, 69
Chumbi. See Belts, handwoven (chumbis)
Cinta (hair wrap), 65, 118, 183
Closed double chain stitch, 86–87. See also Embroidered decoration
Cocán area costume, 223–25
Cochineal dyeing, 20, 135, 139, 142, 143
Colepato: costume, 247–50; socio-economics, 243–47; textile production, 251–53
Colorado (now Tsachila) people, 4
Columbe area, 169; men's costume, 202–3; textile production, 182, 199–200; women's

costume, 200–202
Columbus Quincentennial demonstrations, 15, 42
Compadrazgo, 43–44
Complementary-warp weave, 33, 98–99, 163, 182, 191–92, 236–38
Confederación de Nacionalidades Indígenas del Ecuador (CONAIE), 11, 13, 14–15
Conterón, Breenan: on costume, 41
Cost of clothing: Zumbagua community, 113, 115
Costume tradition: ceremonial occasions, 42–44, 177–78; ethnic identity, 41–42, 104, 142, 253, 280–81; history of, 44–49, 280; symbolism of, 39–40
Cotacachi area costume, 76–78. See also Otavalo ethnic group
Cotopaxi Province: children's costume, 114–15; generational costume differences, 117, 120, 122–23; men's costume, 113–14, 123, 125; socio-economics, 41, 110–12; textile production, 115–16; women's costume, 112–13, 117–23, 123–25
Cotton for textiles, 17–18, 22
Crocheting, 112-13, 123, 186, 198
Cuatro Esquinas, 166
Cuenca area, 228, 254, 258
Cuicuno, 35, 123

Decorative weaving, 31–33. See also Belts, handwoven (chumbis); Poncho styles; Shawl styles
Drafting in spinning, 21
Dress style, 187–89. See also Anaku styles
Drop spinning, 21–22
Dyeing: Achupallas area, 228; Cañar Province, 241, 252–53; cotton, 18; Licto area, 212; Loja Province, 266, 267, 279; materials, 20; for plain weave decoration, 31, 47; Pulucate community, 186; Salasaca ethnic group, 135, 139, 142; Saraguro ethnic group, 266, 267

Earrings: Achupallas area, 228; Azuay Province, 262; Cañar Province, 234–35, 242, 250; Chibuleo area, 147–48; cholos cuencana, 258; Columbe area, 201; Cotopaxi valley floor, 119; historical influences, 47–48; Licto area, 212, 213; Llangahua ethnic group, 157; Majipamba-Troje-Cacha communities, 190, 196; Mariano Acosta community, 106; N.E. Pichincha–E. Imbabura, 90; Nizag community, 225; Otavalo ethnic group, 66–67; Paniquindra–La Florida communities, 99; Pulucate community, 183; Quizapincha area, 160; Salamala-Macas communities, 125; Salasaca ethnic group, 136; San Juan area, 206; Sanganao area, 222; Saraguro ethnic group, 268, 269–70

Ecuador: coastal zone, 3–4; highland zone, 4–7; indigenous identity, 11–12; Oriente zone, 7; political history, 7–10, 12–15

Ecuador Runacunapac Riccharimui (ECUARUNARI), 13–14

El Rosario, 159-60

Embroidered decoration: Achupallas area, 227; Azuay Province, 255–56, 257, 258, 262; Azuay valley cholo, 255-56, 257, 258; blouses, Natabuela community, 78–79; Cañar Province, 231–32, 235, 236, 238, 240, 248, 250; Chambo-Alao area, 214; Chibuleo area, 145, 146, 150, 153, 154–55; Columbe area, 200, 201, 202; cooperatives, 85, 94; Cotopaxi valley floor, 118; Guaranda area, 163; La Merced-Zúlac-Cocán communities, 223; Licto area, 212; Majipamba-Cacha communities, shawls, 190; Majipamba-Troje-Cacha communities, 193–95; Mariano Acosta style, 104–6, 109; N.E. Pichincha–E. Imbabura, 85–87, 88; Nizag community, 225; Otavalo costume, 55–56, 57, 62, 78; Palmira Dávalos area, 216, 217; Paniquindra–La Florida communities, 97, 98; Pulucate community, 180–81, 182–83; Rumipamba/San Clemente communities, 95; Salamala-Macas communities, 124; Salasaca ethnic group, 138, 139, 141–42; San Juan area, 203; Saraguro ethnic group, 265, 266, 267, 270–71; Zuleta community 92

Entrega de gallos festival, 103–4

Esterado belt style, 182

Ethnic identity: costume as, 41–42, 104, 177–78, 253, 280–81; in Ecuador, 11–15. *See also* Costume tradition; Otavalo ethnic group; Salasaca ethnic group; Saraguro ethnic group

Evangelical Protestantism, 14, 169, 172

Export of textiles: Otavalo merchants, 53

Fachalinas: Mariano Acosta community, 106; Otavalo ethnic group, 60–62, 64, 76, 78. *See also* Shawl styles

Fachallinas, 209, 212–13. *See also* Shawl styles

Factory-made clothing, 48; Achupallas area, 227; Azuay Province, 255, 261, 262; Cañar Province, 231, 235, 238, 248, 249–50; Chambo-Alao area, 214; Chibuleo area, 150; cholos cuencanos, 255, 261; Columbe area, 201, 202, 203; Cotopaxi valley floor, 122, 123; Guaranda area, 163, 165, 166; Licto area, 212, 214; Llangahua ethnic group, 156–57, 158; Majipamba-Troje-Cacha communities, 195, 198, 199; N.E. Pichincha-E. Imbabura, 91, 100; Nitón community, 159; Quizapincha communities, 159; Nizag community, 226; Otavalo ethnic group, 64, 67, 69–70, 73; Palmira Dávalos area, 216, 217; Pulucate community, 182, 184; Salamala-Macas communities, 125;

Salasaca ethnic group, 130, 137; San Juan area, 203, 206; Sanganao area, 222; Saraguro ethnic group, 268, 270; Zumbagua community, 114. *See also* Fedoras

Fedoras: Achupallas area, 227, 228; Cañar Province, 242, 250; Cantón Colta, 173; Columbe area, 202; Cotopaxi valley floor, 120, 122, 123; Guamote area, 220; Guaranda area, 165, 166; Licto area, 212, 214; Majipamba-Troje-Cacha communities, 198; Mariano Acosta community, 107, 108; N.E. Pichincha–E. Imbabura, 91; Nitón community, 159, 160; Quizapincha communities, 159, 160; Nizag community, 226; Palmira Dávalos area, 216, 217; Paniquindra–La Florida communities, 99; Pulucate community, 184, 185; Rumipamba/San Clemente communities, 95; Salamala-Macas communities, 125; Salasaca ethnic group, 136, 138; San Juan area, 205, 206; Sanganao area, 222; Zuleta community, 92; Zumbagua community, 113. *See also* Hat styles

Felt hats. *See* Hat styles

Felting technique, 19

Fibers for weaving: animal, 18–19; cotton, 17–18; leaf, 16–17; synthetic, 19–20

Fiesta costume: Chimborazo Province, 198–99, 214; *entrega de gallos,* 104; importance of, 42–43; Salasaca ethnic group, 139–41; Saraguro ethnic group, 268

Fiesta-cargo systems, 172

Follón, 106

Footwear: Angochagua–La Rinconada communities, 103; Azuay Province, 258, 261, 262; Cañar Province, 235, 240, 249, 250; Chibuleo area, 150; cholos cuencanos, 258, 261; Columbe area, 201, 202; historical influences, 48, 49; Licto area, 212, 213, 214; Llangahua ethnic group, 157, 158; Majipamba-Troje-Cacha communities, 198; Mariano Acosta community, 107, 108; N.E. Pichincha–E. Imbabura, 90; Otavalo ethnic group, 64–65, 72, 73; Paniquindra–La Florida communities, 99–100; Pulucate community, 184; San Juan area, 206; Saraguro ethnic group, 268, 273

Forman, Sylvia, 192–93

Franck, Harry, 6

Franquemont, Christine, 25

Franquemont, Edward, 25

Frente akcha hairstyle, 190

Frutilla (belt), 133

Fulling technique, 19

Furcraea andina, 16–17, 72-73, 129, 136-37, 192-93, 226, 273, 275, 276-77

Galte, 218; hat styles, 217, 220

Gender roles: embroidery, 85; spinning and weaving, 23–24, 36–37, 115, 185, 252, 276. *See*

also Migration patterns

Generational costume differences: men's, 70, 72–74; women's, 117, 120, 122–23; wool/synthetic preferences, 178

Godparents, 43–44, 74, 115, 141

González Suárez, 84, 86, 91

Gossypium barbadense (cotton), 17–18

Great Skirt Divide, 168, 222, 225–26

Guamote area, 169; costume, 220–21

Guaranda area (Bolivar Province): men's costume, 166; women's costume, 162–65

Gualaceo, 257, 258, 260-61

Hacienda system: and ethnic identity, 41–42; Cañar Province, 244; Cantón Colta, 169–70; Chimborazo province, 168; E. Imbabura, 84. *See also* Agrarian reform effects

Hacienda Zuleta, 85, 91–92

Hair styles: Achupallas area, 227; Azuay Province, 262; Cañar Province, 235, 240, 242, 247–48, 250; Chambo-Alao area, 216; Chibuleo area, 148–49; Chismote area, 217; cholos cuencanos, 258; Columbe area, 202; Cotopaxi valley floor, 118, 122; Guaranda area, 164–65; historical influences, 47, 48, 280; La Merced-Zúlac-Cocán communities, 224; Licto area, 212; Loja Province, 268, 273, 277; Llangahua ethnic group, 157; Majipamba-Troje-Cacha communities, 190–91, 198; Mariano Acosta community, 107, 109; Natabuela community, 82; N.E. Pichincha–E. Imbabura, 90, 91; Nizag community, 225; Otavalo ethnic group, 65, 70–71, 74; Palmira Dávalos area, 216, 217; Paniquindra–La Florida communities, 99; Pulucate community, 183; Salamala communities, 123–24; Salasaca ethnic group, 136–37, 138; San Juan area, 205–6; Sanganao area, 222; Saraguro ethnic group, 268, 273; Zumbagua community, 113

Hair tying ribbon (*akcha watana cinta*), 136, 191

Hair wrap (*akcha watarina*), 65

Hand-supported spinning, 21–23

Hat styles: Achupallas area, 227, 228; Angochagua–La Rinconada communities, 103; Azuay Province, 262; Cañar Province, 235, 240, 242, 249, 250; Cantón Colta, 173; Chambo-Alao area, 216; Chibuleo area, 149–50; cholos cuencana, 258; Columbe area, 202; Cotopaxi valley floor, 119, 120, 122, 123; felting techniques, 19; Galte area, 217, 220; Guamote area, 220; Guaranda area, 165, 166; historical influences, 48, 280; La Merced-Zúlac-Cocán communities, 224–25; Licto area, 210–12, 212, 214; Llangahua ethnic group, 157, 158; Majipamba-Troje-Cacha communities, 191–92, 198; Mariano Acosta community, 107, 108; Natabuela community, 79, 82;

N.E. Pichincha–E. Imbabura, 90–91; Nitón community, 160; Quizapincha communities, 160; Nizag community, 225, 226; Otavalo ethnic group, 62, 71–72, 76; Palmira Dávalos area, 216–17; Paniquindra–La Florida communities, 99; Pulucate community, 183–84, 185; Rumipamba/San Clemente communities, 95; Salamala-Macas communities, 124; Salasaca ethnic group, 136, 138, 139, 141; San Juan area, 205, 206; Sanganao area, 222; Saraguro ethnic group, 267–68; Tiocajas area, 217; Zuleta community, 92; Zumbagua community, 113, 114

Headcloths: Natabuela community, 79; Otavalo ethnic group, 60–62, 76; Rumipamba/San Clemente communities, 95

Heddle rods. *See* Weaving process

Hijos de Imbabura music group, 70

Hoffmeyer, Hans, 130, 143

Huairapungo: costume, 247–50; socio-economics, 243–47; textile production, 251–53

Ikat. *See* Warp-resist dyeing

Ilumán, 61-62, 64, 69, 70, 73, 74, 91; hat manufacturing, 72

Imbabura Province (Eastern): costume, 45, 48, 85–91; socio-economics, 84–85

Inca empire, 7–9; influence on costume, 44–45, 47, 48, 49, 187, 280

Indigo dye, 18, 20, 68, 120, 257, 266

Instituto Ecuatoriano de Reforma Agraria y Colonización (IERAC), 13

Ishkay cara ponchos, 69

Iskhay fachalina headcloth style, 61

Jackets. *See* Factory-made clothing

Jatun chumbi, 146–47

Jerga fabric, 36

Jewelry: Achupallas area, 227–28; Azuay Province, 262; Cañar Province, 234–35, 242, 250; Chibuleo area, 147–48; cholos cuencana, 258; Columbe area, 201; Cotopaxi valley floor, 119; Guaranda area, 164; historical influences, 47–48; La Merced-Zúlac-Cocán communities, 224; Licto area, 212, 213; Llangahua ethnic group, 157; Majipamba-Troje-Cacha communities, 190, 196; Mariano Acosta community, 106–7; N.E. Pichincha–E. Imbabura, 90; Nitón community, 159, 160; Quizapincha communities, 159, 160; Nizag community, 225; Otavalo ethnic group, 66–67; Palmira Dávalos area, 216; Paniquindra–La Florida communities, 99; Pulucate community, 183; Rumipamba/San Clemente communities, 95; Salamala-Macas communities, 125; Salasaca ethnic group, 135–36; San Juan area, 206; Sanganao area, 222; Saraguro

ethnic group, 268–70; Zuleta community, 92

Jimbilla hair styles, 277

Jirga ponchos: Chibuleo area, 150, 152–53; Majipamba-Troje-Cacha communities, 198; Pulucate community, 184

Jivaro (now Achuar or Shuar) people, 7

Kampu anaku, 101

Kanitillu chumbi (cane belt), 60

Kawiña chumbis: Columbe area, 200; Guaranda area, 163; La Merced-Zúlac-Cocán communities, 223; Majipamba-Cacha-Troje communities, 189–90; Nizag community, 225; Palmira Dávalos area, 216, 217; Pulucate community, 182; San Juan area, 204; Sanganao area, 222. *See also* Belts, handwoven *(chumbis)*

Kushmas (tunics): Cañar Province, 235–36; Columbe area, 202; historical influences, 48, 280; Pulucate community, 185; Saraguro ethnic group, 48, 270

La Calera, 55, 76

La Compañia, 55

La Esperanza, 94–95

La Florida costume, 97–100

La Merced area costume, 223–25

La Rinconada costume, 88, 101–3

Las Abras, 84, 94, 100

Law of Agrarian Reform 1964. *See* Agrarian reform effects

Leaf fibers for textiles, 16–17

Licto area: contemporary women's costume, 212–13; men's costume, 214; socio-economics, 207–8; traditional women's clothing, 208–12

Liencillo fabric, 36

Lienzo fabric, 36, 67, 78-79, 108

Linchi, 273, 275

Lishtu (carrying cloth), 183

Llama hair for textiles, 18–19, 158

Llangahua ethnic group, 155–58

Lligllas (shawls): Azuay Province, 262; Columbe area, 201; historical origins, 45–46; Saraguro ethnic group, 267. *See also* Shawl styles

Llinllin, 199

Loom technology: weaving process, 25–31

Looped bags. *See Shigras* (looped bags)

Looping technique, 17

Macanas (shawls), 120, 164, 205, 220. *See also* Shawl styles

Macas costume, 123–25

Magdalena: skirt styles, 88; poncho styles, 95

Majipamba community, 169; contemporary women's costume, 193–98; factory-made clothing, 186; men's costume, 198–99; traditional women's costume, 187–93

Mama chumbis (mother belts): Columbe area, 201; historical influences, 47; Majipamba-Troje-Cacha communities, 189–90, 194; Otavalo valley, 57, 60; Pulucate community, 182; Saraguro ethnic group, 266–67, 270

Mantones de Manila (Chinese shawls), 47. *See also* Shawl styles

Mapuche (formerly Araucanian) people, 49

Mariano Acosta: children's costume, 108–9; history, 103; men's costume, 107–8; women's costume, 104–7

Marketplaces: Alausí, 223, 225; Ambato, 129, 145; Azogues, 232, 258; Cajabamba, 168; Cañar, 232, 234-35, 240-41, 244, 249-50; Cayambe, 84; Cotacachi, 76-77, 79; Cuenca, 232, 255-56; Gualaceo, 232, 257-58, 260-62; Guamote, 169, 220, 221; Guaranda, 162; Ibarra, 84, 103; Latacunga, 118, 123;Licto, 207-8, 209, 211; Otavalo, 53–54, 55, 84, 144, 145; Pelileo, 129, 150; Riobamba, 187, 196, 207; Salasaca, 144; Salcedo, 118, 120, 122; San Juan, 203; Saquisilí, 117-20, 123; Saraguro, 263; Suscal, 242; Zumbagua, 116

Media Colta. *See* Majipamba

Mestizaje policy on costume, 42

Migration patterns: Azuay Province, 255, 260, 261; Cantón Colta, 171; N. E. Pichincha–E. Imbabura, 85; Salasaca ethnic group, 129; Saraguro ethnic group, 265

Millma sumbriru (wool hat), 183–84

Mittenberger, Edward, 279

Molobóg, 207, 209

Morlán, 76-77

Movimiento Indígena de Chimborazo (MICH), 41

Muratorio, Blanca, 172

Mushapa (leather purse), 118

Music groups, traditional: clothing, 67–68; foreign travel, 53; hair styles, 71

N.E. Pichincha–E. Imbabura indigenous group, 84; costume, 85–91

Ñajcha chumbi, 266–67, 270

Natabuela costume, 78–82. *See also* Otavalo ethnic group

Necklaces: Achupallas area, 227–28; Angochagua–La Rinconada communities, 103; Cañar Province, 235, 250; Chibuleo area, 147; Columbe area, 201; Cotopaxi valley floor, 119; Guaranda area, 164; La Merced-Zúlac-Cocán communities, 224; Licto area, 212, 213; Llangahua ethnic group, 157; Majipamba-Troje-Cacha communities, 190, 196; Mariano Acosta community, 106; N.E. Pichincha–E. Imbabura, 90; Nitón community, 160; Quizapincha communities, 160; Nizag community, 225; Otavalo ethnic group, 66; Palmira Dávalos area, 216; Paniquindra–La Florida communities, 99; Pulacate community, 183; Rumipamba/San Clemente communities, 95; Salasaca ethnic group, 135–36, 141; San Juan area, 206; Sanganao area, 222; Saraguro ethnic group, 269; Zuleta community, 92

Nitiluisa, 23, 203, 204, 206

Nitón community, 159

Nizag community costume, 225–26

Obra (commission weaving), 37

Oña textile production, 279

Otavalo ethnic group: children's costume, 74; costume and identity, 41, 54–55; jewelry, 47, 66–67; men's costume, 67–74; textile production heritage, 50–51, 75–76, 281; women's costume, 55–65. See also Otavalo valley

Otavalo valley, 50–54; textile production, 21, 72. See also Otavalo ethnic group

Otavalo wedding shirt, 67

Ovalos. See Natabuela

Pacotillas, 220, 235. See also Shawl styles

Palmira Dávalos area costume, 216–20

Paniquindra costume, 95, 97–100

Paño fabric, 36, 256

Paños, 242, 257, 258. See also Shawl styles

Pant styles: Azuay Province, 261, 262; Cañar Province, 238, 248, 249; Chambo-Alao area, 214; Chibuleo area, 150; cholos cuencanos, 261; Columbe area, 202; Guaranda area, 166; historical influences, 48, 280; Licto area, 214; Llangahua ethnic group, 158; Loja Province, 270–71, 277; Majipamba-Troje-Cacha communities, 198; Mariano Acosta community, 108; Natabuela community, 79; Otavalo ethnic group, 67, 73; Palmira Dávalos area, 217; Pulucate community, 184; Salamala-Macas communities, 125; Salasaca ethnic group, 137, 141–42; Saraguro ethnic group, 270–71; Zuleta community, 92

Pañu sumbriru, 184

Panutzutzu ukufachallina, 139

Papaurco, 120-21

Paute, 254, 258

Pedido (commission weaving), 37

Peguche, 61-62, 65, 73, 200

Pesillo, 84, 88

Petticoat, cotton, 95. See also Underskirts

Pichincha (Northeastern), 84, 85–91

Pichu anaku, 187–89

Pichu jerga, 130–31

Pickup design, 60

Pilahuín ethnic group: children's costume, 153; men's costume, 149–53; shigras, 153; socio-economics, 144–45; women's costume, 145–50

Pindilig parish, 243–44

Plain weaving process, 26, 36

Plying technique, 22

Pollera styles: Achupallas area, 227; Azuay Province, 262; Cañar Province, 231–32, 250; cholo cuencanos, 255–56; historical origins, 45, 280, 281; La Merced-Zúlac-Cocán communities, 223; Nizag community, 225; Sanganao area, 222; Saraguro ethnic group, 266, 267. See also Anaku styles; Bolsicón styles; Centros (skirts)

Pomatúg hats, 119, 227, 136, 149, 191, 203, 211, 217, 224, 235

Poncho Plaza, 53–54

Poncho styles: Achupallas area, 228; Angochagua–La Rinconada communities, 103; Azuay Province, 258–61, 262; Azuay valley cholo, 258-61; Cañar Province, 238–40, 248, 249–50; Chambo-Alao area, 216; Chibuleo area, 150, 152–53; Columbe area, 203; construction time requirements, 25; Cotopaxi valley floor, 123; Guamote area, 220; Guaranda area, 166; historical influences, 48–49; La Merced-Zúlac-Cocán communities, 225; Licto area, 214; Llangahua ethnic group, 158; Loja Province, 265, 270, 271–72, 277, 278; Majipamba-Troje-Cacha communities, 36, 198–99; Mariano Acosta community, 108; Natabuela community, 82; N.E. Pichincha–E. Imbabura, 91; Nitón community, 160; Quizapincha communities, 160; Nizag community, 226; Otavalo ethnic group, 67–70, 73; Palmira Dávalos area, 217; Paniquindra–La Florida communities, 100; pink patterned, 95, 100, 103; Pulacate community, 173, 184–85; Rumipamba/San Clemente communities, 95; Salamala-Macas communities, 125; Salasaca ethnic group, 138, 141; San Juan area, 206; Saraguro ethnic group, 265, 270, 271–72; Zuleta community, 92; Zumbagua community, 113–14

Programa Social Hacienda Zuleta, 91

Puka poncho, 198

Pulacate: men's costume, 173, 184–85; textile production, 185–86; women's costume, 174, 180–84

Pungalá, 207, 214

Purses, 118, 139, 189

Queseras: costume, 247–50; socio-economics, 243–47; textile production, 251–53

Quilanga, 279

Quizapincha area, 159–60

Rebozos: Achupallas area, 227; Azuay valley cholo, 257–58; historical origins, 46, 47; Licto area, 209, 212, 213; Otavalo ethnic group, 62, 64; Salasaca ethnic group, 135. See also Shawl styles

Rings, finger: Cañar Province, 250; Cotopaxi valley floor, 119; Majipamba-Troje-Cacha communities, 190; Mariano Acosta community, 107; Otavalo ethnic group, 67; Salamala-Macas communities, 125; Saraguro ethnic group, 270

Río Blanco, 155-58

Ruana. See Poncho styles

Rumipamba, Cotopaxi province, 120-21, 164, 205, 207, 212

Rumipamba, Imbabura province, 84, 94, 95, 100

Rural versus urban fabrics, 173–74, 177, 179

Sábana, 62, 64

Saddlebags, 261, 273, 279

Salamala costume, 123–25

Salasaca ethnic group: children's costume, 138–39; costume and identity, 41, 142, 281; men's costume, 48, 137–38, 141; socioeconomics, 126–30; textile production, 136, 142–44; wedding costume, 141–42; women's costume, 48, 130–37, 139–41

San Bernardo textile production, 199–200

San Clemente costume, 95

San Juan area costume, 203–6

Sandals. See Footwear

Sanganao area costume, 222

San Isidro, 84, 87

Saraguro ethnic group: children's costume, 273; clothing care, 276–77; colors in costume, 265–66; costume and identity, 41, 281; jewelry, 268–70; men's costume, 48, 267–68, 270–73; socio-economics, 263–65; textile production, 273, 276; women's costume, 266–68

Scarves: men's, 153, 158, 220, 240, 249; women's, 242

School uniforms, 42, 74, 109

Schreuder, Jan, 51, 130

Self-couching stitch, 86–87. See also Embroidered decoration

Shalaganana headcloth style, 61

Shawl styles: Achupallas area, 227, 228; Angochagua–La Rinconada communities, 101–3; Azuay Province, 46, 257–58, 262; Azuay valley cholo, 257-58; Cañar Province, 233, 235, 250; Chambo-Alao area, 214; Chibuleo area, 147; Columbe area, 201; Cotopaxi valley floor, 46, 118, 120, 122; Guamote area, 220; Guaranda area, 163–64, 165; historical influences, 45–47, 280; La Esperanza community, 95; La Merced-Zúlac-Cocán communities, 223–24; Licto area, 209, 212–13; Llangahua ethnic group, 156–57; Majipamba-Troje-Cacha communities, 190, 195–96, 198; Mariano Acosta community, 106; Natabuela community, 79; N.E. Pichincha–E. Imbabura, 88–89; Nitón community, 159, 160; Quizapincha communities, 159, 160; Nizag community, 225; Otavalo, 60–61, 64, 76; Palmira Dávalos area, 216, 217; Paniquindra–La Florida communities, 98–99; Pulucate community, 181; Rumipamba/San Clemente communities, 95; Salamala-Macas communities, 124–25; Salasaca ethnic group, 46, 133–35, 139, 141; San Juan area, 203, 204–5; Sanganao area, 222; Saraguro ethnic group, 267; Zumbagua community, 112. *See also* Carrying cloths

Sheds. *See* Weaving process

Sheep, 129, 142, 170, 251, 264

Sheep's wool: for felting/fulling, 19; spinning techniques, 22

Shigras (looped bags): Chibuleo area, 153; construction techniques, 17; Cotopaxi valley floor, 120; Licto area, 212; Llangahua ethnic group, 158; Majipamba-Troje-Cacha communities, 192–93, 198; Nitón community, 159, 160; Quizapincha communities, 159, 160; Nizag community, 226; Pulucate community, 186; San Juan area, 205; Saraguro ethnic group, 273

Shirt styles: Cañar Province, 235, 248–49, 250; Chibuleo area, 150; cholos cuencanos, 261; Columbe area, 202; historical influences, 48, 280; Licto area, 214; Majipamba-Troje-Cacha communities, 198; Mariano Acosta community, 108; Natabuela community, 79; Otavalo ethnic group, 67, 73; Palmira Dávalos area, 217; Pulucate community, 184; Salasaca ethnic group, 130–31, 137; Saraguro ethnic group, 270; Zuleta community, 92; Zumbagua community, 112

Shoulder wraps. *See* Shawl styles

Shuar (formerly Jivaro) people, 7, 13

Sigsig (spindle), 21. *See also* Spinning of fiber

Sikinchina (shawl), 198. *See also* Shawl styles

Sisid, 230, 234

Skirt styles: Cotopaxi valley floor, 122; Guaranda area, 165; Salamala-Macas communities, 124–25. *See also* Anaku styles; Bolsicón styles; *Centros* (skirts); Pollera styles

Slips, women's, 76, 183, 212. *See also* Anaku styles; Blouse styles

Spindles, hand, 21–23, 280

Spinning of fiber: in households, 24–25; techniques, 21–24

Stitches, embroidery, 86–87. *See also* Embroidered decoration

Suku fachalinas (headcloths), 61

Supplementary-warp decoration, 31–32, 58–60, 65, 79, 83, 117–18, 131–34, 147–49, 156–59, 187–88, 195–97, 200, 204, 209–11, 266-67

Synthetic fibers, 19–20

T-shirts. *See* Factory-made clothing

Tabacundo, 84, 86

Taday parish, 243–44

Textile production: Achupallas area, 227, 228; Azuay Province, 254; Cacha communities, 163, 198–99; Cañar Province, 235, 241–42, 251–53; Chibuleo area, 154–55; Columbe area, 199–200; education for, 76; embroidery decoration, 85, 94; Guaranda area, 166; Hacienda Zuleta, 91, 92; Ilumán, 72; Licto area, 214; Llangahua ethnic group, 158; Loja Province, 273, 276, 279; Otavalo ethnic group, 50–53, 72, 75–76, 176; Palmira Dávalos area, 217; Pulucate community, 185–86; Rumipamba, 120; Salasaca ethnic group, 129–30, 136, 142–44; Sanganao area, 222; Saraguro ethnic group, 273, 276; wool versus synthetic fiber choice, 176; Zumbagua community, 115–16

Tiocajas, 218; hat styles, 217

Tixan 222

Topic, John, 162–63, 164, 165, 166

Treadle looms, 34–36

Troje community, 169; contemporary women's costume, 193–98; factory-made clothing, 186; men's costume, 198–99; traditional women's costume, 187–93

Tsachila (formerly Colorado) people, 4

Tunics, men's. *See* Kushmas (tunics)

Tunshi Grande, 207, 211

Tupus: Achupallas area, 227; Cañar Province, 233, 234; Chambo-Alao area, 214; Chibuleo area, 147; Columbe area, 201; historical origins, 45, 46; Licto area, 208, 209; Majipamba-Troje-Cacha communities, 187, 190, 196; Nizag community, 225; Pulucate community, 181; Quizapincha communities, 159; Salasaca ethnic group, 135, 141; San Juan area, 205; Sanganao area, 222; Saraguro ethnic group, 267, 268–69

Twill-derived weave, 32–33, 36, 60, 65, 118–19, 182, 200, 204, 266–67, 270

Uchilla chumbi, 200–201. *See also* Belts, handwoven (*chumbis*)

Uchilla maki chumbi, 146–47. *See also* Belts, handwoven (*chumbis*)

Ukunchinas (underskirts), 56–57, 106, 112–13. *See also* Anaku styles

Uma tazina headcloth style, 61, 62

Uma watana headcloth style, 61

Uma watarina tazina headcloth style, 61

Underskirts, 56–57, 95, 106, 112–13. *See also* Anaku styles

Urban versus rural fabric choice, 173–74, 177, 179

Ushutas (footwear), 49, 90, 273

Utcu (cotton), 18

Vests, 64

Wallkarinas. See Shawl styles

Walnut bark dye, 20, 125, 260, 265

Wanaku poncho, 272

Warp fringes on shawls, 46–47, 121, 164, 257-59

Warp-resist dyeing, i, iv, 31, 95, 97, 120–21, 164-65, 198–99, 205, 207-8, 212, 223-25, 228, 233–34, 238–40, 242, 256-57, 259, 279

Warp stripes, 31

Warp tension. *See* Weaving process

Washajatana. See Shawl styles

Wawa chumbi (baby belt): historical influences, 47; Majipamba-Troje-Cacha communities, 187–89; Otavalo valley, 57–60, 74; Pulucate community, 182. *See also* Belts, handwoven (*chumbis*)

Weaving process: as household enterprise, 37–38; by commission, 37; decorative techniques, 31–33; described, 25–31; impact of cash economy, 38; with treadle looms, 34–36. *See also* Belts, handwoven (*chumbis*); Poncho styles

Weaving workshops: Casa de la Cultura Ecuatoriana, 51; Palmira Dávalos area, 217; San Bernardo, 199–200. *See also* Textile production

Weddings, 43–44, 69-71, 140–42

Whips, 158, 220, 241, 249, 250

Whorls for spinning, 21

Wool, sheep's: for felting/fulling, 19; spinning techniques, 22

Wool/synthetic dress patterns, 174–80

Wrist wraps: Angochagua–La Rinconada communities, 103; Cañar Province, 242; Columbe area, 201; Licto area, 212; Majipamba-Troje-Cacha communities, 190, 196; Mariano Acosta community, 106–7; Natabuela community, 79; N.E. Pichincha–E. Imbabura, 90; Nizag community, 225; Otavalo ethnic group, 66; Palmira Dávalos area, 216; Paniquindra–La Florida communities, 99; Pulucate community, 183

Yana poncho, 138

Yanandij baita, 190

Yauti Alto, 222-23

Young-Sánchez, Margaret, 257

Yura poncho, 138

Yurak poncho, 198

Zamarros. See Chaps

Zúlac area costume, 223–25

Zuleta, Hacienda, 85, 91; textile production, 92

Zumbagua: children's costume, 114–15; men's costume, 113–14, 173; socio-economics, 41, 111–12; textile production, 115–16; women's costume, 112–13

Contributors

Lynn Hirschkind, Cañar province, Ecuador

Lynn Ann Meisch, Department of Anthropology, Saint Mary's College of California, Moraga

Laura Martin Miller, M.D., Hoopa, California

Marilee Schmit Nason, Registrar, The Albuquerque Museum, Albuquerque, New Mexico

Ann Pollard Rowe, Curator of Western Hemisphere Collections, The Textile Museum, Washington, D.C.

Rebecca Tolen, Bloomington, Indiana

Mary J. Weismantel, Department of Anthropology, Occidental College, Los Angeles, California